# THE ECONOMIC ANTHROPOLOGY OF THE STATE

Monographs in Economic Anthropology, No. 11

Edited by
## Elizabeth M. Brumfiel

UNIVERSITY
PRESS OF
AMERICA

Lanham • New York • London

Copyright © 1994 by the
Society for Economic Anthropology

## University Press of America,® Inc.
4720 Boston Way
Lanham, Maryland 20706

3 Henrietta Street
London WC2E 8LU England

All rights reserved
Printed in the United States of America
British Cataloging in Publication Information Available

Co-published by arrangement with the
Society for Economic Anthropology

### Library of Congress Cataloging-in-Publication Data

The Economic anthropology of the state / edited by Elizabeth M.
Brumfiel.
  p.  cm. — (Monographs in economic anthropology ; no. 11)
      Includes bibliographical refeences.
  1. Economic anthropology.  2. Political anthropology.  3. State,
    The.   I. Brumfiel, Elizabeth M.   II. Series.
  GN448.E265     1994      306.3—dc20        93–38526 CIP

ISBN 0–8191–9367–4 (cloth : alk. paper)
ISBN 0–8191–9368–2 (pbk. : alk. paper)

 The paper used in this publication meets the minimum requirements of American National Standard for Information Sciences—Permanence of Paper for Printed Library Materials, ANSI Z39.48–1984.

# TABLE OF CONTENTS

Introduction
 *Elizabeth M. Brumfiel* 1

## I The State and the Household Economy

An Andean World-System: Production Transformations Under the Inka Empire
 *Darrell E. La Lone* 17

The Peasant Household in the Transition from Socialism: State Intervention and Its Consequences in China
 *Susan Greenhalgh* 43

Government Policies and the Changing Structure of Farm Women's Livelihood: A Case from Southern Illinois
 *Jane Adams* 65

Household Economy in Early State Society: Material Value, Productive Context and Spheres of Exchange
 *Patricia Wattenmaker* 93

## II The Rationality of State-Controlled Production

The Economics and Politics of Maya Meat Eating
 *Mary DeLand Pohl* 119

Palace and Private Agricultural Decision-Making in the Early 2nd Millennium B.C. City-State of Larsa, Iraq
 *Mitchell S. Rothman* 149

Public and Private Economy in the Inka Empire
 *Terence N. D'Altroy* 169

Political Choices and Economic Strategies in the Vijayanagara Empire
 *Carla M. Sinopoli* 223

State Economic Policy and Rural Development in Paraguay
 *Christina Bolke Turner* 243

## III The Limits of State Intervention

Incorporation of Wage Labor into a Foraging Economy on the Periphery of the Venezuelan State
*Ted L. Gragson*   269

A Different Distinction: The Case of Ancient Greece
*David B. Small*   287

Subsistence and the State: The Case of Porfirian Mexico
*Judith E. Marti*   315

Ecology and Politics in the Puebla Basin of Mexico
*Sheldon Smith*   325

# THE ECONOMIC ANTHROPOLOGY OF THE STATE: AN INTRODUCTION

## Elizabeth M. Brumfiel
## Albion College

States are powerful, complex, institutionalized hierarchies of public decision-making and control. They are created to implement the relations of production in stratified societies and to mediate conflict between diverse economic interest groups. Maintaining economic organization is a primary function of all state hierarchies, and this function is the key to political power for state personnel.

To carry out their functions, state personnel must procure certain goods (D'Altroy and Earle 1985, Levi 1988). At the very least, they must provide for their own subsistence and the subsistence of others employed by the state. They must also meet the equipment needs of state organizations (particularly the arms and communications needs of coercive organizations), and they must acquire socially valued goods with which to reward their loyal servants and to win new supporters (Brumfiel 1987, Earle 1987). To obtain such necessities, state personnel must either enter into exchange relations with primary producers or develop state-controlled production facilities. Thus, state personnel enter the economy as 1) organizers and regulators of the economy, 2) consumers, and, at times, 3) producers.

When state personnel engage in economic activity, they resemble other economic actors in some ways. Like private individuals or firms, state personnel must consider the costs and benefits of alternative policies, purchases, and production strategies. But state decision-makers differ from non-state decision-makers in at least three ways. First, states are large-scale organizations, with access to relatively abundant resources. Hence, state personnel have the capacity to organize
 and regulate the economy in ways that are not possible for private individuals or non-state groups. For example, state personnel can use state bureaucracies to monitor economic functions (Wright 1969, Flannery 1972, Johnson 1978). Or, using tax revenues, they can undertake ventures too costly or risky for private investors (Sahlins 1958:7, Rostow 1971:24-25).

Second, states are powerful organizations, with a monopoly over the legal use of coercive power. Hence, state personnel can use their power to enforce exchange relationships that would not otherwise exist. What others

## 2   ECONOMIC ANTHROPOLOGY OF THE STATE

must seek through barter, state personnel may obtain through extortion (Lane 1958, Gilman 1981, Tilly 1985).

Finally, state personnel are political actors, and they intervene in the economy first and foremost to strengthen and perpetuate political control (Earle 1990).  In some circumstances, political power is enhanced by the efficient production and distribution of goods, in which case the economic activity of the state may appropriately be analyzed using conventional measures of efficiency.  But in many circumstances, political power, at least in the short run, is served by activities that impede the efficient production and distribution of goods.  These activities include restricting supplies of valued goods and subsidizing individuals and institutions that yield political power at the cost of individuals and institutions that would provide more widely desired goods and services.  The logic of state economic policy, then, is the logic of power rather than the logic of the market.

How state personnel intervene in the economy, and to what specific ends, depends upon the nature of the state and its position within the wider political economy (Rueschemeyer and Evans 1985, Clark 1991).  For example, the leaders of tribute-based states and capitalist states derive their power from different bases, and they deal with different economic institutions. Consequently, their economic policies differ.

Tribute-based states arise because of the pressures of competition among political elites in pre-industrial economies (Earle 1978, Brumfiel 1983, Brumfiel and Fox 1993).  Internal competition among elites generates the need for surplus wealth with which to substantiate the ideologies and alliances that serve as the basis of power (Brumfiel and Earle 1987). The state precipitates as an array of agencies dedicated to the extraction of wealth from primary producers and the transformation of this wealth into political power.  Wealth-extracting agencies include military bureaucracies which provide the coercive basis of surplus extraction, tax-collecting bureaucracies which organize the collection of surplus, and specialized groups in charge of long-distance trade, religious ritual, and the production of sumptuary goods, all of which contribute to the solidarity and dominance of state-based power holders.  The organization of economic and political processes under this type of political structure has been called the tributary mode of production (Amin 1976, Wolf 1982).

Extraction is the primary concern of tributary states.  But what tributary states extract, both in terms of quantity and quality, and how these states organize extraction, depends upon their institutional settings.  For example, the rate of extraction may depend upon the presence or absence of strong corporate kinship groups within the subject population (Diamond 1951, Gailey 1985a).  The decision to tax in kind or in currency may

INTRODUCTION 3

depend upon the presence or absence of a reliable market system which permits the exchange of currency for needed goods (D'Altroy and Earle 1985). The choice between tax farming or state-run tax collection depends, in part, upon the nature of income distribution within the tax-paying population (Levi 1988:78).

In addition, various considerations can induce state personnel to begin to organize some forms of production. Production in state facilities can be motivated by the need to limit demands upon the peasant population (Gailey 1985b, Tymowski 1991), to enhance control of the peasant population (e.g., Wittfogel 1957, Johnson 1987, Sanders and Nichols 1988, Halstead and O'Shea 1989), or to monopolize goods of unusual strategic or symbolic importance (Earle 1982, 1987; Clark and Parry 1990, Costin 1991, Peregrine 1991). Similar considerations may induce states to initiate or seize control of long-distance trade.

The papers in this volume document significant variation in the economic organization of tributary states. All were involved in some way in surplus extraction, but the Inka state extracted primarily labor (La Lone, Chapter 1) while Ebla extracted agricultural staples and livestock (Wattenmaker, Chapter 4). The Vijayanagara state collected a tribute in foodstuffs and livestock, but in addition it taxed foreign trade, primarily textile exports (Sinopoli, Chapter 8). Larsa also taxed foreign trade, but derived most of the rest of its income from agricultural estates (Rothman, Chapter 6).

Similarly, all these states organized certain forms of production, but they varied significantly in the industries they organized and the units that carried out production. Among the Maya, elite households reared the deer that would be the centerpieces of elite feasting (Pohl, Chapter 5). The Inka organized state farms and craft workshops using the labor of attached specialists (but only in some provinces, not in others) (D'Altroy, Chapter 7). The rulers of Vijayanagara constructed large scale irrigation systems and roads to be used as public goods (Sinopoli, Chapter 8). Systematic comparative studies might reveal the geographic, demographic, and institutional variables that underlie these differences in state activity.

Capitalist states differ from tributary states in that the primary locus of surplus extraction and economic conflict is located outside of the state, in firms, rather than within the state, itself. State personnel derive their power from their ability to manage the owner-worker conflicts which might otherwise disrupt the economic system. How this is accomplished, and what forms of intervention it requires, have been the subject of vigorous debate (Gold et al. 1975, Foley and Yambert 1989:41-48).

"Instrumentalist" theories of the state in capitalist society propose that state personnel are servants of the capitalist class. Occupying political office at the pleasure of capitalists, state personnel use institutional violence to control and suppress the working class (Lenin 1932; Miliband 1969, 1973). The state also maintains and extends the accessibility of land and labor to market forces (Polanyi 1944), and the state defines and defends property rights, corporate law, labor law, commercial relationships and the other institutional arrangements that are necessary for capitalist production.

"Structuralist" theories of the capitalist state argue that the dominance of capitalists is not so complete. Political office holders derive their power from a number of sources: capitalists, workers, and other segments of society (e.g. agrarian elites, peasants, students, etc). Factions exist within capital and labor which obscure the lines of class conflict and produce a range of potential power bases for state personnel. Thus, political power does not rely entirely upon the relentless pursuit of capitalist interests. State personnel are regarded as a somewhat independent political force, able to act with a degree of autonomy to pursue their own interests, principally maintaining their political power (Poulantzas 1969, 1976).

The papers in this volume provide support for both the instrumentalist and structuralist positions. In support of the instrumentalist position, Adams (Chapter 3) and Turner (Chapter 9) describe situations in which the state has acted to extend capitalist penetration. In support of the structuralist position, Marti (Chapter 12) and Smith (Chapter 13) examine cases in which state personnel seem engaged in a more even-handed mediation of class conflict. Gragson (Chapter 10) finds that capitalist development on the Venezuelan frontier is occurring unaided by state intervention. Again, whether a state assumes an instrumentalist or a structuralist stance may depend upon its institutional setting. Variation may even occur within a single state. As D'Altroy (Chapter 7) points out, it is possible for state personnel to be committed to different policies according to their positions in the social hierarchy. Individuals who carry out economic policy at the grassroots level may be forced to pursue a more structuralist stance, making more concessions to subordinate classes than individuals further up the political hierarchy are willing to concede.

Other modes of production imply still other roles for state personnel in organizing the economy. Differing economic roles for the state are implied by Greenhalgh's (Chapter 2) analysis of economic transformations in Communist China and Small's (Chapter 11) discussion of the economic policies in the slave-holding city-states of ancient Greece.

Despite the differing economic roles played by the state in different modes of production, common questions may be addressed concerning the scope, rationality, and limits of state intervention in the economy. These questions provide the organizing themes of this book. The first group of papers examines the extent to which state intervention affects the economic activity of household units. The second group of papers explore the rationality of state-controlled production. The final group of papers defines the material and political limits of state economic control.

States intervene in household economic activity for several reasons. First, in agrarian societies, and even in the agricultural sectors of industrial societies, much production is household based. Thus, states wishing to mobilize a surplus or alter economic output must find some means of articulating with the household economy. In addition, the household is a kinship-based unit, and its access to resources and labor is often legitimated by kinship ideologies. States wishing to free these resources for use by other economic institutions must redefine the meaning of kinship and, in doing so, transform household relations (Gailey 1985a). Finally, even in industrial societies, the households remain the primary unit of reproduction, and they absorb a significant part of the labor required to sustain and replace the workforce. Therefore, states wishing to alter the size and skill of the labor force will necessarily implement family issue policies.

As La Lone (Chapter 1) points out, household production is geared primarily toward the satisfaction of the household's own wants; no "surplus" is spontaneously generated for the support of state institutions. Therefore, in preindustrial states, state personnel must intervene in the household economy to extract needed goods and services. In the Inka empire, intervention was a two-stage process. Initially, state personnel manipulated existing relations of production to mobilize labor for agricultural production and the construction of state facilities such as roads and storehouses. But direct extraction could not be carried very far under traditional norms before generating resistance from subordinate communities. Under these conditions, surpluses could be enlarged only through conquests which increased the size of the subject population. The Inka state did expand to its practical limits, but the surplus generated by direct extraction was still insufficient. Therefore, state personnel instituted new relations of production that were more conducive to generating surplus.

These new relations of production involved uprooting individuals and groups from their native communities where a web of social alliances had supplied some ability to resist state exploitation. These individuals and groups were resettled in settings where their social isolation made them dependent upon state personnel for security and access to resources. Thus, social isolation implemented with considerable coercive force was at least as important as innovative ideology in enforcing the new relations of production. Under these new relations, new economic institutions came into being: houses of cloth-producing *aclla*, state farms, and private estates.

## 6   ECONOMIC ANTHROPOLOGY OF THE STATE

These institutions provided a larger, more secure financial base for the Inka state than had previously existed.

The Communist state in China supported an even more radical transformation of the existing household economy. Agricultural production was taken entirely out of the hands of peasant and land-owning families. Control over land and labor was transferred from family heads to the governing bodies of agricultural collectives. Greenhalgh (Chapter 2) describes how these changes in the control of resources transformed social relations within the family.

When the family head lost his control over family members' access to land, family sentiments of deference and dependence diminished. This had a liberating effect on younger family members, particularly sons, who no longer felt compelled to provide for their father's old age. This, in turn, reduced the value of children to parents. The transformation of sentiments within the family was consistent with the state's policies of limiting population growth, but it frustrated the state's later economic goals. Greenhalgh finds that while the designers of economic reform in China had hoped to revive family-based enterprises, family members are no longer willing to cooperate in such enterprises. Traditional sentiments do not sustain older patterns of cooperation when the rules governing access to resources have been altered.

As described by Adams (Chapter 3), the United States government also favored the transformation of family-based agricultural production in the post-World War II era. Government economic policies discouraged small-scale, diversified farm production in the Midwest and, in doing so, undermined the participation of women in the farming enterprise. Government economic policies were accompanied by efforts to promote the "rational" financial management of farms by disembedding agricultural production from family relations. Traditionally a producing and consuming unit, the family was redefined as a unit of consumption. Adams describes how government-sponsored Home Extension programs encouraged farm families to accept this new definition of the family. In the new definition, farm women were assigned roles within the domestic sphere.

As in China, the state alteration of economic processes within the household changed the social roles of household members. But while the state was successful in breaking down existing social roles, it was unable to command the development of new allegiances -- to family members in China or to the ideal of domesticity in the United States. The farm women described by Adams succeeded in preserving their independent incomes by moving out of their households and finding off-farm employment or developing new home-based enterprises.

Home Extension programs promoted new norms of consumption in farm households. These norms were justified in terms of increased social well-being, i.e., the improved health, education, social development, and comfort of household members. Consumption thus became a moral issue which affected the household's social standing. It would be interesting to know if the household's economic standing was also decided by its consumption patterns. Could "progressive" farm families more easily obtain the credit they needed to expand their operations in an increasingly competitive market? To what extent can the state manipulate consumption patterns as a tool of economic or political policy?

This question is the central focus of Wattenmaker's (Chapter 4) examination of economic change in third-millennium B.C. Turkey. Wattenmaker finds that as the scale and political complexity of society increased, non-elite households relied more heavily upon specialists to supply ceramic serving vessels and textiles. According to Wattenmaker, these goods would have had great social value because they were highly visible and required expensive labor and/or the use of scarce raw materials for their production. Such goods conveyed information about social status, and they could be used to advance social standing. The consumption of such goods at Kurban, Turkey, indicates the extent to which the expansion of state power prompted the renegotiation of social alliances and social standing at lower levels of the social hierarchy. As Wattenmaker points out, state elites were able to influence these negotiations to an extent because they controlled the production of metals and some categories of textiles.

These first four articles demonstrate the extent to which state intervention transforms the economic activity of household units. State intervention affects not only the quantity and quality of household production, but also the quality of social relationships among household members, and the household's own consumption preferences. However, these articles also indicate that state personnel meet with only limited success in harnessing the existing household economy to the state's institutional needs. Households and individual household members retain their own goals and a degree of power to pursue those goals; therefore, households do not cooperate entirely with state purposes. When states find it too difficult or costly to extract needed goods or services from the household economy, they may initiate state-controlled production.

The rationality of state-controlled production is explored by the second group of articles in this book. Specifically, these articles examine how economic decision-making by state and non-state personnel results in different choices of product and production technique.

## 8  ECONOMIC ANTHROPOLOGY OF THE STATE

Pohl (Chapter 5) demonstrates that Maya elites and non-elites practiced different strategies for procuring meat in both Preclassic (c. 400 B.C.) and Postclassic (c. A.D. 1000) times. Maya elites focused on large terrestrial species such as deer and peccary. These game animals were the central symbols in elaborate feasts that conveyed ideologies of elite superiority and power. Commoners pursued more readily available small mammals, birds, and fish. The elites' control of labor allowed them to invest in expensive technologies. Some of these technologies, such as hunting nets, may have been justified in terms of greater returns. Others, such as women feeding maize to home-raised turkeys, dogs, deer, and peccaries, are time-consuming and calorically inefficient (Lappé 1971). As Wattenmaker and others (e.g. Gero 1987, Clark and Parry 1990, Earle 1990, Hayden 1990, Peregrine 1991) observe, it is precisely the conspicuously inefficient production of elite goods that distinguishes them and makes them valuable markers of social status and currencies of political negotiation. In contrast to the elites, Maya commoners more carefully maximized the caloric returns on their labor.

Rothman (Chapter 6) also finds clear differences in the production strategies of political elites and non-elites. The records of agricultural production from second-millennium B.C. Mesopotamia indicate that the ratio of grain production to date production differed on state-controlled lands and private farms. Palace and temple estates produced more grain; private farms produced more dates. Like the Maya elites, the Mesopotamian state enjoyed privileged access to production factors yielding a different production strategy. Larger land holdings, Rothman suggests, gave state administrators the latitude to concentrate on the production of higher-risk, higher-yield grain crops while private families secured a guaranteed annual yield from their smaller holdings by producing dates. Unlike the Maya elites, the Mesopotamian state generally avoided conspicuous inefficiency in production; conspicuous inefficiency was limited to certain forms of elite craft production and, possibly, elaborate food preparation techniques. The Mesopotamian state, burdened with a large corps of specialized personnel and state institutions, chose to maximize output, at least in the production of subsistence staples.

D'Altroy (Chapter 7) argues that different decision-making criteria may be employed by political elites within a single state, according to local circumstances. In the Mantaro Valley, Peru, Inka administrators took advantage of underused valley lands to establish large state farms. These farms produced large agricultural surpluses which were used to feed the Inka army. The crop mix on these lands maximized caloric output. Despite the importance of maize in Inka rituals, state storehouses in the Mantaro Valley contain abundant remains of quinoa and tubers in addition to maize. In the smaller, drier, Calchiquí Valley, state organized agriculture was limited to smaller tracts of irrigated land. Given the lower agricultural potential of the Calchiquí Valley, state-administered agricultural production appears to have been geared toward supporting local state personnel rather than producing large surpluses for use outside the region.

Craft production was also organized differently in the two regions. In the Mantaro Valley, Inka administrators organized specialized installations. In doing so, they were probably guided by considerations of efficiency and control. Large-scale state enterprises staffed by full-time craft specialists probably achieved efficiencies of scale. These enterprises also enabled the state to control the product, making its distribution an unmistakable sign of state favor and largess. In the Calchiquí Valley, Inka administrators requisitioned pottery rather than overseeing its production; the state seems to have been less concerned with sponsoring feasts and maintaining its facade of reciprocity. The state was more interested in controlling the production of metal and lapidary objects, but, even so, control was achieved by overseeing the final stages of craft manufacture rather than maintaining workshops with full-time specialists engaged in all phases of production.

Sinopoli (Chapter 8) also points to the selectivity and variability of state economic decision-making. The Vijayanagara empire of fourteenth- to sixteenth-century India attempted to monopolize trade in strategically important goods such as horses and firearms. It encouraged but did not attempt to control trade in textiles, which was an important source of revenue to the state. The state encouraged agricultural intensification by constructing large-scale water control networks, but it showed no interest in monopolizing or encouraging the production, distribution, or consumption of utilitarian craft goods. Sinopoli suggests that the overall economic strategy of the Vijayanagara empire was one of selective intervention to insure control of strategic goods and steady growth in revenue-generating activities at the lowest possible administrative cost.

Turner (Chapter 9) considers state enterprise of a somewhat different type: government sponsored settlement of the Paraguayan frontier. This settlement occurred during the 1960s and 1970s under the sponsorship of international development agencies. To foster economic well-being through the growth of market-oriented agricultural production, the agencies provided money to subsidize pioneer settlement and infrastructure development. However, grant money flowed from international agencies to state agencies to the pockets of regional elites who were supporters of the presidential regime. An economic infrastructure for the new settlers was

10 ECONOMIC ANTHROPOLOGY OF THE STATE

developed, but the generous profits from the award of construction contracts on the basis of political patronage enabled a few regional elites to acquire large landholdings and monopolize cash crop production. The commercial system came to be dominated by monopolistic pricing that stifled economic growth and generated a highly uneven income distribution.

Spontaneous settlements, those developed without the economic backing of the state, also suffered low rates of economic growth. Growth was impeded by the lack of infrastructure development, particularly, poor transportation that limited access to distant markets. Farmers were forced to deal with the few buyers who were willing to bulk cash crops for transport to the market. This resulted in extremely low prices for cash crops and low profits to farmers, making cash cropping a barely profitable activity.

This second group of articles suggests that the state-controlled production of subsistence staples tends to occur in societies where the institutional needs of states are great, but where subsistence production is geared to meeting household needs. Under state control, subsistence staples are produced as efficiently as possible. When markets and merchants are present and households have geared their production of staples to market sale, states withdraw from production, relying instead on taxation and market purchases to meet their institutional needs (D'Altroy and Earle 1985). However, even when subsistence staples are procured through taxation and market purchase, states continue to oversee the production of strategic military and status goods. They may also organize certain sectors of the economy to provide payoffs to key players within the political system.

Because social scientists are accustomed to thinking of states as powerful entities, they sometimes ignore the limits to state economic control. The final set of articles in this book explores these limits. The first article examines the effects of distance upon state control, a topic also discussed by La Lone (Chapter 1) and Sinopoli (Chapter 8). The second article discusses the economic and cultural conditions that discouraged Greek city-states from seeking economic control. The final two articles explore the difficulties of implementing economic policy in a welter of pressures and counter-pressures that constitute grassroots politics.

Dependency theories of the state propose that the state plays an important role in engineering the articulation between capitalist economies and the non-capitalist economies on their peripheries (Frank 1967). However, Gragson (Chapter 10) finds that the Venezuelan state did not, and probably could not, play such a role on its southern frontier. On the frontier, administrative costs were high, and population densities were low. Under these conditions, the state permitted commercial cattle ranchers to develop their own customary laws regulating access to pastures and water holes. The indigenous Pumé people also acted autonomously. They engaged in wage work on the cattle ranches because this work was advantageous given the existing Pumé subsistence pattern. State power was not needed to bring them into the capitalist system initially, although it may be needed at some future date as commercial production expands and the competition between ranchers and Pumé over the use of water holes intensifies.

According to Small (Chapter 11), the ancient Greek state almost never intervened directly in the economic activities of its citizens. In ancient Greece, wealthy land-owning, slave-owning elites profited tremendously from commercial exchange that crossed the boundaries of individual city-states. Because elites made grain available to the populace of city-states supported state activities such as athletic, religious, and dramatic festivals, the common citizens of Greek city-states had little desire to intervene in or control private commercial production and exchange. At the same time, because elite ritual friendships guaranteed the fulfillment of commercial contracts, the elites had little incentive to draw the state into their economic affairs.

Still, it could be argued that the Greek city-state did play an important economic role in defense of the slave economy. Both the elites and the common citizens of city-states profited directly or indirectly from estate-based slave labor. By the common consent of all its citizens, the state guaranteed the property rights of the elites in land and slaves.

Marti (Chapter 12) and Smith (Chapter 13) examine the determination of economic policy in Mexican towns at two points in time almost a century apart. The similarities are remarkable. In both cases, the implementation of economic policy appears to be inconsistent and contradictory, arbitrary, chaotic and ineffective.

Marti examines actions taken by municipal governments in conflicts among merchants, market vendors, and street vendors. Although the actions favored first one group, then another, Marti suggests that when viewed as a whole, municipal governments might be seen as implementing a consistent policy. Such a policy was based upon three principles: maximizing municipal revenues, maximizing the availability of cheap subsistence goods to urban workers, and appearing to comply with the dictates of federal leaders upon whose good will the tenure of municipal politicians depended.

Smith analyzes recent conflicts over the implementation of environmental protection legislation in contemporary Puebla. Smith voices the frustration of many Mexicans over the lax and inconsistent way in which the government limits pollution and resource depletion despite legislation

legislation is frustrated by populist machine politics operating at the local level. Machine politics produces private profiteering at the expense of public well-being. And yet, if Marti's style of analysis were applied to the Puebla situation, it might reveal that, in addition to profiteering, municipal policy is guided by the conflicting principles of maximizing environmental protection while minimizing its cost in terms of stifling economic growth.

The economic policies of states thus reflect political context. On frontiers where the political stakes are low, states willingly cede control of local economies to local populations. When all politically active parties benefit from the private control of the economy, states will again cede control of the economy to outside groups. The political factions that express the structural tensions and contradictions of economic development under capitalist institutions will produce economic policies that waver and change.

The papers in this volume underscore three generalizations about the economic anthropology of the state. First, there is a great range of variation in the way that states intervene in the economy, and much of this variation can be explained by variation in the institutional organization of the state and the economy. Second, the economic impact of the state extends far beyond its role in organizing or managing production and distribution. In the process of intervening in the economy, the state often transforms social relations, and in doing so, it profoundly changes patterns of consumption. Third, understanding the economic anthropology of the state requires an examination of how state personnel design economic policy not only with reference to the internal requirements of the economy and the internal requirements of the state, but also with an eye to making necessary concessions to those who hold power outside state institutions, even those who are often regarded as powerless.

## Acknowledgments

This introduction has benefited tremendously from the criticisms and suggestions of Lateef Badru, John Clark, Tom Patterson, and all the contributors to this volume. I am grateful for their generosity.

## References

Amin, Samir
    1976   *Unequal Development.* New York: Pantheon.

Brumfiel, Elizabeth M.
    1983   Aztec State Making: Ecology, Structure and the Origin of the State. *American Anthropologist* 85:261-84.
    1987   Elite and Utilitarian Crafts in the Aztec State. In E.M. Brumfiel and T.K. Earle, eds., *Specialization, Exchange, and Complex Societies*, pp.102-18. Cambridge: Cambridge University Press.

Brumfiel, Elizabeth M. and Timothy K. Earle
    1987   Specialization, Exchange and Complex Societies: An Introduction. In E.M. Brumfiel and T.K. Earle, eds., *Specialization, Exchange, and Complex Societies*, pp.1-9. Cambridge: Cambridge University Press.

Brumfiel, Elizabeth M. and John W. Fox, eds.
    1993   *Factional Competition and Political Development in the New World.* Cambridge: Cambridge University Press.

Clark, John E.
    1991   Statecraft and State Crafts: A Reconsideration of Mesoamerican Obsidian Industries. Paper presented at the 56th Annual Meeting, Society for American Archeology, New Orleans.

Clark, John E. and William J. Parry
    1990   Craft Specialization and Cultural Complexity. *Research in Economic Anthropology* 12:289-346.

Costin, Cathy L.
    1991   Craft Specialization: Issues in Defining, Documenting, and Explaining the Organization of Production. *Archaeological Method and Theory* 3:1-54.

D'Altroy, Terence N. and Timothy K. Earle
    1985   State Finance, Wealth Finance and Storage in the Inka Political Economy. *Current Anthropology* 26:187-206.

Diamond, Stanley
    1951   *Dahomey: A Proto-State in West Africa.* Unpublished Ph.D. dissertation. Columbia University.

Earle, Timothy K.
    1978   *Economic and Social Organization of a Complex Chiefdom: The Halelea District, Kaua'i, Hawaii.* Ann Arbor: The University of Michigan Museum of Anthropology, Anthropological Papers, 63.

1982 The Ecology and Politics of Primitive Valuables. In J.G. Kennedy and R.B. Edgerson, eds., *Culture and Ecology: Eclectic Perspectives*, pp.65-83. Washington, D.C.: American Anthropological Association, Special Publication, 15.
1987 Specialization and the Production of Wealth: Hawaiian Chiefdoms and the Inka Empire. In *Specialization, Exchange, and Complex Societies*, pp.64-75. Cambridge: Cambridge University Press.
1990 Style and Iconography as Legitimization in Complex Chiefdoms. In M.W. Conkey and C.A. Hastorf, eds., *The Uses of Style in Archaeology*, pp.73-81. Cambridge: Cambridge University Press.

Flannery, Kent V.
1972 The Cultural Evolution of Civilizations. *Annual Review of Ecology and Systematics* 3:399-426.

Foley, Michael W. and Karl Yambert
1989 Anthropology and Theories of the State. In B.S. Orlove, M.W. Foley, and T.F. Love eds., *State, Capital, and Rural Society*, pp.39-67. Boulder, CO: Westview Press.

Frank, Andre Gunder
1967 *Capitalism and Underdevelopment in Latin America*. New York: Monthly Review Press.

Gailey, Christine W.
1985a The State of the State in Anthropology. *Dialectical Anthropology* 9:65-88.
1985b The Kindness of Strangers: Transformations of Kinship in Precapitalist Class and State Formation. *Culture* 5:241-50.

Gero, Joan W.
1987 The Intensification of Style: Elite Control Over Specialist Labor. Paper presented at the Southeast Marxist Scholars' Conference, Durham, NC.

Gilman, Antonio
1981 The Development of Social Stratification in Bronze Age Europe. *Current Anthropology* 22:1-23.

Gold, David, Clarence Y.H. Lo, and Erik Olin Wright
1975 Recent Developments in Marxist Theory of the Capitalist State. *Monthly Review* 27 (5):29-43, (6):36-51.

Halstead, Paul and John O'Shea, eds.
1989 *Bad Year Economics*. Cambridge: Cambridge University Press.

Hayden, Brian
   1990   Nimrods, Piscators, Pluckers and Planters: The Emergence of Food Production. *Journal of Anthropological Archaeology* 9:31-69.

Johnson, Gregory A.
   1978   Information Sources and the Development of Decision-making Organizations. In C. Redman et al., *Social Archaeology*, pp.87-112. New York: Academic Press.
   1987   The Changing Organization of Uruk Administration on the Susiana Plain. In F. Hole, ed., *The Archaeology of Western Iran*, pp.107-39. Washington, D.C.: Smithsonian Institution.

Lane, Frederick D.
   1958   Economic Consequences of Organized Violence. *Journal of Economic History* 18:401-17.

Lappé, Frances M.
   1971   *Diet for a Small Planet.* New York: Ballantine.

Lenin, I.V.
   1932   *State and Revolution.* New York: International Publishers.

Levi, Margaret
   1988   *Of Rule and Revenue.* Berkeley: University of California Press.

Miliband, Ralph
   1969   *The State in Capitalist Society.* New York: Basic Books.
   1973   Poulantzas and the Capitalist State. New Left Review 82:83-92.

Peregrine, Peter
   1991   Some Political Aspects of Craft Specialization. Paper presented at the 90th Annual Meeting, American Anthropological Association, Chicago.

Polanyi, Karl
   1944   *The Great Transformation: The Political and Economic Origins of Our Time.* Boston: Beacon Press.

Poulantzas, Nicos
   1969   The Problem of the Capitalist State. *New Left Review* 58:67-78.
   1976   The Capitalist State: A Reply to Miliband and Laclau. *New Left Review* 95:63-83.

Rostow, W.W.
   1971   *The Stages of Economic Growth*, 2nd ed. Cambridge: Cambridge University Press.

16 ECONOMIC ANTHROPOLOGY OF THE STATE

Rueschemeyer, Dietrich and Peter B. Evans
    1985    The State and Economic Transformation: Toward an Analysis of the Conditions Underlying Effective Intervention. In P.B. Evans, D. Rueschemeyer, and T. Skocpol, eds., *Bringing the State Back In*, pp.44-77. Cambridge: Cambridge University Press.

Sahlins, Marshall
    1958    *Social Stratification in Polynesia*. (American Ethnological Society, Monograph 29). Seattle: University of Washington Press.

Sanders, William T. and Deborah Nichols
    1988    Ecological Theory and Cultural Evolution in the Valley of Oaxaca. *Current Anthropology* 29:33-80.

Tilly, Charles
    1985    Warmaking and Statemaking as Organized Crime. In P.B. Evans, D. Rueschemeyer, and T. Skocpol, eds., *Bringing the State Back In*, pp.169-91. Cambridge: Cambridge University Press.

Tymowski, Michal
    1991    Wolof Economy and Political Organization: The West African Coast in the Mid-Fifteenth Century. In H.J.M. Claessen and P. van de Velde, eds., *Early State Economics*, pp.131-42. New Brunswick, NJ: Transaction.

Wittfogel, Karl A.
    1957    *Oriental Despotism*. New Haven: Yale University Press.

Wright, Henry T.
    1969    *The Administration of Rural Production in an Early Mesopotamian Town*. Ann Arbor: The University of Michigan, Museum of Anthropology, Anthropological Papers, 38.

Wolf, Eric R.
    1982    *Europe and the People Without History*. Berkeley: University of California Press.

# AN ANDEAN WORLD-SYSTEM: PRODUCTION TRANSFORMATIONS UNDER THE INKA EMPIRE

Darrell E. La Lone
DePauw University

"The reluctant obedience of distant provinces generally costs more than it is worth." -- Thomas Macauley

The rise and expansion of the Inka state provides one of the most dramatic cases we have of the dilemmas of imperialism. Empires present a convincing facade of invincibility and even inevitability as they attempt to absorb ever-expanding spheres of wealth and power. Their growth and continuing survival depends upon their ability to prey upon weaker opponents, and to keep them weak under asymmetrical relations of power and wealth. Yet ultimately empires find themselves extended beyond what it is worth their while to attempt to control. Then, as Macauley observes, what they can extract from others costs more than it is worth. Ultimately centers collapse, leaving peripheries once again to their own devices, perhaps in time allowing them to become new centers in their own right.

What makes the case of the Inka Empire particularly exciting is that its monumental facade was constructed in such a short period of time. The massive accumulation of the empire still stands silently before us in the form of gigantic cities of stone perched at improbable heights, roads extending for thousands of miles throughout the Andes, and museums filled with the remnants of Andean treasures in gold, silver, feathers, and cloth. Yet this is not the accumulation of millennia, nor even of centuries, but of mere decades.

The general lines I shall follow in tracing the story of Inka state expansion are inspired by recent developments in world-systems analysis. These do not follow directly from the assumptions of Immanuel Wallerstein's discussion of *The Modern World System* (1974 and sequels). They reflect, instead, some of the recent debate and modification of the world-systems approach in the light of archaeological and ethnohistorical applications (e.g., Kohl 1978, 1979, 1987; Ekholm and Friedman 1979; Pailes and Whitecotton 1979; Upham 1982, 1986; Blanton and Feinman

18 ECONOMIC ANTHROPOLOGY OF THE STATE

1984; Schneider 1977; Renfrew and Cherry 1986; Kipp and Schortman 1989; Schortman 1989). The most direct connection with the world-systems perspective flows from the challenges presented in Christopher Chase-Dunn and Thomas Hall's Core/Periphery Relations in Precapitalist Worlds (1991).

## Inka State Expansion and World-Systems

As Chase-Dunn and Hall define world-systems, they are

> intersocietal networks in which the interaction (trade, warfare, intermarriage, etc.) is an important condition of the reproduction of the internal structures of the composite units and importantly affects changes which occur in these local structures (1991:7).

The rise and expansion of Andean states produced a mosaic of core/periphery hierarchical relations. In different regions and in different polities these relations had quite variable impact on the internal structures of the component units. Although we now have a far richer understanding of regional variations within the Andes, our knowledge is still spotty on a number of important issues. For example, we seem to find little agreement on when the earliest Andean states emerge. Furthermore, even when we agree that we are dealing with centralized societies, we may not be clear on what is the center and what is the periphery.

With the formation and expansion of the Inka state, we find data adequate to begin to portray core/periphery relations in some detail. Yet even (or especially) here we are handicapped by a remarkable paucity of archaeological exploration of Cuzco, which proclaims itself the "archaeological capital of the Americas"! Our knowledge of Cuzco is then founded on primarily ethnohistoric materials, and these are often contradictory accounts representing varying factional interests.

Although contentious accounts are meant to conceal much, and to reveal much else only selectively, they may still speak reliably on matters that no one thinks necessary to conceal. In this case the traditions clearly suggest that the highlands in the fifteenth century were filled with small to medium-sized competing polities that seemed to resort frequently to war. Existing archaeological data tend to confirm an image of small competing polities in highland regions (Parsons and Hastings 1988). Archaeological exploration of the Wanka region of the central highlands, for example, reveals a number of fortified hilltop settlements (Parsons and Matos Mendieta 1978, D'Altroy 1987). The ethnohistorical documentation for this

AN ANDEAN WORLD-SYSTEM  19

region also clearly portrays the pre-Inka period as a time when small bellicose polities led by small bellicose warlords, or *sinchis*, contended against one another (Hastorf 1983, Levine 1979, LeBlanc 1981, D'Altroy 1981).

The Inka dynastic traditions portray pre-Inka polities as *behetrías* ruled (or perhaps even tyrannized) by their *sinchis*. *Behetría* is a particularly interesting term, since it denotes a community that is free to choose its own lords, while also connoting a condition of chaos or savagery. Absorption into the Inka Empire is then portrayed as bringing an end to *behetría*, and, obviously depending upon where one is standing, that means the coming of "civilization" or the end of autonomy. We may suspect that the Inka were not the first to proclaim themselves the harbingers of civilization in the Andes, and we certainly know they were not the last to do so.

Before the rise of the Inka state under the first emperors, Cuzco itself is described in the same terms:

> Y era tanto lo que cada pueblo pugnaba por su libertad con sus *cinchis* y sin ellos, queste procuraba subjetar a aquel y el otro al otro, especialmente en el tiempo de los ingas, que aun dentro del mismo Cuzco los de un arrabal, llamado Carmenga, traian guerra con los de otro arrabal, llamado Cayocache (Sarmiento [1572] 1906:56, cited in Bauer, in press).

> [And each people fought so greatly for its liberty with and without its *sinchis* that one managed to subjugate another, and the other yet another, especially in the time of the Incas, so that even within Cuzco itself those of one district, called Carmenca, warred with another district called Cayocache] (my translation)

Attack from an aggressive outside polity, the Chanka, gave Cuzco its start as an increasingly expansive polity. As even late twentieth-century industrial states recognize, a quick and successful war against an underprepared enemy can do wonders for promoting authority and perhaps even legitimacy. When such victories bring spoils, such rewards make imperialism seem well worth the trouble. Such spoils of war were, according to Maria Rostworowski (1988), the very foundation for the Inka state and empire.[1] She argues that over time Cuzco engaged in three types of warfare:

1. *Raids and looting* ("guerras de rapiña")
   During the Late Intermediate and at the beginnings of Cuzco's rise, the most common actions seem to be aimed at looting neighboring communities. Conquest of territory appears not to be the objective, since the same places appear to be attacked repeatedly.
2. *Conquest and incorporation*
   These conquests took the form of promises of generosity and reciprocity. Rich gifts, sumptuous feasts, and the exchange of women were intended to bond incorporated regions to Cuzco, with the clear message also that it would be impolite and impolitic to be less than gracious with amiable Cuzqueños accompanied by several thousand soldiers.
3. *Conquest and blunt intimidation*
   At the farthest reaches of Inka expansion the conquests were directed toward "great reprisals against the conquered, creating a climate of terror and imposing punishment in order to avoid future confrontations or uprisings" (Rostworowski 1988:132-133).

Although I might argue with Rostworowski on several points (for example, her argument that violence was greater on the frontiers because the principle of reciprocity was unknown), her discussion is an interesting account of the expressions of Inka militarism over both time and space. It is interesting also in its parallels and contrasts with Roman statecraft as described in Luttwak's *Grand Strategy of the Roman Empire* (1976). He describes the development of the Roman Empire in the first three centuries in terms of three systems of imperial security:

1. *Hegemonic expansionism* as conquests benefit largely the few who lived in the city.
2. *Territorial security* to serve the interests of the many rather than the few.
3. *Struggle to survive threats of chaos* in the face of external threats and internal weakness (Luttwak 1976:4-5).

Each of Rostworowski's three stages in Inka warfare fits within Luttwak's category of hegemonic expansionism. Nonetheless, the establishment of Inka centers and outposts along the roads of the empire also reflects an effort to attain territorial security in the face of external as well as internal threats. Although we should, of course, find more points in contrast than in similarity between the Roman Empire and the Inka Empire, both were built perhaps less from a grand strategy than from continuing struggle to sustain hegemonic expansionism.

The undisguised violence of this struggle sharpens the edge of what world-systems analysis refers to as core/periphery relations. "Unequal relations of exchange" between core and periphery is too tame a characterization. The formation of hierarchical relations between cores and peripheries reveals often ferocious struggles between and within regions, classes, and factions. Exploration of the Inka expansionist state allows us to see something of a mosaic of such relations, with each piece of the mosaic composed of a complex variety of local and regional conditions in interplay with an expansionist state seeking to transcend the merely local and regional interests. To this end, the Inka state took significant steps toward transforming modes of production in the Andes.

## Transformations in Mode of Production

I use the term "mode of production" to refer to

the basic logic revealed in the processes of the mobilization of social labor, the production of the material requisites of life, and the reproduction of social institutions which enable material production and accumulation to be accomplished (Chase-Dunn and Hall 1991:3).

Following this sense of mode of production, my argument will be that expansion of the Inka state brought in many cases fundamental changes in these processes. However, the overall outcome, at least up to the time of the Spanish conquest, was that the basic logic was incompletely transformed from kin-based modes of production to tributary modes. This followed in part from contradictions at the center--the royal elites wanted to maintain the advantages of narrowly restricting access to their own lands and privileges (hence retaining centrality of kinship), while seeking also the advantage of alienating land and labor from others without regard to the nexus of kin and community. The incompleteness of the transformation reflects also the still inchoate development of core/periphery hierarchy. Cuzco's status as core was indisputable (which is to say it would respond violently if disputed), while the status of other regions as relative periphery was still in contention.

## 22 ECONOMIC ANTHROPOLOGY OF THE STATE

*The Andean Kin-Based Mode of Production*

Throughout the Andes, the mobilization of social labor, production, reproduction of social institutions, and also modes of exchange were organized in terms of kinship. The vast majority of the population was engaged in village-level farming. Access to agricultural land was then the single most important issue in the productive system, and that access was determined through kin-defined rights and obligations.[2] Allocation or reallocation of lands reflected demographic fluctuations within the kin groups, and no apparent place existed for outsiders. One indication of this is the severe disruption accompanying the appearance of such uprooted people (termed *forasteros*) in the aftermath of the Spanish conquest.

As Pease (1986) argues, private ownership of agricultural land was an alien concept in Andean communities. Land was held collectively, and usufruct rights were allotted among the membership of clearly defined groups. Traditionally these groups would be the *ayllus*, which were, and are, kin-groups. Although we are uncertain of the precise kin criteria for membership, we are not at all uncertain that the *ayllu* was a land-holding group. As in other societies, kinship may be sometimes more a metaphor about access to land than a metaphor about biology.

Access to land given through the *ayllu* was subject to readjustment according to varying household needs. Descriptions of community ceremonies reaffirming usufruct rights can be found both in ethnohistoric accounts and in contemporary ethnographic accounts. Access to labor to work agricultural land was also organized along the kin lines of the *ayllu*. *Ayllu* membership and access to land were predicated upon a commitment to reciprocal co-operative labor. This equation of community membership, access to resources, and reciprocal labor obligation is one of the most deeply rooted of all Andean institutions.

Despite the ideological premises emphasizing kinship, community, reciprocity, and generosity, some members of the community enjoyed some advantages over others when it came to claims on reciprocity. In the absence of a medium of exchange, the most secure means to wealth was in access to the labor of others. Some members of the community, known as the *kurakas*, were entitled to labor services beyond those given in normal reciprocity. Having access to a larger labor pool, *kurakas* also had access to greater amounts of land. As the Spaniards interpreted it, this meant that the *kurakas* were privileged both with land and labor.

Nonetheless, it is quite clear that the *kuraka* had to *request* the labor services, and it is quite clear that he was expected to be generous in providing beer and food to those who served him. However, given that what constitutes generosity is subject to opinion and negotiation, we should not be surprised to find that many opportunities arose for the reciprocity to be asymmetrical.

Despite the inequalities within the community that came from some privileged kin statuses, it remained a community bounded by a moral order in which kin relations were the matrix for production, exchange, and consumption. It was a community from which neither land nor labor could be alienated. It was a community in which many things had value, but nothing had a price.

*The Andean Tributary Mode of Production*

The explosive expansion of the Inka state brought rapid and yet incomplete transformations from the kin-based mode of production. Although the Inka state retained and attempted to manipulate the language of kinship, reciprocity, and generosity, it brought fundamental changes in the mobilization of social labor, the production of material requisites of life, and reproduction of social institutions.

The mobilization of social labor is perhaps the most dramatic achievement of the Inka state. As portrayed in the dynastic traditions, the first major transformations occurred in the Cuzco Valley. Potentially disloyal peoples were expelled, initiating the practice later institutionalized as *mitmaq*, populations temporarily or permanently relocated for state interests. Following relocation of questionable subjects, those allowed to remain in Cuzco were called to meet with the Inka, who *requested* that they provide labor services for such projects as channeling the rivers and building a new city of monumental masonry.

Reciprocal labor service now meant that all members of the expanding Inka "family" owed labor to the state on a rotating basis, known as *mit'a*. If ultimately the family included some ten million people and every household owed labor service to the head of the family, opportunities for asymmetrical reciprocity abounded. To be sure, the Inka had to be generous in return, but generosity increasingly took relatively inexpensive forms of ritual service and providing laborers with beer and cloth during their labor rotation.

Success of the Inka state in mobilizing labor was the most obvious legacy of the empire. Massive stone structures, terracing, roads, and administrative centers spread over thousands of kilometers in little more than a century stand in stolid witness to the state labor mobilization.

## 24  ECONOMIC ANTHROPOLOGY OF THE STATE

Production of the material requisites of life also underwent transformation under state impetus. Apart from the massive projects carried out under the state labor mobilization, production was also altered at the local level. Communities were assessed tribute to be given to the state and to the state cults. However, since the rule was that communities must not be assessed tribute from their own lands, new lands had to be created. In other words, the state demanded agricultural intensification, which could mean little more than working lands previously unworked, but often required terracing, irrigation, fertilization, or other intensification techniques. It was this drive to intensify production and to absorb or even create new lands and resources that fueled the Inka impulse to conquer.

In addition to demanding increases in the quantity of agricultural production, the state also promoted fundamental change in the very crops produced. The foundations for village subsistence had been primarily tubers, and it would appear unlikely that any community could have been viable if it were unable to be self-sufficient in tuber production. However, the Inka state had particular interest in fomenting maize production as *the* state crop (Murra 1960, Hastorf 1990a). The elaborate terracing at so many Inka sites is one remnant of the state interest in maize production, since it is maize and *not* tubers that requires terracing and irrigation. Further indication of the importance of maize comes from the records of ceremonies and songs centering on maize (Inka tradition provides ample discussion of maize ritual, yet has little to say about potato rituals -- for these see Cock and Doyle 1979).[3]

We see archaeological evidence of the dietary shift in the surveys of state storehouses, and in the very bones of the Wanka population. Trace element analysis gives clear evidence of a dietary shift following incorporation of the Wanka within the Inka state. It was, furthermore, commoners as well as elites who benefited from the move to maize production (Hastorf 1990a, Costin and Earle 1989).

That commoners showed evidence of added maize in their diet should not be surprising. It is most likely that their opportunities to eat (or more likely drink) maize came during their periods of labor service. Providing maize beer was one of the principal expressions of state generosity. Through generous provisioning of a highly valued food item, the state enhanced its legitimacy at the expense of local elites. In this way, the state attempted to co-opt the population at large rather than the elites alone.

Although commoners may have benefited from a shift to maize production, we should not ignore the broader significance of such a shift for state policy. Community autonomy and self-sufficiency under the kinship mode of production was in large part built around the ability of every community to produce tubers by using ancient techniques. The appearance of a wonderful new state crop, accompanied by wonderful new rituals, required fundamental changes in the way communities organized production, consumption, and exchange. Maize production has quite different labor and land demands than does tuber production. This is particularly the case in the Andean highlands, which reach the upper altitude limits of maize production. Furthermore, given its importance in state rituals and prestations, maize was not to be consumed according to the will of the community, but was strictly controlled by the state.

Although maize might have been one of the most visible state interventions in local production, archaeological evidence reveals intervention in local craft production as well. Again, data from the Wanka region show that the state controlled access to materials used in metal craft production as well as in ceramic production. Consequently, "locally manufactured high-value items were replaced by items produced by state artisans in the state style" (Costin and Earle 1989:711).

Under this tributary mode of production, the state attempted to replace the control of local elites over production, exchange, and status with its own control. Its ability to do so was based in part on manipulating ideologies of generosity and legitimacy, as well as in providing visible evidence of generosity to local communities. Costin and Earle show four of the major means the state achieved this in its incorporation of the Wanka:

1. By providing highly valued foods, such as maize, high-value utilitarian items, and some luxury items, the gap between local elites and commoners was narrowed under Inka rule.
2. Household storage among Wanka elites was replaced by a state storage system directed more to interests of commoners.
3. Hosting of feasts became a state function rather than local elite generosity.
4. Social differences between elites and commoners came to be marked by state rather than local symbols.
(Costin and Earle 1989:710-711).

Through such strategies the state was able to impose tribute demands and at the same time attempt to tie the loyalties of the subject populations to the state rather than to the local elites. Large quantities of beer seem to have been an important lubricant in this process.

# 26 ECONOMIC ANTHROPOLOGY OF THE STATE

Attempts to transfer loyalties from the community or regional elites to those of the state were one form of attack on the kin mode of production (although, as argued below, this was done also by manipulating idioms of kinship). Perhaps one of the most dramatic strategies, however, came with the extraction of women from communities to serve state interests.

We may turn to Chincha where we find one of our earliest documents on Inka strategies of incorporation in the "Relación de Chincha" of 1558. Exchange of women is one of the major preoccupations of this document. Conditions before the Pax Inkaica in the region are described in the by now familiar image of competing polities whose members seemed rather enthusiastically dedicated to bashing one another. Conflict resolution is directly associated with exchange of women:

> y el precip(a)l remedio que tenían pa(ra) bibir en paz era darse mugeres los unos a los otros.
>
> [the principal means they had to live in peace was to give women to one another].

When the Inka state entered the scene, it too demanded women from Chincha. These women, however, were not part of attempted conflict resolution through marriage exchange. Instead they were to be removed permanently from the kin-based community to serve the state as *aclla* (the famous "chosen women"). Although this document fails to elaborate on what customarily happened with *aclla*, we have ample testimony from other sources on the importance of prestations of women (Silverblatt 1987, 1988).

The labor services of *aclla* were of some considerable importance in the Inka state. They were chicha brewers in the state hospitality centers so vital in the state control system (Morris comments that Huanuco Pampa looks more like a great beer hall than a monument of bureaucracy). They were also weavers of fine cloth, perhaps the single most important wealth item in Inka economy. We have probably not begun to appreciate the value of women's forced labor in textile production for the Inka (we may see close parallels in Mycenae, Crete, and Sumer also).

Some of the women taken as tribute to the Inka state were taken to Cuzco as *aclla* who might then be given as wives to favored elites in Cuzco or in other regions. Some were returned to their home communities to be offered as human sacrifices who then became founding deities of local branches of the Cuzco-sponsored cult. Accompanying rituals then established kin connections between Cuzco and the home region.

The Inka state reproduced its control strategies by intervening directly in control over reproduction in incorporated regions. In addition to demanding tribute from women or women *as* tribute, the state also directly intervened at times to assign marriage partners. If we are to speak of the means of reproduction of social institutions, the literal reproduction of the population itself is certainly at the heart of the matter. State command over the labor and reproduction of women represents a profound challenge to a kin-based mode of production.

Ironically, perhaps even cynically, the Inka state exchanged women at times in an attempt to establish kin connections between Cuzco and the provinces. Removal of a woman to Cuzco as an *aclla* and "bride of the Inka", or a gift of a royal *aclla* to a provincial *kuraka* established symbolic affinal ties. However, the stronger connections were those of descent, and to establish this special connection required a very special ritual institution, the *capacocha*.

In this ritual, the daughter of a *kuraka* was taken to Cuzco to be honored as an *aclla-capacocha*. Following great celebrations in the presence of her provincial gods and the important men of her province, she was then returned to her home province. There she was buried alive as sacrifice to the Sun. The Inka then commanded that she be worshipped, and lands and priests would be assigned to her cult. Her father was then promoted to something beyond a mere provincial *kuraka*; he was the father of a Cuzco-approved goddess. Thereby his descent line held a sacred connection to Cuzco (Silverblatt 1988).

In the name of kinship, reciprocity, and generosity, women could be torn from their communities and their lives torn from them. To be sure, the majority of *acllas* did not become human sacrifices, but all were permanently removed from their community for state interests. Christine Gailey aptly portrays the larger significance of the extraction of people, particularly women, from their kin-based communities:

> Both women *and conquest* can produce new producers. The identity of captives, slaves or citizens vis-a-vis the state classes is not as kin, but as producers -- of food, of crafts, of production projects -- as service workers who support the lifestyle of the elite (servants, porters, etc.), or as producers of both goods and people (concubines, slave women, secondary wives, etc.) (Gailey 1985:81).

This then poses a fundamental tension in the transformation from the kin-based mode of production to the tributary mode of production. Under the former, production as well as exchange were understood as relations of reciprocity and generosity between kin. Under the latter, production and exchange are relations between *producers*, with clear understanding that increasing specialization in production implies that some will play a larger role than others in producing the material means for social reproduction.

Under the kin-based mode of production, projects requiring resources and labor beyond the means of individual households could be undertaken by appealing to the broader kin connections of *ayllus* and moieties. Demands of an expansionist state soon exceeded the limits of kin-bounded groups. Increasingly asymmetrical demands on kin-based communities from increasingly distant elites soon cracked the facade of traditional relations of reciprocity and generosity. As Irene Silverblatt concisely phrases the issue:

> Like other precapitalist states, the Inca project, as set forth in its scant hundred years of rule, seemed condemned by the contradictions of its own making: building an empire on its antinomy, relations of kin (Silverblatt 1988:101).

*Resistance, Rebellion, and Relations of Production*

Cobo's comment that

> the whole foundation of their policy of government rested on means designed to keep their people subject and deprive them of the zeal to revolt against them [1653]

underscores the stark reality that the Inka empire was constantly threatened and frequently racked by violent resistance and rebellion (Murra, 1986). Our understanding of the brittleness of the empire and its dependence on policies combining rewards with threats may again be furthered by recalling Rostworowski's and Luttwak's discussions of expansionism.

The initial phases of Inka expansion correspond to what Rostworowski terms "guerras de rapiña" and to what Luttwak terms "hegemonic expansionism". This allowed Cuzco to undertake a project of "primitive accumulation" perhaps quite aptly symbolized in the very name of the emperor credited with its beginning -- Pachacutec. The name Pachacutec can be understood as "world-upheaver", and it was to him that the transformation of Cuzco from a village of mud huts to a city of monumental masonry was credited. Whoever was responsible, the traditions make it clear that the great energy required for this project was mobilized through promises both of generosity and violence.

In short order, Cuzco was able to monopolize its valley and adjoining region. As an apparently peripheral area for centuries, this part of the southern highlands offered no serious organized competition to Cuzco. Once Cuzco began a successful campaign of commanding its own region, it faced no immediate resistance group organized on a comparable scale. Unlike the situations in Mesopotamia, the Aegean, or Mexico, where dense trading networks led to competitive centers, Cuzco was quickly able to establish a power monopoly (Ekholm and Friedman 1982).

Rostworowski describes the initial expansion as a time of simple raiding and looting without territorial conquest, since the same communities were apparently repeatedly conquered. However, I would suggest the issue is not a lack of territorial ambition so much as a common problem of cores expanding against peripheries where organization is far less centralized. The small kin-based communities Cuzco attacked could flee to higher places or disperse. What Cuzco could achieve in such cases was *hegemony* -- it would be sufficient to offer "friendship" and threats. When such communities failed to meet their obligations to Cuzco, then Cuzco would simply be obliged to return to renew the friendly exchanges forcibly.

Such hegemonic strategies in the Inka case may in fact leave little archaeological evidence, since the Inka army did not require permanent bases. For example, what may well have been the largest Inka military force ever gathered was present at Cajamarca at the time the Spaniards arrived, and they were sheltered in tents. Nonetheless, even in the absence of permanent military structures, the success of the Inka hegemonic strategy was contingent upon effective infrastructure and organization. This above all meant the Inka had to work out an effective supply and transport system. Military strategies, whether directed largely toward hegemony or toward conquest and incorporation, were costly and grew even more costly when they were successful in bringing ever more distant regions under their sway. As with other empires, the more the Inka state expanded, the more it *had* to expand to feed the growing needs of empire.

In the absence of a monetary or commoditized economy, and lacking other core regions to trade with, the state and its military apparatus could not be supplied through trade or purchase of needed items. To gain these, the state needed to acquire more *producers*. A kin-based mode of production, with its moral imperatives to observe proper reciprocities, set inconvenient brakes on such demands. When increasing amounts of community labor appear to be directed toward extra-community needs or demands, when the *mit'a* (corvée labor) keeps laborers away from the community for extended periods of time, when laborers are increasingly assigned to non-agricultural tasks, the problem of providing the material means for social reproduction of the community becomes critical. In these conditions, we should not be surprised to find that rebellion was a perennial response.

One short-term solution is to continue the effort to incorporate ever broader regions of resources and labor. Conquests abroad may lessen the need for repression at home, at least until the adventures into distant provinces become more trouble than they are worth. As modern states also realize, those troubles increase rapidly with distance. Supplying, or preparing to supply, distant armies consumes much of the industrial world's wealth, and it was surely no less a problem in the preindustrial world.

Thus, as the Inka state expanded far beyond Cuzco, it attempted to resolve some of the critical contradictions between the tributary mode of production that drove the state and the kin-based mode of production that continued as the foundation for social reproduction. Two major steps in this direction involved changes in the social mobilization of labor and allocation of access to land.

*Changes in Labor Mobilization*

Two state institutions were direct assaults on the kin-based mode of production. The first was the policy of forced resettlement of local populations. It is first mentioned in the dynastic traditions in the context of the expansion of the Inka state within the Cuzco Valley. Dissident or potentially disruptive communities were simply exiled and replaced by others of more certain loyalty. Soon we see the use of loyal communities as settlers in distant regions to bring them under state control. We also see such people sent to work in unpopulated or depopulated areas or otherwise unproductive areas. Yet others came to be assigned to specialized productive tasks (Murra 1978).

These state colonists, known as *mitmaq*, broke the previously unbreakable association between kin-group membership and access to lands held "since time immemorial". Such laborers could then be moved to meet state needs and could be resettled permanently. Since they were severed from the lands of their home communities and were not to be rotated back to their original communities, the problem of long-distance provisioning was obviated. As we can see from testimony in many of the later lawsuits of the Colonial era, *mitmaq* were assigned lands to provision themselves in the regions to which they were assigned. Although later students may occasionally confuse the similar sounding *mit'a* with *mitmaq*, the distinction seems quite clear in the lawsuits: those on *mit'a* service were not granted lands, while *mitmaq were* allocated land.

A second direct assault on the kin-based mode of production came with the taking of women as *aclla*. What the *aclla* had in common with the *mitmaq* was that they too were removed from the network of kin and moral ties that linked them to the people and land of their home communities. They, too, were state-mobilized labor who were assigned productive tasks without regard to the material and social reproduction of their home communities.

Thus these two pivotal institutions in Inka statecraft appear to have been some of the earliest foundations for a labor mobilization system that attempted to crush the contradiction between kin and state. In what appears to be a later development, we find increasing references to yet another form of state-mobilized labor, those known as *yana*. *Yana*, sometimes misinterpreted as "slaves" in older literature, were retainers assigned to state service, service to cults, and in service to private elite estates as well. As was the case with *aclla* and *mitmaq*, the *yana* were removed from their communities of origin and were not subject to the rotating labor draft. With these three state institutions we find a radical severing of labor obligations from rights within a kin-based community.

Labor and land were the foundations for Andean production. With the expansion of the tributary mode of production, labor was increasingly removed from its entanglement with kin and community lands. Following the extraction of labor from the nexus of kinship, we come finally to the extraction of land as well.

*Changes in Land Mobilization: State Farms*

The logistical problem an expansionist agrarian state confronts when it moves its armies into distant peripheral regions may be addressed by what I have termed "land mobilization". One attempted solution for the Inka empire's problem in provisioning armies on lengthy campaign in the far north was to establish what might be called *state farms*.

The most elaborate of these was established in the Cochabamba Valley of what is now Bolivia. In this very large and fertile valley we find another world-upheaval. Once again, this time far to the south of Cuzco, the inhabitants of a rich fertile valley were evicted. This time, however, the Inka did not come to build a city or a state. They came to make a farm to feed soldiers on campaign far to the north of Cuzco.

According to sixteenth century documents, a permanent labor force numbering some fourteen thousand strong was brought in to work the fields, and to stock and maintain the storehouses so that ultimately maize could be

## 32 ECONOMIC ANTHROPOLOGY OF THE STATE

taken to Cuzco, and from there to provision the army fighting for Huayna Capac in the far north. Testimony on this point seems quite clear:

> [Los testigos] conforman en que el maíz que se sembraba en los dichos suyus que así repartieron para todas las naciones de indios que andaban en la guerra con el dicho Inca Guayna Capa (Morales 1977 [1570]:26).

> [[The witnesses] confirmed that the maize grown in these fields was for all the nations of Indians that marched in the war with Inka Huayna Capac].

The lands necessary to produce such vast quantities of maize that over 2400 storehouses can still be identified today were not *ayllu* lands worked by *ayllu* members. They were *state* lands, worked by state laborers. The lands had been extracted from their kin nexus. The labor also had been extracted from its kin nexus, since the permanent labor force was made up of *mitmaq*. The heavier labor demands during sowing and harvest were supplemented with *mit'a* rotation labor. The *mitmaq* were allocated about ten percent of the agricultural land to provide for their own subsistence (Wachtel 1982).

Another state farm was located much closer to Cuzco in the Abancay Valley. Here also the state claimed the land and brought a permanent labor force composed of *mitmaq* from many polities. Here the state labor force worked state lands to produce coca, chile peppers, cotton, and a number of local fruits. Here also the witnesses were quite clear on the reasons so much was being produced and moved to state storehouses:

> E que estando en Tomebamba el dicho Guayna Capa envio un indio llamado Sacapacha para que le llevase todo el algodón y ají y otras cosas que se habían cogido y estaban en depósito para el sustento de la guerra que tenía entonces (Espinoza 1973 [1575]:287).

> [And being in Tomebamba, Huayna Capac sent an Indian named Sacapacha to bring all the cotton and chile peppers and other things that had been harvested in order to support the war then underway].

The development of state farms to meet the increasing demands of provisioning state expansion represented a significant departure from the kin-based mode of production. Perhaps put to purposes other than or in addition to the militaristic expansion of the state, such new ventures in labor and land mobilization offered unprecedented possibilities for state production and investment. However, although this state land and labor mobilization could ultimately have supplanted the kin-based mode of production, it was accompanied by a parallel contradiction.

*Elite Private Estates*

The state farms exemplify extraction of both land and labor from the nexus of kinship. However, I have not yet examined the kin-based mode of production as it applied not to commoners, but to the Cuzco elites. Although the state may have had an interest in undermining the kin-based mode of production as it applied to Cuzco's periphery, the very elites who constituted the rulership factions of that state had strong interests in preserving the kin-based mode of production in the heart of the empire.

The heart of the city of Cuzco was an elite preserve. Within it lived the people who belonged to the ten royal lineages, the *panacas*. Membership in a *panaca* was defined in kin terms, and the *panacas* also were land and wealth holding units. Members were supported, in many cases quite lavishly, from *panaca* estates, each of which was jealously guarded as *panaca* and *not* state property.

Although we cannot in all cases separate claims that an estate belonged to an emperor or queen from claims that it truly belonged to the emperor or queen's *panaca*, private estates were vastly rich. Closely adjoining Cuzco, the Yucay Valley was certainly one of the richest in all the Andes. Within the Yucay we find such major Inka sites as Ollantaytambo and the magnificent Inka "city" known as Pisac. These, however, were not cities as we understand them, but rather private estates. For that matter, John Rowe argues that the magical "city" of Machu Picchu was also one of Inka Pachacutec's private estates (Rowe 1990). *Yana* laborers worked the private estates of the emperors and their *panacas*, and we are told that Huayna Capac's estates in the Yucay Valley required over two thousand *yana*.

Here again we find land and labor extracted from the nexus of kinship in communities, only to be attached to the kinship nexus of the Inka elite class. Just as state military expansion called for the vast mobilization of labor and ultimately land, sustaining the elite lineages of Cuzco also required a massive mobilization of resources. The cost of maintaining this expensive body of elites and elite corpses (the ostensible founder of each of the royal *panacas* was a royal mummy, and it was in the name of the mummy that the estates were preserved and worked) was apparent to the Inka rulers themselves. In fact, at one point the Inka Huascar threatened to burn the royal mummies--a proposal that no doubt gained him little popularity among some of the *panaca* clubhouses!

To the extent that the rivalry among the *panacas* for the power and wealth of the empire was directly responsible for the fratricidal war that contributed to the collapse of the empire, we may conclude that the contradiction between the kin-based mode of production and a still incomplete separation of state and elite kin interests proved to be fatal for the Inka state.

## An Archaic Empire: The Fragility of the Stones

As we examine the rapid expansion of the Inka empire, we find behind its monumental facade a number of weaknesses it shared with other archaic empires. Growth, once undertaken, requires nourishment, which may then allow greater growth, and then demand greater growth. The care and feeding of states and empires is a formidable task, and, as the Inka knew well, one cannot feed on stone.

The Inka state certainly demonstrated uncommon genius in its ability to incorporate or maintain hegemony over highly diverse regions. In its expansion it applied a number of control strategies incorporating varying mixtures of blunt force, rewards, and attempts to claim legitimacy in terms of enduring Andean values. As it rose to increasing strength as a core state, it reorganized the Andean world.

Those peoples it could not organize, it threatened or terrorized. Those it could organize were to varying degrees incorporated within the empire as peripheral regions owing tribute to the center. In the case of the more powerful regional polities, particularly those of the coast, the relationship appears to have been semi-peripheral. Polities such as Chincha and Chimu on the coast, and perhaps the Lupaqa in the southern highlands, were assigned tribute obligations to the Inka empire, yet allowed to command or exchange resources on their own with lesser polities.

Part of the Inka empire's success may be attributed to lack of competition from comparable core polities. This, however, may also account for part of its ultimate failure. As Diamond puts it, "civilization originates in conquest abroad and repression at home" (Diamond 1974:1). As an empire expands, it begins to run out of "abroad". When it manipulates ideologies of legitimacy, it claims to broader and broader regions that it *is* home, so that the circle of repression grows ever wider. Distant provinces indeed become more reluctant to obey, as do not-so-distant provinces. Perhaps the absence of other core polities, who may serve not only as enemies but perhaps at times also as allies and trade partners, helped force the Inka state increasingly to consume itself.

An expansionist state growing from and upon communities in which production, exchange, and consumption are defined in terms of kinship-based obligations and rights faces severe challenges to its ability to extract labor and resources from increasingly reluctant communities. Expansion helps pay the costs of expansion, yet it also increases those costs.

The Inka empire presents a case of an expansionist state still struggling with these contradictions. It had only recently begun its effort to extract labor and land from their nexus of kinship, while at the same time attempting to reduce the costs of doing so by manipulating traditional symbols of legitimacy and by introducing new state symbols. Detaching labor and finally land from the kin-based communities was a significant step in increasing the vertical separation of core and periphery. Nonetheless, at the time of the Spanish conquest, many of the institutions of empire remained inchoate.

As we see so dramatically from Andean archaeology, the Inka empire was wonderfully skilled at moving huge stones. It was effectively organizing the infrastructure of imperialism, though, as had earlier empires before, it was discovering that great distances ultimately pose some of the most serious organizational problems.

Finally, although the Inka empire demonstrated what might be fairly called organizational genius, genius has its limits. What remained inchoate was institutionalization of the state organization itself, which had not yet transcended the limitations of kin-based modes of production. As Christine Hastorf so wonderfully puts it:

> Fundamentally, political hierarchy marks a shift from *power to organize* to *power over the organization* (Hastorf 1990b: 149).

Despite its monumental architecture, the Inka state was still far from monolithic. The vision that states project of coherent or even monolithic decision-making apparatuses is illusory. The Inka state reveals the internal factions and contradictions that we might find to varying degree in any state we examine closely. Although it was uncommonly successful in its power to organize (given its limited technology and overwhelming environmental challenges), it was still struggling with building the organization of its power.

## Acknowledgments

Since its original presentation at the 1991 Meeting of the Society for Economic Anthropology, this paper has benefited greatly from very extensive and thoughtful comments from Joyce Marcus, Christine Hastorf, M. Estellie Smith, and, of course, Liz Brumfiel. Continuing discussions with Tom Hall have also played a large role in exploring the potential of revisionist world-systems theory.

## Notes

1. However, Rostworowski explicitly rejects the term "empire" in regard to the Inka, since the term has "too many connotations from the Old World" and since the Inka followed their own evolution and their own original solutions to their problems and necessities. For that matter, she also rejects even the term "state" and argues simply that we should call whatever it is *Tawantinsuyu* (though she argues that even this was more ideal than reality!).

2. For a very thorough discussion of land tenure in the Andes from Inka times through the colonial era, see M. La Lone (1985).

3. Joyce Marcus (personal communication) points out that many terraces in coastal valleys were constructed in Late Intermediate times. This indicates that agricultural intensification, including maize production, was a fundamental part of the growth and strength of coastal polities *before* the emergence of the Inka state in the highlands. In fact, the ethnohistoric documents frequently refer to pre-Inka coastal polities as *kingdoms*, a term not commonly applied in the highlands. As others also have suggested, important elements of Inka statecraft may have originated in the coastal polities.

## References

Bauer, Brian.
  in press *The Development of the Inca State*. Austin: University of Texas Press.
Blanton, Richard, and Gary Feinman.
  1984 The Mesoamerican World System. *American Anthropologist*: 673-82.
Chase-Dunn, Christopher, and Tom Hall.
  1991 *Core/periphery Relations in Precapitalist Worlds*. Boulder: Westview Press.
Cock, Guillermo and M.E. Doyle.
  1979 Del culto solar a la clandestinidad de Inti y Punchao. *Historia y Cultura* 12:51-73. Lima.
Costin, Cathy L. and Timothy Earle
  1989 Status Distinction and Legitimation of Power as Reflected in Changing Patterns of Consumption in Late Prehispanic Peru. *American Antiquity* 54:691-714.
D'Altroy, Terrence N.
  1981 *Empire Growth and Consolidation: the Xauxa Region of Peru Under the Inca*. Unpublished Ph.D. dissertation. University of California at Los Angeles.
  1987 Transitions in Power: Centralization of Wanka Political Organization Under Inka Rule. *Ethnohistory* 34:78-102.
D'Altroy, Terrence N. and Ronald L. Bishop
  1990 The Provincial Organization of Inka Ceramic Production. *American Antiquity* 55:120-38.
Diamond, Stanley
  1974 *In Search of the Primitive*. New York: E.P. Dutton.
Ekholm, Kasja, and Jonathan Friedman
  1979 Towards a Global Anthropology. In L. Blusse, H.L. Wesseling, and G.D. Winius, eds., *History and Underdevelopment*, pp.61-76. Leiden: Center for the History of European Expansion.
  1982 "Capital" Imperialism and Exploitation in Ancient World-systems. *Review* 4:87-109.
Espinoza Soriano, Waldemar
  1973 Colonias de mitmas multiples en Abancay, siglos XV y XVI. *Revista del Museo Nacional* 39:225-99. Lima.

Gailey, Christine W.
    1985   The State of the State in Anthropology. *Dialectical Anthropology* 9:65-89.

Hastorf, Christine A.
    1983   *Prehistoric Agricultural Intensification and Political development in the Jauja Region of Central Peru.* Unpublished Ph.D. dissertation. The University of California at Los Angeles.
    1990a  The Effect of the Inka State on Sausa Agricultural Production and Crop Consumption. *American Antiquity* 55:262-90.
    1990b  One Path to the Heights: Negotiating Political Inequality in the Sausa of Peru. In S. Upham, ed., *The Evolution of Political Systems*, pp.146-76. Cambridge: Cambridge University Press.

Kipp, Rita S. and Edward M. Schortman
    1989   The Political Impact of Trade in Chiefdoms. *American Anthropologist* 91:370-85.

Kohl, Philip
    1978   The Balance of Trade in Southwestern Asia in the Third Millennium B.C. *Current Anthropology* 19:463-92.
    1979   The "World Economy" of West Asia in the Third Millennium B.C. In M. Taddei, ed., *South Asian Archaeology 1977*, pp.55-85. Naples.
    1987   The Use and Abuse of World Systems Theory: The Case of the Pristine West Asian State. In M. Schiffer, ed., *Advances in Archaeological Method and Theory*, Vol.11, pp.1-33. New York: Academic Press.

La Lone, Darrell
    1978   *Historical Contexts of Trade and Markets in the Peruvian Andes.* Unpublished Ph.D. dissertation. The University of Michigan.
    1982   The Inca as a Non-market Economy: Supply on Command Versus Supply and Demand. In J.E. Ericson and T.K. Earle, eds., *Contexts for Prehistoric Exchange*, pp.291-316. New York: Academic Press.

La Lone, Mary
    1985   *Indian Land Tenure in Southern Cuzco, Peru: From Inca to Colonial Patterns.* Unpublished Ph.D. dissertation. University of California at Los Angeles.

La Lone, Mary and Darrell La Lone
    1978    The Inca State in the Southern Highlands: State Administrative and Production Enclaves. *Ethnohistory* 34:47-62.

Leblanc, Catherine J.
    1981    *Late Prehispanic Huanca Settlement Patterns in the Yanamarca Valley, Peru*. Unpublished Ph.D. dissertation. University of California at Los Angeles.

Levine, T.Y.
    1979    *Prehistoric Political and Economic Change in Highland Peru: An Ethnohistorical Study of the Mantaro Valley*. Unpublished Master's Thesis, Archaeology Program, University of California at Los Angeles.
    1985    *Inka Administration in the Central Highlands: A Comparative Study*. Ph.D. dissertation, University of California at Los Angeles.
    1987    Inka Labor Service at the Regional Level: The Functional Reality. *Ethnohistory* 34:14-46.

Luttwak, Edward
    1976    *The Grand Strategy of the Roman Empire*. Baltimore: Johns Hopkins University Press.

Marcus, Joyce
    1987    Prehistoric Fishermen in the Kingdom of Huarco. *American Scientist* 75:393-401.

Moore, Sally Falk
    1958    *Power and Property in Inca Peru*. New York: Greenwood Press.

Morales, A. (comp.)
    1977    *Repartimiento de Tierras por el Inca Huayna Capac (Testimonio de un Documento de 1556)*. Cochabamba: Universidad Boliviana Mayor de San Simón, Departamento de Arqueología, Museo Arqueológica.

Murra, John V.
    1960    Rite and Crop in the Inca State. In S. Diamond, ed., *Culture and History*, pp.393-407. New York: Columbia University Press.
    1972    El control vertical de un máximo de pisos ecológicos en la economía de las sociedades andinas. In J.V. Murra, ed., *Visita de la Provincia de Huanuco*, vol. 2, pp.427-76. Huanuco: Universidad Nacional Hermilio Valdizan.

1978   Los olleros del Inka: hacia una historia y arqueología del Qollasuyu. In F. Miro Quesada C., F. Pease G.Y. and D. Sobrevilla A., eds., *Historia Problema Promesa*, pp.415-23. Lima: Pontífica Universidad Católica del Perú.

1980 [1956]   *The Economic Organization of the Inka State*. New York: JAI Press.

1982   The *Mit'a* Obligations of Ethnic Groups to the Inka State. In G.A. Collier, R.I. Rosaldo, and J.D. Wirth, eds., *The Inca and Aztec States, 1400-1800*, pp.237-62. New York: Academic Press.

1986   The Expansion of the Inka State: Armies, War, and Rebellions. In J.V. Murra, N. Wachtel, and J. Revel, eds., *Anthropological History of Andean Polities*, pp.49-58. Cambridge: Cambridge University Press.

Parsons, Jeffrey R. and Charles M. Hastings
1988   The Late Intermediate Period. In R.W. Keatinge, ed., *Peruvian Prehistory*, pp.190-229. Cambridge: Cambridge University Press.

Parsons, Jeffrey R. and R. Matos Mendieta
1978   Asentamientos prehispanicos en el Mantaro, Peru: informe preliminar. In R. Matos Mendieta, ed., *Actas y Trabajos del III Congreso del Hombre y la Cultura Andina, II*, pp.540-56. Lima: Editora Lasontay.

Pease, Franklin G.Y.
1986   La noción de propiedad entre los Incas: una aproximación. In S. Masuda, ed., *Etnografía e Historia del Mundo Andino*, pp.3-33. Universidad de Tokio.

Renfrew, Colin and John Cherry, eds.
1986   *Peer Polity Interaction and Socio-Political Change*. Cambridge: Cambridge University Press.

Rostworowski de Diez Canseco, María
1970   Mercaderes del valle de Chincha en la época prehispánica: un documento y unos comentarios. *Revista Española de Antropología Americana* 5:135-78. Madrid.

1988   *Historia del Tahuantinsuyu*. Lima: Instituto de Estudios Peruanos.

Rowe, John H.
1990   Machu Picchu a la luz de documentos del siglo XVI. *Histórica* 14:139-54.

Sarmiento de Gamboa, Pedro
    1906 [1572] Segunda parte de la Historia general llamada Indica...In R. Pletschmann, ed. *Geschichte des Inkareiches von Pedro Sarmiento de Gamboa.* Berlin: Weidmannsche Buchhandlung.

Schneider, Jane
    1977 Was There a Pre-Capitalist World System? *Peasant Studies* 6:20-9.

Schortman, Edward M.
    1989 Interregional Interaction in Prehistory: The Need for a New Perspective. *American Antiquity* 54:52-65.

Silverblatt, Irene
    1987 *Moon, Sun, and Witches.* Princeton: Princeton University Press.
    1988 Imperial Dilemmas, the Politics of Kinship, and Inca Reconstructions of History. *Comparative Studies in Society and History* 3:83-102.

Upham, Steadman
    1982 *Polities and Power.* New York: Academic Press.
    1986 Imperialists, Isolationists, World Systems and Political Realities: Perspectives on Mesoamerican-Southwestern Interaction. In F.J. Mathien and R.H. McGuire, eds., *Ripples in the Chichimec Sea*, pp.205-19. Carbondale: Southern Illinois University Press.

Wachtel, Nathan
    1982 The Mitimas of the Cochabamba Valley: The Colonization Policy of Huayna Capac. In G.A. Collier, R.I. Rosaldo, and J.D. Wirth, eds., *The Inca and Aztec States 1400-1800*, pp.199-235. New York: Academic Press.

Wallerstein, Immanuel
    1974 *The Modern World System: Capitalist Agriculture and the Origins of the European World-Economy in the 16th Century.* New York: Academic Press.

Whitecotton, J. and R. Pailes
    1986 New World Precolumbian World Systems. In F.J. Mathien and R.H. McGuire, eds., *Ripples in the Chichimec Sea*, pp.185-204. Southern Illinois University Press.

# THE PEASANT HOUSEHOLD IN THE TRANSITION FROM SOCIALISM: STATE INTERVENTION AND ITS CONSEQUENCES IN CHINA

Susan Greenhalgh
The Population Council

## The Role of the Peasant Household in the Transition from Socialism

In recent years members of the Communist and ex-Communist world have launched a series of sweeping reforms aimed at solving the nagging problems of the socialist economy.[1] While the aims of different states vary -- some hope to "perfect" socialism, others to dismantle it and usher in capitalism -- a centerpiece of all the reform efforts is the privatization of economic assets and activities previously under the control of the state and quasi-state collective sectors.

Privatization has proceeded furthest in the agricultural sector. (Indeed, Poland never collectivized agriculture and Yugoslavia did so only partially and for a few years [Wädekin 1982: esp. 63-82].) The most far-reaching changes have taken place in China, where mass enthusiasm for privatization turned the leadership's tentative experiments in the late 1970s into wholesale reform in the early 1980s. The Chinese reforms were successful beyond all expectation,[2] leading other members of the socialist group, including the former Soviet Union, to look east for lessons in stimulating the rural economy (Desai 1989).

The family plays a crucial role in the transition from socialism, especially in the agricultural sector. This important yet little-recognized point has been underscored by the Hungarian economist János Kornai (1992:455-459) in his monumental synthesis of the political economy of the socialist system. Under "classical socialism" -- exemplified by the Soviet Union under Stalin and China under Mao[3] -- the sphere of activities coordinated by the family shrank drastically. In the areas of production, consumption, and, to a lesser extent, social welfare, the family found its prerevolutionary activities removed from its control and placed in the hands of state and collective bureaucracies. In the reform era these activities, all critical to the reform effort, are thrust back upon the family as the state and collective retreat from social life. Agriculture is placed under household management, individuals and households are expected to become entrepreneurs, consumption is fully privatized, and state promises to support the elderly and infirm, never adequately fulfilled in any case, are finally and officially withdrawn. Since the legal framework for economic activity is not yet firmly established, Kornai (1992:456) argues, the mutual trust "ensured by family ties" provides the social glue needed to smooth economic transactions in the transitional period.

In reassigning production, consumption, and welfare activities to the peasant household, the policies of reform socialism assume that the peasant family will simply take up where it left off when the revolution arrived, reconstructing itself to organize activities it had not managed, or managed in much reduced fashion, for decades. But is this assumption warranted? Is the post-collective peasant family equipped to take on these weighty responsibilities? The answer to this question, which Kornai does not ask, depends on what kind of family has emerged after decades of collective life. Not surprisingly, perhaps, this subject has been little explored; under socialism how things ought to be tends to gets more attention than how they actually are.

In China and, apparently, elsewhere as well (Netting 1989), the economic effectiveness of the pre-collective peasant family was rooted in its flexible access to a potentially large pool of family labor noted for its high reliability and commitment to shared goals, the "mutual trust ensured by family ties" of which Kornai spoke. The importance of these two features of the peasant household -- the elastic quantity and "high quality" of its labor--is suggested by research on the peasant economies of pre-revolutionary China and contemporary Taiwan (e.g., Cohen 1976, Huang 1990).

Students of pre-1949 China were struck by the flexibility of the Chinese family (*jia*) in the face of environmental change. The *jia*, C.K. Yang (1959:9) said, was "like a balloon, ever ready to expand whenever there was wealth to inflate it" or shrink back in response to environmental threats (Skinner 1971). A patrilineal, patrilocal, and patriarchal institution, the family as an enduring corporation was built on the father-son tie.[4] Children generally, and sons specifically, were the family's major mobility and security assets, playing critical roles in agricultural production, economic diversification, property accumulation, and the provision of old-age support, among other things (Yang 1945, Cohen 1976). By contrast, relations between brothers tended to be brittle (see Freedman 1963).[5] The close connection between family size and wealth suggests that the labor force could be readily expanded in times of prosperity (Lang 1946:147-154). Depending on what stage in the family cycle good times arrived, the number of sons in the labor force was boosted by adding children (primarily through fertility) or by delaying the time sons divided to form their own family units.[6]

The "high quality" of the family work force was evident in the willingness of family subordinates -- both the young, discussed here, and females, discussed elsewhere (e.g., Yang 1945, Johnson 1983, Greenhalgh 1985) -- to accept the authority of the head and to work unstintingly for the good of the whole.[7] Lest we romanticize, it should be noted that the qualities of trust and cooperation among family members were rooted not in altruism, but in an intergenerational exchange of resources, which in turn was based on control of the family property by the family head. In this exchange, sons were expected to contribute to the family economy and provide for their elderly parents in return for economic support and a share of the family property at the time of division. Unmarried daughters were expected to contribute to the family economy in exchange for support and a small share of the family property in the form of a dowry at the time of marriage.[8]

The scholarship on collective-era China -- roughly the mid-1950s to the late 1970s -- suggests that many if not most of these features of the traditional peasant family economy were preserved under classical socialism. Students of the Maoist period argue that Chinese socialism not only conserved, but also restored, utilized, and even strengthened traditional village and family institutions (Johnson 1983, Shue 1988). The peasant household retained such traditional functions as the provision of family social security and subsistence production in a pared-down but still important domestic economy centered on the private plot (Parish 1975, Parish and Whyte 1978:200-234, Johnson 1983, Nee 1985). The major study of peasant family economy during classical socialism, Parish and Whyte's *Village and Family in Contemporary China*, argues that, although a few features of the rural political economy tended to loosen the intergenerational bond, even more strengthened it, with the result that young people's ties and obligations to their parents were "not dramatically altered" (1978:231). This literature leads us to expect that once the state retreats from the economy, something resembling the traditional peasant household will reappear and answer the call to develop agriculture, diversify the rural economy, and support the elderly.

Using field data from Shaanxi Province, this paper looks closely at the peasant household economy that has emerged in the reform era. The central concern is the economic role of children, the keys to family mobility and security in the past. In the villages studied, it finds that, almost a decade after the reforms were instituted, children played important roles in agricultural production, but their contributions to entrepreneurship outside agriculture were negligible and their participation in the old-age social security system was contested and insecure. It argues that the state itself was responsible for weakening the family labor regime. State intervention in the social system, a process that began under classical socialism and continued during the reform era, limited the household's ability to adjust its resources to the environment, and loosened the intergenerational bonds that had made it an effective agent of mobility and security in the presocialist past. Of course, people fiercely resisted these interventions (e.g., Greenhalgh 1993). But the balance of power weighed heavily in favor of the state. As of eight years into the reform period, the household's ability to perform the tasks assigned it by the state appeared to be partial at best. It seems that by intervening in and profoundly altering the family system, the state may have unwittingly jeopardized achievement of its own developmental goals.

This study is part of a larger project on the political economy of family change in peasant China over the four decades 1947-87. Field research was carried out during the first six months of 1988.[9] The research focused on three villages in the northwestern province of Shaanxi, an area whose social terrain has never been mapped by anthropologists.[10] The primary source of information used here is a set of family social and economic histories gathered from 150 families randomly selected from the study villages.

## Economic Reform in Village Shaanxi

Located in the Wei River Basin just west of the provincial capital of Xi'an, the villages studied are part of Weinan Township (a pseudonym; 1987 population 26,102), which in turn is part of Xianyang City (1986 population 3.97 million). The three villages varied in size -- their 1982 populations ranged from 1,436 to 707 -- but, with shared cultural backgrounds and political-economic histories, had evolved similar social, economic, and political institutions.

Vegetable growers for the nearby urban populations, the villagers were moderately well-off by Shaanxi standards, though only lower-middling by China-wide criteria. Township records put the 1987 per capita income at 402 *yuan*, 122% of the provincial average (for the agricultural population), but only 87% of the national average.[11]

The township's modest level of prosperity was largely a product of the economic and political reforms of the late 1970s and early 1980s. As in China generally, the reforms were introduced in two broad phases (a convenient overview is Riskin 1987:284-315; for more detail see Griffin

1984, Parish 1985, Perry and Wong 1985, Saith 1987). The first, inaugurated in 1979, was an experimental phase entailing the introduction of limited market incentives within an unreformed collective structure. In Weinan, 1979 brought the return of small private plots to peasant households and the reopening of free markets. In 1980 short-term wage labor outside the commune was officially permitted, enabling peasants to boost their private incomes with short-term work in urban construction and transportation.

Phase II, launched in 1982 in one of the villages and 1983 in the other two, involved the dismantling of the collective structure itself and the introduction of the household responsibility system, which transferred rights to use of the land and management of agriculture to peasant households. Since that time peasants in the three villages have had virtually total control over the use of their plots and marketing of their produce. Although parcels were reshuffled a few times after the initial division of land, from 1984 on the allocations have been relatively permanent. A related set of political changes, known collectively as commune reform, was carried out in 1983. Designed to reduce party control over the economy, these reforms entailed establishing a township government and turning the commune into an economic organization. The production brigade and production team were also abolished, replaced with the villagers' committee and villagers' small group.

The reforms had striking effects on the organization of and rewards to economic activity, especially after decollectivization in Phase II. Some of these changes are documented in Table 1. In Weinan Township peasants shifted land out of grain into vegetables for the market. The proportion of cultivated land in grain (primarily wheat and corn) fell from 42% during 1979-81 to about 30% in 1982-87. That devoted to cash crops, virtually all vegetables, rose from about 40% in 1979-80 to 60% in 1982 and 70% in 1987. While the organization of agriculture underwent major overhaul, little change occurred in the sectoral distribution of economic activity. The share of the township's labor force in agriculture fell slightly, from 96% to 91%, while that in other sectors, in particular commerce, industry, construction, and transportation, increased a few percentage points.

As a result of these and other changes, per capita income soared, rising from 100-200 *yuan* in 1979-83 to about 300 in 1984-85 and 400 *yuan* in 1986-87 (about 300 in real, inflation-adjusted terms [Shaanxi Provincial Bureau of Statistics 1987:240]). Rising incomes brought a flurry of new home construction and acquisition of consumer goods. By 1988, the year I was in the village, one in two families had managed to buy a television set, and a few had contrived to purchase washing machines, motorcycles, and other paraphernalia of modern life.

TABLE 1. ECONOMIC CHANGE IN WEINAN TOWNSHIP, 1979-87

| Year | Population | Cultivated Land by Crop[a] Grain | Vegetables | Labor Force by Sector Agriculture | Industry | Commerce | Net Annual Income Per Capita[b] |
|---|---|---|---|---|---|---|---|
| | | (% of land) | | (% of labor force) | | | (yuan) |
| Reform Phase I | | | | | | | |
| 1979 | 23,283 | 41.9 | 39.6 | 96.2 | 2.1 | .0 | 136 |
| 1980 | 23,454 | 41.8 | 40.0 | 96.4 | 2.1 | .0 | 115 |
| 1981 | 23,723 | 41.5 | 46.6 | 95.8 | 2.2 | .2 | 91 |
| Reform Phase II | | | | | | | |
| 1982 | 24,052 | 29.4 | 60.4 | 95.4 | 1.8 | .3 | 130 |
| 1983 | 24,473 | 31.0 | 65.4 | 94.1 | 1.5 | .3 | 179 |
| 1984 | 24,774 | 27.3 | 72.6 | 95.0 | 1.6 | .3 | 314 |
| 1985 | 25,210 | 31.0 | 68.6 | 92.5 | 1.6 | 1.0 | 327 |
| 1986 | 25,599 | 28.6 | 67.1 | 93.1 | 1.6 | .9 | 371 |
| 1987 | 26,102 | 29.5 | 70.0 | 91.0 | 2.2 | 1.3 | 402 |

Source: Township records

Notes: [a] After distribution of land to households in 1982-83, virtually all vegetables were grown for the market and all grain was grown for home consumption.
[b] 1 yuan = US$.27. Income expressed in current yuan values.

An economic portrait of the 150 households (see Table 2) reveals a community heavily engaged in market transactions but still largely agriculture- and village-bound. Despite their proximity to two urban centers (Xianyang was about 20 minutes away by bicycle, Xi'an 1 1/2 to 2 hours), in 1987 fully 99% of households were engaged in agriculture and 91% of the sample labor force was in agriculture. Migration to work places outside the village was very rare: only 9% of the households had members resident outside the village, and an even lower 3% of the households' members lived elsewhere.

Nor is there evidence of the sorts of commercial and industrial entrepreneurship taken up by peasants on China's southeast coast. The response to economic opportunity was strong, but the villagers' energies were thrown almost entirely into vegetable production. Perhaps because vegetable cultivation was relatively lucrative, few households took advantage of the opportunity to lease their land out and devote full-time to other pursuits. In the first eight years of the reform era, village households had managed to accumulate some privately-owned productive assets, but they were small in scale and limited in expansionary potential. Nearly all households owned the items needed for vegetable cultivation and marketing: bamboo poles and plastic sheets for cold-weather tents, and bicycle-pulled carts. However, only 7% possessed larger-scale properties, and those assets (tractors, trucks, small-scale shops) were hardly the stuff of which fortunes could be built. The overall picture, then, suggests an environment of substantially improved mobility opportunity, but limited response except in vegetable cultivation.

## The Unit of Economic Organization

Since rights to land use, production, and marketing had been handed over to the peasant household, it is not surprising that the household, rather than the family or a group of non-relatives, was the basic unit of economic organization. By household I mean the usually (but not always) co-residential group that shared a budget and cooked and ate together (cf. Wilk and Netting 1984). All households were composed entirely of family or part-family groups (i.e., individuals related by blood, marriage, or adoption); not all families, however, formed single households. The study households were small -- mean household size fell at 4.9 -- and simple in structure. The vast majority were either nuclear (about 55%) or patrilocal stem (41%), suggesting the importance of parent-child, and relative unimportance of brother-brother, ties in organizing economic activity.

TABLE 2. HOUSEHOLD ECONOMIC ORGANIZATION,
150 WEINAN HOUSEHOLDS,[a] YEAR-END 1987

| | |
|---|---:|
| **HOUSEHOLD SIZE AND SPATIAL DISTRIBUTION** | |
| Total Number of Persons | 730 |
| Mean Household Size | 4.9 |
| Proportion Households with Members Resident Outside Village | 8.7% |
| Proportion Population Resident Outside Village | 2.6% |
| **LABOR FORCE** | |
| Total Size | 468 |
| Mean Size per Household | 3.1 |
| Distribution by Male/Female | 49/51% |
| **SECTORAL DISTRIBUTION OF LABOR FORCE**[b] | |
| Agriculture | 91.0% |
| Industry | 3.0% |
| Commerce | .9% |
| Transportation and Construction | 2.4% |
| Service (Government, Education, Medicine) | 2.8% |
| **AGRICULTURE** | |
| Proportion of Households Engaging in | 98.7% |
| Distribution of Cultivating Households by Crop Mix | |
| Vegetables Only | 46.9% |
| Vegetables and Grain | 51.7% |
| Grain Only | 1.4% |
| **NONAGRICULTURAL JOBS**[c] | |
| Total Number | 71 |
| Proportion of Households with Worker Holding | 38.7% |
| Distribution by Full-time/Part-time and Occasional | 57.7/42.3% |
| **PRODUCTIVE PROPERTY** | |
| Mean Size of Contracted Land per Household | 4.8 $mu$[e] |
| Mean Value of Productive Assets per Household | 1,675 $yuan$[f] |
| Proportion of Households Owning Key Assets | |
| Bicycle Cart[d] | 94.6% |
| Vegetable-Growing Paraphernalia | 92.5% |
| Larger-scale Property (e.g., Tractor, Store) | 6.7% |

Source for Table 2: Calculated from Family Histories
Notes for Table 2: [a]Defined as groups sharing a budget and cooking and eating together; see text.
[b]Full-time jobs only.
[c]Includes part-time work.
[d]Main means of transporting crops to market.
[e]1 $mu$ = .1647 acre; 15 $mu$ = 1 hectare.
[f]1 $yuan$ = US$.27. 1,675 $yuan$ is 85% of estimated mean household income for 1987.

After twenty-five years of collective agriculture, one would expect to find some remnants of collectivism in the organization of economic activity. In particular, one might expect that households whose members had worked together in the same production team for many years might pool their efforts, especially at peak periods during the agricultural cycle. The Shaanxi villages, however, showed little evidence of such team-based cooperation. In 1987 only a small portion of the households cooperated with members of other households in economic production, usually during the busy spring season when seedlings had to be transplanted. In every case the partner was a relative, usually an agnate, and usually a son.

### The Mobility and Security Values of Children

In the male-centered family system of pre-revolutionary China, children, particularly sons, were crucial mobility and security assets. The ethnographic literature suggests that they played critical roles in agricultural production; in economic diversification and property accumulation, both indications of entrepreneurial tendencies; and the provision of old-age support. Because daughters married out, they were but minor assets to their natal families, contributing their labor to housework and, in some localities, work in the fields before being lost to their husbands' families at marriage (e.g., Fei 1939, Yang 1945). To what extent had these economic roles of children persisted into or been revived during the post-collective era?

As shown in Table 3, children had important productive roles, especially in agriculture. Of roughly 150 unmarried children who had completed their schooling and were available to work during the reform years, fully 98% engaged in income-producing work. The great majority -- 89% -- worked in agricultural production, helping their parents transplant,

TABLE 3. CONTRIBUTION OF CHILDREN TO HOUSEHOLD
ECONOMY DURING THE REFORM ERA, 1979-87,
150 WEINAN HOUSEHOLDS

| Unmarried Children Available to Work During 1979-87[a] | Percent engaged in economic activity[b] | Economic Activity |  |  | Number of Children |
|---|---|---|---|---|---|
|  |  | Agriculture | Nonagricultural Job[c] | Military Service |  |
| Sons | 97.3 | 82.4 | 6.8 | 8.1 | 74 |
| Daughters | 98.7 | 94.8 | 3.9 | .0 | 77 |
| Both Sexes | 98.0 | 88.7 | 5.3 | 4.0 | 151 |

Sources: Calculated from Family Histories

Notes: [a]Includes children who had finished their schooling but had not yet married.
[b]Defined as income-producing work in fields or in nonagricultural jobs.
[c]75 percent of children working in nonagricultural jobs remitted all or part of their wages to their parents.

weed, fertilize, harvest, and transport the vegetables to market. Indeed, youngsters' help in growing these highly labor-intensive crops was so important that parents had begun to pull their children (especially their daughters) out of school early to enlarge the family labor force.

If children were vital to agricultural production, did they facilitate entrepreneurship outside of agriculture? We saw earlier that the extent of entrepreneurial activity, as measured by the ownership of productive assets, was very limited in these villages. It is possible, however, that the seeds of enterprise had been sown yet not had a chance to grow to fruition. To see children's roles in incipient entrepreneurial activities, we can explore their contributions to diversifying the family economy -- usually the route to the

PEASANT HOUSEHOLD IN CHINA 53

acquisition of skills and capital later used in the establishment of businesses, and to the acquisition of larger-than-minuscule productive assets.

A look at the economic activities children undertook indicates a minor role in diversifying the household economy. Only 9 % of children (15% of sons and 4% of daughters) held non-agricultural jobs (Table 3). About half of these were sons who had joined the army, an unlikely source of capital or skills useful to village enterprise (the army was, however, a source of political contacts valuable at higher levels of the administrative system). Most of the other sons and nearly all the daughters worked in state- or collective-run enterprises, usually in nearby Xianyang City. Such jobs, which were extremely hard to get, could be important sources of savings and entrepreneurial skills. One son worked full-time in construction. This was a potentially fruitful arena for enterprise development. Not only was the market for construction work excellent, ensuring fairly handsome returns to labor, but work in this sector permitted the acquisition of technical skills and the building of social networks that would locally useful. In sum, although a few children did help diversify the household economy, working at jobs that promoted the acquisition of skills, savings, and other useful resources, their limited numbers translate into a small contribution to household enterprise overall.

Resources provided by children also facilitated property accumulation. As we have seen, though, the acquisition of productive assets beyond those required for vegetable cultivation was very limited. Of the five households owning a store at some time during the 1980s, only one had relied on the resources of a child. In this case a daughter who had married out of the family loaned her father 2,000 (of a total of 3,000) *yuan* with which to purchase it. The other stores were acquired individually, usually by leasing the property from the former production brigade or team and buying the goods with individual savings. Children's contribution was somewhat more important in the purchase of tractors, which, at about 5,000 *yuan* each in the mid-1980s, represented sizable expenditures for most households (the equivalent of three to four months' income). During 1979-87 seven households had bought a tractor, purchasing it in hopes of hiring themselves out to till their neighbors' land. Virtually all the machinery was bought with the resources of more than one person. In four of the cases the tractor was purchased with the savings of a stem or joint household. In the other three cases an individual bought the equipment, using his own savings and loans from affinal (two) or agnatic (one) relatives.

A close look at this handful of cases of relatively (by local standards) large-scale property accumulation reveals some of the constraints on family cooperation in economic endeavor. First, even where father-son cooperation could be managed, it was generally shortlived. In the cases of joint acquisition of a tractor by an extended household, the enlarged household turned out to be very fragile, coming apart within a few years of being formed. Members of the household of Shi Zhanlan (a pseudonym), for example, joined forces to purchase a tractor in May of 1984. At that time the household labor force was large, consisting of the older-generation couple, aged 51 and 42, one married son and his wife, and two unmarried sons, who together cultivated 9.2 *mu* of land. In 1986, however, the second son got married, and began to press for division of the family. Unable to delay the inevitable, Shi acceded. Division occurred in July of 1987, and, three years after it was bought, the tractor was partitioned along with the rest of the family holdings. One son got the tractor, his brother a larger portion of the Shis' other assets.

Second, even where fathers or sons were physically available to cooperate, they were not necessarily socially available -- that is, willing -- to do so. Wang Mufa is a case in point. When making preparations to buy a tractor in 1987 he sought help not from his older brother and father, from whom he had formally divided 18 months earlier. He went instead to two of his older sisters, who had married out the family nearly two decades earlier, and from them borrowed the sums needed to purchase the machine. Family division apparently ended all possibility of productive relations, even those that might be mutually beneficial. Thus, while a shortage of sons might have constrained household entrepreneurship (remember the small average size of the households), the fragility of family relationships was also a contributing factor.

If children offered little in the way of economic advancement, what about old-age security? Evidence from the three villages suggests that nearly a decade into the reform era sons continued to perform this duty, but parents were beginning to entertain doubts about the reliability of filial support. In 1987, all 19 household heads who were no longer self-sufficient were financially supported by their sons. However, support by sons was not universally considered ideal. Of those cared for by their sons, only two-fifths believed that such an arrangement was ideal. Doubt about filial support was even stronger among younger informants, who had not yet had to face the question of how they would make it through old age. Among the 131 household heads who were still economically self-sufficient, only two-fifths said they intended to rely entirely on their sons, while another quarter intended to obtain support from their sons and some other source, such as savings or purchased insurance. Only one-third of these younger household heads considered children the optimal means of support.

Eight years after the reforms were launched, the mobility and security values of children had been partially reinstated at most. Children played central roles in family agriculture, but their contribution to entrepreneurial endeavors outside agriculture was limited. Sons were virtually the only source of old-age support for their parents, but the older generation was edgy about the future, unsure that filial obligation would carry as much weight as it had in the past.

### State Intervention in the Household Economy

Despite the expansion of economic opportunities and a return of economic power to the peasant household, peasant households did not fill up like balloons, nor did children recover all their mobility and security values. Shaanxi's relative poverty, and hence paucity of mobility opportunities, may help explain the weakness of the familial response to economic change. Anthropological research in richer areas of the country, however, casts doubt on this proposition. In parts of Guangdong, Fujian, Hebei, and Sichuan Provinces, households in the 1980s were generally small, averaging 3.5-5.5 members, and simple in structure, with nuclear and stem units making up 85-100% of the total. Aspiring entrepreneurs exploited family ties, but family-run enterprises were small in scale, embracing such activities as petty commerce (peddling, small shopkeeping), long-distance trade, and handicraft assembly. Sons supported their elderly parents, but growing numbers of old people living alone, often in pitiable circumstances, suggests some weakening of the family social security system (Huang 1989, Potter and Potter 1990, Harrell 1993, Johnson 1993, Selden 1993).

Part of the reason for this muted household response lies in continuing political constraints on household economic activities, especially of an entrepreneurial sort. Under reform socialism generally, the tendency to develop the private sector is offset by a counter-tendency, led by ambivalent bureaucracies, to restrict and even obstruct private activities (Kornai 1992:450-455). In China, state bureaucracies remain the dominant actors in the economy, and political capital in the form of contacts with state officials and access to state-provided goods are the *sine qua non* for large-scale entrepreneurship (e.g., Nee 1989, Siu 1989). Such political constraints, however, apply in more limited fashion to the modest sorts of entrepreneurial activities undertaken in the Shaanxi villages and not at all to the familial provision of social security. Indeed, the Constitution of the People's Republic of China obliges children to support their elderly parents, and local society provides few alternatives.

The reasons for this shrinkage in the scale and scope of activities organized by the peasant household are complex and explored in full elsewhere.[12] Here I focus on a small sub-set of these causal forces related to state intervention in the labor regime of the peasant household. I argue that a long history of state tampering with domestic arrangements has weakened the two features of the household labor regime that underlay its economic effectiveness in pre-collective days, namely, flexibility in labor mobilization and strong intergenerational ties.

**Flexibility in labor mobilization.** In pre-collective times the size of the household workforce was highly elastic, expanding when economic opportunities brightened, contracting when they dimmed. The number of sons in the labor force was increased in two main ways: by adding children, primarily through reproduction, and by delaying family division. During the collective era, both strategies of labor recruitment were curtailed, undermining the household's ability to adapt its resources to changing environmental conditions.

First, as is well-known, a forceful population policy has drastically limited the number of children Chinese couples are allowed to have. Under the "later-longer-fewer" (*wan-xi-shao*) policy of 1971-78, peasant couples were allowed, first, three and, from 1977, two children each. The policy called for later marriage, longer spacing between children, and fewer children (for details see Chen and Kols 1982). Under the one-child policy (1979-present) couples are expected to limit themselves to one. Although peasant resistance to the policy has forced policymakers to liberalize the conditions under which second children are permitted, the rules on childbearing remain extremely restrictive. In the Shaanxi villages, the *de facto* policy in effect in the mid- to late 1980s allowed couples to have two children. Only if the first two were girls could a couple get away with paying a fine and having a third (for the politics involved see Greenhalgh 1990 and 1993).

Even if the "one-child" policy were lifted, though, other changes initiated under collectivism and furthered during the reform era have worked to reduce the number of children peasants want.[13] Asked how many children they considered ideal, the great majority of my informants, both male and female, young and old, replied one son and one daughter. Having a son was deemed essential; who else would work the family plot and provide economic support in old age? Notably, neither economic diversification nor property accumulation was cited as an advantage of having sons. They wanted a daughter to help with housework before marriage and lend emotional support when they grew old. The major reason the villagers wanted *only* one child of each sex was clearly economic. Asked their reactions to the old saying "more children, more happiness," most of my informants indicated strong disagreement. Many children meant not prosperity, but economic burdens. Indeed, the costs associated with raising children have skyrocketed in reform era. Everything from subsistence goods such as food and clothing, to schooling and health care, to life-cycle celebrations such as the one-month ceremony and weddings, has escalated in cost, in some cases dramatically. The cost of a typical dowry, for example, had risen from about 200 yuan in the 1970s to well over 500 *yuan* in the 1980s. The costs of these items were on the tip of everyone's tongue, suggesting their salience in daily life and decisionmaking.

The second major strategy for increasing the size of the household workforce, delaying the division of sons from the family, was also a victim of state intervention in the social system, this time in an earlier historical era. The research of Parish and Whyte indicates that during the collective era sons began to divide from the family not long after marriage (1978:133-135). Early division was rooted most fundamentally in the socialization of property in the 1950s; with family property removed from their control, fathers found themselves with little clout and no solid economic rationale, such as joint exploitation of the estate, for keeping their sons in the fold. In the Weinan villages, the tendency to divide early had not been checked by the dismantling of collective institutions. The great majority of sons divided within two years of marriage. Only sons who had no brothers generally remained with their parents, often to their wives' distress. It is possible that, in the future, privatization of land ownership and increases in ownership of non-agricultural assets might provide the economic basis for delaying partition. So far, however, there is little indication that this is occurring, even where land is considered virtually private and ownership of non-agricultural properties is more widespread than in Shaanxi. Indeed, the evidence from a number of locales suggests just the opposite: increased prosperity is promoting earlier rather than later division (Potter and Potter 1990, Huang 1989, Johnson 1993). (There is some evidence that the introduction of economic reform led to delayed partitions in Hebei and Sichuan, but the delays were of short duration; see Harrell 1993 and Selden 1993). In the Shaanxi villages, the openly distant, sometimes even hostile relations between the young and old, born of decades of shared poverty and socialist policy, would seem to make a trend toward later division unlikely.

**Intergenerational ties.** Not only the quantity, but also the quality of family labor has been declining. In the past it, was the social glue of intergenerational obligations that ensured the commitment of the younger generation to achievement of family mobility and security goals. The bond between the generations, however, is under assault, and has been for decades. We saw that parents no longer fully trust their sons to fulfill their old-age support obligations. For their part, adult sons no longer trust their parents to make the best economic decisions. The reforms ushered in a whole new economic ball game and young people believe, no doubt rightly, that they are better equipped than their parents to figure out the rules and how to get around them.

The weakening of the intergenerational bond, like the loss of flexibility, was a residue of the political economy of classical socialism. The first and probably most critical blow was the collectivization of family property, which had been the mainstay of the intergenerational exchange system traditionally. Other changes associated with the construction of a socialist society -- in particular, the introduction of mass education -- had the same effect of altering the balance of resources in favor of the young. Deprived of many of their traditional sources of authority, such as tangible property and greater amounts of socially relevant knowledge, parents were no longer able to cement the loyalty of their sons.

Although I have presented only part of a complex and historically variable argument, the points developed here should suffice to convince the reader that the state itself was largely responsible for weakening the labor regime of the household. The policies of classical socialism (in particular, the collectivization of family property and a highly restrictive population policy) and of reform socialism (state-mandated or -sanctioned increases in the price of goods or a yet more restrictive population policy) undermined household labor recruitment strategies and loosened the bonds between the generations. State intervention in household affairs went too deep and went on for too long, sapping the household's flexibility and solidarity. In reaction, households remade themselves into small, structurally simple units, and children sought to redefine their obligations to their parents in increasingly minimalistic, short-lived terms.

## Conclusion

As Kornai has pointed out, the peasant household plays, or is expected to play, a crucial role in the transition from socialism. Whether the household is equipped to take on all the tasks thrust upon it is another question. The evidence from the Shaanxi villages suggests that traditional household economic arrangements do not simply bounce back when collective institutions are removed. Changes instituted both during the collective era, when the state sought to dominate nearly every domain of social life, and the reform era, when it endeavored to make room for private initiative, were simply too deep to be readily reversed. By intruding too far into the domestic domain, state policies have enfeebled the very institution that was supposed to lead the agricultural sector into reform socialism and beyond. With diminished levels of flexibility and weakened internal ties, the Shaanxi households appeared to have limited developmental potential. While capable of developing family-scale agriculture on vest pocket-sized plots, they demonstrated little readiness for non-agricultural entrepreneurship, and they were gradually losing their capacity to support their own dependents. This is a far cry from the robust peasant household assumed by reformist state policy.

Clearly, alternative institutions will emerge to fill the gaps left by the peasant household. The specific character these institutions take in different countries will depend on the nature of pre-socialist traditions as well as the depth and form of socialist transformation in the countryside. From current trends in the Chinese countryside, it seems that in that country entrepreneurial groups may involve networks of individuals connected by ties of kinship, locality, and/or patron-client relations, often organized by present or former cadres. Old-age support is likely to be provided by one adult son living with or, increasingly, apart from his parents. Parental savings and insurance will no doubt supplement the financial contributions of sons. Trends in social change to date suggest that family, household, and kinship will not be absent from the post-socialist future, when and if one arrives, but they will play vestigial roles compared with the pre-socialist past.

## Notes

Financial support was provided by the National Science Foundation, Grant Number BNS-8618121. This article is based on hand tabulations of a small part of a very large data set.

1. Among the characteristic difficulties are lags in technical development, inefficiencies and backlogs in production, backwardness in consumption, and waste, all of which lead to public dissatisfaction and loss of confidence in the system.

2. Between 1978 and 1984 agricultural output grew by at least 9% a year; sidelines grew 19% a year. During the same period rural per capita income more than doubled, and peasant diets improved in quantity and quality (Riskin 1987:190-199).

3. Kornai's analysis of classical socialism is based on the experience of fourteen countries whose Communist parties held power for at least three decades, allowing the political structure and economy to consolidate into a coherent political economic system (see Kornai 1992: 4-9).

4. Students of the Chinese family generally recognize two distinct but cross-cutting familial institutions, the descent line, a transhistorical group of males that held corporate property transmitted by inheritance, and the family (*jia*), a contemporaneous group of males and females concerned with the tasks of livelihood. Sons were more central to both units. See Wolf and Huang 1980.

5. Cohen's (1976) research in contemporary Taiwan shows how fraternal tensions can be mitigated by an opportunity-filled environment that makes it economically rational for married brothers to remain together in the family unit formed by their father.

6. Other methods of expanding the family labor force included adoption, marriage, especially at an early age, taking a second wife, and fostering in a "little daughter-in-law."

7. The use of family labor was also advantageous because of its low recruitment, educational, and supervision costs (see Netting 1989, esp. pp. 228-30).

8. The flow of resources from old to young also included training for productive and reproductive work and help in arranging marriage.

9. The research was conducted in collaboration with members of the Population Research Institute of Xi'an Jiaotong University.

10. Other Western observers have, however, reported on life in the area. See Hinton 1966 and Myrdal 1965.

11. Provincial and national income figures from State Statistical Bureau 1988:826.

12. "The Post-Collective Household Economy in Village China," ms.-in-progress.

13. For example, during the collective era women generally worked in the fields and had less time for childcare. New health programs reduced infant and child mortality. These and other changes in village life, which persisted into the reform era, worked to lower peasant childbearing desires.

## References

Chen, Pi-chao and Adrienne Kols
    1982    Population and Birth Planning in the People's Republic of China. *Population Reports* Series J, no. 25:J577-J618.

Cohen, Myron L.
    1976    *House United, House Divided: The Chinese Family in Taiwan.* New York: Columbia University Press.

Davis, Deborah and Stevan Harrell, eds.
    1993    *Chinese Families in the Post-Mao Era.* Berkeley: University of California Press.

Desai Padma
    1989    *Perestroika in Perspective: The Design and Dilemmas of Soviet Reform.* Princeton: Princeton University Press.

Fei Hsiao-tung
    1939    *Peasant Life in China.* London: Routledge & Kegan Paul.

Freedman, Maurice
    1963    The Chinese Domestic Family: Models. *Vle Congrès international des Sciences anthropologiques et ethnologiques* 2, part 1:97-100.

Greenhalgh, Susan
   1993   The Peasantization of Population Policy in Shaanxi. In D. Davis and S. Harrell, eds., *Chinese Families in the Post-Mao Era*. Berkeley: University of California Press.
   1990   The Evolution of the One-Child Policy in Shaanxi. *The China Quarterly*:191-229
   1985   Sexual Stratification: The Other Side of 'Growth with Equity' in East Asia. *Population and Development Review* 11, no. 2:265-314.
Griffin, Keith, ed.
   1984   *Institutional Reform and Economic Development in the Chinese Countryside*. Armonk: M.E. Sharpe.
Harrell, Stevan
   1993   Strategies of Survival and Strategies of Advancement: Geography, Demography, and Family Composition in Two Southwestern Villages. In D. Davis and S. Harrell, eds., Chinese Families in the Post-Mao Era. Berkeley: University of California Press.
Hinton, William
   1966   *Fanshen: A Documentary of Revolution in a Chinese Village*. New York: Vintage.
Huang, Philip C.C.
   1990   *The Peasant Family and Rural Development in the Yangzi Delta, 1350-1988*. Stanford: Stanford University Press.
Huang Shu-min
   1989   *The Spiral Road: Change in a Chinese Village Through the Eyes of a Communist Party Leader*. Boulder: Westview.
Johnson, Graham E.
   1992   Family Strategies and Economic Transformation in Rural China: Some Evidence from the Pearl River Delta Region. In D. Davis and S. Harrell, eds., *Chinese Families in the 1980s*. Berkeley: University of California Press.
Johnson, Kay Ann
   1983   *Women, the Family and Peasant Revolution in China*. Chicago: University of Chicago Press.
Kornai, János
   1992   *The Socialist System: The Political Economy of Communism*. Princeton: Princeton University Press.
Lang, Olga
   1946   *Chinese Family and Society*. New Haven: Yale University Press.

Myrdal, Jan
    1965    *Report from a Chinese Village*. New York: Signet.
Nee, Victor
    1985    Peasant Household Individualism. In W.L. Parish, ed., *Chinese Rural Development: The Great Transformation*, pp.164-90. Armonk, N.Y.: M.E. Sharpe.
    1989    Peasant Entrepreneurship and the Politics of Regulation in China. In V. Nee and D. Stark, eds., *Remaking the Economic Institutions of Socialism: China and Eastern Europe*, pp.169-207. Stanford: Stanford University Press.
Netting, Robert McC.
    1989    Smallholders, Householders, Freeholders: Why the Family Farm Works Well Worldwide. In R.R. Wilk, ed., *The Household Economy: Reconsidering the Domestic Mode of Production*, pp.221-44. Boulder: Westview.
Parish, William L. ed.
    1985    *Chinese Rural Development: The Great Transformation*. Armonk: M.E. Sharpe.
    1975    Socialism and the Chinese Peasant Family. *Journal of Asian Studies* 34, no.3:613-30.
Parish, William L. and Martin King Whyte
    1978    *Village and Family in Contemporary China*. Chicago: University of Chicago Press.
Perry, Elizabeth J. and Christine Wong, eds.
    1985    *The Political Economy of Reform in Post-Mao China*. Cambridge: Council on East Asian Studies, Harvard University.
Potter, Sulamith Heins and Jack M. Potter
    1990    *China's Peasants: The Anthropology of a Revolution*. Cambridge: Cambridge University Press.
Riskin, Carl
    1987    *China's Political Economy: The Quest for Development Since 1949*. Oxford: Oxford University Press.
Saith, Ashwani, ed.
    1987    *The Re-emergence of the Chinese Peasantry: Aspects of Rural Decollectivisation*. London: Croom Helm.
Selden, Mark
    1993    Familial Strategies and Structures in Rural North China. In D. Davis and S. Harrell, eds., *Chinese Families in the Post-Mao Era*. Berkeley: University of California Press.

Shaanxi Provincial Bureau of Statistics
  1987  *Shaanxi Tongji Nianjian, 1987* (*Statistical Yearbook of Shaanxi, 1987*). Xi'an: SPBS.
Shue, Vivienne
  1988  *The Reach of the State: Sketches of the Chinese Body Politic.* Stanford: Stanford University Press.
Siu, Helen F.
  1989  Socialist Peddlars and Princes in a Chinese Market Town. *American Ethnologist* 16:195-212.
Skinner, G. William
  1971  Chinese Peasants and the Closed Community: An Open and Shut Case. *Comparative Studies in Society and History* 13:270-81.
State Statistical Bureau
  1988  *Zhongguo Tongji Nianjian, 1988* (*Statistical Yearbook of China, 1988*). Beijing: Zhongguo Tongji Chubanshe.
Wädekin, Karl-Eugen
  1982  *Agrarian Policies in Communist Europe: A Critical Introduction.* The Hague: Allenheld Osmun.
Wilk, Richard R. and Robert McC. Netting
  1984  Households: Changing Forms and Functions. In R.McC. Netting, R.R. Wilk and E.J. Arnould, eds. *Households: Comparative and Historical Studies of the Domestic Group*, pp. 1-28. Berkeley: University of California Press.
Wolf, Arthur P. and Chieh-shan Huang
  1980  *Marriage and Adoption in China, 1845-1945.* Stanford: Stanford University Press.
Yang, Martin C.
  1945  *A Chinese Village: Taitou, Shantung Province.* New York: Columbia University Press.
Yang, C.K.
  1959  *The Chinese Family in the Communist Revolution.* Cambridge: M.I.T. Press.

# GOVERNMENT POLICIES AND THE CHANGING STRUCTURE OF FARM WOMEN'S LIVELIHOOD: A CASE FROM SOUTHERN ILLINOIS

Jane Adams
Southern Illinois University at Carbondale

After World War II, farm life in the United States underwent a profound transformation. As farm families adopted new technologies they also reorganized their production systems in ways that severed functional ties between the farm enterprise and the household.[1] In the process most farm women adopted middle class urban standards in household architecture and consumption patterns and, within the home, accepted hegemonic definitions of their role as "homemakers". At the same time, many farm women retained a commitment to gainful employment, seeking to retain home-based enterprises or finding off-farm jobs. Two questions are raised by the this process: first, why did farm families not adopt urban standards of household organization for so long, and second, when they did "modernize", why did they not adopt core definitions of feminine domesticity?

The answer to the first question -- why farm women for so long did not accept the doctrine of separate spheres -- lies primarily in the different ways in which farm and urban middle-class women integrated themselves into the nineteenth-century industrial capitalist political economy. Urban middle class women found themselves largely removed from extra-household distribution circuits as their household manufactures were industrialized and their homes were redefined as spheres of private consumption. In contrast, nineteenth-century farm women became petty commodity producers. Their poultry and small-scale dairy (largely cream and butter) operations provisioned the growing urban working classes (Jensen 1986, Osterud 1991). Women produced feathers, flowers, dried fruits, corn husks for tamales and other products for market. In Southern Illinois, the site of this case study, women were deeply involved in horticultural production. Farm owning wives generally managed the packing process and participated in other phases of small fruit and vegetable production; non-owning women and youths worked for wages in the fields and packing sheds. Whereas nineteenth-century urban middle-class women managed servants, farm women managed their children and worked cooperatively with neighbors and relatives. When they managed wage workers it was in the domain of commodity production (e.g., packing sheds). Not only poverty (widespread after World War I), but structural participation in a farming enterprise contributed to farm women seeing themselves as producers and workers. Their control over the proceeds of their labor and over their parts of the labor process, although not equal with men, gave farm women a degree of autonomy and independence different from urban middle-class women.[2]

After World War II, government policies, predicated on notions of an appropriate "feminine sphere", a narrowly defined domesticity, undercut women's productive agricultural functions and created the conditions in which farm families were forced to accept a new gendered division of labor as the price of greater affluence. Agricultural policies that assumed women were not agricultural producers and that severed ties between farm and home have been analyzed elsewhere (Fink 1986, 1992; Adams 1988; Flora 1988). At the same time, government programs directed specifically at farm women were important in transforming farm households from centers of commodity production to loci of consumption. The narrow domestic focus of home extension programs points up the _failure_ of government policies and programs to enhance the historically unique relationship of farm women to the larger economy, and must be seen as a major determinant of the removal of farm women from farming.

This article examines the role of government policies and programs, particularly Home Extension, in channeling farm women into roles parallel to their urban counterparts and the responses of farm women to these policies and programs. Using a close study of a completely rural county, Union County, in extreme southern Illinois, I first analyze the roots of U.S. agricultural development programs in the nineteenth century. Then I examine Home Extension in Union County, Illinois. County level data come from annual reports and minutes of Farm Extension and Home Extension meetings, case studies of seven farms made in 1984 and 1990, and interviews and discussions with many Union County residents. In addition, I grew up on a farm in the county adjoining Union County during the post-World War II period dealt with here. My family was active in Farm Bureau, Home Bureau, and 4-H, as well as school consolidation and other "development" programs, such as creating a department of public health.

This case study suggests that the experience of farm women in controlling the proceeds of their labor and their parts of the labor process, together with the economic pressures experienced by family farms after World War II, explains why farm women, when they did "modernize", moved outside their ideologically assigned domestic roles and sought off-farm employment.

## Nineteenth Century Roots of Women's Roles

The roots of home extension, like the roots of farm extension, lie in the nineteenth century. Both are lineal descendants of the advocates of progress who viewed democratically organized, practical education as a primary foundation of United States society (True 1924, Scott 1970). The two forms of adult education followed somewhat different paths, however, embodying increasingly differentiated notions of appropriate male and female roles. Farm extension grew out of Farmers' Institutes, which were programs of itinerant lecturers generally sponsored by a state agricultural society or midwest land-grant college. These programs began at least as early as the 1840s but were not organized on a regular basis until nearly two decades later. The lectures were poorly received by the majority of farmers and remained an elite-led "movement." The demonstration system, initiated in the South in the early 1900s to reach farmers who resisted "book farming," became the primary vehicle for state extension of agricultural information by the 'teens (Scott 1970:64-8, 100-1, 221-36). Agricultural extension work began in Illinois in DeKalb County in 1912 and in 1918 in Union County (True 1924:89, Union County Farm Extension Service Records, [hereafter FESR] Annual Report 1918). Government sponsored agricultural education provided practical research and information on production techniques and, to a far lesser extent, management practices, including organizing cooperatives. Along with farm magazines and informational materials disseminated by agricultural industries, government sponsored agricultural education channeled largely through the Land Grant colleges aggressively extended their research results to U.S. farmers (Marcus and Lowitt 1990).

Home extension was first organized in the south in 1914 and in Illinois in 1918. Union County was one of the last Illinois counties to hire a home adviser, in 1947 (True 1924:201; Home Extension Service Records [hereafter HESR] 1947; FESR 1946:6, 1947:4). Its mission was very different from that of agricultural extension, deriving from a different tradition than farm extension. Its ideological and institutional roots were in home economics, a movement derived from the redefinition of urban homes that occurred when industrial production removed men's working life from the household.

Two early nineteenth-century traditions merged to form the home economics/domestic science movement. In Calvinist New England Catherine Beecher and other progressive reformers vigorously promoted the idea that women were especially capable of educating young people and inculcating them with elevated moral values, while in the south the cavalier tradition upheld the model of the leisured lady whose primary role was as hostess and as symbol of her husband's status. As the household lost its centrality in social production to factories and distant offices, middle- and upper-class women's productive functions were eliminated or lost their social valuation. But even as middle-class urban women's domestic sphere became ever more privatized, these women opened new avenues of public action and organization. Utilizing the ideology of domesticity and morality as women's "natural" venue, they organized against slavery, for women's suffrage, temperance, labor reforms, international peace, and a variety of other progressive programs. They also organized to elevate the domestic sphere to one co-equal with men's public sphere through the domestic science movement (Taylor 1961, Welter 1966, Lerner 1969, Sklar 1973, Morantz 1977, Bloch 1978, Cott 1978, Degler 1980, Bordin 1981, Hartman 1981, Matthaei 1982, Ryan 1982, Zaretsky's 1986, Matthews 1987). As Home Economics developed in the nineteenth century its creators were so concerned with legitimating women's domestic functions that they completely relinquished the world of commerce and social production to men. In trying to defend women's traditional productive activities they became complicit in creating a conception of the home as abstracted from production, as a site solely of consumption and the development of private life. Because of their commitment to this definition of the home, even those home economists who tried to redefine women's domestic work as important productive activities could not incorporate women's income-producing activities into their analytic frameworks (see, e.g., Reid 1934).

Two phases in the home economics movement can be distinguished. The first arose in mid-nineteenth-century and was rooted in notions of Victorian domesticity. It centered on the image of the Mother who embodied piety, purity, and submissiveness (Ryan 1982). The home was a "haven in a heartless world" (Lasch 1979); like the women who cared for it the Victorian home was associated with nature, linked to the polluting world of industrial production and commerce only through consumption. Prescriptive writing in this period focused on the moral and aesthetic virtues with which women enriched their families and enabled their husbands to make the proper public impression (East 1980, Wright 1980).

By the late nineteenth century science became the hegemonic standard for evaluating worth, and those who sought to elevate the status of women and of housekeeping adopted the language and forms of science. Isabel Bevier, the founder of the University of Illinois department of home economics, like Cornell University's Ellen Richards and the "founder" of Home Economics, was a chemist and assiduously stressed the professional and research aspects of the fledgling discipline. With others she sought status as a peer with other scientific disciplines. While "science" became the hegemonic framework through which all activity was valued, "efficiency" became the means through which scientific practices were institutionalized in productive life. "Taylorization" -- the efficient organization of the assembly line, time and motion studies, and so forth -- became the fundamental principle of business management. Domestic scientists, who met in an important series of annual conferences at Lake Placid, New York, between 1899 and 1908, largely accepted these as defining conditions for their new discipline (East 1980:36; Elbert 1988:253, also Bruere and Bruere 1912, Pattison 1915, Gilbreth 1927, Wright 1980). These women tended to stress the important productive functions that occurred in the house. These included cooking, laundry, furnishing and cleaning the house, and perhaps sewing; the cultivation of the family's moral and aesthetic sensibilities, including providing clothing and inculcating manners appropriate to the family's social class; and responsibility for good sanitation and nutrition (e.g., Parloa 1910, Pattison 1915, Frederick 1920, Gilbreth 1927, Balderston 1936). The need for housewives to be discerning and educated consumers became increasingly important; by the 1930s consumer education became a greater focus of home economics education, but it did not become a specific course of study until the 1960s. By the 1930s child care was also elevated to a specific area of concern (East 1980:54; see also Kyrk 1933, and Reid 1934, esp. pp. 14-5, 376-7).

The founders of home economics were associated with the Country Life Movement which, with other participants in the Progressive movements of the early twentieth century, understood social problems in evolutionary terms. They associated modernity, progress, and civilization as lived by the upper and middle classes as the future for all humanity, mapping class relations as temporal transformation (Danbom 1979, Fabian 1983). They saw their role as raising "backward" people, including farmers, to their level. This entailed, in part, promoting a "rational" division of labor that required, as Elbert notes in her study of early home extension to New York farm women, "a functional gender separation of spheres" (Elbert 1988:250-1).

There is little indication that farm women nationally related to these prescriptions nor, initially, did the U.S. Department of Agriculture. In 1913 the Secretary of Agriculture addressed a letter to the wives of the Department's crop correspondents, asking how the Department of Agriculture could better meet the needs of farm housewives (USDA 1915; see also Bowers 1974, Danbom 1979, Elbert 1988, Knowles 1988). Despite the fact that the respondents would have been among the more prosperous and educated, and therefore in class terms corresponded to the middle-class urban women who increasingly defined themselves through the ideology of domesticity, their complaints centered on the drudgery their lives entailed. Further, their labor was highly valued. An Iowa correspondent, writing for his wife, wrote that "The country club for women has not bettered the condition, as they are invariably dominated by the town club, where washing dishes, cooking for harvest hands and plowmen is not at all fashionable, and sweeping floors and dusting is considered as detrimental to the color of the cuticle of the hand. So if a country club is organized, let it be by the country women and women who are proud of their ability to labor and who consider labor honorable" (USDA 1915:33).

The USDA recognized the economic importance of farm women in their literature. For example, it suggested organizing "the boys and girls in their rural communities into agricultural clubs, the purpose of which is to teach advanced methods of farming, animal husbandry, and home making in a practical way which yields a monetary profit to the children taking part in the work .... The girls will be interested in the canning, gardening, apple, poultry, and pig clubs; the boys will be stimulated by clubs for the raising of corn, potatoes, pigs, apples, baby beef, peanuts, or poultry ...." In its 1915 pamphlet directed to farm women it listed government publications concerned with protection of the food supply (FDA and USDA), sanitation and hygienic water supplies, road improvement, crop diversification, farm management, education, and informative pamphlets on flora and fauna, as well as publications dealing with topics more traditionally associated with women such as gardening, dairy, poultry, foods and cooking, and canning and preserving. It is notable that this publication lists no pamphlets on house decorating or design, sewing, first aid, or psychology, topics that would dominate home extension fifty years later (USDA 1915:77-89; also 900-100). In other words, in 1915 the United States Department of Agriculture considered women as agricultural producers who were potentially as intellectually interested in the natural world and civil society as were men. USDA policies towards women in this period was oriented to improving their quality of life by creating producer cooperatives: in its 1915 report the U.S. Department of Agriculture suggested the formation of cooperative laundries, creameries, canneries, sausage making, lard rendering, fruit and vegetable evaporation, and bakeries (USDA 1915:62-6).

On the state level, women were considered qualified to educate both men and women about dairy and poultry production, addressing farmers' institutes. For example, Miss Kate Maxey addressed the 1910 Illinois Farmers' Institute on "Illinois and the Poultry Interest; What Ought To be Done; Large Profit in the Business;" another woman spoke on "Production of Clean Milk." Farm men were considered to be concerned with topics that were later to be largely relegated to women such as the moral climate of the home, health, household sanitation, and children's education (Illinois Farmers' Institute 1910:263-7, 328-335, 182-191; Illinois Farmers' Institute 1911:69-81).

Despite the integration of women into the regular Farmers Institute program of agricultural education, household science was developing as a complementary but discrete program. At the 1910 Illinois Farmers' Institute, for example, the representative from the University of Illinois' decade-old Department of Household Science outlined the Department's work to the assembled farmers (Illinois Farmers' Institute 1910:121-4). This included courses at the university, work with Illinois Federation of Women's Clubs and Farmers' Institutes, short courses for housekeepers, summer school courses, and high school extension work. The Department offered courses and instruction in foods, especially cooking, sewing, and house planning and decoration (see also Bevier 1907).

The prescriptions for "domestic science" were considerably different than those for agriculture. At an Illinois Farmers' Institute Short Course in Agriculture at the Eastern Illinois State Normal School in 1911 Miss Anna Lois Barbre said that "Agriculture...provides the means whereby food, clothing, and shelter for men are obtained,...household science...adapts these things to the needs of the family." "Housekeeping" and "homemaking," she said, were a girl's "natural destiny and her God-given right." In order to do this properly, however, "she should be trained to perform her household tasks in an orderly, efficient manner." Another speaker, Miss Bertha Miller, stated that "Home-making is a profession on an equal with medicine, with the law, with the ministry and with teaching." She went on to argue that homemakers needed training in science, particularly chemistry, dietetics, bacteriology, and house-building, in economics, and in sociology. She defined the man as producer and woman as spender, and defined women's task as primarily one of managing the home in such a way that domestic harmony and stability were maintained in an aesthetically uplifting environment. "The true home-maker must thoroughly understand the forces which are tending to pull her home apart, and she must meet those forces intelligently," she maintained (Illinois Farmers' Institute 1911:283-5).

That same year, in a Short Course at Southern Illinois State Normal School, the Director of Domestic Science in the city schools of Carbondale, Miss Elsie Kratzinger, gave a paper that stressed the importance of cleanliness and hygiene, and of the mother's responsibility for keeping her family healthy. The Domestic Science curriculum, begun in 1909, taught sewing for grades 4 through 9 and cooking for grades 7, 8, and 9. From the text it is apparent that the students were taught cleanliness as well as orderly and efficient arrangements (Illinois Farmers' Institute 1911:291-93). Unlike the USDA orientation, which still presented farm women as producers, the domestic science movement either ignored or actively opposed the development of women as producers of publicly valued and distributed goods. In 1911, unlike the previous year, no women addressed the farmers attending the Institute on agricultural issues.

Home economists increasingly took over the role of linking farm women to the U.S. Department of Agriculture. The 1940 *Yearbook of Agriculture* is indicative of the shift in USDA thinking. In describing "patterns of living of farm families," home economist Monroe (USDA 1940:867) focuses virtually all her attention on consumption patterns, noting only in passing, and only in reference to farmers' relative ability to withstand the economic depression, that "a considerable degree of self-sufficiency is another characteristic of the patterns of living of farm families. ....Food and fuel are produced....Many elements in farm living reflect this tendency to carry on production for household use" (United States Department of Agriculture 1940:848-69).

For a brief period during World War II, when large numbers of men left the civilian labor force for the armed forces, government and industry encouraged women to assume many jobs that men had formerly held. After World War II, however, the "cult of domesticity" was given a new impetus. Men returning from the war needed jobs, and many women, exhausted from holding down full-time jobs and full-time housekeeping responsibilities, were willing to retreat to the domestic sphere (Friedan 1963).

By the time Union County women established Home Extension in 1948, it was completely under the sway of home economics and had abandoned all connection to agricultural production, to remunerative activities, or to any other form of economic activity such as cooperative canneries, laundries, etc. Farm and Home Extension, while generally linked through shared office space and a close collaborative relationship on county-level issues such as school consolidation and health insurance, programmatically shared little regarding farm and household. Farm extension dealt with the technical aspects of agricultural production and marketing and with farm management; home extension dealt with "home-making," a job that could be placed in any farm or non-farm setting.

## Union County Home Extension Service/Home Bureau

Union County is a relatively small county located in the Shawnee Hills of extreme southern Illinois. Fruit and vegetable growing historically predominated in the central uplands, served since the 1850s by the Illinois Central Railroad, while grain and livestock farming predominated in the Mississippi Bottoms to the west and in the eastern uplands. Early nineteenth-century southern Illinois farm households were largely patriarchal in organization, with the male head of household the authority over all other household members (wife, children, apprentices, servants and laborers).

Women did not organize nor, except for church membership, join organizations in their own right. In contrast, leading Union County men were active in contemporary commercial and political trends. As early as the 1840s some farmers organized a shipping association, and the county was among the first to institute a state-sponsored county fair in 1859. After the Civil War, county farmers organized in professional associations and, beginning in 1873, they participated in the agrarian and cooperative movements of the period. The organization of a Farm Bureau and hiring a county extension agent in 1918 was, therefore, based on a long history of organizing (Adams 1992a, 1992b, 1986).

Congruent with national trends, town women developed various church- and community-based organizations in the late nineteenth century, and Women's Clubs organized in the early twentieth century (Perrin 1883:379, Miller n.d.). Unlike their urban counterparts, farm women became increasingly involved in commodity production, particularly of poultry and dairy products (Adams 1993). Many Union County farm women also developed new roles in relation to fruit and vegetable production, both as wage workers in the fields and packing sheds and as "bosses" in these fields and sheds. By the 1890s women also began to serve on local school boards and to act as reporters from their communities to the county newspapers, and a number of farm women joined the Rebekahs, the women's sodality associated with the International Order of Odd Fellows (IOOF) that had several chapters around the county. This pattern, established by at least 1890, lasted, with some modifications (and impoverishment), until after World War II.

Fruit and vegetable production is very labor intensive; medium to large growers depended on resident laborers. The seven farms I have studied intensively all had resident laborers, both in the house and in separate small dwellings. Larger farms approached plantation conditions; one farm studied had, through the 1930s, seven dwellings for tenants plus other residential facilities for seasonal labor. During the 'teens, when the Farm Bureau was organized in the county and Home Extension begun nationally, farmers intensified production of a wide variety of agricultural commodities, most of which required women's labor and, in the case of farm-owners, their managerial skills.

After World War II the farm economy changed radically, greatly stimulated by government policies. Rural electrification (a government program), begun in the late 1930s but arrested by the war, reached virtually all farm houses in Union County by the mid-1950s (94.9% by the 1954 Census of Agriculture). Farm to market roads began to be improved by the Civilian Conservation Corps (CCC) and Works Projects Administration

(WPA); in the decade after the war virtually all populated rural roads were graveled and gradually these roads were blacktopped (Adams 1987a:390).

The period following World War II was a harsh one for Union County farmers. The federal interstate system made possible the rapid transport of fruits and vegetables from California, Texas, and Florida. Growing conditions and tenure patterns in these regions allowed growers to provide large quantities of predictably high quality produce to the growing supermarket chains and undercut markets for Union County's small-scale production. Industrial expansion attracted labor to cities, leaving horticulturalists with a scarce and increasingly expensive labor supply. At the same time, increasingly stringent state health codes limited access to the market by farmers, largely women, who raised dairy products, fryers, and eggs, and increasing scale of commercial production undercut small producers' ability to compete. The market for cream and butter produced in ungraded dairies and for home-produced fryers virtually vanished by the mid-1950s; the market for small quantities of eggs declined somewhat more slowly because local market sales through feed stores, small groceries, and direct sales were largely unaffected by health codes until the mid-1970s.

The proportion of farms raising dairy cows decreased from 87% in 1935 to 20% in 1964, and those raising poultry decreased from 93% in 1935 to 10% in 1969. The attempt by women to retain their income-producing production is indicated by the relatively long retention of small-scale production: as late as 1959 the 38% of farms with milk cows averaged only five cows per farm. Women maintained their poultry operations even more tenaciously: as late as 1964, 68% of farms still raised chickens, with an average of 57 chickens per farm, a decrease from previous years, suggesting that farmers had turned from commodity production to raising for home consumption (see Adams 1987a:381, 383 for tabulations from U.S. Bureau of the Census 1936 County Tables 2, 5; 1961 County Table 8; 1967 County Table 10; 1972 County Tables 7, 16, 18). However, as Fink (1986) documents, because agricultural experts did not consider women to be agricultural producers they were not included in either opportunities to increase in scale, or in research and extension programs that helped farmers change their crop mix in order to survive in the post-war economy. The particular development path chosen by U.S. policy-makers gave those farmers who chose to stay integrated in the larger American economy little choice but to reorganize cropping regimes, investment patterns, and labor and family relations to more closely conform to urban industrial norms (Adams 1988).

Those farmers who stayed in business reoriented their production. While the number of farms with peach and apple orchards and with small fruits and vegetables declined precipitously, those few that persisted increased in scale. At the same time the proportion of farms raising wheat, soybeans, and sorghum (milo) increased (Adams 1987a:Appendix F). Farming in Union County remained unusually diversified, but it shared the national trend to concentrate in less labor-intensive row crops and beef cattle.

The path of development promoted by government and industry buffeted farm families with contradictory currents. At the same time that they were being encouraged to capitalize their farms and homes with new technologies and as a proliferation of consumer goods offered them greater comfort and convenience, their ability to earn money from their farm operations was undermined. Farm income decreased after the war (see Table 1) and gross value of the county's agricultural products did not recover to World War II levels until 1959; net farm incomes did not show any gain until the 1964 census, a reflection of the sharp rise in expenditures (other than farm labor) required by the new agricultural regime. The poverty accompanying this drop in farm income is indicated by rural farm family income. In 1960, the median rural farm family income in Union County was only $3,476, compared to median income for Illinois families of $6,566 (U.S. Bureau of the Census 1963, Tables 66, 93).

By the 1960s, most farm families had become heavily dependent on off-farm work. In 1950, non-farm income exceeded income generated by farming on 26% of farms; by 1959 the proportion had risen to 45.7% (U.S. Bureau of the Census 1952, County Table I; 1961, County Table 5). By 1964, most Union County farm families were heavily reliant on non-farm income (see Table 2). Seventy-seven percent of farm operators and 44% of the members of farm families, other than the operator, worked off the farm; 29% of females living in farm households were reported working off the farm.[3] Average off-farm earnings per family were $3,842 (U.S. Bureau of the Census 1967 County Table 7). The high proportion of farm operators and, presumably, their wives working off the farm is remarkable because the average age of farm operators in 1964 was over 52 years; approximately 500 of the estimated 965 females between 15 and 65 years old were over 45. In contrast, in 1940 only 5% of operators worked off the farm 250 days or more, and only 21% reported any off-farm work at all.

The poverty that accompanied post-war agricultural adjustment, and the strong need for workers in industry, led many people in the area to leave. Even more than in other Illinois farming regions the number of farms declined precipitously and young people left the farm in large numbers. The rural farm population fell from 9,989 in 1940 to 6,426 in 1950 and 3,441 in 1960, a decline of nearly two-thirds. The number of farms fell from 1724 in 1939 to 1535 in 1949 and 1097 in 1959, a 37% decline. The farms that

TABLE 1. GROSS FARM INCOME AND EXPENDITURES

| Year | 1944[a] | 1949 | 1954[b] | 1959 | 1964[c] | 1969 |
|---|---|---|---|---|---|---|
| Value of farm products sold-County: | $4,565,513 | $3,489,117 | $4,411,878 | $4,960,252 | $5,774,450 | $7,639,649 |
| Value per farm | 2,713 | 2,273 | 3,689 | 4,317 | 6,059 | 8,811 |
| Expenditures | --- | 1,123 | 1,171 | 3,347[d] | 2,383 | 4,362[e] |
| Est. per farm net farm income | --- | 1,150 | 2,518 | 870 | 3,686 | 4,449 |

[a] Source for 1944 and 1949: U.S. Bureau of the Census 1952, County Table 4.

[b] Source for 1954 and 1959, U.S. Bureau of the Census 1961, County Table 4.

[c] Source: U.S. Bureau of the Census 1972, County Table 4; for expenditure data, County Table 5.

[d] On the 50% of commercial farms.

[e] These expenditures are comparable to those tabulated in 1964. Expenditures per farm tabulated in 1969 equalled $7,387 per farm.

TABLE 2. 1964 INCOME OF ALL PERSONS IN HOUSEHOLD
FROM SOURCES OTHER THAN FARM OPERATED[a]

| Income source | Households No. | % | Gross amt. | Amt. per farm |
|---|---|---|---|---|
| All farm households | 953 | 100.0 | --- | --- |
| All sources | 809 | 84.8 | $3,108,036 | $3,841.83 |
| Wages & salaries | 582 | 61.0 | 2,466,411 | 4,237.82 |
| Non-farm business or profession | 66 | 6.9 | 183,709 | 2,777.12 |
| Social Security, pension, Vet. benefits, welfare | 248 | 26.0 | 183,709 | 740.76 |
| Rent, interest, dividends | 246 | 25.8 | 274,626 | 1,116.36 |
| Income of members of farm operator's household (excluding operator) from sources other than farm operated | 416 | 43.7 | 816,210 | 1,962.04 |

[a] Source: U.S. Bureau of the Census 1967, County Table 7.

## 78  ECONOMIC ANTHROPOLOGY OF THE STATE

did persist used far fewer laborers; the county as a whole lost nearly 4,000 in population during these two decades.

The development policies and processes of the post-War period affected virtually all aspects of social life. In the late 1940s, a strong push was made to consolidate schools. School consolidation was vigorously promoted by the State (Weaver 1944, Nickell 1956), and sharply declining rural populations, particularly of school aged children, eroded the viability of rural schools. The number of rural children between 5 and 14 dropped from 4,271 in 1930 to 3,021 in 1940, to 2,719 in 1950 and to 1,780 in 1960 (U.S. Bureau of the Census 1932 Table 14; 1943 Tables 26, 17; 1952 Tables 48, 49; 1963 Table 30). Between 1947 and 1953 most rural schools consolidated with town schools; by 1959 virtually all rural districts had consolidated with town-based districts (Adams 1987a:350-2). Schools had been a center of rural social life and a domain in which women often functioned as political equals with men on school boards and in planning activities.

The new technologies and social arrangements also required farm families to develop new skills quickly. They had to learn to choose and use electric appliances wisely and safely, and organizations like Home Bureau (and the Rural Electric Cooperatives) were excellent vehicles for developing these new skills.

It was in this context -- of rapid changes in farm labor relations and crop mix, of rapid technological innovation, and of reorganization of important aspects of rural social life with declining population, the elimination of rural schools, and development of all-weather roads -- that Union County Home Bureau was organized.[4] The first attempts occurred in 1945 when some women in the northern part of the county joined the Home Bureau in the adjoining county. The following year the district representative from the state Home Bureau spoke to the Farm Bureau Annual Meeting, encouraging the development of a county Home Bureau. Two months later organizing began with assistance from the county farm extension agent and home extension agents from the University of Illinois. Of the 565 women invited to attend a planning meeting, 75 attended. This core group canvassed the rural school districts and continued to organize "until June when due to the busy farming season in which the women of Union County play a vital part it was thought to postpone the work until fall." A goal of 400 members was set; finally, the goal still not reached, an organizing meeting was set for April 6, 1948. That year was largely spent establishing the organization. By September there were 15 units; a year later there were 18. The number of units declined gradually to 11 in the early 1960s. Membership stood between around 370 and 460 through 1949, declining to 211 paid members in 1958 and 186 in 1962. Since oral accounts indicate that most members were young, and since women frequently joined for only a few years, quitting when they got off-farm jobs or otherwise changed their life situation or because of dissatisfaction with the program, at least half of younger farm women were probably involved in Home Bureau at some point. A core of women remained active throughout their lives.

Union County Home Bureau, true to its home economics roots, dealt solely with those activities common to all homemakers. Each year the county board, in consultation with unit representatives, chose a series of major and minor programs from those offered by the state extension service. The extension service then provided training for local unit leaders or, in some cases, conducted major programs themselves. This program was aimed at developing local leadership skills as well being an effective transfer of the demonstration system developed by farm extension.

In 1949, the first full year of organization, the county Home Bureau created an ambitious program, choosing the following 17 major lessons, 3 special lessons, and 9 minor lessons:

    arrangement of furniture
    basic principles of landscaping
    wills and inheritance laws in Illinois
    efficient kitchen arrangements
    problems in dress design
    personal dress design problems
    pressing equipment and its uses
    sauces to complement the dish
    variety of meats
    serving groups, how and what to serve
    understanding ourselves and others
    growing older graciously
    how to obtain ease and charm
    recreation for family and community

Major alternatives:
    window treatments
    better use of sewing machines
    oven and broiler meals

County wide - Cancer

Special lessons:
    sewing machine clinic
    upholstering
    textile painting

80 ECONOMIC ANTHROPOLOGY OF THE STATE

Minor Lessons:
  2 first aid
  2 better English
  3 garnishes -- meats, salads, desserts
  2 meringues
  3 spot and stain removers
  1 or 2 know your fabrics
  leather tooling
  glass etching
  clothing construction

These lessons dealt with clothing construction and care (8), cooking (5), household design, upholstering, and landscaping (5), legal advice (1), etiquette and personal development (4), health (2), crafts (3), and recreation (1). While the 1949 program includes more projects than became usual, the distribution of topics represents the annual selection through the 1950s and '60s. They ranged from utilitarian, as in choosing small appliances and mending tips (1955), to decorative, as in decorating cakes (1954).

These programs were part and parcel of the process through which farm women transformed their homes from production sites to foci of consumption and "homemaking". As among urban middle- and upper-class families in the nineteenth century, farm women's daily life, stripped of its integral role in agricultural production, was newly privatized and isolated. Like their nineteenth century counterparts, many farm women turned to involvement in civic affairs that were congruent with their roles as mothers, particularly education, health care, and community betterment.

The Home Bureau served as a vehicle for farm women to exercise civic influence on a county-wide basis. It was involved in community-wide health programs, including bringing in a mobile X-ray unit and forming a County Health Organization. This program may have arisen out of an Infantile Paralysis Board that was organized in 1951 (HES Minutes 2/8/49, 2/9/53; 1/7/1952; and 10/30/51, 12/3/51) and out of work on obtaining a health insurance carrier for Home and Farm Bureau members in 1952 (HES Minutes 10/5/48, 1/7/52; Farm Adviser letter 4/11/52 in HES, Minutes 5/9/52, 5/22/52; 8/4/52; Union County Farm Bureau Annual Meeting Proceedings 1959, in FES records). The organizing drive for a county health department does not appear prominently in the farm and home adviser's records or in the Home Bureau minutes. However, oral recollections from participants in this project suggest it took a great deal of time, skill, and perseverance to get the county health department organized. According to these accounts, most men who could have been instrumental in creating such a department were indifferent to or, in the case of doctors, often actively opposed its formation. Elderly women looked back with pride at their accomplishment in the face of this perceived male resistance.

Some Home Advisers tried to extend programs into ones concerned with broader issues, as in the 1957 program "What's Your Prejudice." The Home Adviser wrote in the Farm Extension Service Annual Report that "The lesson was chosen because of the prevalence of racial and religious prejudice in the county....It is hoped that this lesson will pave the way for desirable relationships if and when negroes [sic] begin living in the county" (Home Adviser's Report in FESR Annual Report 1957:24).[5] Such programs around social issues were infrequent.

The Home Bureau also took an active interest in education, both in regard to the public schools and to 4-H clubs. Home Bureau women promoted school consolidation; on a local level they were active in various community development activities. The organization was directly involved in 4-H clubs, and it was common for active Home Bureau and Farm Bureau members to be 4-H club leaders (e.g., FES Annual Report 1956:14, 1957:5, 1960:3). 4-H, organized by project, was theoretically open to both sexes but in practice tended to be boys' clubs and girls' clubs. Records of club project participation appear for the first time in 1940. Projects that year were corn, soybeans, home gardens, dairy cattle, poultry, and clothing. Only corn (with 21 boys), soybeans (with one boy) and clothing (with 12 girls) were gender specific. Poultry was evenly split with 6 boys and 6 girls, while in home gardening and dairy cattle one girl and 4 boys participated in each (FES Annual Report 1940). The number and kind of projects varied widely in the ensuing years, but some patterns emerge: no girl ever participated in corn or soybean projects and no boy ever participated in clothing, food, or home beautification projects. However, other projects, although biased toward one or the other gender, were not exclusive. In addition to the projects mentioned, beef cattle, swine, rabbits, sheep, horses and mules, agricultural engineering and shop, and dogs were predominantly boys' project, while more girls than boys participated in crafts and beautification of home grounds (Adams 1987a:394-96). Young peoples' participation in 4-H projects indicates that row crops were the exclusive domain of men; cooking, sewing, and home decoration were the exclusive domain of women. A wide range of agricultural and other productive activities were not so firmly associated with either male or female spheres.

The home economics program, which was predicated on the assumption that a woman's sphere was in the home or, in public, related to "feminine" concerns of morality and the expressive and aesthetic side of life, was only partially successful in converting farm women to its vision of femininity. Many farm women learned the practical and normative practices associated with middle-class homemaking but expanded their sphere to include remunerative activities and, frequently, husband's assistant. What explains this highly selective adoption of the home economists' program?

## Bases for Adoption with Modification of Home Economics Prescriptions

Large numbers of farm women welcomed the Home Bureau programs. Like the Farm Bureau, Home Bureau's membership was largely drawn from the leading elements of the farming community. Few if any Home Bureau members were poor tenants; most tenants quickly left the farm for wage labor in the expanding industrial and service economy. Most Home Bureau members embraced "modern" ways of doing things and promoted progressive reforms such as public health and school consolidation within the community and middle-class standards in the home. They welcomed labor-saving technologies that released them from drudgery.

They generally accepted the new standards that, even as heavy labor was eased, continued to require large amounts of housework: numerous changes of clothes, frequent cleaning and pressing of all clothing, greater attention to personal hygiene and etiquette, more intensive care for the fewer children in the home, and a tastefully decorated home (Cowan 1974, 1983). As child labor became less important on farms (and as farm technologies made farm work more dangerous to young children) farm women joined their urban counterparts in being given and assuming the primary care of their children's psychological, moral, and intellectual development.

There is no doubt that farm women adopted many aspects of the doctrine of separate spheres as it was represented in the post-War period. Most girls took home economics courses, so even if their mothers were not active in Home Bureau and they were not active in girls 4-H clubs, they learned the rudiments of middle-class standards of etiquette, diet, and home decoration. During the 1950s and '60s, virtually all home owners who could afford to do so significantly remodeled their homes, not only adding electricity and running water but also furnishing the home as tastefully as possible (Adams 1993). To most of the women who persisted in farming, many of the Home Extension prescriptions seemed useful and helped them make the transition to industrialized farming.

However, the government's home extension service, along with the various print and broadcast media, failed to acknowledge other dimensions of life that farm women perceived as central to their own identity and to the family's well-being, that of being gainfully employed. With their commitment to transforming women into consuming homemakers, Home Extension and other agencies responsible for farm-oriented research and education developed no opportunities for women to remain gainfully employed on the farm. With this avenue foreclosed by development policies, large numbers of farm women found off-farm jobs. In 1940 only 9.3% of farm women were listed as in the labor force;[6] by 1960 one-fourth of farm women were listed as in the labor force and by 1980 36% were so listed. While these are comparable in percentage terms to women's labor force participation nationally, they reflect opposing trends: non-farm women's participation either declined or held steady, while farm women for the first time entered the enumerated labor force. Additionally, given the age structure of farming noted above, in which more than half of farm women over 15 years old were 45 or older in 1964, the movement of farm women into the labor force must be seen as a major phenomenon. The jobs women reported also shifted: in 1940 17% of employed women were domestics; by 1960 only 4 individuals reported working in this capacity. The proportion of "operatives and kindred workers" rose from 27% in 1940 to 35% in 1960, and service and clerical workers increased from 8.3% in 1940 to 21.6% of the farm women in the labor force (U.S. Bureau of the Census 1943, 1963; see also Rosenfeld 1985). A state mental hospital and shoe factory in the county's main market town, as well as the proximity of a rapidly expanding state university and other smaller industries and government services (including prisons) provided jobs to many who sought them.

Women reported, both to me and to the Home Adviser, that they sought off-farm work in order to earn money to keep the farm afloat during the difficult period of the 1950s. I believe that this was not the only reason, for women reported to me that their husbands did not want them to work off the farm, indicating that the assessment of financial necessity was different for husband and wife. I believe that farm women were accustomed to earning disposable income through their on-farm production, and that they were not content to be assistants to their husbands with no independent access to money. Additionally, they wanted to improve their homes and help educate their children, investments for which they had previously been largely responsible. Some women who did not seek off-farm work maintained their poultry enterprises long after they had ceased to be economically profitable and in fact were costing the farm money for feed (money taken out of the farm side of the accounts and not out of the egg money received), suggesting that many farm women valued gainful activity. A few farm women maintained poultry flocks into the 1990s, selling eggs to individuals because state laws prohibit their sale through retail outlets. Other farm women developed cottage industries like custom sewing and catering. In some cases, these enterprises reproduced strong reciprocal relationships between husband and wife: a seamstress' husband assisted her in altering patterns and cutting out the fabrics; she owned her own tractor (a birthday gift from her husband) with which she did field work.

Farm women were among the last to experience the structural separation of domestic space and social production and they were among the first property-owning classes to experience the common mid- to late-twentieth century phenomena of a man's income being insufficient to support the entire family. Further, because they abruptly lost their ability to sell their agricultural products and to participate autonomously in the farm enterprise, the challenge to standards of hard work and partial economic autonomy which undergirded farm women's self-valuation was jarring. At the same time the 1950s, a period of unprecedented prosperity in which the "cult of domesticity" could appear as a viable form of family life for urban Americans was difficult for middle-level farmers. They lost economic security and, although they were able to live better than they had during the Depression years, their relative standard of living could not keep pace with either their parents at the turn of the century, or with their urban counterparts. Farm women's entry into the labor market can therefore be attributed both to their attempt to retain an inherited class status and to retain a form of autonomy based on independent access to cash income. In the process, they accepted Home Extension education to learn the forms of urban middle-class living, replacing earlier domestic arrangements but, anticipating developments of the next decades, failed to internalize the restrictive boundaries of "bourgeois domesticity". They not only acted as leaders in civic organizations oriented to "domestic" concerns, particularly health and education, but they entered the non-farm labor force in large numbers. Structurally removed from the farm they, like the other farm laborers displaced by new technologies, became members of the working classes.

It is not possible to re-write history but it is possible to imagine a different historical trajectory in which adult education for farm women could have helped them recreate their working lives as partners, not assistants, with their husbands in the farm operation. It is ironic that expert advice to farmers struggling through the farm crisis of the 1980s included enlisting the wife as a partner in the farm operation. Her ideal role, they advised (in addition to "go-fer" and general pinch-hitter), was to take care of the books and other aspects of the increasingly complicated managerial aspects of the farm. After a half century of viewing the farm as men's domain in which women were, at best, marginalized assistants, the joint phenomena of economic crisis and women's liberation may restore a vital role to women in some farm operations.

## Acknowledgments

Thanks to Home Advisers Ruby Lingle and Judy Wagner, Extension Secretary Joann Leadbetter, early Home Bureau members Clara Davidson (dec.), Lulu Dillow (dec.), Helen Kimber, Maud Kinder, Clara Bell Miller (dec.), Edith Rendleman, Elaine Rushing, Arilla Spiller (dec.), Ruby Weaver (dec.), and other Union County men and women who shared their memories with me. Thanks also for editorial comments by Peggy Barlett.

## Notes

1. A number of groups followed a different route, from the Hutterites who adopted new technologies but developed alternate labor systems, to the Amish who rejected both technologies and social organization, and other smaller enclaves who more-or-less explicitly rejected "modernization". Such groups include intentional "utopian" communities, many rural African-American communities, and "conservative" ethnic settlements and individuals. On the latter, see Salamon 1992.

2. The growing body of research on farm women's lives suggests that symbolic representations of and restrictions on women's appropriate sphere varied considerably from region to region and/or ethnic group to ethnic group. In the southern Illinois hill region, most farm women interviewed defined themselves as workers engaged in various forms of agricultural production and appear to have had greater flexibility in work roles (e.g., plowing and doing other field work) than women in many other parts of the country, (see Bush 1982, 1987; Jensen 1985; Fink 1986; Osterud 1987, 1991; Adams 1988; Elbert 1988; Flora 1988; Barlett 1993).

3. This figure was derived by calculating that females made up 47.7% of farm population, calculating that the number of people on farms between 15 and 65 was 2023, estimating that 965 (2023 x .477) were female, and dividing the 278 females reported working off the farm during the year by total estimated females -- 965.

86 ECONOMIC ANTHROPOLOGY OF THE STATE

4. This account is synthesized from Union County Home Extension Service [HES] "History of Union County Home Bureau" n.d. and HES minutes archived in HES office, Anna, Illinois; interviews with several charter members of the Union County Home Bureau; and interviews with two County Extension Home Advisers.

5. In fact, a number of African-American families lived in the county, largely in the northern third in and around the village of Cobden which, prior to World War II, had a large enough population to support a "colored" school and church.

6. This low percentage masks the large number of farm women who worked seasonally in the fields and packing sheds and who were engaged in remunerative enterprises like poultry and dairy. It does reflect the low participation in the non-farm labor force, and should be read as such.

## References

Adams, Jane
    1993    Resistance to "Modernity": Southern Illinois Farm Women and the Cult of Domesticity. *American Ethnologist* 20:89-113.
    1992a  Agrarian activism: Mediator between two worlds. *Social Science History.* 16:365-400.
    1992b  'How can a poor man live'? Resistance to Capitalist Development in Southern Illinois, 1870-1890. *Rural History: Economy, Society, Culture* 3:87-110.
    1988    The Decoupling of Farm and Household: Differential Consequences of Capitalist Development on Southern Illinois and Third World Family Farms. *Comparative Studies in Society and History* 30(3):453-82.
    1987a  *The Transformation of Rural Social Life in Union County, Illinois, in the Twentieth Century.* PhD Dissertation, University of Illinois.
    1987b  Business Farming and Farm Policy in the 1980s: Further Reflections on the Farm Crisis. *C&A: Culture and Agriculture* 32 (Spring/Summer):1-6.
    1986    Farmer organization and class formation. *Canadian Journal of Anthropology/RCA* 5:35-42.

Balderston, Lydia Ray
    1936    *Housewifery: A Textbook of Practical Housekeeping.* 5th Edition. Chicago: J.B. Lippincott Co.

Barlett, Peggy F.
    1993    *American Dreams, Rural Realities: Family Farms in Crisis.* Chapel Hill: University of North Carolina Press.

Bevier, Isabel
    1907    *The House: Its Plan, Decoration and Care.* Chicago: American School of Home Economics.

Bloch, Ruth H.
    1978    Untangling the Roots of Modern Sex Roles: A Survey of Four Centuries of Change. *Signs* 4(2):237-52

Bordin, Ruth
    1981    *Woman and Temperance: The Quest for Power and Liberty, 1873-1900.* Philadelphia: Temple University Press.

Bowers, William L.
 1974 *The Country Life Movement in America 1900-1920.* Port Washington, NY: Kennikat Press.
Bruere, Martha B. and Robert W. Bruere
 1912 *Increasing Home Efficiency.* New York: The MacMillan Company.
Bush, Corlann G.
 1982 The Barn is His, The House is Mine: Agricultural Technology and Sex Roles. In G.H. Daniels and M.H. Rose, eds., *Energy and Transport*, pp.235-59. Beverly Hills, CA: Sage Publications.
 1987 "He Isn't Half So Cranky as He Used to Be": Agricultural Mechanization, Comparable Worth, and the Changing Farm Family. In C. Groneman and M.B. Norton, eds., *"To Toil the Livelong Day"*, pp.213-36. Ithaca, NY: Cornell University Press.
Cott, Nancy F.
 1978 Passionlessness: An Interpretation of Victorian Sexual Ideology, 1790-1850. *Signs* 4(2):219-36.
Cowan, Ruth Schwartz
 1983 *More Work for Mother: The Ironies of Household Technology from the Open Hearth to the Microwave.* New York: Basic Books, Inc.
 1974 A Case Study of Technological and Social Change: The Washing Machine and the Working Wife. In M.S. Hartman and L. Banner, eds., *Clio's Consciousness Raised* pp.245-53. New York: Harper Torchbook.
Danbom, David B.
 1979 *The Resisted Revolution: Urban American and the Industrialization of Agriculture, 1900-1930.* Ames: Iowa State University Press.
Degler, Carl
 1980 *At Odds: Women and the Family in America from the Revolution to the Present.* New York: Oxford University Press.
East, Marjorie
 1980 *Home Economics: Past, Present, and Future.* Boston: Allyn and Bacon, Inc.
Elbert, Sarah
 1988 Women and Farming: Changing Structures, Changing Roles. In W. Haney and J.B. Knowles, eds., *Women and Farming*, pp.245-64. Boulder, CO: Westview Press.

Fabian, Johannes
    1983    *Of Time and the Other: How Anthropology Makes Its Object.* New York: Columbia University Press.

Fink, Deborah
    1986    *Open Country, Iowa.* Albany: State University of New York Press.
    1992    *Agrarian Women: Wives and Mothers in Rural Nebraska, 1880-1940.* Chapel Hill: University of North Carolina Press.

Flora, Cornelia Butler
    1988    Public Policy and Women in Agricultural Production: A Comparative and Historical Analysis. In W. Haney and J.B. Knowles, eds., *Women and Farming*, pp.265-80. Boulder, CO: Westview Press.

Frederick, Mrs. Christine
    1920    *Household Engineering: Scientific Management in the Home. A Correspondence Course....* Chicago: American School of Home Economics.

Friedan, Betty
    1963    *The Feminine Mystique.* New York: Dell.

Gilbreth, Lillian
    1927    *The Homemaker and Her Job.* New York: D. Appleton-Century.

Hartman, Heidi
    1981    The Family as the Locus of Gender, Class and Political Struggle: The Example of Housework. *Signs* 6(3):366-94.

Illinois Farmers' Institute
    1910    *Fifteenth Annual Report. For the Year Ending June 30, 1910.* Springfield: Illinois State Journal Co.
    1911    *Sixteenth Annual Report.* Springfield: Illinois State Journal Co.

Jensen, Joan M.
    1986    *Loosening the Bonds: Mid-Atlantic Farm Women, 1750-1850.* New Haven: Yale University Press.

Knowles, Jane B.
    1988    "It's Our Turn Now": Rural American Women Speak Out, 1900-1920. In W. Haney and J.B. Knowles, eds., *Women and Farming*, pp.303-18. Boulder, CO: Westview Press.

Kyrk, Hazel
    1933    *Economic Problems of the Family.* New York: Harper and Brothers.

Lasch, Christopher
    1979    *Haven in a Heartless World.* New York: Basic Books, Inc.
Lerner, Gerda
    1969    The Lady and the Mill Girl: Changes in the Status of Women in the Age of Jackson. *Midcontinent American Studies Journal* X(1):5-15.
Marcus, Alan I. and Richard Lowitt
    1990    The United States Department of Agriculture in Historical Perspective. Special symposium issue, *Agricultural History* 64(2).
Matthaei, Julie A.
    1982    *An Economic History of Women in America: Women's Work, the Sexual Division of Labor, and the Development of Capitalism.* New York: Schocken Books.
Matthews, Glenna
    1987    *"Just a Housewife": The Rise and Fall of Domesticity in America.* New York: Oxford University Press.
Miller, Clara Bell
    n.d.    "Through the Looking Glass": Cobden Women's Club, 1908-1976. Ms. in author's collection.
Morantz, Regina
    1977    Making Women Modern: Middle Class Women and Health Reform in 19th Century America. *Journal of Social History* 10(4):490-507.
Nickell, Vernon L.
    1956    llinois Public Schools Provide Educational Opportunities to All. In *Illinois Blue Book 1955-1956*, pp.404-13. State of Illinois.
Osterud, Nancy Grey
    1991    *Bonds of Community: The Lives of Farm Women in Nineteenth-Century New York.* Ithaca: Cornell University Press.
    1987    "She Helped Me Hay It as Good as a Man": Relations among Women and Men in an Agricultural Community. In C. Groneman and M.B. Norton, *"To Toil the Livelong Day."*, pp.87-97. Ithaca: Cornell University Press.
Parloa, Maria
    1910    *Home Economics.* New York: The Century Co. New and Enlarged Edition. (First edition, 1898).

Lasch, Christopher
    1979    *Haven in a Heartless World.* New York: Basic Books, Inc.
Lerner, Gerda
    1969    The Lady and the Mill Girl: Changes in the Status of Women in the Age of Jackson. *Midcontinent American Studies Journal* X(1):5-15.
Marcus, Alan I. and Richard Lowitt
    1990    The United States Department of Agriculture in Historical Perspective. Special symposium issue, *Agricultural History* 64(2).
Matthaei, Julie A.
    1982    *An Economic History of Women in America: Women's Work, the Sexual Division of Labor, and the Development of Capitalism.* New York: Schocken Books.
Matthews, Glenna
    1987    *"Just a Housewife": The Rise and Fall of Domesticity in America.* New York: Oxford University Press.
Miller, Clara Bell
    n.d.    "Through the Looking Glass": Cobden Women's Club, 1908-1976. Ms. in author's collection.
Morantz, Regina
    1977    Making Women Modern: Middle Class Women and Health Reform in 19th Century America. *Journal of Social History* 10(4):490-507.
Nickell, Vernon L.
    1956    llinois Public Schools Provide Educational Opportunities to All. In *Illinois Blue Book 1955-1956*, pp.404-13. State of Illinois.
Osterud, Nancy Grey
    1991    *Bonds of Community: The Lives of Farm Women in Nineteenth-Century New York.* Ithaca: Cornell University Press.
    1987    "She Helped Me Hay It as Good as a Man": Relations among Women and Men in an Agricultural Community. In C. Groneman and M.B. Norton, *"To Toil the Livelong Day."*, pp.87-97. Ithaca: Cornell University Press.
Parloa, Maria
    1910    *Home Economics.* New York: The Century Co. New and Enlarged Edition. (First edition, 1898).

1952 *Census of Agriculture, 1950. Volume I, Counties and State Economic Areas, Part 5, Illinois*. Washington, DC: U.S. Government Printing Office.
1953 *Census of Population, 1950. Volume II, Characteristics of the Population, Part 13, Illinois*. Washington, DC: U.S. Government Printing Office.
1961 *Census of Agriculture, 1959. Volume I, Counties and State Economic Areas, Part 12, Illinois*. Washington, DC: U.S. Government Printing Office.
1963 *Census of Population, 1960. Volume I, Characteristics of the Population, Part 15, Illinois*. Washington, DC: U.S. Government Printing Office.
1967 *Census of Agriculture, 1964. Statistics for the State and Counties. Part 12, Illinois*. Washington, DC: U.S. Government Printing Office.
1972 *Census of Agriculture, 1969. Volume I, Area Reports, Part 12, Illinois, Section 2, County Reports*. Washington, DC: U.S. Government Printing Office.

United States Department of Agriculture
1915 *Social and Labor Needs of Farm Women, Report No. 103*. Washington, DC: Government Printing Office.
1940 *Yearbook of Agriculture: Farmers In a Changing World*. Washington, DC: U.S. Government Printing Office.

Weaver, Leon H.
1944 *School Consolidation and State Aid in Illinois*. Urbana: The University of Illinois Press.

Welter, Barbara
1966 The Cult of True Womanhood: 1820-1860. *American Quarterly* XVIII(2, pt. 1):151-74.

Wright, Gwendolyn
1980 *Moralism and the Model Home*. Chicago: University of Chicago Press.

Zaretsky, Eli
1986 *Capitalism, the Family and Personal Life*. New York: Harper and Row.

# HOUSEHOLD ECONOMY IN EARLY STATE SOCIETY: MATERIAL VALUE, PRODUCTIVE CONTEXT AND SPHERES OF EXCHANGE

Patricia Wattenmaker
University of Virginia

Textual and archaeological data reveal that ancient Near Eastern political elites derived their strength, in part, from agricultural and pastoral resources extracted from the rural sector (e.g., Archi 1981; Heltzer 1976; Stein and Wattenmaker 1990; Wright 1984:56; Zeder 1988: 9-11; 48-49). However, little is known about the impact of political centralization or increased tributary demands on production and consumption patterns among non-elite households producing the surpluses. This paper examines household economies during a period of political centralization, using data from mid-late third millennium B.C. houses excavated at the site of Kurban Höyük, in southeast Turkey. Previous analysis has revealed that non-elite households at Kurban became increasingly reliant on specialists for craft goods during this period of state development (Wattenmaker in press). To investigate the relationship between political centralization and economic specialization, this study considers : 1) evidence for a tributary economy during a period of early state development, 2) consumption patterns among non-elite households at Kurban, and 3) factors guiding production organization and consumption among both the non-elite and political elite. T h e spatial distributions of artifacts from Kurban provide insights into the organization of production and consumption. Evidence for a tributary economy is examined through a study of faunal remains. Chipped stone, ceramics and spindle whorls inform about the production and use of craft goods. Archives from the royal palace at the site of Ebla, 180 km. to the southwest of Kurban provide additional information on the organization of craft production. Establishing those categories of goods produced by households and those produced by specialists provides insight into why households became increasingly reliant on specialists as state societies developed.

Increasing sociopolitical complexity is closely associated with intensified economic specialization and exchange in early state societies (e.g. Brumfiel and Earle 1987:1-4; Clark and Parry 1990:320), but the nature of

## 94 ECONOMIC ANTHROPOLOGY OF THE STATE

this relationship is not well understood. Most discussions of changing economic patterns in early states focus either on increasing demand for sumptuary goods among the political elite or else on the need to provision state-supported workers (located primarily at centers). Household consumption patterns have generally been overlooked in considerations of economic reorganization in early state societies. However, there is now abundant evidence (primarily from surveys) for widespread use of specialist-produced craft goods at small communities, both in the Old World (Johnson 1973; Wright 1981) and New World (e.g. Blanton et al. 1982; Marcus 1983:217). Research in Mesoamerica (Blanton et al. 1982:22-3) has drawn attention to the relationship between political centralization and household economy. Surface collections from sites in the Valley of Oaxaca revealed an increase in specialist-produced goods at smaller sites. The researchers proposed that increased tributary demands may have created a conflict in the scheduling of food and craft production, resulting in increased demand for specialist-produced goods among households. Kurban provided an opportunity to investigate the relationship between political centralization and household economic organization in a Near Eastern case of state formation.

### Urbanism in Third Millennium Northwest Mesopotamia and Reorganization at Kurban Höyük

Kurban is located in the Karababa Basin of the southern Turkish Euphrates Valley, at the border between the Taurus mountains and the north Mesopotamian steppe (Figures 1 and 2). The area falls within the dry farming zone of north Mesopotamia. State societies first developed in the late fourth millennium B.C., but these had collapsed by the beginning of the third millennium B.C. In the mid- third millennium a series of urban centers (50-100 ha.) with associated towns and villages developed across the north Syro-Mesopotamian plain. The scale of mid-third millennium B.C. urbanism was unprecedented for this part of the Near East.

Numerous surveys and excavations were conducted in the southern Turkish Euphrates Valley as part of an international salvage effort to document the archaeological record before it was flooded by the filling of the Ataturk dam. As part of this salvage project, mid-third millennium B.C. occupational levels were uncovered at two town-sized sites (5-25 hectares) (Lidar Höyük and Kurban) and two village sized-sites (less than five hectares) (Gritille Höyük and Hayaz Höyük) before they were flooded. Ongoing excavations at Titriş Höyük (Algaze et al. 1992), which falls outside the flooded area, continue to provide data from the regional center.

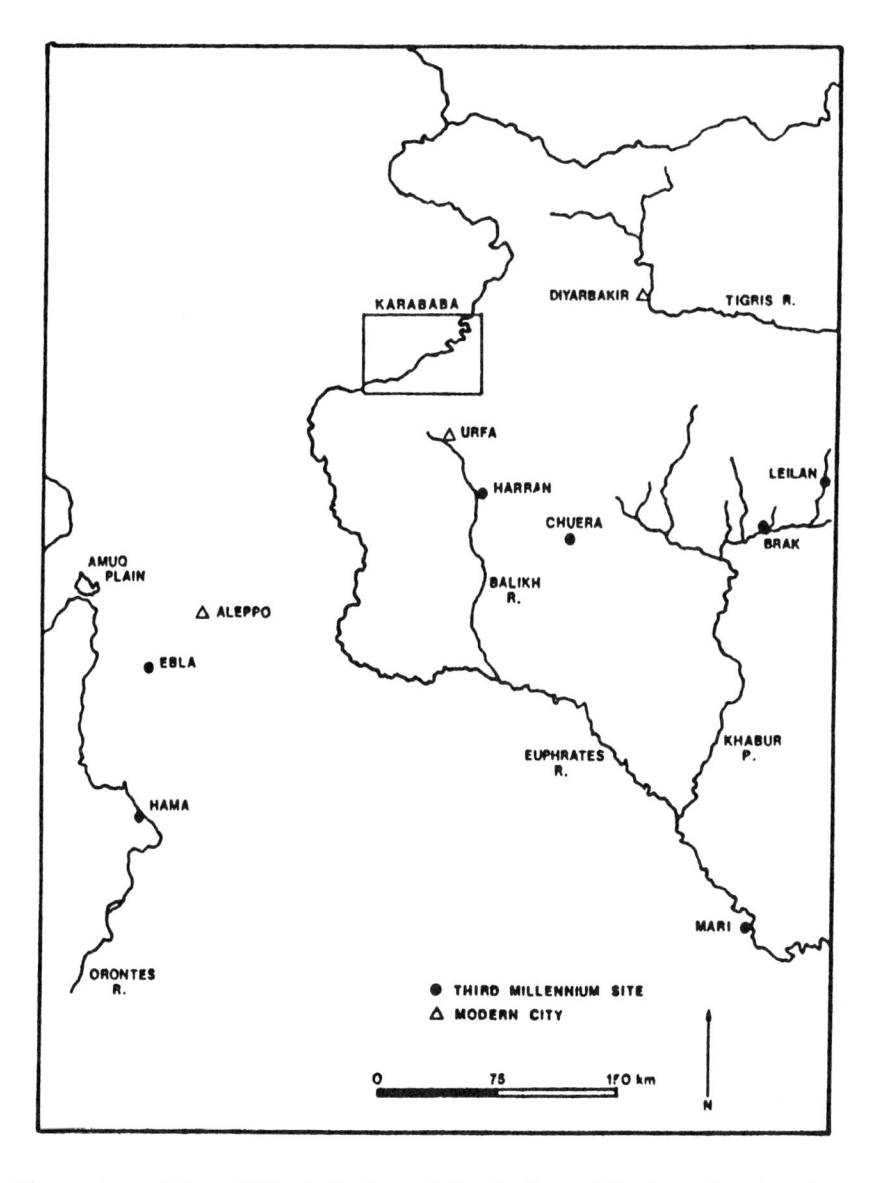

Figure 1. Map of North Syria and South-Central Turkey showing the location of the Karababa Basin

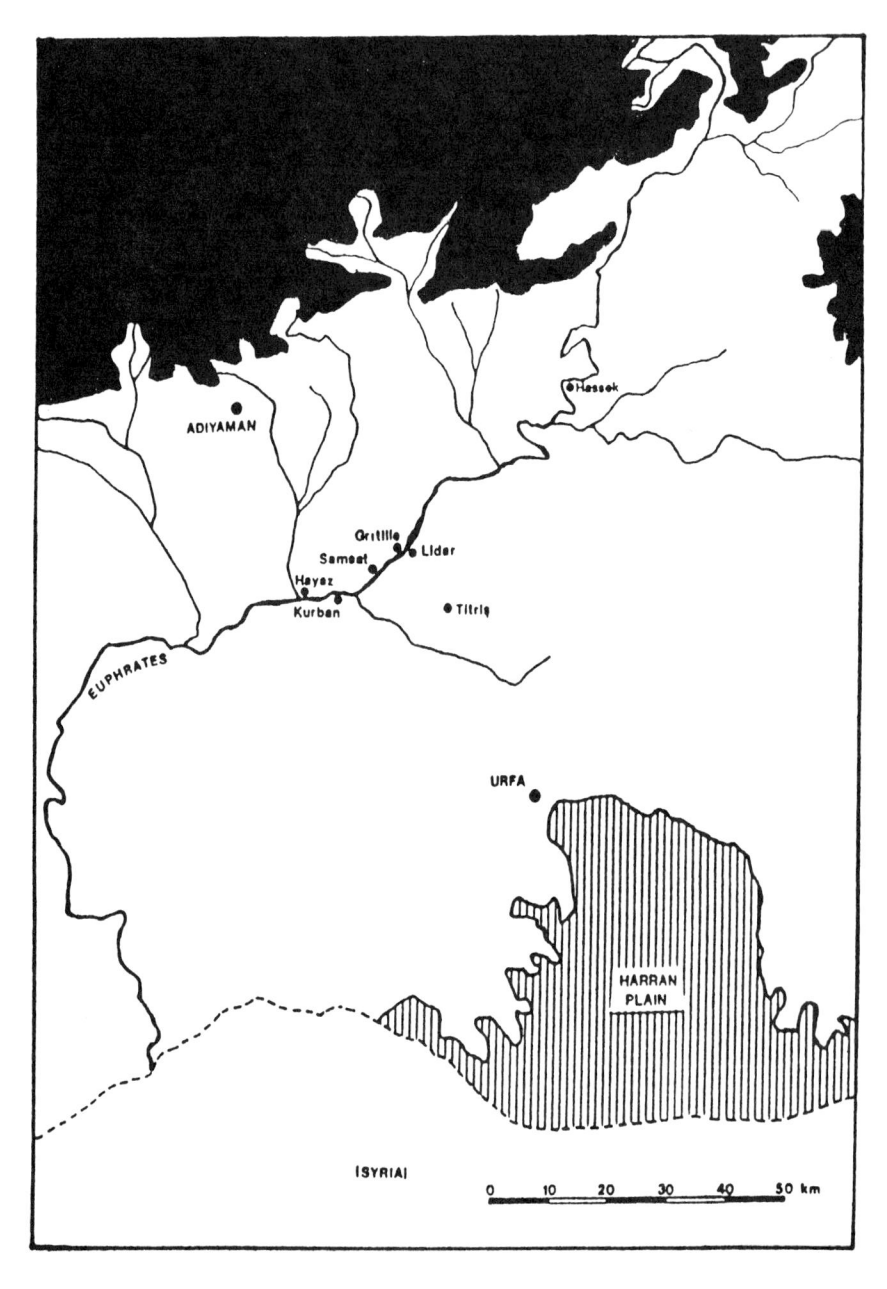

Figure 2. Location of Kurban Höyük and neighboring excavated third millennium B.C. sites.

Settlement patterns from the Karababa Basin suggest a major shift in political organization during the mid-late third millennium B.C. The total settlement area in the Kurban region increased more than three-fold, and the early third millennium B.C. settlement pattern of uniformly small village sized sites was replaced with one that included a regional center (Titriş, 43+ ha) (Algaze et al. 1992:46), large and small towns (Lidar ca. 15 ha, Kurban ca. 6 ha), and villages or hamlets (Şaşkan ca. 1.1 ha; Yaslica .3 ha) (Wilkinson 1990). The settlement at Titriş was established during this period and it rapidly reached urban proportions (Algaze et al., 1992). Kurban expanded from a one-hectare single-mounded site to a double-mounded site of six hectares (Algaze 1990a).

Kurban was selected for excavation because mid-late third millennium deposits were located just below the mound surface, providing an ideal opportunity to investigate political centralization during this time[1]. Four years of excavation at the town site of Kurban by the University of Chicago yielded a fairly extensive clearance of relatively elaborate structures toward the central part of the site (Algaze 1990b) (Figure 3, Areas A and C). To investigate changes in non-elite household economy, additional excavations were concentrated toward the edge of the site, where more modest residential areas were located (Figure 4, Areas B and G) (Wattenmaker 1990). Approximately 900 m$^2$ of Period IV occupational remains were available for this study.

The mid-late third millennium settlement (referred to as **Period IV** of the Kurban sequence; see Algaze 1990b) can be divided into four subperiods spanning ca. 400 years (Wattenmaker 1990). During the earliest subperiod, the "village phases", the site was confined to the large mound. Excavations were limited to a deep sounding. In the second subperiod, the "town formation" phases, the fortification wall was constructed and shortly afterward, settlement expanded to the small mound. Excavations toward the center of the site yielded several fairly elaborate structures which probably represent elite houses. One excavated structure may have been a public building. The walls were fairly massive and one room of the structure contained a large storage jar and evidence of administrative activity in the form of a door lock sealing and jar sealings. During the third subperiod, the "town development" phases, the site reached its maximum size of 6 hectares. Houses include both fairly elaborate and more modest structures. Finally, during the sub-period of increased settlement nucleation, population density at the site was high and houses were closely spaced. The findings from these excavations provide the data with which to examine the tributary economy and its potential impact on non-elite production and consumption.

## The Tributary Economy

Political centralization in the mid-third millennium B.C. may have led to new tributary demands placed on households. Faunal remains from Kurban provide the primary data source with which to examine evidence for a tributary economy in the Karababa Basin. Herd animals would have been an ideal tributary item, since they could be moved between sites on hoof, and kept alive until their meat was needed, thereby avoiding the problem of spoilage (see Zeder 1988:10). No written records have been found at sites in the Karababa Basin, but the importance of sheep and goat in the ancient Near Eastern state economy is well documented in texts from sites such as Ebla, where 800 to 4600 animals were slaughtered for palace and temple use each month (Archi 1982:214). Texts record the movement of large numbers of animals (as well as agricultural surpluses) from other settlements to Ebla; the scale of the deliveries from such a large number of settlements (Pettinato 1981:162-5, 202) suggests that the animals were sent as tribute from hinterland settlements. Due to the large numbers of sheep and textiles listed in the Ebla archives, Ebla has been characterized as "an empire built on the backs of simple shepherds" (Gelb 1986:158).

Although the Kurban region did not fall under the control of Ebla (Archi 1980:3), and economic patterns in the two regions may have differed in some ways, data from Ebla on economic organization provide a useful source of hypotheses on economic patterns in the Karababa region. Records attest to exchange between the two areas (Pettinato 1981:226), and ceramic assemblages were in many ways similar (Algaze 1990b:346), suggesting extensive contact between the two areas.

To evaluate evidence for a tributary economy at Kurban, the ages of sheep and goat at death were determined through a study of tooth emergence and wear patterns (following Payne 1973). If sheep and goat were raised at Kurban but not exported as tribute, we would expect to find animals in all age categories, including immature animals that died of natural causes, older animals representing a breeding population, and animals that survived only until the ages of two to three years, the age when we would expect most male caprines to be slaughtered. By the age of three most animals have reached their maximum size, so it is often no longer advantageous for herders to keep them alive for meat alone (Payne 1973:282). A small number of males will be kept alive for breeding, and female caprines are generally kept alive for breeding and secondary products until they become infertile or ill. Throughout most of the Kurban Period IV sequence, most animals represented were killed after the age of three, beyond the prime-age

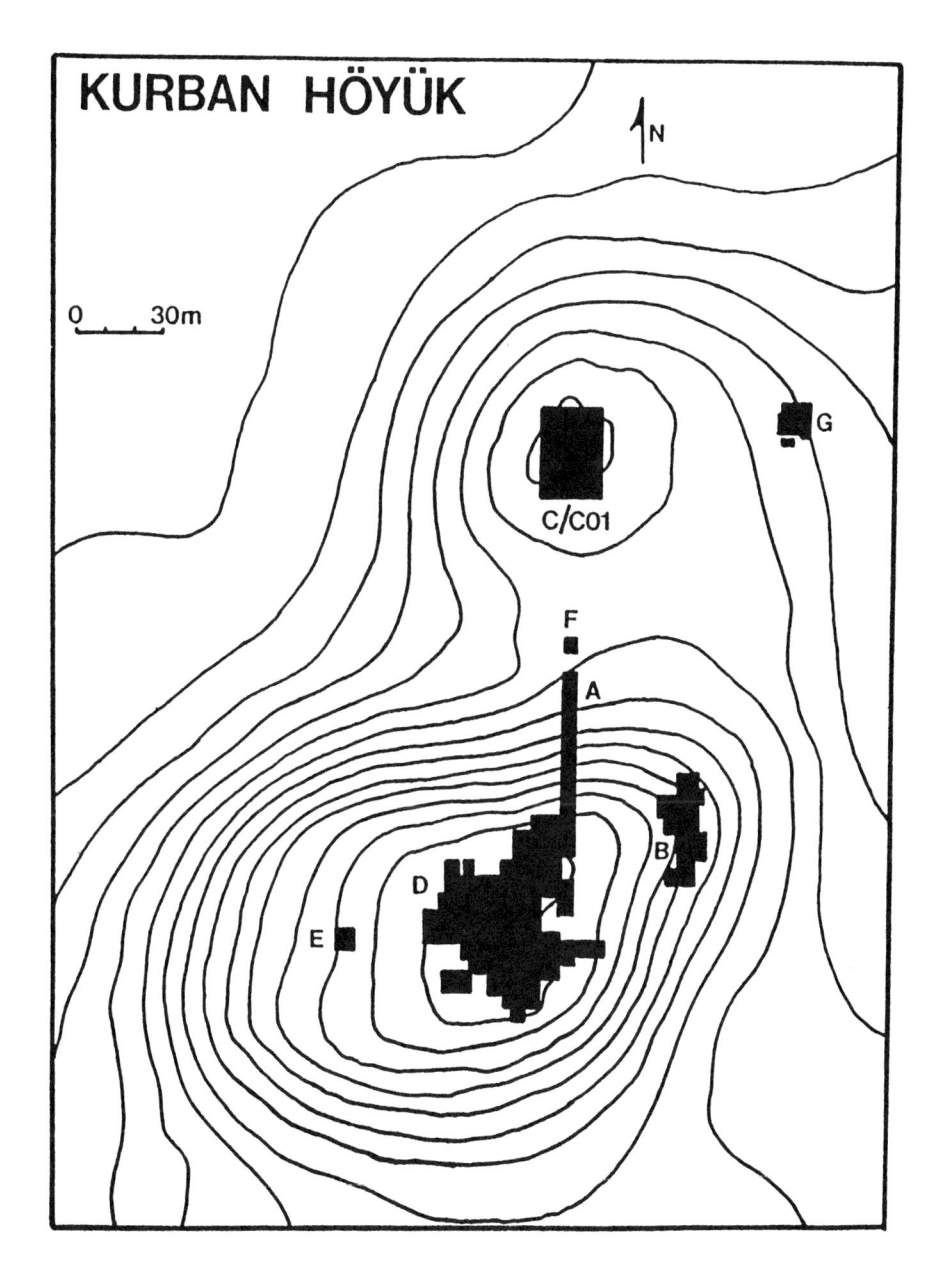

Figure 3. Map of Kurban Höyük, with excavated areas shown.

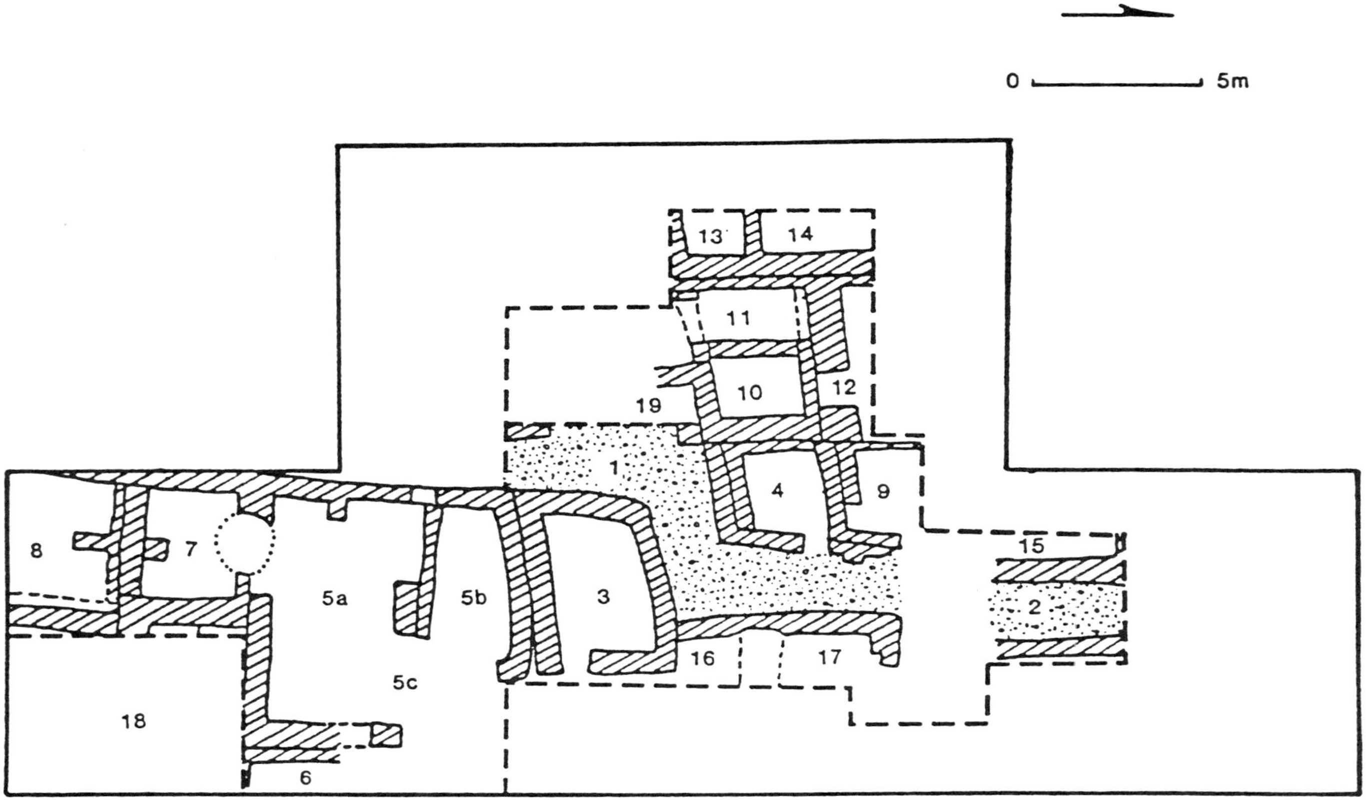

Figure 4. Plan of Kurban Höyük Area B (Periods IV and III) (after Verhaaren 1986).

range (Figure 5). While some younger animals were represented, there is a near absence of animals killed between the ages of 2-3, the age group we would expect to be best represented. This suggests that animals were exported from domestic areas at Kurban, possibly as tribute.

A low proportion of animals in the prime-age category might, in some cases, be interpreted as evidence for an emphasis on wool production. If animals were raised primarily for wool or hair, they would probably be kept alive until a fairly late age, when the quality of wool declines (Payne 1973: 281; 283). However, in this case the animals were not kept alive as long as might be expected if they were raised primarily for fibers (ibid.). Moreover, faunal analysis at two other mid-third millennium B.C sites in the region yielded kill-off patterns consistent with a meat production strategy, with the majority of animals slaughtered in the prime-age category (Stein 1988; Kussinger 1988). Finally, if animals were raised primarily for wool, younger animals might be slaughtered only if they became ill or if meat was needed. This herding strategy would result in a steady decline in the proportion of animals surviving, with at least some animals slaughtered between the ages of two to three. Instead, the data reveal a selective absence of animals in the prime-age category, suggesting the export of animals in that age category, possibly as tribute.

Agricultural products were also important in the ancient Near Eastern tributary economies. Economic tablets record the transport of agricultural products from surrounding settlements to the Ebla palace; at least some of the deliveries may represent tributary payments. In the Karababa Basin, evidence is strong for agricultural expansion and intensification during this time. There are signs of deforestation (Miller 1986:89) and the onset of gully erosion and alluvial aggradation by the end of the period (Wilkinson 1986:46). This suggests intensified production in an effort to produce surpluses.

An extensive storage area from Titriş provides suggestive preliminary evidence for centralized mobilization and storage of agricultural surpluses. An area with storage pits and at least one silo was located (Algaze et al. 1992), and magnatometer survey revealed that additional round stone features similar in shape to the excavated silo extended for at least 2400 m2 (Algaze pers. comm). Future excavation at Titriş should yield more conclusive evidence about the function of this area.

In summary, the tributary economy may have had a major influence on the ages of animals consumed at the site, and by the end of Period IV, agricultural production was sufficiently intense to cause noticeable environmental changes in the area immediately surrounding Kurban. Although data from Kurban are only suggestive, they are consistent with

## 102 ECONOMIC ANTHROPOLOGY OF THE STATE

expectations that tribute pressures would escalate following political centralization. An analysis of the spatial distribution of chipped stone, ceramics and spindle whorls provides insight into the organization of craft production among non-elite households and the impact of political centralization and increased surplus production on household economies.

### Consumption Patterns Among Non-Elite Households: Chipped Stone Tools

Chipped stone tools were well represented in domestic contexts at Kurban.[2] A sample of chipped stone tools and debitage from non-elite domestic contexts (964 pieces from Areas B and G) was analyzed to determine whether households were manufacturing their own tools or procuring stone tools from specialists (Wattenmaker 1990, in press; see also MacDonald 1986). The lack of standardization in the tool forms and the distribution of debitage suggest that stone tools were produced by households.

Most of the chipped stone tools were made from flint, readily available from the nearby Euphrates river or limestone hills within 2 km of the site. The tools appear to have been made in a very casual, expedient manner. The assemblage was so informal that it was difficult to identify tool types, and tools that had the similar functions (e.g. scrapers) varied in form (including flakes, chunks and blades), working edge and direction of retouch (MacDonald 1986). The lack of standardization suggests that households produced their own stone tools, and this conclusion is supported by the spatial distribution of debitage. Debitage represented 70% of the stone tool assemblage and was recovered from all excavated rooms and exterior areas. The ubiquitous spatial distribution of debris, combined with the informal nature of the industry, suggests that stone tools were produced by households. With the exception of large blades, there is no evidence for specialized chipped stone production in any period. Available evidence from two non-elite domestic areas (Areas B and G) indicates that, in general, the organization of stone tool production did not vary spatially or chronologically.

An absence of large blade cores at Kurban suggested that larger blades, which are relatively difficult to manufacture, may have been produced by specialists. A surface survey at Titriş revealed that blade cores were concentrated in one site sector, providing additional evidence that production of large flint blades may have been specialized.

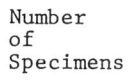

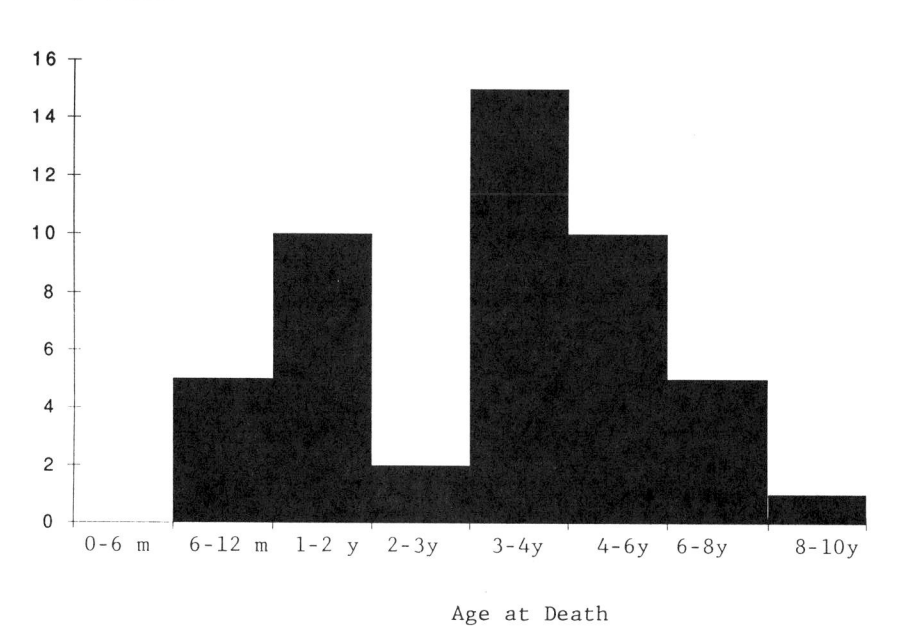

Figure 5. Kill-off patterns for Period IV Sheep and Goat at Kurban Höyük.

104 ECONOMIC ANTHROPOLOGY OF THE STATE

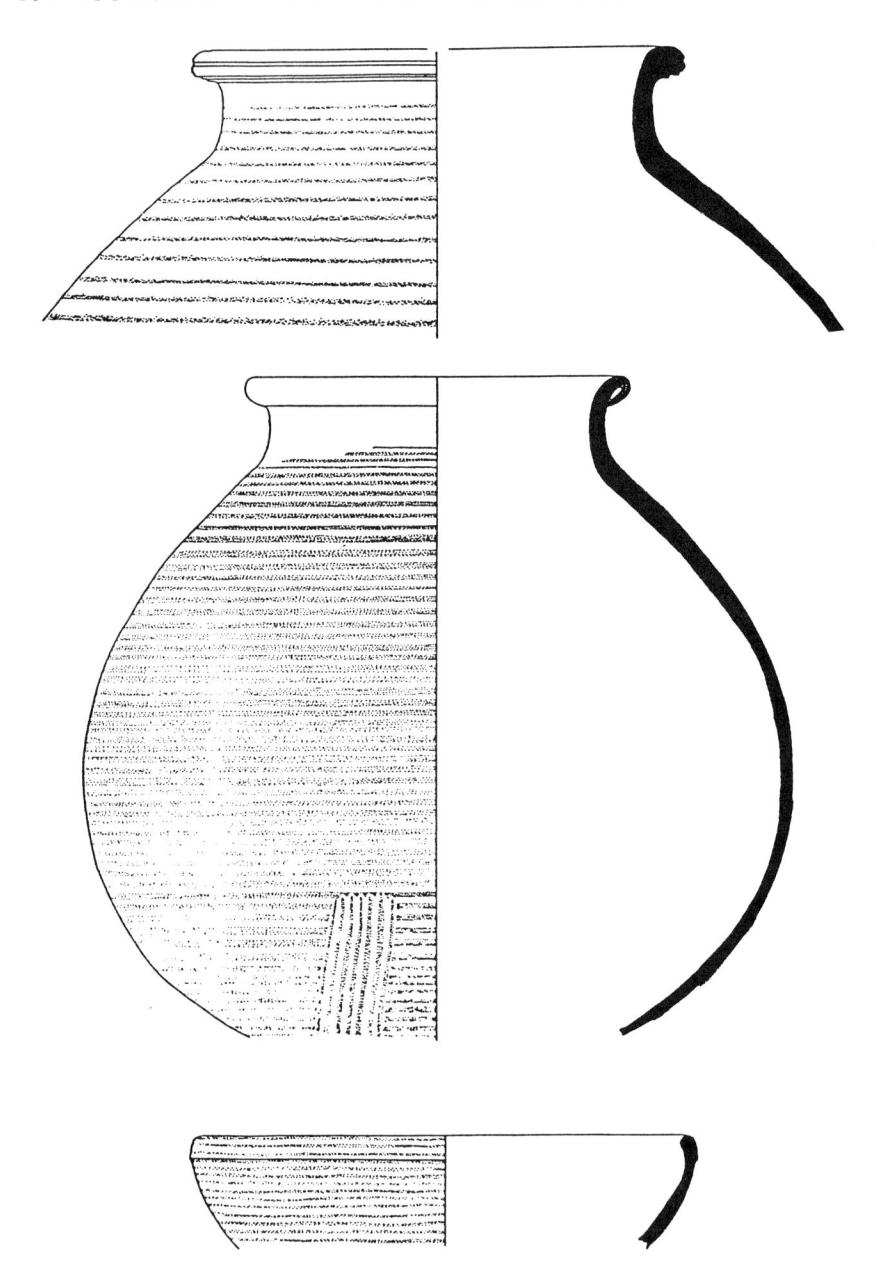

Figure 6. Examples of wheel-thrown pottery from Kurban Höyük (Horizontal Reserve Slip Ware) (from Algaze 1990a; scale 2:5).

## Ceramic Usage Among Non-Elite Households

Ceramics were recovered from all domestic contexts at Kurban, providing one of the primary sources of information on consumption patterns.[3] Two major groups of pottery were represented in Kurban Period IV deposits (Algaze 1990a). The first group -- pottery that was at least finished on a fast wheel -- appeared to be well made and highly standardized. This category of pottery included a number of ware types, such as "Plain Simple Ware" (the most common wheel-made ware), "Horizontal Reserve Slip Ware" (Figure 5) and " Metallic Ware" (Figure 6). A few sherds had potters' marks, and many were decorated. Forms include pot stands, cups, bowls and jars. The second category -- hand-made pottery -- is composed primarily of lugged hole mouthed pots probably used for cooking. It also includes some trays, bowls and jars (Figure 7).

The handmade forms were highly variable in shape and size. Handmade ceramics are often made by specialists, but, in this case, the forms were highly variable. The lack of uniformity suggests that they were made very informally, probably by individual households. Ethnographic data on ceramic manufacture reveals that the use of wheel and kiln are associated with production by specialists (see Rice 1987:182). Therefore, in this analysis, ceramics made on a fast wheel were categorized as specialist-produced.

Wheel-made pottery produced by specialists was heavily relied on throughout the period. However, throughout time, the wheel-thrown pottery increased from 54% to 68% of the ceramic assemblage (Wattenmaker 1990, in press). Within the category of hand-made pottery, open vessels, possibly used for serving food, declined steadily in proportion to the number of cooking pots (19% to 5%). Overall, the ceramic data suggest that households became increasingly reliant on ceramics produced by specialists working in large-scale workshops. By the final subperiod, households obtained almost all their ceramics from specialists, with the exception of cooking pots.

## Textile Production and Exchange Among the Non-Elite

Textiles were not preserved at Kurban, but this category of craft goods was considered because the Ebla archives reveal their economic and symbolic importance in the ancient Near East. The distribution of spindle whorls, used to spin fibers into yarn, was examined to determine whether households at Kurban procured textiles from specialists or manufactured their own cloth. If households manufactured at least some of their own textiles, we would expect to find spindle whorls in domestic contexts.

Only two definite spindle whorls were recovered from Kurban and, additionally, eight clay chariot wheels may have served as spindle whorls (see Yener 1990). Four of these were clustered in one structure (in Area B) from the final sub-period. Although their near absence in the earliest two sub-periods may be due to limited exposures, their absence from deposits dating the sub-period of town development is noteworthy given the broad clearances of both elite and non-elite areas. It suggests that households did not spin their own yarn, an initial step in textile production. The exclusive presence of spindle whorls in one of four exposures from the final sub-period further supports the inference that textile production was a specialized activity during this time.

Although spinning does not seem to have been an important activity at Kurban, cloth production appears to have been an essential part of the Ebla economy (Gelb 1986:158; Pinnock 1984:22). There are references to weaving factories, and inventories of cloth in store rooms. Since the Ebla archives record transactions of interest to the political elite, they do not directly provide insight into production of textiles utilized by non-elite households. However, they do demonstrate that textiles were highly valued in the ancient Near East. It is likely that textiles were highly valued among the non-elite, although textile production in the private non-elite sector was probably organized differently that in the public elite sector. The low density of spindle whorls at Kurban suggests that even non-elite households may have relied on specialists for textiles during this time.

### The Organization of Specialized Craft Production

Of the three categories of craft goods examined (chipped stone, ceramics and textiles), ceramics and possibly textiles appear to have been produced by specialists for use among non-elite households. To determine whether the political elites directly contributed to increasing economic specialization in the non-elite sector by administering production of goods (cf. Johnson 1987:116), evidence for the social context of production is considered below.

Available data suggest that ceramics were produced in a number of locations in the Karababa Basin. An extensive pottery workshop with over 19 kilns was recovered from the town site of Lidar, (20 km from Kurban). A second smaller workshop was associated with a private house (Hauptmann 1987:204-06). No ceramic workshop was found at Kurban, but ceramic wasters were well represented (Algaze pers. comm.), and a concentration of

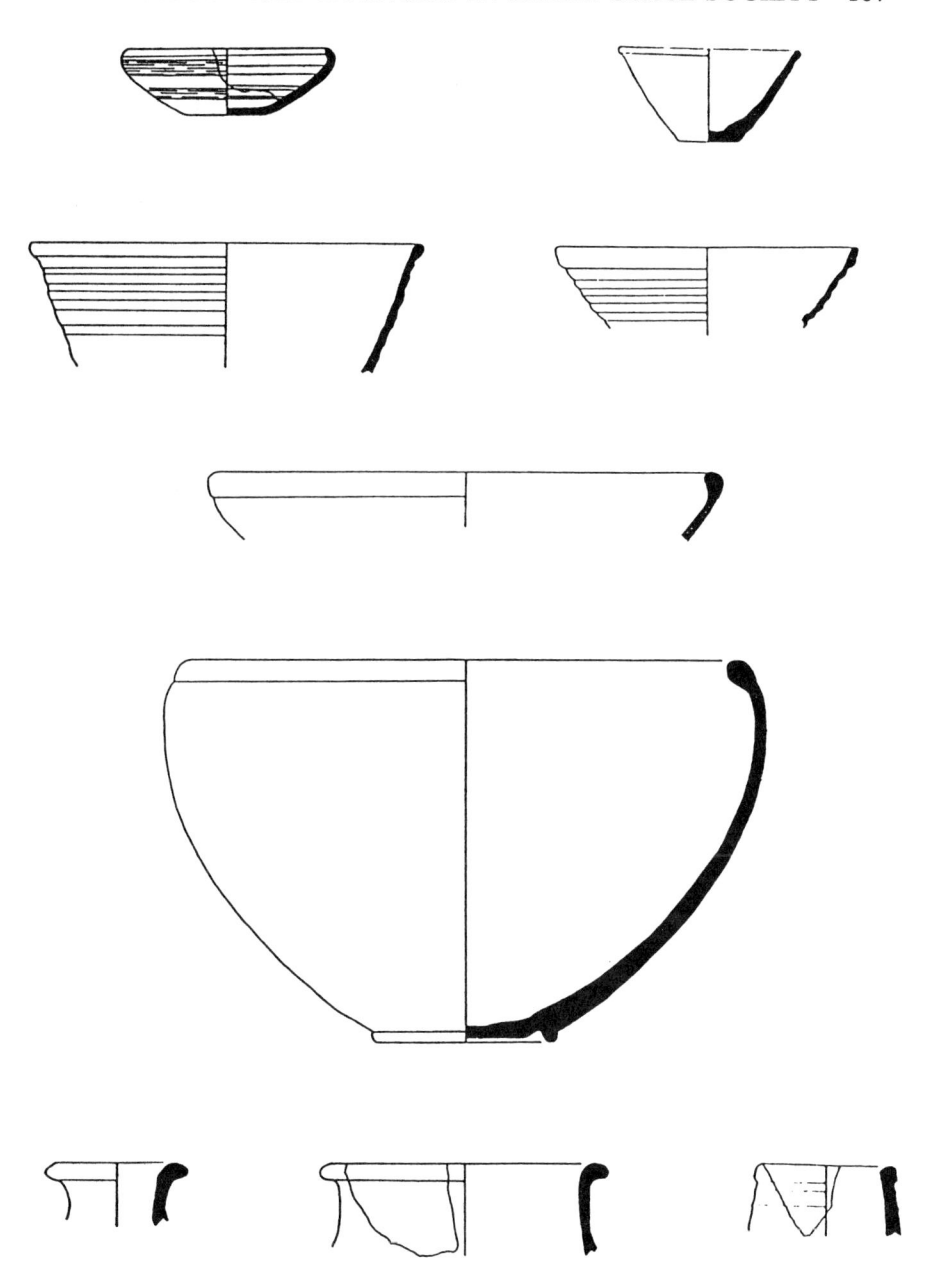

Figure 7. Examples of wheel-thrown pottery from Kurban Höyük (Metallic Ware) (Figures 7B through E from Algaze 1990a) (scale 2:5).

108  ECONOMIC ANTHROPOLOGY OF THE STATE

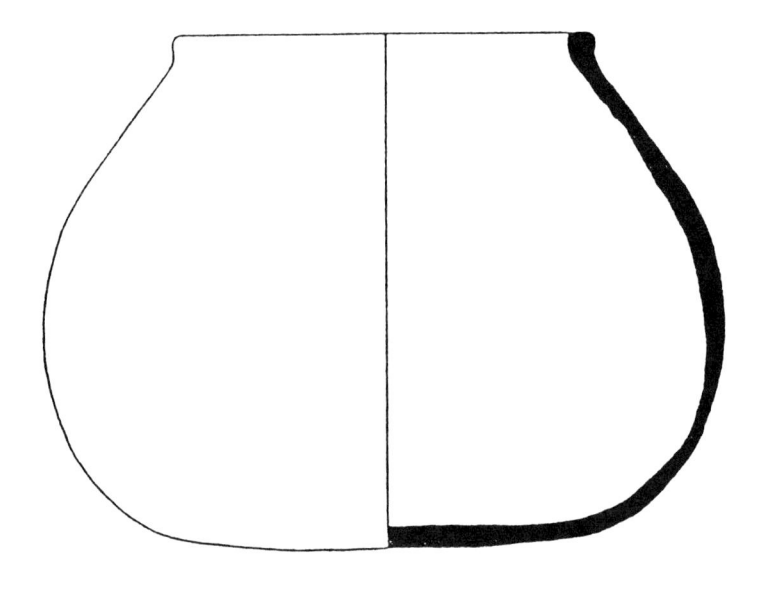

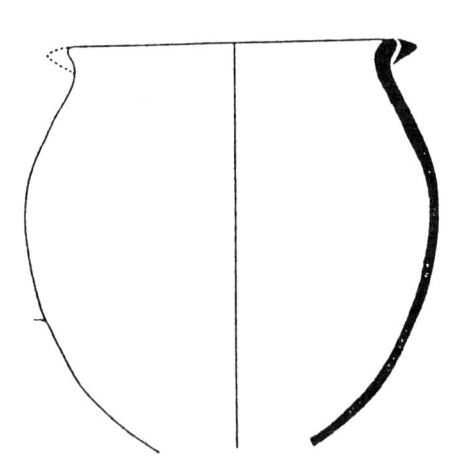

Figure 8. Examples of hand-made pottery from Kurban Höyük (from Algaze 1990a; scale 1:5).

ceramic slag in a domestic area on the small mound may have resulted from ceramic production (Wattenmaker 1990:190). The discovery of two spatially discrete pottery workshops at Lidar and the possibility of a third on the small mound at Kurban suggests that pottery was made in multiple workshops. The evidence for multiple workshops, along with apparent lack of interest in ceramics among the palace elite, suggests that pottery production and distribution was not administered. When jars (presumably made of clay) are listed in the Ebla tablets, they are mentioned only in the context of listing their contents (e.g. oil and wine), with no details provided about the containers (e.g. Archi 1982:212, 216).

References to weaving factories in the Ebla texts (Archi 1982:209), rations for state-supported weavers (ibid.:204), and lists of garments in store rooms (ibid.:211) indicate that textile production was at least partially administered. Garments from the palace were used as gifts, payments, and trade exports (ibid.:208-219), or were distributed to palace officials (Archi 1981:12; 1982:218). However, it is unlikely that the administered workshops were a major source of cloth for the non-elites, with the possible exception of palace-sponsored workers.

The evidence for production of textiles and ceramics suggests that some aspects of the specialized economy were administered, while others were not. As specialist-produced goods, textiles and ceramics contrast with chipped stone, which was produced on a household basis throughout Period IV. Specialist-produced ceramics were consumed by households throughout the period, but the reliance on specialist-produced pottery increased through time. Given the rare occurrence of spindle whorls throughout the sequence, it is difficult to determine whether household reliance on specialists for textiles increased during Period IV.

## The State and Household: Factors Guiding Non-Elite Production and Consumption Patterns

In summary, available evidence indicates that specialized craft production intensified following political centralization in the area. The data on chipped stone and ceramics suggest that some, but not all, aspects of the economy were reorganized as the state society developed. Most households continued to produce at least some craft items after a state society was formed and a tributary economy established. Study of animal bones and the distribution of agricultural tools revealed that both non-elite and elite households produced their own food throughout most of this period (Wattenmaker 1987, 1990). Overall, the data show that household economic patterns were uneven, with households producing food, stone tools and some ceramics, while obtaining other ceramics and possibly textiles from specialists. This evidence for non-elite consumption patterns and how these changed through time provides the basis for considering factors guiding production and consumption decisions among non-elite households.

Findings from the Karababa Basin suggest that tributary demands may have an impact on household food production and consumption patterns. Households may have used prime-age caprines to meet tributary demands, and agricultural intensification during this period may have been a result of tributary pressures. However, the select nature of the goods produced by specialists (cups, bowls, jars and probably textiles) suggests that, in the Kurban case, increasing involvement of households in a specialized economy was initially an indirect result of political centralization, rather than a direct response to tributary pressures.

The goods examined can be divided into two categories: those used in social events and household goods. Of the limited categories of goods examined, those of relatively low social visibility (see Wobst 1977), cooking pots and stone tools, were produced informally , probably by households. Those of higher visibility, vessels used to serve food and textiles, appear to have been produced by specialists.

Vessels used for serving food have a high degree of social visibility (Pollock 1983), since meals are generally a social activity. When vessels are used to serve guests, they often function as display goods, communicating information about the significance of an occasion or the social identity of the sponsoring individual, family, or group.

Several lines of evidence show that although the mid-late third millennium B.C. ceramics used by households were highly standardized, they did in fact have symbolic significance and function as display goods. Although many of the ceramics were undecorated, they were well-made and carefully fired. Ceramic types similar to those from domestic contexts at Kurban were recovered from the Ebla Palace in north Syria (Mazzoni 1988:85) and in graves at Kültepe, in central Anatolia (Özgüç 1986:34-38), illustrating that ceramics were used in long-distance trade. Ceramic vessels were used as burial goods; in the Karababa Basin, ceramics were common in stone-lined graves from Lidar (Hauptmann 1983:96-110) and Titriş (Algaze et al. 1992:38-39). These findings demonstrate that some categories of goods had multiple functions, and their use in non-elite household contexts did not preclude their use as bearers of social information in either domestic or other social domains.

Textiles and garments often serve to convey social information such as ethnicity or ranking. They are well-suited as markers of rank, since they are highly visible, are made of raw materials of limited availability, and require replacement more regularly than other forms of material culture such as metal objects. Their manufacture may require detailed workmanship and considerable skill. The Ebla tablets reveal that the palace officials paid close attention to the details of textile color and decoration (Pinnock 1984), perhaps because of the information they conveyed as well as their economic value.

Those craft goods produced by households, stone tools and cooking pots, were of lower social visibility and would probably be viewed primarily by family members. By this time, metal had become an important display item, and may have replaced chipped stone as a medium for conveying social information such as rank. The finding that households farmed throughout most of the period supports the conclusion that specialization among the non-elite focused on display goods, until the final subphase of the period.

The emphasis on display goods in the specialized economy suggests that increased specialization among the non-elite initially stemmed from changes in the role of goods in the information system due to increased sociopolitical complexity. In large-scale state societies, characterized by both vertical and horizontal complexity, competition for power, access to information and goods is more intense than in less complex societies. Since there is more variability in identity, status and wealth, there is a greater need for symbols of social identity, and the use of goods becomes more important as a means of conveying social information.

Rowlands (1973) has argued that specialized production of craft goods represented an attempt by the elite to prevent commoners from imitating their goods. However, the use of prestige goods to verify rank can only be effective if there is some recognition of the goods symbolizing prestige, and demand for them, among the non-elite. Emulation of these craft goods by the non-elite to advance their own standing would be especially effective in a large-scale and diverse society. The greater inaccessibility of specialist-produced goods would have facilitated communication of information on rank. Therefore, demand for specialist-produced prestige goods, such as textiles, may have increased at Kurban due to efforts by the non-elite to imitate the prestige goods of the elite. This suggests that craft production was initially reorganized on the non-elite household level only as an indirect consequence of elite political strategies.

Currently available data on the organization of production suggest that the political elite were not involved in specialization among the non-elite sector. The organization of production was apparently guided by the social visibility of the goods being produced, the scarcity of the materials they were made of, and the labor required to produce them. Flint and clay were readily available in the immediate vicinity of Kurban. The casual appearance of the flint tools and discard of barely used pieces suggests that flint tools were not highly valued and were not carriers of social information. They appear to have been manufactured on a household basis.

Although the non-elite relied on specialists for ceramics, available data suggest that ceramic production was not administered by the elite. The lack of elite interest in ceramics may indicate that they were not important markers of rank, although they may have conveyed other categories of social information, such as group affiliation.

Textiles, in contrast to ceramics and chipped stone tools, were of considerable interest to the political elite. This may be related to the fact that they were made of raw materials less accessible than clay or chert, since their availability depended on the success of flax crops or herds. Moreover, their manufacture is fairly labor intensive, involving a wide range of activities such as herding or farming, harvesting or shearing, cleaning, spinning, and dying (Schneider and Weiner 1986). Textiles are potentially of high social visibility (see Wobst 1977). Goods in this category -- of high visibility and restricted resources -- used to express ranking as well as other kinds of information, were apparently produced by specialists and partially administered. Variability in the quality of the raw materials, amount of labor involved, and skill of specialists, would serve to restrict access and signal rank. However, since textiles are made from self-renewing resources, they might not be as important for signifying rank as goods of even scarcer materials, such as metal.

Non-elite households appear to have manufactured their own goods of minimal significance for bearing social messages. However, where reliable exchange systems and adequate surpluses for exchange were available, they may have obtained goods of higher visibility, such as ceramics, through exchange. Some goods might require specialization regardless of their social significance, due to the skill involved in manufacture, such as sickle blades. Exceptional situations, such as the need for large quantities of containers for storing surpluses, might require mass production due to the potential for greater efficiency.

The labor involved, scarcity of raw materials, and social visibility of goods appear to have played a key -- but not exclusive -- role in determining whether goods were produced by households, specialists, or administered specialists. The results from Kurban suggest that the relationship between social visibility of goods, scarcity of raw materials used to make them, and production organization applies to the non-elite household as well as the political elite, although the quality and quantities of the goods would be different, and only small quantities of prestige goods would end up in low-ranking households.

By the end of the mid-late third millennium B.C., just before the collapse of this society, households appear to have become involved in a specialized subsistence economy (Wattenmaker 1990) and were more reliant on specialists for ceramics than they had been in earlier subperiods. Perhaps by this time tribute demands were sufficiently high to require major reorganization of household economies. We often think of specialized economy as a means of attaining greater surpluses; in this case the non-elite do not appear to have profited from the benefits of specialization. On the eve of the collapse of this state society, overexploitation of the environment had led to deforestation and erosion, meat utilization by households may have declined (Wattenmaker 1990:235), and non-elite families appear to have lived in small, closely spaced structures (Fig. 4). Artifacts were limited almost exclusively to cooking pots, stone tools and wheel-made pottery, with objects such as ornaments and figurines very rare. Declining economic and dietary conditions among the non-elite may have contributed to the collapse of this society.

Increased sociopolitical complexity and scale led to critical changes in how goods were valued and used. Archaeologists recognize these changes on the elite level; this study shows that such changes were profound on the non-elite household level as well. The material culture of the non-elite households appears to have been dynamic, highly variable, and responsive to changes in political and socioeconomic organization, rather that static and invariate. Although most data encountered by archaeologists on surveys or in excavations represent non-elite domestic debris, the non-elite component of society has played a minimal role in studies of early states. Paradoxically, the household may prove to be a key source of information on the organizational dynamics of early state societies.

## Notes

1. Excavations at Kurban were sponsored by the University of Chicago and directed by Leon Marfoe.

2. Much of the chipped stone sample from Areas B and G was recorded by Kathy Ataman and Gil Stein. Preliminary results of a study by Mary MacDonald (1986) of 5000 pieces from Area C on the center of the small mound provided data from a third area.

3. A total of 40,000 sherds were used in this analysis including pottery from the areas excavated by the Chicago team and recorded by G. Algaze (1990a).

## References

Algaze, Guillermo
    1986   The Ceramic Sequence. *Anatolica* XIII:54-60.
    1990a  The Ceramic Sequence and Small Finds. In G. Algaze, ed., *Town and Country in Southeastern Anatolia. Volume II: The Stratigraphic Sequence at Kurban Höyük*, pp.211-395. The University of Chicago Oriental Institute, Publications 110. Chicago: The Oriental Institute of the University of Chicago.

Algaze, Guillermo, ed.
    1990b  *Town and Country in Southeastern Anatolia. Volume II: The Stratigraphic Sequence at Kurban Höyük*. The University of Chicago Oriental Institute Publications, Volume 110. Chicago: The Oriental Institute of the University of Chicago.

Algaze, Guillermo, Adnon Misir and Tony Wilkinson
    1992   Şanliurfa Museum/University of California Excavations and Surveys at Titriş Höyük, 1991: A Preliminary Report. *Anatolica* XVIII:33-53.

Archi, Alfonso
    1980   Notes on Eblaite Geography. *Studi Eblaiti* 11/1:1-17.
    1981   Notes on Eblaite Geography II. *Studi Eblaiti* IV:1-17.
    1982   About the Organization of the Eblaite State. *Studi Eblaiti* V:201-220.

Blanton, Richard E., Stephen Kowalewski, Gary Feinman, and Jill Appel
    1982   *Monte Alban's Hinterland, Part I: The Prehispanic Settlement Patterns of the Central and Southern Parts of the Valley of Oaxaca*. Ann Arbor, University of Michigan Museum of Anthropology, Memoirs 15.

Brumfiel, Elizabeth and Timothy Earle
    1987   Specialization, Exchange and Complex Societies: An Introduction. In E.M. Brumfiel and T.K. Earle, eds., *Specialization, Exchange and Complex Societies*, pp.1-9. Cambridge: Cambridge University Press.

Clark, John and William Parry
    1990   Craft Specialization and Cultural Complexity. *Research in Economic Anthropology* 12:289-346.

Gelb, I.J.
    1986   Ebla and Lagash: Environmental Contrast. In H. Weiss, ed., *The Origins of Cities*, pp.157-67. Guilford: Four Quarters.

Hauptmann, Harald
 1983 Lidar Höyük, 1981. *Turk Arkeoloji Dergisi* 26:93-110.
 1987 Lidar Höyük and Nevali Çori, 1986. *Anatolian Studies* 37:203-07.
Heltzer, M.
 1976 *The Rural Community in Ancient Ugarit.* Wiesbaden: Reichert.
Johnson, Gregory
 1973 *Local Exchange and Early State Development in Southwestern Iran.* Ann Arbor: The University of Michigan Museum of Anthropology, Anthropological Paper, 51.
 1987 The Changing Pattern of Uruk Administration on the Susiana Plain. In F. Hole, ed., *The Archaeology of Western Iran*, pp.107-139. Washington, D.C.: Smithsonian Institution Press.
Kussinger, Sonja
 1988 *Tierknochenfunde vom Lidar Höyük in Südostanatolien (Grabungen 1979-86).* Munich: Universität Müchen.
MacDonald, Mary
 1986 The Chipped Stone Sequence. *Anatolica* XIII:60-66.
Marcus, Joyce
 1983 On the Nature of the Mesoamerican City. In E.Z. Vogt and R.M. Leventhal, eds., *Prehistoric Settlement Patterns: Essays in Honor of Gordon R. Willey*, pp.195-242. Albuquerque: University of New Mexico Press.
Mazzoni, S.
 1988 Economic Features of the Pottery Equipment of Palace G. In H. Hauptmann and H. Waetzoldt, eds., *Wirtschaft und Gesellschaft von Ebla*, pp. 81-105. Heidelberg: Heidelberger Orientverlag, Heidelberger Studien zum Alten Orient-Band 2.
Miller, Naomi
 1986 Vegetation and Land Use. *Anatolica* XIII:85-89.
Özguc, Tahsin
 1986 New Observations on the Relationship of Kültepe with Southeast Anatolia and North Syria during the Third Millennium B.C. In J. Vorys Canby, E. Porada, B. Sismondo Ridgeway, and T. Stech, eds., *Ancient Anatolia: Aspects of Change and Cultural Development. Essays in Honor of Machteld J. Mellink*, pp.31-47. Madison: University of Wisconsin Press.
Payne, Sebastian
 1973 Kill-off Patterns in Sheep and Goats: The Mandibles from Asvan Kale. *Anatolian Studies* 23:281-303.

Pettinato, Giovanni
    1981    *The Archives of Ebla: An Empire Inscribed in Clay.* New York: Doubleday.
Pinnock, Francis
    1984    Trade at Ebla. *Bulletin of the Society for Mesopotamian Studies*, 7:19-36.
Pollock, Susan
    1983    Style and Information: An Analysis of Susiana Ceramics. *Journal of Anthropological Archaeology* 2:354-390.
Rice, Prudence
    1987    *Pottery Analysis: A Sourcebook.* Chicago: University of Chicago Press.
Rowlands, Michael
    1973    Modes of Exchange and the Incentives for Trade, with Reference to Later European Prehistory. In C. Renfrew, ed., *The Explanation of Culture Change: Models in Prehistory*, pp.589-600. London: Gerald Duckworth.
Schneider, Jane and Annette Weiner
    1986    Cloth and the Organization of Human Experience. *Current Anthropology* 27(2):178-184.
Stein, Gil
    1988    *Pastoral Production in Complex Societies: Mid-Late Third Millennium B.C. and Pastoral Medieval Faunal Remains from Gritille Höyük in the Karababa Basin, Southeast Turkey.* PhD Dissertation, University of Pennsylvania. Ann Arbor: University Microfilms.
Stein, Gil and Patricia Wattenmaker
    1990    The 1987 Tell Leilan Regional Survey: Preliminary Report. In N. Miller, ed., *Economy and Settlement in the Near East: Analyses of Ancient Sites and Materials*, pp.8-18. MASCA Research Papers in Science and Archaeology 7 (supplement).
Verhaaren, Bruce
    1986    The Excavations at Kurban Höyük: Cross-Sectional Views. *Anatolica* XIII: 66-76.
Wattenmaker, Patricia
    1987    Town and Village Economies in an Early State Society. *Paleorient* 13/2: 113-122.
    1990    *The Social Context of Specialized Production: Reorganization of Household Craft and Food Economies in an Early Near Eastern State.* Ph.D. Dissertation, University of Michigan. Ann Arbor: University Microfilms.

in press State Formation and the Organization of Domestic Craft Production at Third Millennium B.C. Kurban Höyük, Southeast Turkey. In S. Falconer and G. Schwartz, eds., *Village Communities in Early Complex Societies*. Washington, D.C.: Smithsonian Institution Press.

Wilkinson, Tony
    1986 Environmental Change and Local Settlement History. *Anatolica* XIII:69-76.
    1990 *Town and Country in Southeastern Anatolia. Volume I: Settlement and Land Use at Kurban Höyük and Other Sites in the Lower Karababa Basin*. Chicago: The Oriental Institute of theUniversity of Chicago, Publications, 109.

Wobst, Martin
    1977 Stylistic Behavior and Information Exchange. In C. Cleland, ed., *For The Director: Research Essays in Honor of J.B. Griffin*, pp. 317-34. Ann Arbor: The University of Michigan Museum of Anthropology, Anthropological Papers 61.

Wright, Henry T., ed.
    1981 *An Early Town on the Deh Luran Plain: Excavations at Tepe Farukhabad*. Ann Arbor: The University of Michigan Museum of Anthropology, Memoirs 13.

Wright, Henry T.
    1984 Prestate Political Formations. In T. Earle, ed., *On the Evolution of Complex Societies: Essays in Honor of Harry Hoijer*, pp.41-78. Malibu: Undena.

Yener, Aslihan
    1990 The Small Finds: The Ceramic Sequence and Small Finds. In G. Algaze, ed., *Town and Country in Southeastern Anatolia. Volume II: The Stratigraphic Sequence at Kurban Höyük*, pp.397-410. Chicago: The University of Chicago Oriental Institute, Publications 110.

Zeder, Melinda
    1988 Understanding Urban Process through the Study of Specialized Subsistence Economy in the Near East. *Journal of Anthropololgical Archaeology* 7:1-55.

# THE ECONOMICS AND POLITICS OF MAYA MEAT EATING

Mary DeLand Pohl
Florida State University

## Introduction

Marrying in and dining in go together argues Jack Goody (1982: 206); both establish social distance and maintain ranked hierarchy. In hierarchical societies different social groups have different lifestyles. They eat different foods. Elites demand special menus embellished by ingredients obtained through exchange or tribute. The emergence of haute cuisine in Eurasian states resulted in the reorganization of food preparation; men replaced women in performing tasks that gained high status (Goody 1982).

The prehistoric Lowland Maya used animal consumption to mark social boundaries (Pohl 1976, 1985, 1990; Pyburn 1989). I have chosen case studies from the Preclassic and Postclassic periods to illustrate elite and commoner or egalitarian patterns of Maya meat eating. During the development and denouement of Maya statelets, conflicts over the assertion of high status would have been particularly acute, and changes in faunal remains will delineate social transformations. I will first trace the emergence of class stratification through the emergence of feasting patterns culminating in the Late Preclassic period between 400 B.C. and A.D. 250. I will draw on data from three northern Belize sites (Figure 1), Cuello (Wing and Scudder 1991), Colha (Shaw 1991), and Cerros (Carr 1986).

The second case study comes from the Postclassic period after A.D. 1000 when the political and economic structure of the southern Lowlands was rapidly changing, and the center of power was shifting to the northern Lowlands. In the southern Lowlands, the site of Lamanai (Pendergast 1981) grew through the Postclassic period as an urban elite center while Tipu (Jones, Graham, Kautz 1985), Tikal (Culbert 1973), and Cerros were small rural communities. The fauna from these sites (Pohl 1976, Carr 1986, Emery 1990) reflect these political events.

The data are among the best that we have from the Maya Lowlands. The Cerros, Cuello, Tipu, Tikal, and Colha samples include material screened through 1/4 inch screen and fine-screened or water-screened through fine-mesh screening. Samples from these sites also include deposits specifically identified as middens.

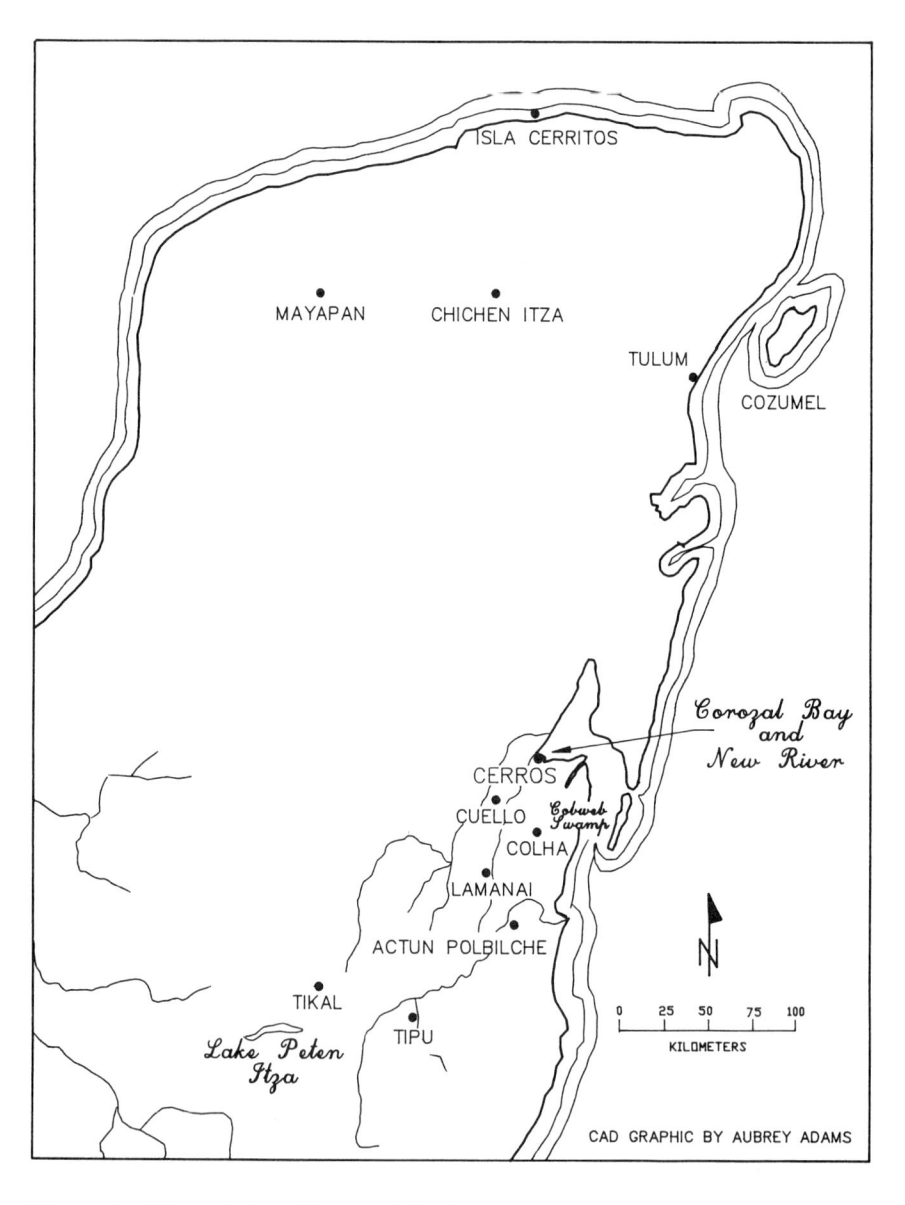

Figure 1. Map of sites discussed in the text.

The elaboration of meat-eating among the ancient Maya parallels elaboration of other types of archaeological remains, e.g., monumental architecture, jewelry, and decorated pottery. One might consider production of food for a lord and his clients a kind of craft production. Political symbolism directed the choice of meats just as it did the choice of images on pottery. Evidence for long distance exchange in meats demonstrates that maximization of return on labor was not the primary concern. Substantial effort might be expended on getting the right kind of meat.

Prehistoric Maya art and ethnohistoric data suggest that elite men monopolized hunting, and women assumed the task of raising animals for feasts the lords sponsored and for tribute. Women may have taken on animal rearing because they saw an opportunity for involvement with a high-status commodity.

## Ethnohistoric Record of Meat Consumption

Ethnohistoric accounts dating from the sixteenth and seventeenth centuries indicate that meat consumption was a significant aspect of elite status and elite-controlled activities. Elites feasted among themselves in exclusive circles of gift giving and political maneuvering (Tozzer 1941:27, Roys 1943:29), and they ate meat regularly (Roys 1943). Commoners ate meat only rarely, usually at elite sponsored fiestas (Relaciones de Yucatán 1898-1900, I:244, 271; López de Cogolludo 1688, I:228, 235, 296; Roys 1943). These fiestas were lavish public displays in which elites recounted the myths of the ruling lineage, re-enacted their military victories, and took tribute to support their political activities (Edmonson 1982, 1986).

Maya elites garnered meat supplies through tribute payments. At the time of the Spanish Conquest live chickens, which had rapidly supplanted the difficult native turkeys, were prominent in tribute lists, and some coastal communities paid part of their taxes in sun-dried or salted fish (Pohl 1985:Table 3.1). A party returning from a deer hunt or those celebrating the New Year would give part of their catch, especially the prized haunch of venison, to their rulers and priests (Tozzer 1941:57,141).

> They also joined together for hunting in companies of fifty, more or less, and they roast the flesh of the deer on gridirons, so that it shall not be wasted, and when they reach the town, they make their presents to their lord and distribute the rest as among friends (Tozzer 1941:57).

Maya nobles, like many elites throughout Central and South America, led animal round-ups that took place on ceremonial occasions (Relaciones de Yucatán 1898, I:301; Bourke 1892). In the interior of Peten, Guatemala, the Itza Maya may have restricted hunting, perhaps to such elite round-ups. In 1525, Cortés and his men encountered docile deer in savannas south of Lake Peten-Itza, and when they asked why the animals did not run away, they were told that the deities, who took the form of deer, had ordered the local people not to molest the animals (Díaz del Castillo 1927:452).

While Maya lords passed their time hunting, women raised fowl, deer, and dogs in their homes and dooryards for the ceremonial feasts and tax payments (Pohl and Feldman 1982). They suckled fawns, and when the animals grew older, they trained them to designated locations in the woods (Tozzer 1941:127). The fauna that women may tend are not always small, dooryard animals as Friedl (1975) suggests.

Maya women devoted great attention to preparations for public fiestas. For example, they raised numerous turkeys, which are hard to tend.

> so great is the confluence of persons attending any of these festivities, and if one could tell the multitude of turkeys eaten on that day, it would be difficult to believe as they raise them all year for that day (López de Cogolludo 1971 [1688] I:296).

Women have traditionally been the cooks.

> They killed them by twisting their heads and [by] putting a foot over the turkey and pulling [the head] off....and later they threw them into a fire to burn off the feathers. Deplumed, they washed them and put [them] to cook (Hellmuth 1977: 426).

The Maya kept deer on hand for blood sacrifices accompanied by feasts, in which both men and women participated:

> They took a live deer to the courtyard of the...temple...and there they throttled...him....They cooked the deer by itself and the blood, by itself, and while these were cooking, they had their dances....When the dance was finished, the head and feet were scorched in the fire before the idol as an offering and afterwards taken to the house of the high priest and eaten (Tozzer and Allen 1910:349).

The ethnohistoric record demonstrates that meat was a highly valued commodity whose consumption was subject to close regulation. Meat was an essential ingredient in feasts that took place in political and religious contexts, and the Maya went to considerable trouble to see that their lords had supplies available when needed.

## The Emergence of Elite Consumption Patterns in the Preclassic Period

Substantial, nucleated agricultural communities appeared throughout the Maya Lowlands in the early Middle Preclassic period about 1000 B.C. The elaboration of artifacts of social interaction provides evidence of incipient inequality. The fineness of the pottery used to present food and the existence of a pan-Lowland ceramic tradition (Valdez 1987) are significant. Traditional personal insignia of authority such as necklaces marked emergent status. At Cuello and Colha beads were made from exotic materials such as jade, greenstone, and marine shell and were deposited as grave goods after death (Hammond 1977, Robin 1989, Dreiss 1982, Potter 1982).

By the Late Preclassic period social stratification became widely institutionalized in many parts of the Maya Lowlands, including northern Belize. Archaeologists can trace these social changes through the elaboration of public architecture and fiesta paraphernalia. At Cerros, for example, elites destroyed the residential core of the community and constructed a large plaza flanked by pyramids and high-status residences between 100 and 50 B.C. (Freidel 1979, Cliff 1986). The elaboration of pottery shapes and decoration including special ritual types (Robertson 1983, Valdez 1987) in the Late Preclassic period marks the continued use of feasting as a vehicle for building elite coalitions and extracting surplus.

Physical remains of sacrifice, perhaps of captive warriors, also point to the acceleration of political competition. At Cuello two mass burials consisting of 32 and 15 individuals, almost exclusively young males and dating to about 400 B.C. and A.D. 100 respectively, occurred in the Late Preclassic pyramid, Platform 34 (Saul and Saul 1991; Robin, Gerhardt, and Hammond 1991). Unhealed puncture wounds and dismemberment strongly suggest warfare.

The animal bones from Cuello, Colha, and Cerros (Carr 1986, Shaw 1991, Wing and Scudder 1991) show distinctive patterns of meat consumption in the Preclassic period (Tables 1-4). All three sites contain plentiful bone from medium and large mammals especially deer suggesting that the

TABLE 1. PERCENTAGES OF SELECTED ANIMALS
CALCULATED ACCORDING TO FRAGMENTS PRESENT
(From Wing and Scudder 1991, Shaw, 1991)

|  | CUELLO Preclassic Early Middle | Late | COLHA Preclassic Early Middle | Late Late |
|---|---|---|---|---|
| Dog | 7 | 11 | 4 | 10 |
| Deer[a] | 22 | 19 | 4 | 11 |
| Peccaries[b] | 1 | -- | .5 | tr[c] |
| Lrg/Med Mammal | na | na | 15 | 33 |
| Small Mammal[d] | 11 | 13 | 1 | 1 |
| Cat[e] | -- | -- | - | tr |
| Wild Turkey | tr | -- | - | - |
| Bird | tr | tr | tr | 1 |
| Freshwater Turtle | 6 | 14 | 25 | 5 |
| Bony Fishes | 1 | 11 | 41 | 18 |
| Percent of Fauna | 48 | 68 | 91 | 79 |
| Total Frags. | 1545 | 918 | 1805 | 946 |

[a]Includes white-tailed deer (*Odocoileus virginianus*), brocket deer (*Mazama*), and Cervidae.

[b]Includes white-lipped peccary (*Tayassu pecari*) and collared peccary (*Tayassu tajacu*).

[c]"Trace" signifies a frequency of less than .5.

[d]Includes rabbit (*Sylvilagus*), opossum (*Didelphis marsupialis*), armadillo (*Dasypus novemcinctus*), agouti (*Dasyprocta punctata*), and paca (*Agouti paca*).

[e]Includes jaguar (*Felis onca*), puma (*Felis concolor*), and ocelot (*Felis pardalis*).

exploitation of such animals was universal by early Middle Preclassic times. Differences occur in the relative abundance of fish and turtle, reflecting differences in the environment of the sites. Cuello hunters living at the ridge-top site exploited aquatic resources only rarely while Colha residents with access to aquatic and wetland habitats of Rancho Creek and Cobweb Swamp caught more fish and turtle. Inhabitants of Cerros, situated on Corozal Bay, concentrated on reef and estuarine fish.

What is striking as that over time the faunal assemblages at the three sites became increasingly similar to each other. By the Late Preclassic period a meal, especially for elites, included deer, dog, and turtle meat with some peccary and fish, frequently imported from the coast. Inhabitants of Cuello continued to emphasize deer in the Late Preclassic period and increased consumption of dog and freshwater turtle (Wing and Scudder 1991). They were also getting a surprising number of marine and peripheral fish, perhaps from Corozal Bay down the New River. The ratio of freshwater to coastal fish species went from 2.5:1 in the early Middle Preclassic to 1:3 in the Late Preclassic period (Wing and Scudder 1991:85). The choice of coastal fish is noteworthy since freshwater fish would have been available nearby in the New River. At Colha deer, dog, and the unidentified large-medium mammal category increased significantly in Late Preclassic samples while turtle and fish declined (Shaw 1991:Tables 6.4, 6.5, 6.7). This trend is contrary to what one might expect since rising water levels in Late Preclassic times would probably have made more fish available in Cobweb Swamp (Pohl 1990a, Shaw 1991). Thus, the fish at these two sites demonstrate that efficiency was not the primary factor in their exploitation.

Cerros shows the convergence in diet most clearly. After the transformation of the site to a ceremonial and political center, marine fish declined significantly; fish make up as little as 9% of the bone fragments in one operation (Carr 1986:371). Instead terrestrial animals made a substantial contribution to the diet, and deer, dog, and peccary were concentrated in elite residential and ceremonial contexts at the site (Tables 3 and 4). Forest clearance and milpa agriculture around Cerros would have been beneficial for populations of game mammals such as deer, but botanical data suggest that more was involved.

Botanical data on fruit remains at Cerros (Cliff and Crane 1989, Crane 1991) reinforce the idea that the changes in fauna represent the elaboration of elite feasting. Remains of nance (<u>Byrsonima crassifolia</u>) and coyol palm (<u>Acrocomia mexicana</u>) increased dramatically during the course of the Late Preclassic period. The ubiquity or percentage of samples containing nance seeds rose from 44% in second and third centuries

TABLE 2. PERCENTAGES OF SELECTED ANIMALS AT LATE PRECLASSIC CERROS CALCULATED ACCORDING TO UBIQUITY (NUMBER OF SAMPLES IN WHICH AN ANIMAL OCCURS)
(data from Carr compiled by Crane)

|  | CERROS 275 - 100 B.C.[a] | CERROS 100 - 50 B.C.[b] |
|---|---|---|
| Dog | 12 | 44 |
| Deer | 16 | 36 |
| Peccaries | 1 | 8 |
| Small Mammals | 1 | 6 |
| Cat | 0 | 1 |
| Wild Turkey | 2 | 1 |
| Bird | 2 | 3 |
| Freshwater Turtle | 14 | 26 |
| Aquatic Fauna[c] | 86 | 65 |
| Total samples | 208 | 115 |

[a]Stages II and III

[b]Stage IV

[c]Marine and estuarine fishes, turtles, crabs

TABLE 3

RELATIVE ABUNDANCE OF AQUATIC AND TERRESTRIAL
ANIMAL FRAGMENTS IN REPRESENTATIVE ELITE AND
NON-ELITE CONTEXTS AT CERROS
(From Carr 1986:Table 20)

|  | Elite % | Non-Elite % |
|---|---|---|
| Aquatic | 12 | 50 |
| Terrestrial | 43 | 16 |

TABLE 4

RELATIVE ABUNDANCE OF MINIMUM NUMBERS OF DOG,
DEER, AND PECCARIES IN REPRESENTATIVE ELITE AND
NON-ELITE CONTEXTS AT CERROS
(From Carr 1986:Table 22)

|  | Elite % | Non-Elite % |
|---|---|---|
| Dog | 14 | 7 |
| Deer | 15 | 4 |
| Peccary | 5 | 0.5 |

B.C. samples to 78% in first century B.C. samples, and the ubiquity of coyol palm rose from 9% to 38% (Cliff and Crane 1989). Probable cacao remains also occurred in the later samples (Crane 1989). The Maya have traditionally made alcoholic beverages or ceremonial drinks from these plants (Tozzer 1941:200; Cliff and Crane 1989:311; Arturo Gómez-Pompa, personal communication 1991), and drinking has always been as essential as meat-eating to these banquets. The Maya probably brought these and other edible fruits into Cerros since low-lying soil conditions are unfavorable for these tree species there today (Crane 1989), and conditions in the Late Preclassic period were most likely more swampy (Pohl 1990a).

## Status and Consumption in the Late Prehistoric Period

*Southern Lowland Sites*

Political disintegration began in the ninth century and accelerated in the southern Lowlands between A.D. 900-1000 when the focus of political power was shifting to Yucatan. Tikal (Culbert 1973) in northeast Peten, Guatemala, declined early. In Terminal Late Classic and Early Postclassic times, a remnant population was camping out on top of palace structures and throwing rubbish into collapsed rooms below. Cerros (Freidel 1979) had actually been in decline since the beginning of the Classic period, but a small settlement continued as late as Late Postclassic times. As conditions of political instability widened in the Postclassic period, Lamanai and Tipu continued as organized communities with population levels at least comparable to those of the Classic period. Tipu (Jones, Graham, and Kautz 1985) was a small site with an estimated core of 500-1000 people. In contrast, Lamanai (Pendergast 1986) gained in prominence through the Postclassic period as a political center located strategically on the New River with access to increasingly active coastal exchange networks. It was a center of copper manufacturing and may have exchanged this commodity with the north. Lamanaians emulated fashions in northern centers, adopting Mayapan style vessels and Tulum style architecture and pottery (Emery 1990).

The faunal assemblages allow a comparison of a large elite center (Lamanai) with three small non-elite sites (Tikal, Tipu, and Cerros) in the southern Lowlands during the Postclassic period. One can also assess the effect of environment and resource availability. Lamanai, Tipu, and Cerros all had access to aquatic fauna in a river, lagoon, or the sea. Tikal had no natural source though the Classic period reservoir might still have held some water.

The difference in species diversity illustrates the difference in faunal patterns between the high and low status sites. Tipuans, for example, hunted a wide range of animals throughout the Postclassic period; the index of diversity averaged about 25 through the Middle and Late Postclassic periods. At Lamanai the diversity index dropped from 30 in the Early Postclassic period to seven in the Late Postclassic period (Emery 1990:69-70).

Late Postclassic Lamanaians were eating a lot of dog and deer, which made up 50% of the minimum numbers of individuals (Table 5). The Lamanaians also raised turkeys (14% of MNI) (Emery 1990). Birds, including turkeys, are generally more characteristic of sites in Yucatan (Ray 1956, Wing 1981, Wing and Steadman 1980, Hamblin 1984).

Analysis of bone chemistry suggests that Postclassic Lamanaians, even those from the high-status contexts studied, did not eat much meat. Meat-eating remained at Classic period levels (White and Schwarcz 1989: 463) despite a general decline in human population in the southern Lowlands that would have resulted in conditions favorable for populations of deer and other game. The relatively low level of Postclassic meat consumption is noteworthy in view of the fact that Lamanaians had iron deficiencies. One-third of the individuals suffered from this problem at some point in their lives (White 1989). Its cause was primarily infections and parasites resulting from high population aggregation. The condition was probably exacerbated by cultural practices; the relatively limited intake of iron-rich foods, along with alkali processing of corn, which may have inhibited absorption of iron (White 1989), the use of grinding stones introducing chelating agents in the stomach (Saul and Saul 1991:146), and the practice of ritual blood-letting, which may have been particularly common among elites.

At Tikal and Tipu, small-sized game mammals such as rabbit, agouti, paca, armadillo, and opossum are well-represented (Pohl 1977, Emery 1990). At Late Postclassic Cerros, the residents went back to fishing though they also ate some small game mammals and turkey (Carr 1986:486-88).

The distinctiveness of the Postclassic high-status diet at Lamanai is underlined by changes in fauna in the colonial period when the site became a small community with a remnant elite and a veneer of Christianity represented by a church. Deer dropped to a mere 9%, and dogs virtually disappeared from the site refuse. Bony fishes, a readily available and reliable meat source given the location of Lamanai on the New River Lagoon, jumped from an average of 8% in the Postclassic period to 57% in colonial times, and freshwater turtles also increased (Emery 1990:Appendix B). Thus, the colonial Lamanai diet came to approximate diets at small Postclassic sites.

TABLE 5. PERCENTAGES OF MINIMUM NUMBERS OF
SELECTED ANIMALS AT TERMINAL LATE CLASSIC AND
POSTCLASSIC SITES
(from Pohl 1977, Carr 1986, Emery 1990)

|  | TIKAL Terminal Late Classic- Early Postclassic | TIPU Postclassic Middle | TIPU Postclassic Late | CERROS Postclassic Late | LAMANAI Postclassic Early | LAMANAI Postclassic Late |
|---|---|---|---|---|---|---|
| Dog | 3 | 2 | 2 | 5 | 6 | 7 |
| Deer | 8 | 23 | 14 | 0 | 31 | 43 |
| Peccaries | 5 | 9 | 9 | 0 | 6 | 5 |
| Small Mammals | 48 | 26 | 25 | 9 | 19 | 5 |
| Cat | 4 | 0 | 7 | 0 | 6 | 4 |
| Primates [a] | 1 | 0 | 2 | 0 | 0 | 0 |
| Domestic Turkey [b] | 0 | 0 | 0 | 0 | 0 | 14 |
| Wild Turkey [c] | 2 | 4 | 2 | 0 | 0 | 0 |
| Turkey ? sp. | 0 | 0 | 1 | 5 | 0 | 0 |
| Bird | 20 | 4 | 7 | 0 | 6 | 22 |
| Freshwater Turtle | 3 | 6 | 7 | 9 | 6 | 1 |
| Bony Fishes | 1 | 11 | 4 | 59 | 6 | 10 |
| Percent of Fauna | 95 | 85 | 80 | 87 | 86 | 111 |
| Total MNI | 130 | 47 | 134 | 22 | 16 | 94 |

Notes for Table 5:

[a]Includes howler monkey (*Alouatta*), spider monkey (*Ateles geoffroyi*), and Cebidae, perhaps capuchin monkey (*Cebus capucinus*). No primates occurred in Preclassic faunal assemblages.

[b]*Meleagris gallopavo* - Central Mexican domestic turkey

[c]*Agriocharis ocellata* - Ocellated turkey

*Meat in Late Prehistoric Exchange Networks*

Lamanaians or other Maya from the southern Lowlands may have participated in Postclassic exchange networks traversing and circling the greater Yucatan Peninsula that included meats. Island sites off the coast of Yucatan provide the best documentation of meat in regional exchange networks. Deer would definitely not have been available on the island sites of Cozumel, a trade center, or Isla Cerritos, which may have been a port for the center of Chichen Itza. In Early Postclassic contexts at Cozumel and Isla Cerritos, deer was rare, but 29 and 52 percent respectively of the deer bones were "major meat cuts" (i.e., vertebrae, limb girdles, and upper limbs) (Carr 1989).

The Postclassic elites of Cozumel were not able to get much venison. They had to make do with other mammal meats, and they invested heavily in animal rearing. The Cozumel fauna follows certain patterns that characterized Preclassic Cerros. Mammals were clustered in ceremonial-administrative contexts and burials while non-elite domestic contexts yielded more fish and other marine biota. Nevertheless, peccaries replaced deer as the high-status dietary staple. Women raised domestic and tamed ocellated turkeys and dogs, judging from the number of immature bones. They may also have nurtured coatis, raccoons, and peccaries since about one third of the procyonids and one fourth of the peccaries were subadult. These domesticated mammals make up 57 percent of the minimum numbers of mammals at the Cozumel sites and 16 percent of all fauna (Hamblin 1984:124, 132, 147).

There is evidence that Lamanai was participating in the meat and animal exchange network of the Late Postclassic period. The turkey bones at Lamanai are those of the Central Mexican domestic turkey (*Meleagris gallopavo*) (Emery 1990:Appendix B), which also occurred on Cozumel, probably because of its role as a center of long-distance exchange (Hamblin 1984). Lamanaians appear not only to have copied architecture and pottery from Yucatan; they also acquired special foods that northerners ate, and they, in turn, might have supplied venison to those in the north.

We may be underestimating the frequencies of high-ranked animals procured by elites at late prehistoric sites because of exchange in meat as well as animal sacrifices. The Maya made pilgrimages to perform sacrifices in lineage and rain ceremonies at cenotes and in caves. Deer, dog, peccary, and marine organisms were food fit for both gods and ancestors. Deer, dog, and peccary bones made up 58% of the fauna from the cenotes at Mayapan but only 9% of the bones from Late Postclassic elite contexts at the site (Pohl 1983). Deer bones, marine shells, and the remains of over 200 dogs occurred in Terminal Late Classic deposits at the cave of Actun Polbilche (Pendergast 1974). Since these cave and cenote ceremonies were principally validations of right to rule (Pohl and Pohl 1983), elites were most likely performing the sacrifices, and the animals probably came from their sources or stores.

## Discussion

The patterns of bone distribution at Maya sites reflect political ideology and the politics of meat procurement and distribution in Maya society. Evidence for the influence of politics on Maya foodways comes from prehistoric iconography and ethnography. Maya elites have traditionally been militaristic; the continual dominance of victors over the vanquished served as the Maya elites' theory of history (Bricker 1981). Ancient Maya art suggests that prehistoric elites cast this dominance as a predator-prey relationship with themselves in the role of top predators, jaguar and vulture, and their victims in the role of deer or peccary. An early example is the Leiden plaque, which presents the ruler of Tikal at his accession to office in A.D. 320 dressed in jaguar headdress and standing on an elite captive wearing deer antlers (Figure 2). An eighth century, Late Classic style vase from Yucatan shows a lord dressed as a vulture feeding on a deer with human mandible (Figure 3). Thus, as Maya elites feasted in celebration of their victories, they metaphorically ate their defeated rivals as they ate venison. This interpretation is consistent with the fact that in the Late Classic period scenes of both deer hunting and human sacrifice involving characters dressed as animals (Figures 4 and 5) frequently decorate the pottery from which celebrants ate and drank (Pohl 1981).

The politics of food procurement and distribution also helps explain how bones of specific animals ended up in elite contexts. If the customs documented for the early historical period, specifically tribute payment in staple surplus such as venison, restriction of hunting favored species to elites perhaps in the context of ritual round-ups, and women raising deer,

Figure 2. The Leiden plaque shows the ruler of Tikal dressed as jaguar standing on an elite captive, who wears deer antlers (from Schele and Miller 1986).

Figure 3. A Late Classic style vase from Yucatan shows a lord dressed as a vulture feeding on a deer with human mandible (from Coe 1975).

dogs, and turkeys for ritual feasts sponsored by elites, extended back into the prehistoric period, the result would be a preponderance of bones of these species in elite archaeological contexts.

The best evidence exists for women raising animals. Pottery figurines showing women holding dogs or other animals such as coatis are relatively common (e.g., Willey 1972:Fig.34f), and they demonstrate that women were nurturing animals at least by the Classic period. Elemental analysis (Sr, Mg, Zn) suggested that three of nine herbivore bones studied from Postclassic ceremonial contexts at Lamanai came from deer and peccary that were maize-fed and probably semi-domesticated (White and Schwarcz 1989:46061). The isotopic composition of one Late Preclassic dog bone from Cuello (Nicholas van der Merwe, personal communication to Mary Pohl and to Norman Hammond 1991:238) indicates about 70% maize consumption (comparable to that of humans) suggesting that women were fattening up some dogs in house compounds at an early date. (Men fed their hunting dogs lots of meat and bones, cf. Vickers 1989.) The presence of over 70% subadult individuals in a cache of 35 deer skulls in Cuello Platform 34 (Wing and Scudder 1991) may indicate that these animals were culled from a semi-domesticated herd (Pohl 1989). There are no definite indications from isotopic studies of deer bones that this was so, however (van der Merwe, personal communication to Pohl 1991). Some of the herding techniques that Maya women are known to have used historically may have made semi-domestication hard to detect. Fawns born to does trained to a location in the woods might not eat foods different from wild animals.

Domesticated animals would have provided a convenient and reliable source of meat for political and ceremonial activities. Nevertheless, effort and resources go into animal raising. Elite men did not themselves expend the energy required; women most likely did. Domestic animals might have appealed to women because they provided some access to a valuable commodity that could be used in reciprocal social relations, and tending animals dovetailed with raising children (Pohl 1989).

Women's involvement with the production of high-status meats may have contributed to their retaining control of food preparation and presentation. Even as feasting emerged as a focus of elite activity, women probably continued to cook. Ethnohistoric traditions place women in this role, and Late Classic period art shows women grinding corn and serving lords (e.g., Anton 1973, Coe 1975). One might think of their work as a kind of craft production since the food was highly symbolic, and elites used banquets to manipulate social obligations to their advantage.

Figure 4. Late Classic style vase from southern Campeche, Mexico, or northern Peten, Guatemala, shows jaguar and vulture impersonators preparing to sacrifice a man whose hair is arranged like deer antlers (from Coe 1975).

The Maya case contrasts with historic China (Goody 1982) where women have traditionally raised pigs and fowl but lost positions as directors of food preparation with the elaboration of upper class banqueting. China was, however, a far more hierarchical society with a more complex culinary culture.

To what extent were the Maya attempting to maximize rate of return on labor in procuring meat? Desirable fauna would have increased in

Figure 5. Late Classic Jaina figurine showing a captive like that in Figure 4 (Dallas Museum of Art, from Taube 1988). Taube (1988:334) points out that the historic period *Book of Chilam Balam of Chumayel* identifies those who execute war captives as deer-slayers (*ah-cehob*) and their prisoners as prey.

abundance beginning in the Preclassic period. John Jones' study of pollen data from Cobweb Swamp near Colha (Jacob 1991) indicates that forest clearance was significant as early as 2500 B.C. Such disturbance would have increased browse available for white-tailed deer, and shortly thereafter crops in garden plots would have attracted peccaries, paca, and agoutis (Linares 1976). One might expect that the Maya would have targeted deer because the animals are relatively large in contrast to the generally small size of most neotropical animals, and returns per unit effort would have been better (Ted Gragson, personal communication 1991). The deer might have been particularly attractive to elites and their helpers trying to provision a feast where a considerable amount of meat would be consumed in a short time.

Both technology and labor may have been significant factors in elite and commoner hunting patterns and their relative efficiency. Elites may have employed group hunts perhaps with nets, which are particularly good for capturing small and medium sized ungulates. Data from tropical Africa (Willke and Curran 1991) indicate that net hunters are ten times more effective than archers in getting the ungulates. There are some hints of elite net hunting from Maya archaeology. The high-status Late Classic polychrome pottery shows deer with nets. At Lamanai (Pendergast 1981, Helmuth and Pendergast 1988) the Early Classic period burial of a high-status male contained remains of cordage that might have been netting. Net hunting might explain how the Late Preclassic Cuello Maya were so effective in getting many young deer for their skull caches. Elites would have been in the position to make the substantial investment in construction and upkeep of nets and to use their political status to organize large hunting parties. Of course nets were not the only hunting equipment that elites used. Painted scenes on pottery show them with spears, blowguns, and dogs, which might have been used in conjunction with nets or alone.

In contrast to elites, commoners would have been spending most of their time in small numbers in their fields though they may also have participated in group day hunts in the vicinity of their settlements. For poor farmers, the smaller mammals are more common and more reliable than larger species (Redford and Robinson 1987, Hames 1990:92-93). The small game mammals, birds, and monkeys that characterize Postclassic non-elite sites (and elite Lamanai in the case of birds) suggest that these late prehistoric hunters were using cheap technology such as blowguns and bow and arrow. Early Postclassic lithics from Colha and Lamanai include small, side-notched "dart" points, and tiny, triangular "arrow" points occur at Late Postclassic Lamanai and other lowland sites (Hester 1985).

The late prehistoric and colonial sites raise particular questions about deer as prey. One would expect that deer would have been most abundant shortly after a site went from being a flourishing political center to a small community because emergent brush interspersed with milpa plots would have provided optimal food and cover. Data from a lake core in Peten, Guatemala, suggest that mature rainforest inimical to white-tailed deer did not return until the fifteenth century at the earliest (Brenner et al. 1990). At Postclassic Tikal quail bones deposited by birds of prey on the roof comb of an abandoned pyramid (Raymond Paynter, personal communication 1974) and pollen from dog coprolites (representing inhaled pollen grains) (Fred Wiseman, personal communication 1987) indicate open conditions with much brush and some maize cultivation. Moreover, late prehistoric hunters were killing cats that prey on deer (Table 5), thus allowing deer populations to increase further. Nevertheless, hunters living in small communities ate relatively few deer. Tikaleños ate lots of small game and birds along with some primates. Inhabitants of Postclassic Cerros and colonial Lamanai spent more time fishing. Preliminary studies of Classic and Early Postclassic fauna at Colha show that mammals such as deer declined dramatically in the Postclassic period when the site became a small community; residents concentrated on aquatic species, mostly marine fish and turtles (Scott 1982, Scott and Valdez 1990; Wing and Scudder 1991). Local freshwater food resources had probably disappeared because the swamp had silted in by Postclassic times (Jacob 1991). The rarity of deer bones in these small communities is hard to explain except that non-elite hunters may have observed taboos on these animals, and they may not have been able to invest in nets or hunting dogs.

The non-elite faunal assemblages from Postclassic Tipu, Cerros, Colha, and Tikal and colonial Lamanai are similar to kills of present-day indigenous hunters in New World tropical forests, who are highly opportunistic when it comes to getting meat (Vickers 1984, Redford and Robinson 1987). Small game mammals and birds are common. Modern Indian hunters get more primates because forests are present. Deer kills are rare, probably because of the greater forest cover and perhaps because taboos on hunting of large game such as deer are widespread (Redford and Robinson 1987), as was probably the case for Maya commoners in many areas at least as far back as the late prehistoric period. Fish are the major source of protein where a reliable source is available; "[T]he productivity of fishing must be viewed as probably the major determinant of the scope of hunting (Ross 1978:15)." Colonists, like prehistoric Maya elites, have a narrower range of fauna that they consider acceptable. They eat larger animals based on culturally-shaped ideas, i.e., resemblance to domestic animals, and they supplement their more meager kills with meat from domestic animals (Redford and Robinson 1987).

## Summary

Preclassic and Postclassic faunas reveal how Maya elites worked at establishing a different lifestyle from commoners and maintaining hierarchy. They organized feasts where they celebrated their victories in battle, and the ideology of deer as a substitute for human captives probably influenced their preference for venison. Women became craft specialists raising deer, dogs, peccaries, and turkeys to provide reliable and convenient sources of meat and cooking foods that often carried prestigious symbolic connotations just like other crafts. Elites also used their tribute systems and exchange networks to get the kinds of meat that they wanted. They may have hedged their bets further by restricting deer hunting to themselves, and they probably invested in hunting equipment such as nets, which were particularly effective in capturing these animals. In the long run, elite political strategies would have paid economic dividends, in greater tribute collections, for example.

Commoner hunters might have been officially barred from killing high-status animals. The presence of small numbers of bones of deer or peccary in their refuse most likely indicates their participation in elite-sponsored feasts as well as occasional poaching. Commoner households appear to have been more inclined to practice optimal foraging, relying on the most stable source of meat and considering the efficiency of obtaining food. They would most likely have bagged whatever animals they encountered using bow and arrow and blowgun, resulting in the variety of large but mostly small, terrestrial and arboreal animals that are typical of non-elite faunal assemblages. Where a reliable source of aquatic resources was available, they preferred to exploit it.

There may be long term trends in archaeological faunas of the southern Maya Lowlands, specifically an increase in exploitation of primates and birds. The consumption of birds, especially turkey, may have been an attempt to imitate Yucatecan food preferences. Increased kills of arboreal animals may also be related to use of stone-tipped blowgun and arrow points that are characteristic of the Postclassic period. Late prehistoric non-elite Maya meat consumption is similar in many respects to that of present-day indigenous hunters in the New World tropics.

## Notes

1. In a previous publication (Pohl 1990b) I reported on Tikal fauna scattered around and on top of Group G, which was comparable to fauna from other sites considered. This report includes the fauna protected in Rooms 21 and 23 in Group G.

2. Contemporaneous Moche pottery from Peru shows elites hunting deer with nets, spears, and dogs (Donnan 1978:179)

## References

Anton, F.
    1973    *Woman in Pre-Columbian America.* New York: Abner Schram.

Bourke, J. G.
    1892    Sacred Hunts of the American Indian. *Proceedings of the 8th International Congress of Americanists, Paris,* 1890: 357-68.

Brenner, M., B. Leyden, and M. Binford
    1990    Recent Sedimentary Histories of Shallow Lakes in Guatemalan Savannas. *Journal of Paleolimnology* 4:239-52.

Bricker, V. R.
    1981    *The Indian Christ, the Indian King. The Historical Substrate of Maya Myth and Ritual.* Austin: University of Texas Press.

Carr, H. S.
    1986    *Faunal Utilization in a Late Preclassic Maya Community at Cerros, Belize.* Ph.D. Dissertation, Department of Anthropology, Tulane University.
    1989    Patterns of Exploitation and Exchange of Subsistence Goods in Late Classic-Early Postclassic Yucatan: A Zooarchaeological Perspective. Paper presented at the 54th annual meeting of the Society for American Archaeology, Atlanta.

Cliff, M.
    1986    Excavations in the Late Preclassic Nucleated Village. In R. Robertson and D. Freidel, eds. *Archaeology at Cerros, Belize, Central America. Volume I: An Interim Report,* pp.54-64. Dallas: Southern Methodist University Press.

Cliff, M. and C. Crane
   1989    Changing Subsistence Economy at a Late Preclassic Maya Community. In P. McAnany and B. Isaacs, eds., *Prehistoric Maya Economies of Belize*, pp.295-324. Research in Economic Anthropology, Supplement 4. Greenwich, CN: JAI Press.

Coe, M.
   1975    *Classic Maya Pottery at Dumbarton Oaks*. Washington: Dumbarton Oaks.

Crane, C.
   1989    The Palynology and Archaeobotany of Cerros, Belize. Paper presented at the 54th annual meeting of the Society for American Archaeology, Atlanta.
   1991    Archaeobotanical and Palynological Research at a Late Preclassic Maya Community, Cerros, Belize. Paper presented at the Conference on Ancient Maya Agriculture and Biological Resource Management, Riverside, CA.

Culbert, T. P.
   1973    The Maya Downfall at Tikal. In T. P. Culbert, ed., *The Classic Maya Collapse*, pp.63-92. Albuquerque: University of New Mexico Press.

Díaz del Castillo, B.
   1927    *The True History of the Conquest of Mexico*. M. Keatinge, trans. New York: McBride.

Donnan, C.
   1978    *Moche Art of Peru*. Los Angeles: Museum of Culture History, University of California.

Dreiss, M. L.
   1982    An Initial Description of Shell Artifacts from Colha, Belize. In T. Hester, H. Shafer, and J. Eaton, eds. *Archaeology at Colha, Belize: The 1981 Interim Report*, pp.208-24. San Antonio: Center for Archaeological Research, the University of Texas at San Antonio and Centro Studi e Ricerche Ligabue, Venezia.

Edmonson, M. S.
   1982    *The Ancient Future of the Itza. The Book of Chilam Balam of Tzimin*. Austin: University of Texas Press.
   1986    *Heaven Born Merida and Its Destiny*. Austin: University of Texas Press.

Emery, K.
   1990    *Postclassic and Colonial Period Subsistence Strategies in the*

*Southern Maya Lowlands: Faunal Analyses from Lamanai and Tipu, Belize*. M.A. Thesis, Department of Anthropology, University of Toronto.

Freidel, D.
- 1979 Culture Areas and Interaction Spheres: Contrasting Approaches to the Emergence of Civilization in the Maya Lowlands. *American Antiquity* 44:36-54.

Freidel, E.
- 1975 *Women and Men. An Anthropologist's View*. New York: Holt, Rinehart, and Winston.

Goody, J.
- 1982. *Cooking, Cuisine and Class. A Study in Comparative Sociology*. Cambridge: Cambridge University Press.

Hamblin, N.
- 1984 *Animal Use by the Cozumel Maya*. Tucson: University of Arizona Press.

Hames, R.
- 1990 Sharing among the Yanomamö: Part I, The Effects of Risk. In E. Cashdan, ed., *Risk and Uncertainty in Tribal and Peasant Economies*, pp.89-106. Boulder, CO: Westview.

Hammond, N.
- 1977 The Early Formative in the Maya Lowlands. In N. Hammond, ed., *Social Process in Maya Prehistory: Studies in Honour of Sir Eric Thompson*, pp. 77-105. London: Academic Press.
- 1991 Cuello Considered: Summary and Conclusions. In N. Hammond, ed., *Cuello, an Early Maya Community in Belize*, pp. 235-48. Cambridge: Cambridge University Press.

Hellmuth, N.
- 1977 Cholti-Lancandon (Chiapas) and Peten-Ytza Agriculture Settlement Pattern, and Population. In N. Hammond, ed., *Social Process in Maya Prehistory*, pp.421-48. New York: Academic Press.

Hester, T.
- 1985 The Maya Lithic Sequence in Northern Belize. In M. Plew, J. Woods, and M. Pavesic, eds., *Stone Tool Analysis: Essays in Honor of Don E. Crabtree*, pp.184-210. Albuquerque: University of New Mexico Press.

Jacob, J.
- 1991 Agriculture and Land Use at Colha. Paper presented at the 47th International Congress of Americanists, New Orleans.

Jones, G., E. Graham, and R. Kautz
    1985    Archaeology and Ethnohistory on a Spanish Colonial Frontier: An Interim Report on the Macal-Tipu Project in Western Belize. In A. Chase and P. Rice, eds., *The Lowland Maya Preclassic: Questions and Answers*, pp.206-14. Austin: University of Texas Press.

Linares, O.
    1976    Garden Hunting in the American Tropics. *Human Ecology* 4:331-49.

López de Cogolludo, D.
    1971 [1688] *Los Tres Siglos de la Dominación Española en Yucatán o sea Historia de esta Provincia*, 2 vols. Graz: Akademische Druk-u. Verlaganstalt.

Pendergast, D.
    1974    *Excavations at Actun Polbilche, Belize*. Toronto: Royal Ontario Museum, Archaeology Monograph 1.
    1981    Lamanai, Belize: Summary of Excavation Results 1974-1980. *Journal of Field Archaeology* 8:29-53.
    1986    Stability through Change: Lamanai, Belize from the Ninth to the Seventeenth Century. In J. Sabloff and E. W. Andrews, eds., *Late Lowland Maya Civilization: Classic to Postclassic*, pp.223-50. Albuquerque: University of New Mexico Press.

Pohl, M. D.
    1976    *Ethnozoology of the Maya: An Analysis of Fauna from Five Sites in Peten, Guatemala*. Ph.D. dissertation, Department of Anthropology, Harvard University.
    1977    Fauna de Tikal, Grupo G. Manuscript.
    1981    Ritual Continuity and Transformation in Mesoamerica: Reconstructing the Ancient Maya *Cuch* Ritual. *American Antiquity* 46:513-29.
    1983    Maya Ritual Faunas: Vertebrate Remains from Burials, Caches, Caves, and Cenotes in the Maya Lowlands. In R. Leventhal and A. Kolata, eds., *Civilization in the Ancient Americas*, pp.55-103. Albuquerque: University of New Mexico Press.
    1985    An Ethnohistorical Perspective on Ancient Maya Wetland Fields and Other Cultivation Systems in the Lowlands. In M. Pohl, ed., *Prehistoric Lowland Maya Environment and Subsistence Economy*, pp. 35-46. Cambridge, MA: Peabody Museum, Harvard University, Papers of the Peabody Museum, vol. 77.

Pohl, M.

1989    Women, Animal Raising, and Social Status: The Case of the Formative Period Maya of Central America. Paper presented at the 22nd Annual Chacmool Conference, Calgary.

1990a    *Ancient Maya Wetland Agriculture: Excavations on Albion Island, Northern Belize.* Boulder, CO: Westview Press.

1990b    The Ethnozoology of the Maya. Faunal Remains from Five Sites in Peten, Guatemala. In G. R. Willey, ed., *Excavations at Seibal, Guatemala*, pp.142-74. Cambridge, MA: Peabody Museum, Harvard University, Monographs, vol. 17, no. 3.

Pohl, M. and L. Feldman

1982    The Traditional Role of Women and Animals in Lowland Maya Economy. In K. Flannery, ed., *Maya Subsistence*, pp.295-311. New York: Academic Press.

Pohl, M. and J. Pohl

1983    Ancient Maya Cave Rituals. *Archaeology* 36:28-32, 50-51.

Potter, D.

1982    Some Results of the Second Year of Excavation at Operation 2012. In T. Hester, H. Shafer, J. Eaton, eds., *Archaeology at Colha, Belize: The 1981 Interim Report*, pp.98-122. San Antonio: Center for Archaeological Research, University of Texas at San Antonio and Centro Studi e Ricerche Ligabue, Venezia.

Pyburn, K.A.

1989    Maya Cuisine: Hearths and Lowland Economy. In P. McAnany and B. Isaac, eds., *Prehistoric Maya Economies of Belize*, pp.325-46. Greenwich, CT: JAI Press.

Ray, C.

1956    Preliminary Checklist of Vertebrate Remains from Mayapan, Yucatan. Manuscript.

Redford, K. and J. Robinson

1987    The Game of Choice: Patterns of Indian and Colonist Hunting in the Neotropics. *American Anthropologist* 89:650-67.

Relaciones de Yucatán

1898-1900    *Collección de Documentos Inéditos Relativos al Descubrimiento Conquista y Organización de las Antiguas Posesiones Españolas de Ultramar.* 2nd series, vols. 11 and 13, Madrid.

Robertson, R.

1983    Functional Analysis and Social Process in Ceramics: The Pottery from Cerros, Belize. In R. Leventhal and A. Kolata, eds., *Civilization in the Ancient Americas*, pp.105-42. Albuquerque: University of New Mexico Press.

Robin, C.
    1989    *Preclassic Maya Burials at Cuello, Belize.* Oxford: British Archaeological Reports, International Series 480.

Robin, C., J. C. Gerhardt, and N. Hammond
    1991    Ritual and Ideology. In N. Hammond, ed., *Cuello, an Early Maya Community in Belize*, pp.204-34. Cambridge: Cambridge University Press.

Ross, E.
    1978    Food Taboos, Diet, and Hunting Strategy: The Adaptation to Animals in Amazon Cultural Ecology. *Current Anthropology* 19:1-19.

Roys, R.
    1943    *The Indian Background of Colonial Yucatan.* Washington: Carnegie Institution of Washington, Publication 548.

Saul, F. and J. M. Saul
    1991    The Preclassic Population of Cuello. In N. Hammond, ed., *Cuello, an Early Maya Community in Belize*, pp.134-58. Cambridge: Cambridge University Press.

Schele, L. and M. Miller
    1986    *The Blood of Kings: Dynasty and Ritual in Maya Art.* Fort Worth: Kimbell Art Museum.

Scott, R.
    1982    Notes on the Continuing Faunal Analysis from the Site of Colha, Belize: Data from the Early Postclassic. In T. Hester, H. Shafer, and J. Eaton, eds., *Archaeology at Colha, Belize: The 1981 Interim Report*, pp.203-07. San Antonio: Center for Archaeological Research, University of Texas, San Antonio and Centro Studi e Ricerche Ligabue, Venezia.

Scott, R. and F. Valdez
    1990    Subsistence and Culture Change in the Terminal Classic to Early Postclassic Maya Lowlands: The Colha Case. Paper presented at the 55th annual meeting of the Society for American Archaeology, Las Vegas.

Shaw, L.
    1991    *The Articulation of Social Inequality and Faunal Resource Use in the Preclassic Community of Colha, Northern Belize.* Ph.D. Dissertation, Department of Anthropology, University of Massachusetts, Amherst.

Taube, K.
1988 A Study of Classic Maya Scaffold Sacrifice. In E. Benson and G. Griffin, eds., *Maya Iconography*, pp.331-51. Princeton: Princeton University Press.

Tozzer, A. M.
1941 *Landa's Relación de las Cosas de Yucatán*. Cambridge: Papers of the Peabody Museum, Harvard University, vol. 18.

Tozzer, A. M. and G. Allen
1910 *Animal Figures in the Maya Codices*. Cambridge: Papers of the Peabody Museum, Harvard University, vol. 4.

Valdez, F.
1987 *The Prehistoric Ceramics of Colha, Northern Belize*. Ph.D. Dissertation, Department of Anthropology, Harvard University.

Vickers, W.
1984 The Faunal Components of Lowland South American Hunting Kills. *Interciencia* 9:366-76.
1989 Patterns of Foraging and Gardening in a Semi-Sedentary Amazonian Community. In S. Kent, ed., *Farmers as Hunters*, pp.46-59. Cambridge: Cambridge University Press.

White, C.
1989 Chemical and Trace Element Analyses of Human Bone from Lamanai, Belize. Paper presented at the 54th annual meeting of the Society for American Archaeology, Atlanta.

White, C. and H. Schwarcz
1989 Ancient Maya Diet as Inferred from Isotopic and Elemental Analysis of Human Bone. *Journal of Archaeological Science* 16:451-74.

Willke, D. and B. Curran
1991 Why Do Mbuti Hunters Use Nets? Ungulate Hunting Efficiency of Archers and Net-Hunters in the Ituri Rain Forest. *American Anthropologist* 93:680-89.

Willey, G. R.
1972 *The Artifacts of Altar de Sacrificios*. Cambridge: Papers of the Peabody Museum, Harvard University, vol. 64.

Wing, E. S.
1981 A Comparison of Olmec and Maya Foodways. In M. Coe and D. Grove, organizers, *The Olmec and their Neighbors: Essays in Honor of Mathew W. Stirling*, pp.21-28. Washington: Dumbarton Oaks.

Wing E. and S. Scudder
  1991 The Exploitation of Animals. In N. Hammond, ed., *Cuello, an Ancient Maya Community in Belize*, pp.84-97. Cambridge: Cambridge University Press.

Wing, E. S. and D. Steadman
  1980 Vertebrate Faunal Remains from Dzibilchaltun, Yucatan. In E. W. Andrews IV and E. W. Andrews V, eds., *Excavations at Dzibilchaltun, Yucatan, Mexico*, pp.326-31. New Orleans: Tulane University, Middle American Research Institute, publication 48.

# PALACE AND PRIVATE AGRICULTURAL DECISION-MAKING IN THE EARLY 2ND MILLENNIUM B.C. CITY-STATE OF LARSA, IRAQ

Mitchell S. Rothman
Widener University

## Introduction

The prospectus for the 1991 meetings starts with the premise that "states are both like and unlike other economic actors." In their dual role as economic players and as political power brokers, the leadership institutions of states can have many different economic goals, economic tools, and economic effects on those outside the decision-making apparatus. For want of a better term, we refer to those outside the leadership's inner circle as the "private sector", even while we know that this term includes groups very tightly tied to the policies, favor, and fate of state leaders, as well as those quite separated from and little considered by leaders in making their decisions.

This paper presents a case study that contrasts state administrators and private families as economic actors. The case is that of the Middle Eastern state of Larsa during the early 2nd millennium B.C. Although a sharp line between state and private sectors is often hard to draw (see below), for this one case, the clearest distinction between state and private institutions as economic players is their qualitatively different economic strategies. These strategies are evident in their decisions about agricultural land use, labor organization, and the resulting ratio of risk to potential returns.

A number of agricultural researchers have cited risk and uncertainty in studies of farming, particularly peasant farming in developing states, as a major variable in making production decisions (e.g., Cancian 1972, Ortiz 1967, 1980). Cognition of the factors leading to success or failure judged in cultural terms has proven a critical attribute for understanding the decisions of farmers in such societies (Barlett 1980:562). Particularly important is the effect of uncertainty on labor allocation (Barlett 1976). This article confirms the importance of risk, uncertainty, and perceived goals on agriculture. To those other factors I would add that the perceptions of institutions within the state vary, leading to different strategies. Specifically, the decisions administrators of large state enterprises make in order to support armies, dependent laborers, construction, state religion were and are essentially different that the average farmer without state resources and state responsibilities.

## Isin-Larsa and Old Babylonian Socio-Economics in Southern Mesopotamia

The case of Larsa in what are called the Isin-Larsa and early Old Babylonian periods, approximately 1900 to 1750 B.C.[1] is, for a number of reasons, particularly appropriate for looking at contrasting decision-making strategies. First of all, one characteristic of the pre-oil economies of the southern Mesopotamian alluvium -- what is now southern Iraq and southwestern Iran -- is their dependence on agriculture. Few other resources, including essential sources of wood, tool-making ores, and precious metals, occur naturally in this region. Irrigation agriculture and to a lesser extent pastoralism were the bedrocks of economic life for the state institutions of palace and temples as well as for all other sectors of society. Not surprisingly, most of the documents of the time that we find preserved on clay tablets pertain to agricultural land, labor, and products. While most are from state institutions, significant numbers of records concerning privately held or privately farmed fields and orchards appear in the Isin-Larsa and Old Babylonian Periods for the first time. So, for this period, detailed documentation exists for state and private agriculture, and agriculture is *the* most critical economic enterprise in the society as a whole. There is one additional benefit of this time and place for the analysis of agricultural decision-making. The rule of the Isin-Larsa Period's longest reigning king, Rim-Sin of Larsa, ended abruptly in the middle of this period; the expansionist Old Babylonian Empire of Hammurabi conquered and incorporated Larsa in 1763 B.C. So, we not only get to compare state and private agricultural decision-making when Larsa was the center of a state polity, but how its agricultural economy was restructured when it was a province of the Old Babylonian Empire.

Parenthetically, for those interested in the debate between formalist and substantivist views of economy, this case covers the same region and time as Polanyi's (1957) landmark article, "Marketless Trading in Hammurabi's Time".

What then do we know in general about the society and economy of that time and place? The Isin-Larsa and Old Babylonian states came into being more that a millennium and a half after the earliest states evolved on the southern alluvium of Mesopotamia in the 4th millennium B.C. (Adams

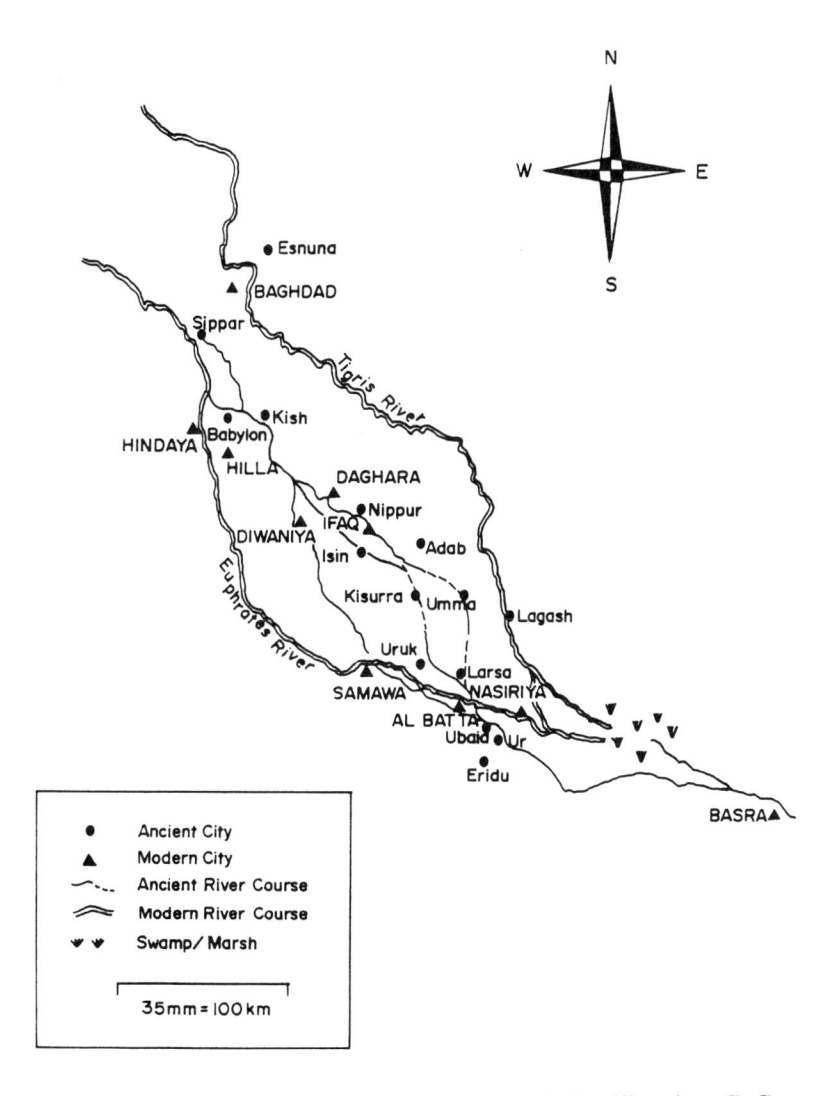

Figure 1. Southern Mesopotamia in the early 2nd millennium B.C.

## 152 ECONOMIC ANTHROPOLOGY OF THE STATE

1981, Wright and Johnson 1975). During the interval from first states to the early 2nd millennium B.C., individual urban economies, the city-states, became the essential building blocks of the region's economic and political organization, and the first two attempts to meld city-states into a territorial empire -- the Akkadian and Ur III Empires -- had come and gone. By the beginning of the second century of the second millennium B.C., the region was again typified by a series of city-states under the rule of various ethnic groups. Through conquest or confederation, various of these city-states merged into a dozen or so relatively equal territorial states. Among these small conquest states were the one centered in Larsa (including Ur), Isin, its major earlier competitor, Lagash on the Tigris, and Babylon, Larsa's eventual conqueror (see Figure 1).

Within these city-states, society was divided into four groupings: the state institutions of the palace and temples, landholding extended families, landless laborers, and rural farmers and herders (Oppenheim 1977). The palace and temples each held very large agricultural estates, although by the previous Ur III Period, the palaces controlled the temples' capital, managing their lands and even storing religious icons in palace vaults (Steinkeller 1987). Whereas in the 3rd millennium slaves constituted a major pool of agricultural labor, by the early 2nd millennium B.C. palace retainers and part-time laborers tilled state and some larger family fields in exchange for grain rations (Evans 1963). Public corvée labor was also engaged through state administrators (Walters 1970). The palace and temples compensated many of their highest administrators by grants of land (see below). At the same time, individuals who appear in texts as community or lineage leaders -- those whom I regard as essentially private individuals -- also were at times given temporary use of temple land in exchange for favors or services to state institutions (Stone 1977).

As implied above, many families were involved with the state on a temporary or contract basis. Yet, the majority of urban-dwelling private families we know of through texts appear to have relied on their own resources for their economic livelihood. Many were neither wealthy nor part of an "elite" class, yet those who appeared in texts were rarely from the large landless laborer class.[2] The state itself recognized the distinction between state and private land, because some of these families' land is designated as immune from state seizure. This we know from a memorandum of the conqueror Hammurabi to his occupation estate manager, Šamaš-hazir,[3] shortly after the conquest of 1763 B.C. Hammurabi wrote, "Sin-išmeani, the...date gardener...brought this to my attention....Šamaš-hazir has appropriated land of my family's estate and has given it to a soldier...Is perpetual land ever to be taken away?....Return the field to him" (TCL 7, 16;[4] translated in Kraus 1968).[5]

Governance reflected this rather fuzzy line between state and local authority. Texts have been interpreted to say that the non-palace urban sector had its own community-based councils of elders with authority for local services, even within the capital of their state. This may reflect a neighborhood type of government within the larger state apparatus (Stone 1987).

The operation of the economy appears to have begun to have some elements of market economics, but remained an essentially barter or redistributive economy. Contrary to what Polanyi wrote, there were market places (Röllig 1976), but prices seem to have been standardized and not based on pure market principles of supply and demand, as Polanyi argued. The setting of prices appears to have depended on custom or on the meddling of the state in the form of *mišarum* edicts or *şimdat šarri* (Kraus 1958). These royal edicts set guidelines for the exchange of goods and also forgave debts in certain categories. Silver was used as a standard of value, yet it rarely seems to have been used as a medium of exchange, even in those land contracts that specify the land's worth in terms of grains of silver (Sweet 1958). Barley is the most often mentioned medium of payment for sales, taxes, etc., although other agricultural goods -- onions, dates, and the like -- are also found. Private entrepreneurship also existed in the form of private merchants, labor recruiters, loan sharks, and so forth, but state bureaucrats influenced many of these enterprises, especially long-distance trade (Leemans 1950).

State administrators derived most of the income for their activities from palace and temple agricultural estates. In addition, the state collected taxes from state sanctioned importers and merchants and also from private community councils. One series of texts from the time of Hammurabi concerned a state officer called the Overseer of Merchants, who received state taxes in dates, garlic, onions, fish, wool and the like on the docks at Larsa, and there exchanged those goods with private distributors for one of the only two goods the palace appears to have wanted -- barley and silver (Stol 1982). According to other texts, the major overseers in each locality had to supply a set amount of barley and silver annually. This they obtained by exchanging the goods produced under their authority. The state's requirement was specified at the beginning of the year in a sealed order of the king. By basing the actual payment on a percentage of the exchange, as long as the minimum was achieved, the state bureaucrats encouraged overseers to get the best return they could. A last source of state income, probably the smallest, was loans to private individuals with up to 33% interest. Almost all loan repayments were due at the end of the barley harvest season.

Private families farmed their own land, sharecropped others' land or sold their labor full- or part-time for various economic tasks. Shorter term indenture for failure to pay debts at harvest time was common.

What is most important here is that wherever the land came from, be it the palace, a temple, or corporate kinship group, the basic production decisions of private farmers appear to have been those of the individual. Similarly, most state fields and orchards were under the direct decision-making authority of high-order administrators. To the degree that it is possible to monitor crop choice, labor organization, etc., these represent actual decisions of the administrator or the non-state family head involved.

### Isin Larsa and Old Babylonian Agriculture

For both state and private sectors, the primary crops of that day were the field crops barley and wheat and the horticultural crop dates. In addition, the interiors of cities were dotted with private plots on which vegetables like garlic, onions, greens and oil seeds were grown (van Zeist 1984, 1985).

All crops depended on irrigation. Yet, there were in effect two distinct types of irrigation systems. Within the circle of land around city and large town centers, there was considerable investment in complex irrigation systems with reservoirs and canals (see Figure 2). A text from contemporary Lagash speaks of sending 1800 men to perform emergency repairs on the Nubitar feeder canal (BIN 7, 30, translated in Walters 1970). One memorandum from Hammurabi to his estate manager in Larsa outlined a very complex division of fields among two field managers to minimize conflict between the managers' overseers in a year of low water volume (Kraus 1968: text 23). Clearly, competition for irrigation water existed in the areas of densest population. However, outside the inner agricultural belt of cities and towns supplies of arable land could be expanded by cutting low investment, easy-to-manage gravity flow canals.

The first major key to understanding the differences in strategy between state and private farming lies in the agricultural and social differences between the two major crops -- grains and dates. Dates require a heavy initial investment to establish a garden. Cultivators must wait three or four years until mature trees produce fruit. Due to their high water needs, date orchards are best placed along the rivers' levees in *ušallu* fields, but competition for those plots are intense because of their easy access to irrigation water (see Figure 2). Once mature, however, date trees yield a very

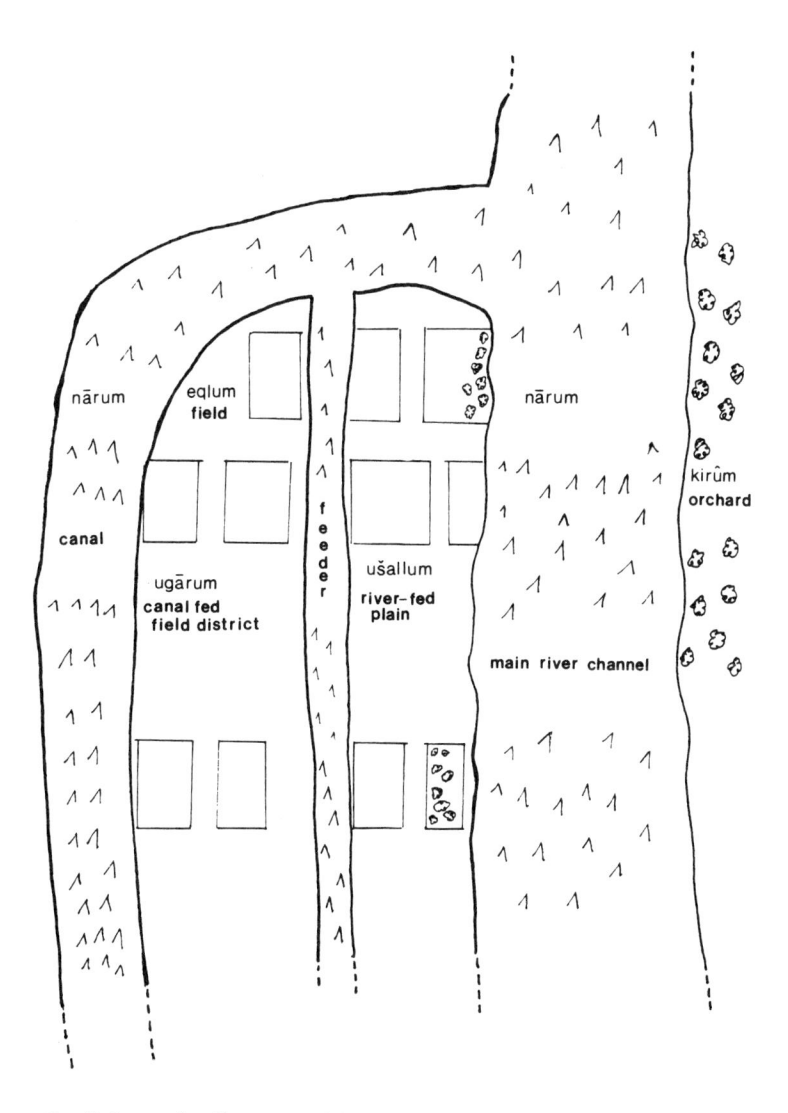

Figure 2. Schematic diagram of irrigation in the Urban Zone, Larsa.

a very reliable return year after year at relatively low labor cost. Labor input is heavy for the gardener at the time of annual pollination, but few pollinators are needed. Also, the maximal labor input for dates is at the season of lowest labor requirements for field agriculture, freeing gardeners for cultivation on their own or others' grain plots. In nutritional terms a small date orchard can produce as many calories as a larger grain field. As the Bedouin say today, "Seven dates make a meal" (Drower 1954:546). However, dates seem to have been a less prestigious food than grains. As the ancient Babylonian saying goes, "the orphan, the widow, the poor man, what do they eat when my sweet dates are scarce?"(*ibid.*).

Contrary to date horticulture, grain cultivation requires much less initial investment and its productivity can be increased by as much as 20% by increased labor inputs in the initial plowing and then weeding stages (Agarwal 1972). But labor demands are very high in the plowing and harvesting phases of grain production both in terms of numbers of individuals and hours of labor input per day. Still, the return on grains in a good year exceeded that of modern mechanized agriculture, according to ancient texts (Jakobsen 1982). This figure is still debated (Powell 1985), but the yields were certainly high. Also, grains were the main medium for payment.

As a number of ethnographers of agricultural decision-making have pointed out, risk and uncertainty affect such crop choice decisions (see above). In this part of Mesopotamia, the risks of agriculture, especially grain production, are high. In modern times, on average, two out of every five years produce substandard crops (Poyck 1962). There is no reason to think the risk was lower earlier in time. Also, improper fallowing or drainage causes serious salinization in grain fields. There is evidence of salinization in state surveys of named fields in the 3rd and 2nd millennia B.C. (Jacobsen 1982). Coincidentally, dates are the most saline-resistant plant grown in the area and barley is more salt-resistant than wheat, although barley can accelerate soil breakdown because of its low evapotranspiration rates (Elgabaly 1971:65).

So, we have in the kingdom of Larsa a focus on one central economic enterprise and a choice of how to allocate labor, means of production, and risk between two major crops -- grains and dates. How do the strategies of private farmers reflect their choices?

## Agricultural Strategies

We know about private agriculture from records of exchanges of arable land, as well as from a few personal letters between individuals.

Among these records are inheritances, exchanges of parcels of lands, court cases disputing land, and what are called sales. The last seem like normal exchanges of goods valued in silver for the permanent alienation of land, except that other documents, called redemptions, record the repayment of exactly the same amount for some of the same fields 5 to 25 years after the date of their sale document. What these texts do tell us is parcel size and location, whether field or orchard, sometimes the number of trees or state of field development, its value in silver for sales and redemptions, owners, sellers and their patronyms.

From the 81 pre-conquest private records tabulated, a clear distinction in the number of fields versus orchards emerges for the agricultural belt

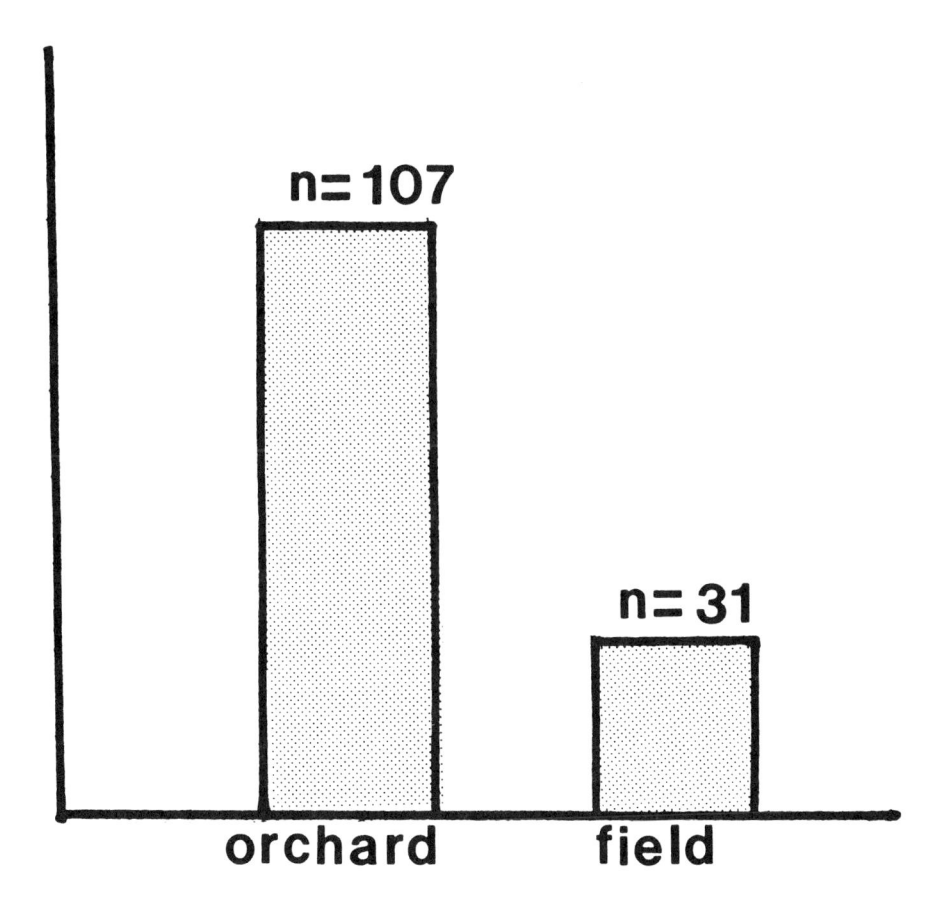

Figure 3. Relative number of fields and orchards in the Larsa private sector.

around Larsa (see Figure 3). That is, date orchards far outnumber grainfields. However, the total area of fields is greater than orchards. In terms of nutritional capture -- certainly per hectare of land -- dates seem to provide a high percentage of subsistence. This is supported by a private letter from Larsa, in which a long-distance trader authorized his son to remove the family's basic annual subsistence from their storehouse as needed (UCP 9/4, 15). The letter specifies 6000 liters of barley, 9000 liters of dried dates, and 1500 liters of linseed oil. Although figure 3 presents a clear contrast, we know that agglomerated data for a large number of people can mask individual strategies. To compensate for that, inheritance documents that list the entire holdings of one family, can be used to reflect an individual family's choices. Figure 4 lists the total hectares in each of eight wills and specifics the proportion that was allocated to orchards, *ušallu* fields with a border of trees (see Figure 2), and grain fields. It is evident that the fewer hectares of land held, the greater the percentage of orchards and *vice versa*. Although eight texts is certainly a small sample, the same general pattern seems to hold at contemporaneous up-river Nippur. One of the most informative cases we have from Nippur records five generations of one family, starting with the will of the founder Ninlil-zimu to his four sons in 1880 B.C. The four sons start with a large estate, but one scattered over many small orchards and fields. By the end of the first generation, they had exchanged various fields and orchards so that they had a series of larger contiguous fields to leave to their sons. As their heirs, the cousins inherited, some did well and retained grain fields, but others began to fail. Their land transactions show that they exchanged smaller field holdings for orchards in higher and higher proportions through time. In other words, at their most successful point they do emphasize grains, but as inheritance splits field size and poor decisions or luck diminish returns, their strategy changed.

In sum, given the choice between the high initial investment, but reliable and low maintenance orchard, with its nutritious but lower status dates, or the riskier, higher input, but potentially more productive fields with their higher status grains, most private farmers adopted what looks like a classic minimax strategy. That is, they produced that mix of crops that reliably guaranteed a subsistence return, plus whatever extra was possible, without risking minimal needs (Coombs 1980). In one case, a very wealthy, quasi-governmental entrepreneur, Balmunamhe, appeared in transactions involving large quantity of fields, but also many orchards in a rural district named for him (van der Mieroop 1985). With his potential wealth in land, a minimax strategy would not seem to be necessary. Yet, one of his major side businesses was trading in slaves or indentured servants, mostly field-

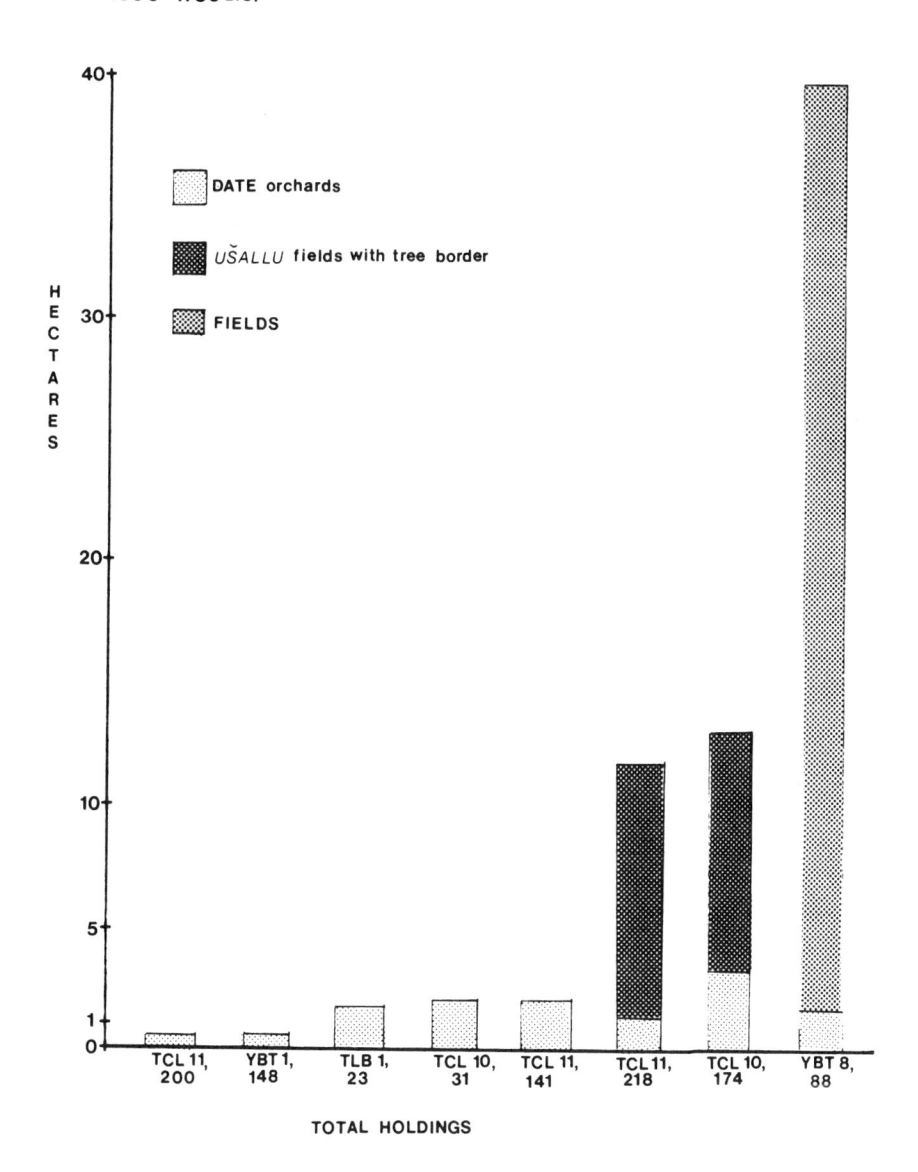

Figure 4. Inheritance documents from Larsa, 1800-1750 B.C.

160 ECONOMIC ANTHROPOLOGY OF THE STATE

hands. The feeding of slaves with the cheap to produce, reliable dates would seem a good way to minimize costs and possible shortfalls.

Thus, most of the individual private farmers found in texts are following a minimax strategy, except those with large, stable, contiguous plots. If the palace and temples have large estates, and their functions and goals are essentially different than private farmers, one would expect state administrators to follow a more extreme version of the strategy of wealthy individual owners.

In fact, we know much more about state agriculture than private. Documents include registers of fields in different categories. Among the different categories are *biltu* fields farmed by state retainers, *miksu* fields farmed by sub-contractors, and *ilku* land granted to individual families or occupational groups in exchange for long-term military, craft, or administrative service (Ellis 1976). The state received the whole yield of the field from *biltu* fields and 1/2 to 2/3 of the yield from *miksu* and *ilku*, in all cases after production costs were deducted. *Šuku* plots for rations also existed. Presumably, all the return was taken by the person assigned the plot. Other texts list expected yields, details of seed, feed, and workers' rations at each stage of production. From this mass of detail, let me select a few critical factors.

The first factor is crop choice. Clearly, the state did have date orchards. Large state date orchard holdings are documented a thousand years later (Coquerillat 1968). Some argue that a few seemingly private date producers were working state orchards. Perhaps, this is so. However, in all the detail alluded to above, the subject of the state records we *actually have* is almost always barley seed and returns in barley. The Larsa state under Rim-Sin was producing vast quantities of grain. For example, one text from Rim-Sin lists the barley "receipt for one year" as 1,582,866 liters of barley from three contiguous fields (YBT 5, 176).

The organization of this production is clear from production cost accounts and *biltu* field registers. In two newly created state agricultural plantations outside of the inner band of Larsa, Mašum and Nur-libi, contiguous fields totalling 359 and 98 hectares respectively were divided into 69 and 15 plots averaging 5 1/4 and 6 1/2 hectares apiece. For each plot a cultivator was appointed. Gangs of oxhandlers and irrigators were assigned to the field as a whole to aid in the production of many cultivators. As far as I can tell, overseers and workers were paid in grain rations. Sometimes, overseers were granted small šuku plots for their sustenance.

In other words, rather than small plots, diversified by crop and geared toward minimal subsistence plus -- the minimax solution -- Rin Sin appears to have adopted a Baysian strategy in which returns of the most productive crop are maximized with less concern for risk (Coombs 1980).

If proposing such a low intensity Baysian agricultural production strategy is possible for Rim Sin, it is clear and explicit in records after the conquest of Hammurabi. After his annexation of Larsa and neighboring Isin and Lagash, Hammurabi's occupational overseers confiscated all the palace and temple lands. They also seized some percentage of privately farmed land in exchange for inferior plots of similar size to consolidate large field holdings. This we know because some texts refer to Hammurabi's land grants to his retainers as coming "from family lands." The philosophy of Mesopotamian kings before the late 1st millennium B.C. Achaemenids was to seize all governmental functions, impose its own government, and use captured resources to support armies, craftspersons, and administrators. After seizing lands, Babylon split their new holdings into *biltu, šuku, miksu* and *ilku* lands. Like Rim Sin before him, Hammurabi divided *biltu* fields into plots for individual cultivators, the *iššaku*. But there was a real difference. Instead of paying cultivators -- now more like overseers -- a set ration, they were given larger fields from which they received 1/3 to 1/2 of the yield after expenses were deducted (Birot 1-11). That is, like the Overseers of Merchants and Production mentioned above, they were paid on commission. Their profit was dependent on the productivity of their one set plot and the labor they could bring to it. The *iššaku*, like other state economic agents, were given tremendous incentive to follow an even more extreme Baysian strategy than Rim Sin appears to have.

In Figure 5, this strategy is characterized in the differing field sizes of private farmers' plots, Rim-Sin's state *biltu* field sub-plots, Hammurabi's *biltu* overseen sub-plots, *miksu, ilku* fields, and modern sharecropper and private land-owners' fields. The Mašum and Nur-libi average field sizes from Rim-Sin's time were comparable to average private field size during Rim-Sin's reign and *šuku* field size during Hammurabi's reign. However, the *biltu, miksu* and *ilku* field plots of Hammurabi's time are significantly larger, just as modern tenant farm plots are larger than private family plots. The different sizes reflect the desire for increased productivity. Again, as mentioned above, the best way to increase barley yields is to increase labor input in plowing and weeding. In the records of Hammurabi's *iššaku* at Lagash, they were assigned fieldhands to enable them to intensify their production. On average 4 1/2 field hands per hectare were assigned to a *biltu* field of 1166 ha. (BIN 7, 161), compared to an average one adult per hectare necessary for a modern non-mechanized Middle Eastern grain field (Salmanzadeh 1980:179). The *iššaku* had to get enough work and yield out of each parcel to get a high return. Again, they would receive a percentage

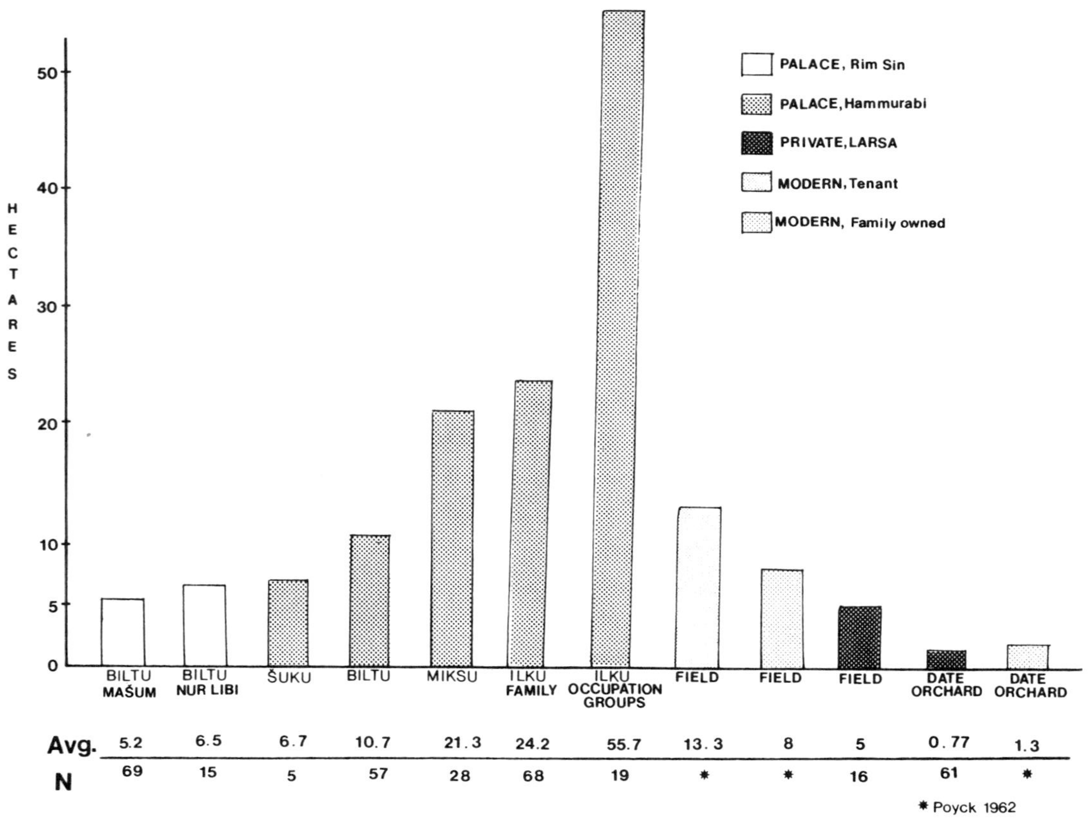

Figure 5. Relative plot size in southern Mesopotamia/Iraq.

of that yield *after* the rations for fieldhands, seed, etc. were paid. Because the added laborers raised the level of expenses, larger fields created an economy of scale, where added expenses were more than compensated for by the added productivity, if *iššaku* succeeded. If they failed, at least state administrators did not need to guarantee the less successful *iššaku* a set ration.

Top state decision-makers imposed a management style geared toward a Baysian strategy emphasizing high production of one key crop. From their point of view, they maximized the return needed to maintain their army, the administrative corps, craft specialists, the buildings and goods that were the necessary symbols of state authority.

Parenthetically, the private sector in Larsa almost disappears in records of post-conquest Larsa. The only private transactions that have been identified are wills, redemptions, and loans.

One of the possible effects of this Baysian strategy was a general decline in the agricultural regime of southern Mesopotamia. Whether it was caused by violation of fallow, salinization, overplowing, gradual declines in irrigation water, or social conflict, after Hammurabi, the population of the Larsa area declined and the city was abandoned within a couple hundred years of the conquest.

## Conclusion

As ethnographers of agriculture predict, risk and uncertainty were key factors in deciding on agricultural strategy among small private farmers in ancient Larsa. They appear to have followed a minimax solution that guaranteed subsistence by diversifying their crops and relying on the date tree.

However, for the decision-makers in state institutions with large estates of their own to manage, the heavy requirements of supporting state dependents and activities produced a different mindset, in which a Baysian solution was more fitting. That solution relied on increasing labor input and productivity of one key crop to maximize returns rather than guaranteeing a minimal return through diversification. Private farmers with large estates or with temporary land grants from palace or temples, were closer in their strategy to the Baysian, although probably not so much as state managers.

Although the sample of texts is small and some kinds of information are lacking in clay records, I take comfort in Adams' statement that "the basic features of a pattern can often be recognized even when a very large number of elements are missing in the totality" (Adams 1981:53). I think there is a pattern here, one that distinguishes state and private sectors.

## Notes

1. All dates are uncalibrated.

2. As to the truly rural segment of society and nomadic pastoralists, both of whom must have played a significant role in Larsa's economic life, we know little from texts.

3. In the Akkadian, š is pronounced [sh], ṣ [ts].

4. The way cuneiform texts are cited is by the volume in which autograph copies of texts were drawn, the text number, and line. The abbreviations for volumes cited are listed below. The major dictionaries, organized by citation from tablets, are cited by initials-CAD, *Chicago Assyrian Dictionary*, AHW *Assyrische Handworterbuch* -- volume and page.

5. The term Hammurabi used for perpetual, *dūrum*, also applies to occupational tenure or social status, that is, as a kind of right or privilege built into the social system (CAD D). The existence of family land holdings is also evidenced in field markers -- *kudurru*'s. These private land holdings were negotiated from the palace, and the stone markers themselves date to the mid-second into first millennia B.C. (Oppenheim 1977:286). A variety of property rights existed, in part determined by geographical distance from the city centers (Adams 1982).

## Acknowledgments

I want to thank Liz Brumfiel for encouraging me to participate in this session. I also want to thank Bob Hunt for his comments following my presentation and M. Estellie Smith for her lengthy letter with questions. Both helped me clarify my presentation.

## Text Editions and Dictionaries

UCP= University of California Publications
BIN= Babylonian Inscriptions in the collection of J.B. Nies.
YBT= Yale Babylonian Texts
TCL= Textes Cunéiformes du Louvre
Birot= Tablettes Economique et administratives d'Epoque Babylonienne Ancien.
TLB= Tabulae Cuneiformes a F.M. de Liagre Bohl Collectae

## References

Adams, Robert M.
>1981 *Heartland of Cities.* Chicago: University of Chicago.
>1982 Property Rights and Functional Land Tenure in Mesopotamian Communities. In J.N. Postgate, ed., *Societies and Languages of the Ancient Near East*, pp.1-14. Warminster: Aris and Phillips.

Agarwal, D.C.
>1972 *Agricultural Efficiency in Vndhya Pradesh.* India: University of Indore Press.

Barlett, Peggy
>1976 Labor Efficiency and the Mechanism of Agricultural Evolution. *Journal of Anthropological Research* 32:124-40.
>1980 Adaptive Strategies in Peasant Agricultural Production. *Annual Review of Anthropology.* 9:545-73.

Buccellati, Giorgio
>1985 Mozan: Historical and Methodological Considerations. *ASOR Annual Meetings.* Chicago.

Cancian, Frank
>1972 *Change and Uncertainty in a Peasant Economy.* Stanford: Stanford University Press.

Cocquerillat, Denise
>1968 *Palmeries et Culture de l'Eanna d'Uruk.* Berlin: G. Mann Verlag.

Coombs, Gary
>1980 Decision Theory and Subsistence Strategies: Some Theoretical Considerations. In T. Earle, et al., eds., *Modelling Change in Prehistoric Subsistence Economies*, pp.187-208. New York: Academic Press.

Elgabaly, M.M.
>1971 Reclamation and Management of Salt Affected Soils. In *Salinity Seminar Baghdad* IDP 7. Rome: UNESCO.

Ellis, Maria DeJ.
>1976 *Agriculture and the State in Ancient Mesopotamia.* Philadelphia: Occasional Publications of the Babylonian Fund.

Evans, D.G.
>1963 The Incidence of Labour-Service in the Old Babylonian Period. *Journal of the American Oriental Society* 83(1):20-27.

Jacobsen, Thorkild
    1982    *Salinity and Irrigation Agriculture in Antiquity.* Malibu: Undena Press.

Kraus, F.R.
    1958    *Ein Edikt von des Königs Ammi-saduqa von Babylon.* Leiden: Brill.
    1968    *Briefe aus der Šamaš-hazir im Paris und Oxford.* Altbabylonische Briefe 4. Leiden: Brill.

Leemans, W.F.
    1968    *The Old Babylonian Merchant.* Studia et Documenta III. Leiden: Brill.

van der Mieroop, Marc
    1985    The fortunes of an Old Babylonian Landowner: The Archive of Balmunamhe. Paper presented at the American Oriental Society Meetings. Ann Arbor.

Oppenheim, A. Leo
    1977    *Ancient Mesopotamia.* Chicago: University of Chicago Press.

Ortiz, Sutti
    1967    The Structure of Decision-making among Indians of Columbia. In R. Firth, ed., *Themes in Economic Anthropology*, pp.191-228. ASA Monographs 6. London: Tavistock.
    1980    Forecasts, Decisions, and the Farmer's Response to Uncertain Environments. In P. Bartlett, ed., *Agricultural Decision Making*, pp.177-200. New York: Academic Press.

Polanyi, Karl
    1957    Marketless Trading in Hammurabi's Time. In K. Polanyi, C.M. Arensberg, and H.W. Pearson, eds. *Trade and Market in Early Empires*, pp.12-26. Glencoe, IL: Free Press.

Powell, Marvin
    1985    Salt, Seed, and Yields in Sumerian Agriculture: A Critique of the Theory of Progressive Salinization. *Zeitschrift für Assyriologie und Vorderasiatische Archäeologie* 75(1):7-46.

Poyck, A.P.G.
    1962    *Farm Studies in Iraq.* Wageningen: H. Veeman and Zonen N.V. for Medelingen van der Landbauscogeschool.

Röllig, Wolfgang von
    1976    "Der Altmesopotamische Markt." *Die Welt des Orients* VIII(2):286-95.

Salmanzadeh, Cyrus
    1980    *Agricultural Change and Rural Society in Southern Iran.*

Cambridge: Middle East and North African Studies Press.

Steinkeller, Piotr
    1987    The Administrative and Economic Organization of the Ur III State. In M. Gibson and R. Biggs, eds., *The Organization of Power: Aspects of Bureaucracy in the Ancient Near East*, pp.19-41. Chicago: Oriental Institute.

Stol, M.
    1982    State and Private Business in the Land of Larsa. *Journal of Cuneiform Studies* 34/3-4:127-230.

Stone, Elizabeth
    1977    Economic Crisis and Social Upheaval in Old Babylonian Nippur. In L. Levine, and T.C. Young, eds., *Mountains and Lowlands*, pp.267-90. Malibu: Undena.
    1987    *Nippur Neighborhoods*. Chicago: Oriental Institute, Studies in Ancient Oriental Civilizations 44.

Sweet, Ronald
    1958    *On Prices, Moneys and Money Use in the Old Babylonian Period*. Ph.D. dissertation, University of Chicago.

Walters, Stanley
    1970    *Water for Larsa*. New Haven: Yale University Press.

Wright, Henry and Johnson, Gregory
    1975    Population, Exchange, and Early State Formation in Southwestern Iran. *American Anthropologist* 77:267-89.

van Zeist, Wilhem
    1984    List of names of wild and cultivated cereals. *Bulletin of Sumerian Agriculture*. I:8-16.
    1985    Pulses and Oil Crop Plants. *Bulletin of Sumerian Agriculture* II:33-37.

# PUBLIC AND PRIVATE ECONOMY IN THE INKA EMPIRE

Terence N. D'Altroy
Columbia University

Many commentators have sought explanations of decision-making rationality in the Inka economy in terms of a standard model built on features particular to the region's cultures. The first Spanish accounts often commented on the distinctiveness of the Andes, sometimes taking pains to explain how Andean economies differed from those of Europe (e.g., Falcón 1946 [1567], Polo 1940 [1561], Garcilaso 1960 [1609], Cobo 1979 [1653]). Novel features, at least to the Europeans, included virtually exclusive rendering of taxes through labor service, the inalienability of the peasantry's resources, complex practices of ritual exchange and hospitality that provided the context for political relations, and elaborate ceremony central to productive activities ranging from farming to shearing wool. Market systems and money were missing in most of the Andes; instead, exchange was frequently structured through dyadic or polyadic trade relationships or through shared access to productive resources. Together, these qualities pointed to an economy shaped by distinctive social conventions. From this analytical perspective, the Inka state economy built upon existing forms and used existing organizations as convenient means for implementing state directives (see Murra 1980a; Rostworowski 1977, 1978, 1988).

By the time of the Spanish conquest in 1532, there had been profound changes under a century of Inka rule.[1] A pivotal change lay in the creation of independent state resources and labor cadres in the empire's latter decades (Murra 1980a; Espinoza Soriano 1973, 1975, 1983, 1987). Similarly, state labor demands, population shifts to lower elevations among sierra populations, and the reduction of local hostilities had important consequences for household economies, in access to resources, dietary mixes and labor scheduling. Even within the distinctive Andean context, economics were therefore not a straightforward product of convention, extant organization, or traditional practices.

How, then, did the Inkas set their economic goals? Under what circumstances did existing practices govern state decision-making, and how did state economics accommodate varied conditions? Where did innovation appear in Inka decision-making, and how was it manifested? How did state choices ripple down to the private economies of subject groups? How did

170 ECONOMIC ANTHROPOLOGY OF THE STATE

decision-making differ between state and subject within comparable spheres?

Although we are only beginning to gain insight into some of these issues, it is apparent that state administrators were well aware of the material consequences of economic decisions and planned accordingly. State administrators exhibited a predilection for accounting of labor and material resources, periodic reallocation of labor assignments, reformation of labor institutions, and heavy investment in the agricultural, transport, and storage infrastructure. Together these managerial activities suggest that the Inkas took into account cultural tradition, the availability of resources and the material outcomes of decisions, and maintained a flexible approach to policy design and implementation.

Although economic decision-makers in subject communities encountered comparable environmental circumstances and the same social foundations as state managers, their decisions were likely quite different. As other papers in this volume observe, state and elite interests are often driven by considerations of maximization or control of output or by security concerns (see also Feinman et al. 1984, Brumfiel and Earle 1987). Decision-makers in private economies are more often concerned with risk or labor minimization, optimization of labor input and productive output, or satisfaction of culturally defined levels of output (e.g., Wolf 1968, Sahlins 1972, Earle and Christensen 1980, Rutz and Orlove 1989).

Nonetheless, some emphasis on intensified agricultural production and craft specialization for political purposes was widespread among the pre-Inka political economies (e.g., Topic 1982, Hastorf and Earle 1985, Costin 1986). Similarly, many of the pre-Inka societies were not entirely self-sufficient, but produced surpluses of localized resources to participate in exchange networks. Finally, Inka storage facilities, especially in the Peruvian sierra, demonstrate at least a degree of concern with containment of risk.

Thus, decision-making under the Inka cannot be phrased simply as either (1) Andean cultural and ecological tradition or (2) maximization of production by the state versus minimization of risk or labor by its subjects. The situation was far more complex. In the present paper, I would like to focus upon the competing and intersecting variables that created a mosaic of decision-making situations. The paper will proceed by sketching out the nature of the Inka economy and the organization of the decision-making hierarchy. I then consider economic decision-making in two spheres of activity that had an important role in both state and subject economies: agricultural land use and craft production.

I draw on documentary and archaeological evidence from two regions in which my colleagues and I have been conducting research on state/subject

ECONOMY IN THE INKA EMPIRE 171

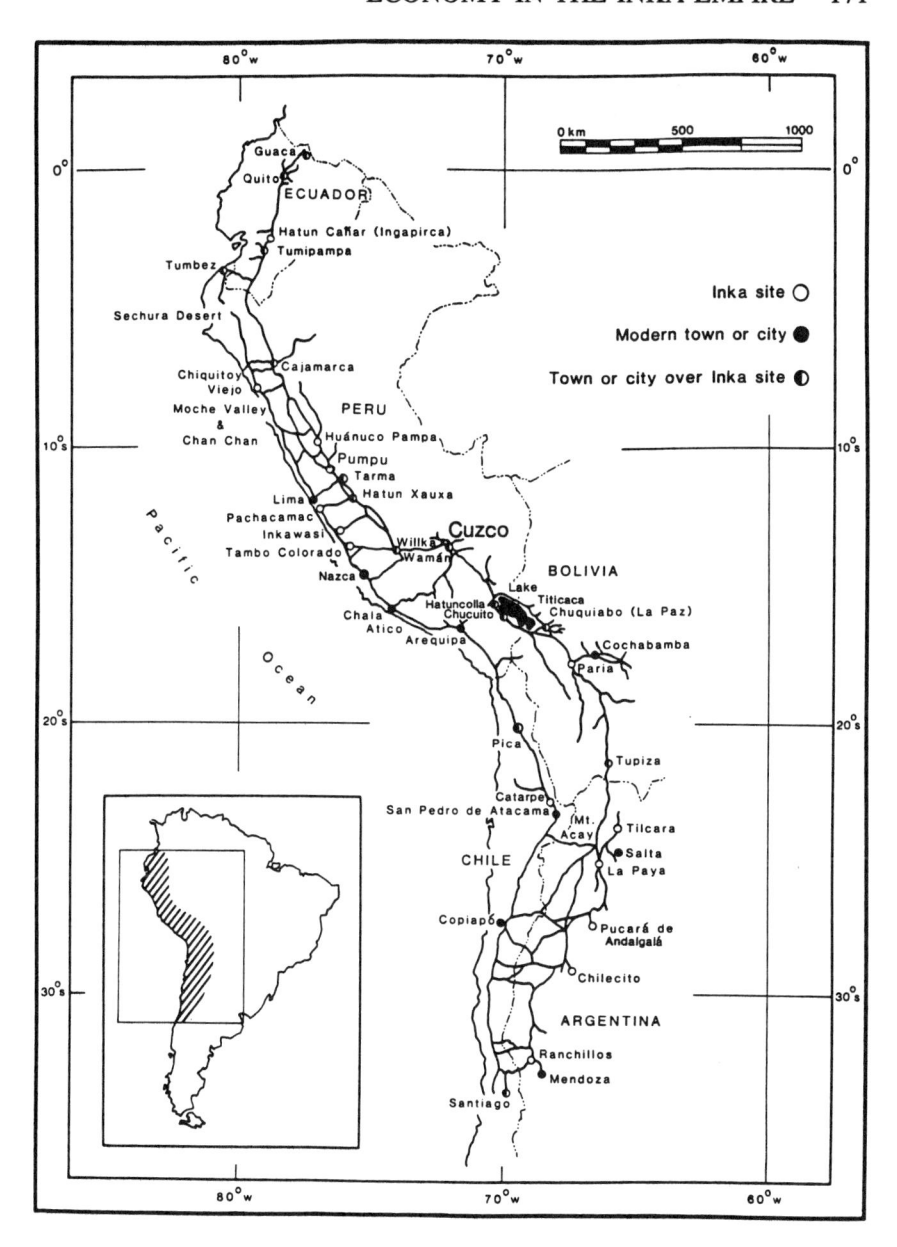

Figure 1. The Inka road system, showing two main routes along the coast and in the highlands, with trunk routes joining them at intervals (after Hyslop 1984: frontispiece).

relations. These areas are the Upper Mantaro Valley of the central Peruvian highlands and the Valle Calchaquí in the northwest Argentine Andes (Figure 1). The Upper Mantaro region constituted a critically important province of the empire because of its agricultural productivity and central logistical position (Figure 2). The provincial center, Hatun Xauxa, was one of the great links in the chain of imperial settlements from Cuzco to Quito. Although the Valle Calchaquí lies toward the southern margin of the empire, it was a focus of imperial settlement and resource development in the southeastern imperial quarter, called Kollasuyu (Figure 3). It is hoped that comparing the data from these areas can provide insight into commonalities of state practice and subject responses.

## The Nature of the Inka Economy

The Inka economy was an elaboration of the Peruvian sierra economies present at the time of the Inka expansion (Murra 1975, 1980a). These economies were generalized in subsistence production and only modestly specialized in craft production. The *ayllu*, a corporate kin group, formed the basic resource-holding unit in Peru and northern Bolivia, while analogous social units were found elsewhere. With populations that could attain several thousand individuals, *ayllus* allocated member households access to resources through usufruct. *ayllus* and communities often attempted to distribute their members among a range of complementary ecological zones, so that the products obtained could be pooled and economic independence maintained (Murra 1972). Apart from household service, specialization in services was apparently rare, but our data on this subject are scant. Among many Andean societies, the Inkas included, property rights passed through both male and female lines (Rostworowski 1988). Elites had rights to have their lands worked, herds tended, and some craft products manufactured, in return for their leadership (Murra 1980a). It may be noted, however, that numerous oral histories taken down by the Spaniards described the immediate pre-Inka period as one in which the military elites augmented their personal wealth and status through conflict and forcible appropriation (e.g., Toledo 1940 [1570], LeBlanc 1981, D'Altroy 1987b).

In the Andes, household and corporate decision-making focused around manipulation of customary relationships within stable social structures. Reciprocity and redistribution (see Polanyi 1957) were the key means by which traditional societies organized exchange. Reciprocity assumed two forms: balanced and asymmetrical. The classic form of balanced reciprocity is *waje waje*, in which households of equal status ex-

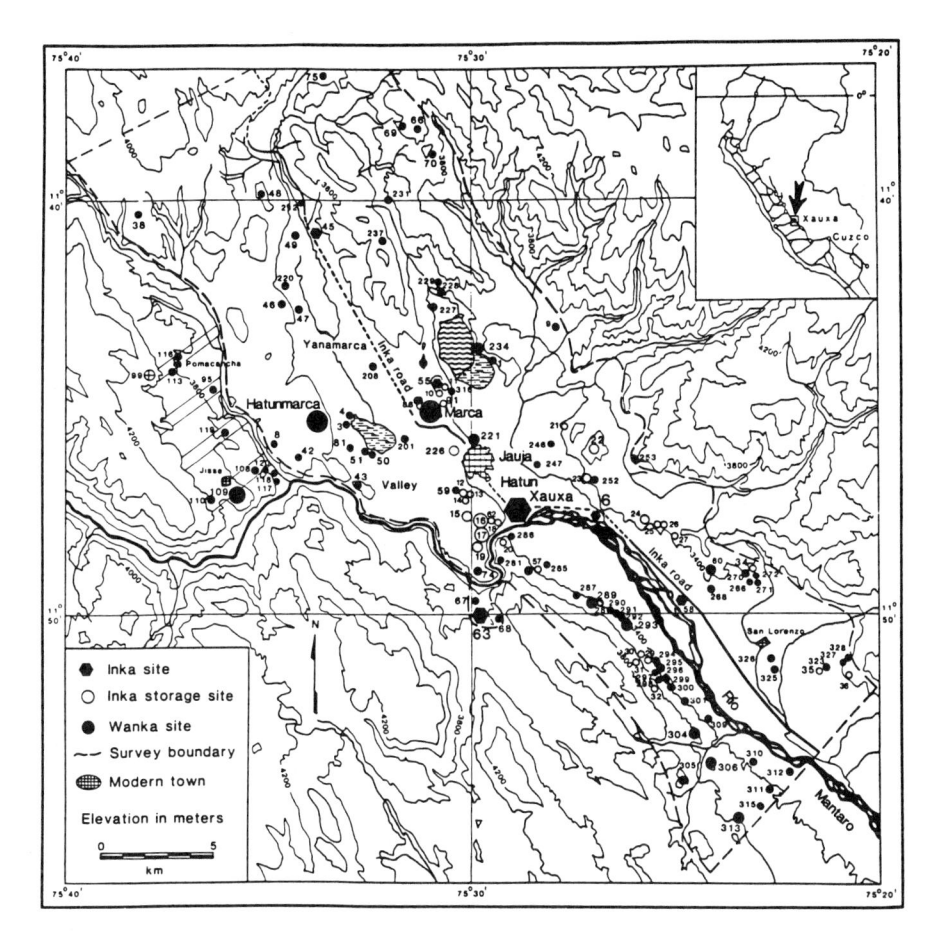

Figure 2.   Distribution of sites in the Upper Mantaro region during the Inka occupation.

change services in expectation of a return of equivalent value (Fonseca 1974; Stanish 1992:24). Asymmetrical reciprocity, or *minka*, takes various forms, such as the services provided to in-laws or contributions of agricultural labor to upper-status by lower-status households who expect to share in the produce. In *minka* exchange, inequality between the parties is the key to defining the nature of the exchange.

Andean redistribution consisted of two central elements. The first was the elite's provisioning of certain kinds of material goods and edibles, especially cloth and *chicha* (maize beer), to the subordinate populace as part of the elite's obligations to his group (e.g., Wachtel 1977, Netherly 1978, Rostworowski 1988). The second consisted of the allocation of particular specialized resources, controlled by the elites, to the general populace; coca and capsicum peppers were among the key goods provided in this manner (see Murra 1972). In each case, the goods were often produced by specialists working directly for the elites and were distributed through ceremonial hospitality. This kind of redistribution was not a substitute for basic subsistence production or a market system. Instead, it bonded sociopolitical groups, reinforced unequal statuses, and provided the general populace with access to goods that might otherwise be difficult to obtain. In the volatile pre-Inka era, the ceremonial distributions likely also served to attract followers to the more powerful elites or groups, thus providing a means of restructuring political relationships.

The Inka state economy built upon these existing organizations, using the ideology of local reciprocity and redistribution as a way of legitimizing and dampening the effects of the exploitative new economy. Upon conquering a region, the Inkas appropriated rights to all resources, which were then divided among the state, the state religion, and the subject communities. The available evidence suggests that the administration had substantially more resources at its disposal than did the religion (see La Lone and La Lone 1987). In exchange for rotating corvée (*mit'a*), the state allocated access to productive agricultural and pastoral lands back to the communities. Certain wild and mineral resources, especially metals, were ostensibly controlled by the state, although the purported monopoly may not have been achieved (Berthelot 1982). In practice, communities retained a high proportion of their original resources, but yielded many prime lands to the state.

Households within the local communities performed a welter of duties for the state. In 1549 and 1562, for instance, members of the Chapachu ethnic group of the Huánuco region reported having fulfilled 31 distinct duties (Helmer 1955-56; Ortiz de Zúñiga 1967, 1972; see below). Each assignment was allocated according to the population of the region, as assessed by a periodic census. In return for their efforts, the laborers were entitled to be supported with food and chicha while they were carrying out state directives. Other reported rights included an annual bestowal of sandals and a new set of clothing to soldiers.

State goods were stored in enormous facilities at Cuzco, provincial centers, and *tampu* (way stations), principally for use by the imperial armies and state laborers. Personnel housed at state settlements and itinerant state travelers also drew from the stocks. A sense of the scale involved can be

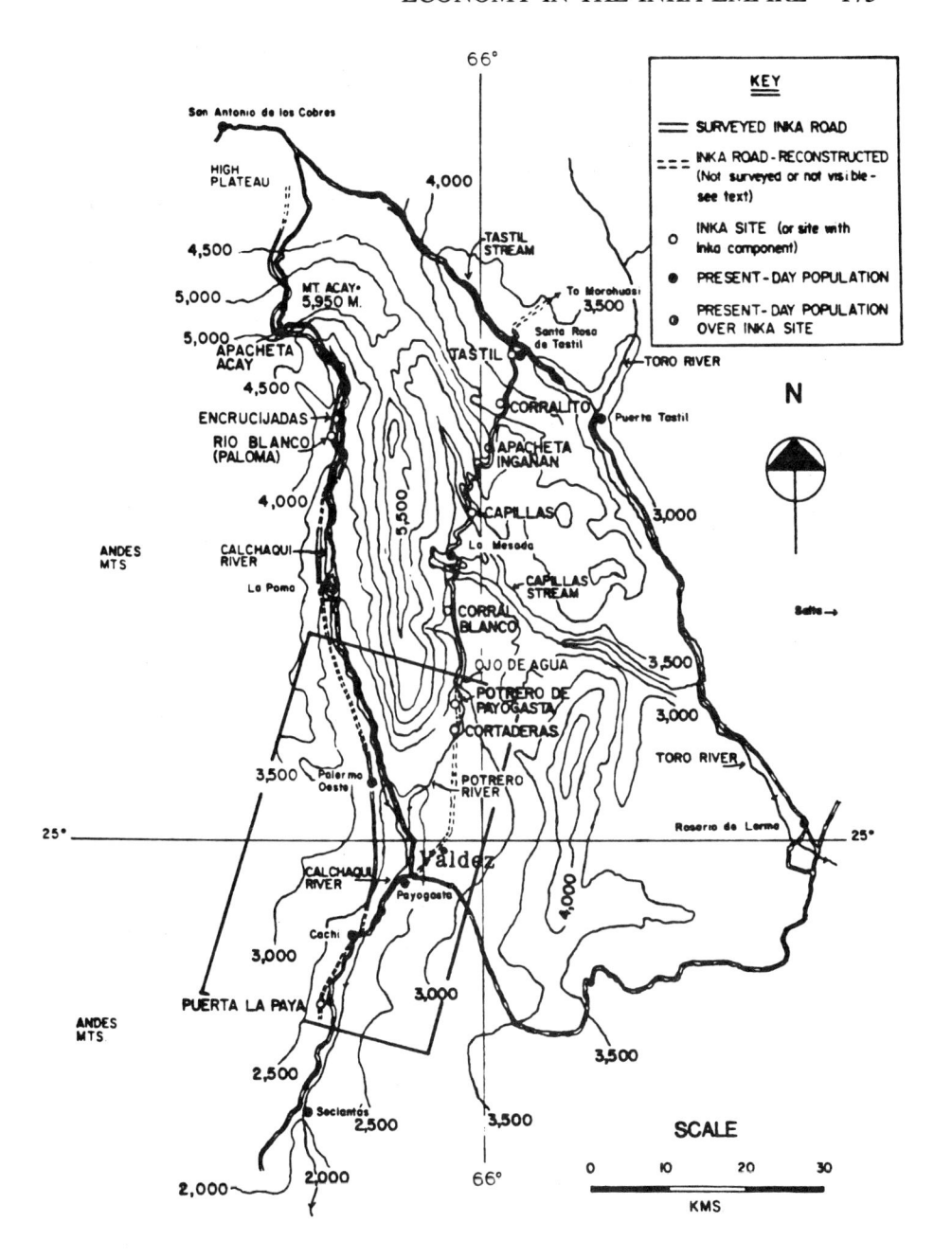

Figure 3. Northern Calchaquí Valley (after Hyslop 1984:169).

obtained by observing that one of the largest of these storage facilities, in the Upper Mantaro Valley, could have supported an army of 35,000 for about a year on the food potentially stockpiled in the 3000 storehouses (*qollqa*) (D'Altroy 1992).[2]

One key decision in the development of the state economy concerned changes in the relations of production between the Inkas and their subjects. Initially dependent upon the capacities of the general populace, the state was moving its production from corvée toward attached specialization in the latter decades of its rule (see La Lone, Chapter 1; Murra 1980a:183-86).

The Inkas created several specialized labor statuses. The most important were the *mitmaqkuna*, the *yanakuna*, and the *aqllakuna*. The first of these were forcibly resettled colonists installed to meet military and economic needs (see Espinoza 1973, 1975, 1987). Colonists also tended crops, such as maize, coca, and peppers, and made craft items, such as cloth and pottery. The *yanakuna* were individuals detached from their kin group and assigned permanent duties, including farming and household service for the elites. Although often viewed as slaves by later commentators, yanakuna could attain positions of high status within the administration. The last category -- the *aqllakuna* -- were young women separated from their families and assigned to live in segregated precincts within state installations. There, they wove cloth and brewed chicha, until awarded in marriage to men honored by the state (see Morris 1974).

Not all Andean regions conformed to this sketch. The central and northern Peruvian coast and the Ecuadorian Andes, especially, differed in important ways from the Inka heartland. On the north coast, entire communities or local sociopolitical groups specialized as potters, weavers, farmers, fishers, traders, and sandal-makers, exchanging their products for those made by others (Rostworowski 1977, 1978, 1983; see also Netherly 1978; Stanish 1992:4-5). The region differed also in the scale of irrigated agricultural systems, as the most expansive canal networks in the New World lay in the Lambayeque-La Leche region. The leadership of the Chimu state, which governed the coast and was the last major power to fall to the Inkas, favored enormous investments of its public labor in agricultural projects rather than in monumental architecture (Moseley and Cordy-Collins 1990). The small-scale chiefdom societies of Ecuador were markedly less complex sociopolitically than the Chimu, but used monetary goods in regional marketing systems. Even in the Bolivian altiplano, where the mixed herding-farming economy was roughly comparable to that of the Inkas, the balance much more heavily favored the pastoral sector.

Numerous authors have described variations in Andean economies over the last couple of decades (e.g., Albert and Mayer 1974; Brush 1976;

Rostworowski 1977, 1978; Masuda, Morris, and Shimada 1985). This research has detailed local variations on a limited number of basic themes, such as exploitation of complementary ecological zones (called "verticality"), types of exchange, and the relationship between social structure and access to resources. Apart from the literature based on marxist perspectives (e.g., Espinoza Soriano 1978; Patterson 1985, 1986), explanations consistently draw from substantivist or structural viewpoints. Authors often couch their explanations in terms of *lo andino*, the distinctive Andean mode of thought and life. Rationality in decision-making, from this perspective, is explicable only in terms that the actors themselves would accept.

As these investigators emphasize, decision-making does not occur in a sociocultural vacuum. Nonetheless, economic decisions unavoidably have material consequences. The complex agricultural systems and planning entailed in the Inka political economy indicate that managers were aware of the outcomes of their choices. Because the trajectory of the Inka economy suggests that the state modified its policies to accommodate material outcomes, I would like to rethink some features of Andean economies in terms of concepts infrequently employed in this context, such as maximization of output, risk minimization, efficiency, and optimization. We can then think about how these were balanced against cultural goals and existing economic formations. We are not yet in a position to venture many quantitative assessments in this area, but a re-evaluation of the relationship between institutions and decision-making may shed light on how decisions were made.

### The regional structure of state decision-making

The Inkas often used existing sociopolitical hierarchies as convenient structures to implement state directives. The decimal hierarchy, where installed, typically used local elites as state managers below the level of provincial governor. The formation of the cadres of specialists suggests that the Inkas found this system somehow inadequate (Murra 1980a). Nonetheless, because the corvée system yielded extensive services and vast quantities of supplies, it is worth some effort to consider how it worked.

Because most taxes were assessed in terms of labor, it is easy to lose sight of the fact that labor taxes were not constant. Instead, the exactions balanced administrators' estimates of needs for products and services against the available personnel. The chronicler Cobo (1979 [1656]:234) explained the situation as follows:

> One thing that should be pointed out with respect to the amount of tribute that they brought to the king, and it is that there was no other rate or limit, either of the people that the provinces gave for the *mita* labor service or in the other requirements, except the will of the Inca. The people were never asked to make a fixed contribution of anything, but all of the people needed were called for the aforementioned jobs, sometimes in larger numbers, other times in lesser numbers, according to the Inca's desire, and the result of those labors was the royal tribute and income; and in this way the people extracted all the gold and silver that the Incas and the *guacas* had.

In Chucuito, witnesses in the Spanish inspection of 1567 said that the Inkas annually specified the area to be farmed, or the amount of seed to be sown, and the amount of wool to be woven by local communities (Diez de San Miguel 1964 [1567]:9, 31, 39). The notion of periodic reassignments may also be found in other documents (e.g., Falcón 1946 [1567]:137-40, Murúa 1987 [1606]:Bk. 2, Ch. 21, pp. 402-04). Regardless of how much or how often the exactions, we may infer that labor obligations resulted from administrators' appraisal of the state's needs and informed estimates of the material outcome of labor investment.

The data are sketchy on how the Inkas arrived at the proportions assigned to each kind of labor service. Some clues may be gained by looking at known state labor categories and the numbers of individuals assigned to each category in areas for which we have data. The chroniclers Falcón (1946 [1567]:137-40), Murúa (1987 [1606]:Bk. 2, Ch. 21, pp. 402-04), and Guaman Poma (1980 [1613]:/191[193], p. 183) itemized lists of labor service due the state. Falcón specified 32 categories for coastal societies and 37 for highland populations, not counting the two kinds of taxes that likely demanded the greatest input -- agricultural labor and military service (Table 1). Among the coastal categories were specialists responsible for human sacrifice; miners; people who worked with stones, colored earth, and salt; artisans, including weavers, sandal-makers, potters, wood-workers, and masons; guards for Women of the Sun, priestesses, llamas, and storehouses; coca farmers; and fishers. Additional highland specialists included individuals to serve the bodies of the deceased Inkas, and artisans who made earspools and cords of lead with which the emperors played. A review of Table 1 shows that Murúa's list generally corresponds well with Falcón's and that both chroniclers often distinguished between artisans producing fine quality objects and more ordinary goods.

The best evidence on how these labor categories were locally assigned comes from Spanish inspections, called *visitas*, recorded in the first few decades after the Inka demise. The 1549 and 1567 inspections in the province of León de Huánuco, in north-central Peru (Helmer 1957; Ortiz de Zúñiga 1967 [1567], 1972 [1567], and the 1562 inspection in Chucuito, Bolivia (Diez de San Miguel 1967 [1562]) are especially rich in detail. Prior analyses, by Julien (1982, 1988) and LeVine (1987), show systematic relationships between census counts and labor exactions, as recorded on the mnemonic knot records called *khipu* (see also Cobo 1979 [1653]:233-34). Julien observes that some populations, such as the Qolla, were restructured into administratively convenient units by dividing large groups, whereas other units were created by merging small groups that had previously been under fragmented leadership, such as the Chachapoyas. The Inkas similarly combined the Xauxas and Wankas into three provincial subdivisions, each under its own native paramount (LeVine 1979; D'Altroy 1987). Elsewhere, the administration accommodated its units to the scale of the indigenous population; the accounting of the Lupaqa, for example, worked around the seven population nuclei that were already present (Julien 1988:268). Julien argues that the standardization of administrative units eased the application of labor exactions and facilitated comparisons in productivity among subject groups. In turn, the needs for administrative personnel could have been minimized and competition stimulated among productive units. Finally, notions of fairness could have been met by assigning comparable tasks across census units.

Labor requirements were assessed according to the census counts of these administrative units. According to the Huánuco visita of 1549, the Chupachus and Yachas together constituted 4108 households. This total was divided into four *waranqas* (units of 1,000households) and 40 *pachacas* (units of 100 households). Many labor requirements were assessed as 40 households or a multiple thereof, perhaps indicating that the assessments were spread evenly across all *pachacas* (Julien 1988:264-66). For those few cases in which the assessments were not evenly divisible by 40, Julien argues plausibly that some specialized personnel, such as silver miners, coca cultivators, or salt miners might have been drawn from certain *pachacas*, thus bringing the accounting into balance. LeVine (1987) additionally shows that labor exactions that resulted in production of goods were apparently assessed evenly at the *pachaca* level, whereas exactions that required services as output were assigned evenly at the *waranqa* level. This suggests that decisions about production of material goods were tailored to

TABLE 1. LABOR SERVICE OWED THE INKAS, ACCORDING TO MURUA (1987) [CA. 1605]: BK. 2, CH.21, PP.402-04) AND FALCON (1946 [1567]):137-40).

| Murúa | Falcón: coast | Falcón: highlands |
|---|---|---|
| miners: gold, silver, pigments | human sacrifice administrators | human sacrifice administrators |
| smiths: gold, silver | gold miners | guardians of the Sun? |
| feathered-cloth weavers: fine, ordinary | lapidary workers | servants of dead Inkas |
| weavers: fine, ordinary | pigment workers | gold specialists |
| dyers | guardians of sacred objects/locations | silver specialists |
| sandal-makers | feathered-cloth weavers: fine, ordinary | copper (?) specialists |
| sacrificial llama keepers | weavers: fine, ordinary | pigment (?) specialists |
| gardeners | dyers | guardians of sacred objects/ locations |
| field workers | sandal-makers: fine, ordinary | feathered-cloth weavers: fine, ordinary |
| coca farmers | guards: women of the Sun and services | weavers: four classes |
| salt miners | llama keepers | sandal-makers: fine, ordinary |
| aji farmers | storehouse guardians | hunting noose specialists |
| maize sprout workers | coca farmers | guards for women of the Sun |
| orchard workers | ash/lime loaf makers | oclla farmers |
| granary guards and their supervisors | aji farmers | potato farmers |

| | | |
|---|---|---|
| guards: landmarks, rivers, fords, bridges, basket bridges | salt miners | coca farmers |
| town accountants for state resources | fishers | llama keepers: two kinds |
| gate-keepers: palaces, houses of retreat of Inka and daughters of the Sun | potters | ash/lime loaf makers |
| | carpenters | aji specialists |
| record-keepers | masons: three kinds | salt specialists |
| *mitmaq*: guards for forts, farmers | shell messengers | maize sprout specialists |
| masons | feather specialists | early maize specialists: two kinds |
| fishers | porters | potters: fine, ordinary |
| hunters: guanaco, vicuña, deer | colonists | orchard keepers |
| hunters: cuys, viscachas, small animals | general farmers, porters | river (?) specialists |
| hunters: birds and fowl | other public workers | bridge keepers |
| carpenters: fine, ordinary | | masons |
| potters: find, ordinary | | messengers |
| spies | | earspool makers |
| anti-insurgency specialists | | lead cord makers (bolas?) |
| | | colonists |
| | | agricultural workers for Inka |
| | | agricultural workers for lords |
| | | laborers on other public works: temples, roads, bad passes, bridges, houses, corrals buildings |
| | | porters |

environmental variations, but that decisions concerning services did not need to take into account such local detail.[3]

The laborers assigned to categories in the 1549 Huánuco *visita* provide insight into the proportions in a specific regional exaction; these are itemized in Table 2. The 4108 Chupachu laborers can be partitioned analytically as follows: 15.0% (640) to extract natural materials, 13.1% (560) to manufacture material goods, 22.9% (980) to cultivate state fields, 9.4% (400) to build or maintain the physical infrastructure, and 39.7% (1698) to provide services that did not yield a material product (e.g., guard duty). Although it is unwise to generalize from a single data source, the balance among these categories is intriguing. For example, less than 10% of the labor was assigned to construction or maintenance of the physical infrastructure, and all of these workers were sent to toil in Cuzco. This assessment was put into practice even though the Chupachu inhabited the province administered from Huánuco Pampa, architecturally the greatest of all preserved provincial centers (see Morris and Thompson 1985). This anomaly may possibly be attributed to the completion of the center by the time that the reported apportionment of duties was assigned; earlier assessments may have included more construction workers.

We often think of labor specialists in terms of craft production, but it is intriguing to observe that only about one of eight of the Chupachu specialists was an artisan. Only 40 (1.0%) were potters, whereas 200 worked with feathers and 400 (10%) made tapestry cloth. The same ratio (1:10) of potters to weavers is found in the mitmaqkuna settlement of Cupi, Bolivia, suggesting that state administrators conceptually linked the two kinds of production (see Murra 1978; D'Altroy, Lorandi and Williams in press). Melissa Hagstrum (pers. com., 1991) has suggested that these proportions may partially stem from the amount and intensity of labor needed to make the particular specialized products. Textiles, for example, are far more labor-intensive than are ceramics and therefore required greater investment for any product.

The allocation of almost 40% of labor to services that would not have directly produced material objects focuses our attention on several issues. Many individuals in these categories were either military guards or security personnel for high status individuals, perhaps reflecting Inka anxieties about the safety of their position. This situation almost certainly differed strikingly from the pre-imperial circumstances in the highlands, when most permanent services were presumably restricted to household servants for the elites. Conversely, only 440 individuals labored at tasks that yield the two principal kinds of remains that archaeologists employ to study the Inka economy in the sierra -- physical infrastructure and ceramics. The relative imbalance of labor assignments and material remains should encourage us to think carefully about how to model economic sectors for which we do not have written records. Archaeological assessment of such important service sectors of the imperial economy, which leave scant trace in the material record, presents a special challenge.

A related issue concerns how the individuals or households were chosen for labor service. Certain groups were favored for particular kinds of duty because special skills were attributed to them. For instance, the Rucanas were employed as litter bearers, the Lake Titicaca peoples as stonemasons, the Chumbivilcas as dancers, and the Chachapoyas, Cañares, Chuyes, and Charcas as warriors (Rowe 1946). Among those central sierra provinces, labor duty ostensibly rotated among households. However, Moore (1958) has observed that the local administrators' discretion in assigning odious or easy service gave them enormous power over their subordinate populations. We can therefore surmise that political favor or kin ties played a meaningful role in labor assignments and that democratic notions of equal division of labor could be construed in a variety of ways in practice.

The Huánuco data are important because they show how the labor allocations were applied administratively in the central part of the empire, but they leave unanswered the key issues of how the directives were set and how the assessments affected the subject economies. To put this another way, a structural understanding of the implementation of state labor directives is not in itself sufficient to discern the principles underlying state decision-making rationales. To address these issues, we may turn to some of the evidence for agricultural and craft production, using the archaeological record in the Mantaro and Calchaquí regions to complement the documentary evidence.

## Land Use

Farming was the most important productive enterprise undertaken by the state and by Andean societies under Inka rule. The early chroniclers stated that rights of access to lands entailed apportionment of lands equally among the state, the state religion, and the subject communities. But even if we grant an unequal allotment of lands among these categories and accept that most community lands were probably alienated only in principle, this characterization is no longer tenable. The development of royal estates, the granting of productive resources to resettled colonists for private use, and the awarding of private estates to favored *kurakas* all contributed to a more

TABLE 2. CHUPACHU LABOR SERVICE TO INKA, AS REPORTED IN 1549 AND 1562.

| Assignment | Total Households | Paucarguaman 1549 Extraction | Manufacture | Agriculture | Building/ Maintenance | Service | Xagua 1562 |
|---|---|---|---|---|---|---|---|
| gold miners: 120 men, 120 women | 120 | 120 | | | | | + |
| silver miners: 60 men, 60 women | 60 | 60 | | | | | + |
| construction, Cuzco area | 400 | | | | 400 | | + |
| agriculture, Cuzco area | 400 | | | 400 | | | |
| retainers of Wayna Qhapaq, Cuzco | 150 | | | | | 150 | + |
| guards for body of Thupa Yupanki, Cuzco | 150 | | | | | 150 | |
| guards for weapons of Thupa Yupanki, Cuzco | 10 | | | | | 10 | |
| garrison in Chachapoyas | 200 | | | | | 200 | |
| garrison in Quito | 200 | | | | | 200 | |
| guards, for body of Inka, Cuzco | 20 | | | | | 20 | |
| feather workers | 120 | 120 | | | | | + |
| honey gatherers | 60 | 60 | | | | | + |
| weavers of tapestry cloth (*qompi*) | 400 | | 400 | | | | + |
| dye makers | 40 | | 40 | | | | |
| herders of Inka's flocks | 240 | | | | | 240 | + |
| guard for maize fields | 40 | | | | | 40 | + |
| aji cultivators | 40 | | | 40 | | | + |

| | | | | | | |
|---|---|---|---|---|---|---|
| salt miners (40, 50, 60) | 50 | 50 | | | | + |
| coca cultivators | 60 | | | | | + |
| hunters for royal deer hunt | 40 | 40 | | 60 | | |
| sandal makers, Cuzco and Huánuco | 40 | | 40 | | | + |
| wood workers, products to Cuzco | 40 | | 40 | | | + |
| potters, products to Huánuco | 40 | | 40 | | | + |
| guards for Huánuco Pampa | 68 | | | | 68 | |
| porters, carrying loads to Pumpu | 80 | | | | 80 | |
| guards for women of the Inka | 40 | | | | 40 | |
| soldiers and litter bearers | 500 | | | | 500 | |
| cultivators of Inka lands | 500 | | | 500 | | |
| makers of weapons and litters, Cuzco | | | | | | + |
| processors of dried, salted fish | | | | | | + |
| snare makers for hunt | | | | | | + |
| women in service to the Inka | | | | | | |
| Subtotals | 4108 | 450 | 560 | 1000 | 400 | 1698 |
| Percentage | | 11.0 | 13.6 | 24.3 | 9.7 | 41.3 |
| Total | 4108 | | | | | 4108 |

Note. Sources: Helmer 1955-56 [1549], Ortiz de Zúñiga 1967 [1562]; modified from LeVine 1987: Table 1 (p. 23), Julien 1988: Table 4 (p. 265). The figures for miners are ambiguous; the *visita* lists 120 and 60 individuals of each sex for gold and silver mining, respectively, whereas other figures appear to cite men only. Because this table represents households, I have chosen to follow Julien in using the figures 120 and 60 (households), rather than 240 and 120 (individuals).

complex pattern of land tenure and use than the early chroniclers' view allows (see Rostworowski 1962, 1988; Murra 1980b; Salomon 1986).

To address the comparability of state and subject decision-making in land use, it will be useful to begin by looking at cases where we have detailed local information. Here, I will briefly review two lines of evidence: (1) land ownership recorded in 1591 among the Collaguas populace of the south-central Peruvian highlands; and (2) archaeobotanical remains recovered from the Upper Mantaro Valley pertaining to the immediately pre-Inka (Wanka I: A.D. 1000-1350; Wanka II: A.D. 1350-1440) and Inka (Wanka III: A.D. 1440-1533) periods. We can then turn our attention to the development of state farms and their impact on subject economics.

Ayllu *and community resource use*

Since the publication of Murra's (1972) seminal article on spatially extended resource use in late prehistory and the early Colonial era, scholars have elaborated and documented the "verticality" model of land use among highland groups (e.g., Brush 1977, Pease 1981, Lehman 1982, Masuda et al. 1985). In its simplest form, this model posits that a resource-holding social group, normally an *ayllu*, attempts to distribute its population across as wide a range of environmental zones as possible. Optimally, a highland community or *ayllu* will situate its principal settlement at an ecotone between two productive zones, such as the maize and potato-growing zones (see Ortiz de Zúñiga 1967, 1972). Smaller settlements, sometimes only temporarily occupied, will be established in pastoral grasslands and in warmer lands. The members of the extended *ayllu* or community can then pool their output, to be shared among the population as a whole, along lines of kin or political affiliation. This approach to resource use is encouraged by the rugged Andean terrain, in which distinct micro-environmental zones are found in close proximity to one another. The overall intent of this resource procurement strategy is to retain access to key resources within the corporate group, so that its self-sufficiency can be maintained (Murra 1972). It may be noted that this practice is also consonant with a strategy intended to minimize risk by diversifying resource use.

As widespread as the principles of the verticality model may have been, putting them into action was another issue. Where and how practices regularly diverged from or conformed to the model should provide some insight into the criteria underlying economic decision-making at the *ayllu* and community level. Land ownership patterns recorded in 1591 among the Yanque-Collaguas, a subgroup of the larger Collagua ethnic group, illustrate a number of intriguing patterns (Pease 1977).[4] Tomka (1987) shows that the *ayllus'* land ownership configuration was far from the ideal of access to all resource zones. For example, in the town of Callalli, none of the 45 households in its single *ayllu* had any potato lands, whereas 84.4% owned herd animals and 53.3% farmed maize lands. Conversely, in the towns of Yanque and Coporaque, most households held maize and quinoa fields, but ownership of herds and potato and cañihua lands was uncommon (Tomka 1987:18-19); only one of 199 households among three *ayllus* in Yanque, for instance, owned herd animals. In the *reducción* of Tute, situated in a mid-elevation locale, most of the 72 households in the six resident *ayllus* cultivated a wide range of crops, and 41.7% (30) had herd animals.

Tomka concludes from these patterns that *ayllus* living in the same *reducción* tended to exploit the same resources. These resources were generally found in two neighboring production zones, but did not comprise the entire range of productive resources in the region. For households to gain access to the full range of resources, they had to establish some kind of exchange relationships. Documentary evidence from throughout the Andes suggests that this was likely mediated through dyadic or polyadic exchange relationships. Members of one group overproduced the products of their resources with the intent of exchanging the products with other groups. A similar situation may be pointed out for the Huánuco region, in which members of 18 different named ethnic groups tended to exchange the products of their immediate resource zones for goods that could not be produced there (Ortiz de Zúñiga 1967, 1972).

Deustua's analysis (1978) shows an additional status-related distinction within the Collaguas population. The elite households normally held lands in a wider array of pastoral and agricultural zones than did the rest of the populace. They frequently had three or four kinds of lands classed as being productive in maize, quinoa, potatoes, and cañihua, along with pastoral grasslands. A final key point is that exploitation of multiple land-use zones within households depended fundamentally on the composition of the household. As Tomka (1987:24) observes, households with complete nuclear or extended families present had access to a wider range of agricultural crops than did households made up of old, single, or orphaned individuals. He points out that this pattern conforms to Harris's (1978:57) demonstrated relationship between household demographic structure and its ability to practice multi-zonal cultivation in highland Bolivia. Larger households, with a higher proportion of producers to dependents, were capable of exploiting a wider range of resources than those households limited by size or age profile.

We may now turn to the archaeologically-documented case of food production and use in the Upper Mantaro Valley. Hastorf's (1983, 1991,

1993) elegant analyses of crop production, processing, storage, and consumption show that agricultural organization among the Sausa (Xauxa) combined environmental possibilities with political demands and cultural preferences. The patterning exhibited in the botanical remains recovered from residential contexts is too complex to summarize here, but I would like to draw attention to several features. In her analysis, Hastorf (1991) assessed crop production and consumption in three successive periods: Wanka I, II, and III. The first period was one of relatively decentralized regional organization, with the populace distributed in small settlements. In Wanka II, the population aggregated in a series of large sites, situated and constructed defensively. Under Inka rule, in Wanka III, the population again moved down to lower elevations in many smaller settlements. During the first and third periods, the population was settled principally at elevations where maize cultivation was possible nearby. During Wanka II, when the population was concentrated at higher elevations and nearby maize production was usually untenable, tubers would be expected to have been the principal crops grown near the settlements.

Hastorf (1991) shows that the crops recovered from residential contexts in all three periods generally conform to the mixes expected from an optimal use of lands found near (<4 km from) the sites, with some telling divergences. As might be expected, the high-elevation Wanka II settlements favored production of potatoes more than did either the Wanka I or III communities. Similarly, both a center (Hatunmarca) and a town (Umpamalca) with better access to maize lands in Wanka II yielded more maize in the household botanical remains than did another center (Tunanmarca). Access to the preferred crop maize was concentrated in elite compounds in all settlements, a pattern not so clearly marked in the distributions of potatoes, quinoa, and legumes. Significant differences in the per cent presence of maize cobs and kernels at different sites suggest that communities were exchanging foodstuffs.

As the population moved down from the high elevation sites in Wanka II to valley and flank sites in Wanka III, maize and quinoa production was greater than would have been anticipated and, potato production dropped more than expected. Maize ubiquity (percent presence) figures trend from 40% (Wanka I), to 25% (II), to 70% (III) (Hastorf 1991:275). Although part of this progression is attributable to local land use, the difference between the Wanka I and III ubiquities suggests an intensified use of maize under Inka rule. The emphasis on maize in Wanka III is also directly visible in consumption patterns, through analysis of stable isotopes in bone collagen (see DeNiro and Hastorf 1985). At the same time, several lines of evidence indicate that the differences between the elite and commoner members of subject communities was diminishing. Among the key changes were reduction in access to metal wealth among the elites, and radical increases in the amount of camelid meat and maize in commoner households (Sandefur 1988, Costin and Earle 1989). Taking into account that the Inkas were intervening in household activities in other realms -- e.g., doubling spinning activities (Costin 1984) -- Hastorf suggests that the accent on maize under the Inkas may reflect the intervention of the state in household production, not simply preferences on the part of the residents.

Together, the ethnohistorical and archaeological cases illustrate that land use did not conform well to the fully elaborated vertical model, but that multiple concerns affected subsistence production and consumption. In both situations, local populations (*ayllus* or communities) diversified their production in adjacent environmental zones, but tended to exploit lands close to the main community. This pattern conforms to an overall strategy that took into account both labor input and risk. However, both Hastorf's data and the Collaguas land ownership patterns underscore that the elites had preferential access to more prestigious and a wider variety of foods, especially maize. This pattern is reinforced in the Upper Mantaro by Sandefur's (1988) faunal analyses, which show that the elites of both Wanka II and III had preferred access to the better cuts of meat and to labor-intensive forms of preparation. This evidence indicates clearly that political processes played a role in subsistence decision-making among central Andean populations both before Inka rule and after it.

*The imposition of agricultural production for the Inka state*

With the advent of Inka control in new territories, state personnel set about ensuring production of foodstuffs to sustain state personnel. Generally speaking, this was established by setting off lands for state production, on which the local populace was required to render labor service, as we have already seen in the Huánuco visita. These lands seem often to have been located around state administrative centers, but could also be established in particularly favorable agricultural locations, such as the fertile valleys of Abancay and Cochabamba (Wachtel 1982, La Lone and La Lone 1987). The standard sources often emphasize two points concerning the use of state lands and the labor allocated to their cultivation. First, state and state religion lands were cultivated by the subject populace before they were allowed to turn to their own lands (e.g., Polo 1916 [1571]:58-60). Second, the state emphasized the production of maize on its lands to feed state personnel, and especially to provide chicha to soldiers (e.g., Polo in Wachtel 1982). Both points need to be reconsidered.

The rendering of labor service to state farming likely posed labor scheduling dilemmas for the participating households. Mitchell (1980) points out that the altitudinal compression of the Andean landscape obliges farmers to cultivate their crops in a sequence dictated largely by the choice of crop, the agricultural cycle, and location of the fields, especially with respect to elevation. To these factors may be added access to irrigation and micro-environmental variation in rainfall and frost patterns (see Hastorf 1983). As a consequence of the environmental restrictions on agricultural practices, it would have been a practical impossibility for farmers to work all state lands before cultivating their own crops. The labor sequence reported in the chronicles is thus likely elite ideology.

The temporal interdigitation of state and subject needs for labor has several ramifications for the scheduling of labor in the subject populace. Because crops can only be planted and harvested during short windows of opportunity, households likely experienced pressure on labor during these key points of the agricultural cycle. An additional strain arose from the periodic reassessments of state needs (Cobo 1979 [1656]:234), which could not always be predicted by the personnel who were assigned to render labor service. An example of such stresses can be found in the burdensome call to military service that could be applied with little warning. The levies for Wayna Qhapaq's two decades of military action in the northern Andes were surely disruptive, even if they were announced prior to the actual mobilization and even if the donor communities carried on the agricultural and other duties of the soldier's families. During the latter part of Wayna Qhapaq's reign (1493-1526), peoples collectively called the Chiriguanos took advantage of the emperor's long-term preoccupation with the north to invade the southeastern frontier. The sovereign dispatched the general Yasca to mobilize armies from Cuzco and points south in a successful campaign to reassert imperial control (e.g., Cieza de León 1967 [1553]:ch. 63, pp. 211-12). Rapid mobilizations such as these had the potential to tax severely the scheduling of household labor.

Aside from resistance to imperial service, we may expect several possible consequences of such bottlenecks. One likely possibility is that farmers alternated labor devoted to state and personal tasks according to the sequential demands of the complex agricultural cycles (Mitchell 1980). Alternatively, they may have divided tasks among household members. Another possibility is that the subject households manipulated their composition to increase their size and thus reduce the per capita obligation to the state. Possible means of accomplishing this end include having larger families and delaying marriage or taking up new residence. Although the data on this subject are scant, early witnesses from the Upper Mantaro stated that their populations increased under the Inkas (Toledo 1940 [1570]). Archaeologically, we may note that the area of residential compounds in the Late Horizon settlements increased by a factor of almost two under Inka rule (Earle et al. 1987). Although part of this increase may be attributed to a shift of the populace to lower-elevation, less-constricted locales, the increased size of both compounds and residential structures conforms to the notion that household size grew under imperial rule. Commoner households may also have modified the composition of their crop mix, to reduce labor demands or temporal conflicts in agricultural tasks.[5] Finally, the households may have altered their labor exchanges to ensure that their lands were tended. At present, I am unaware of specific information that could be used to assess this possibility.

The state's reliance on corvée for much of its production thus shifted the parameters of agricultural decision-making in the subject populace. State agricultural supervisors, recognizing the problems that ensued, may have seen it to be in their interest to professionalize state farming more fully. Almost 40 years ago, Murra (1980a [1956]) drew attention to the Inkas' shift away from corvée to state farms. By establishing state farms staffed by dedicated farmers, whose lands lay amidst the state fields, the state could partially reduce the scheduling conflicts inherent in using corvée as the principal labor source by minimizing travel time from state to private lands. However, compliance may have been the key advantage of creating farming cadres. Although the evidence for specific state farms remains limited, it is suggestive of radical changes in the political economy.

Throughout the empire, the Inkas appropriated and intensified lands around major state installations and other designated areas. The most notable state farms lay in Cochabamba, Bolivia, where the emperor Wayna Qhapaq ordered virtually all native residents removed from the valley. Fourteen thousand agricultural workers were then brought in to work the lands, both as permanent colonists and as corvée laborers (Wachtel 1982). The food, said to be maize, that was produced in the valley was stored in 2500 storehouses at Cotapachi and ultimately transported to Cuzco, reportedly to feed the Inka armies. Other state agricultural areas were set up, at Abancay, Yucay, and Guiaparmarca/Ocomarca, for example (Espinoza 1973; La Lone and La Lone 1987). In each case, the *mitmaqkuna* were given usufruct rights on lands they used to support themselves.

Areas of state farms have also been tentatively identified archaeologically in the Upper Mantaro and Calchaquí Valleys (D'Altroy et al. 1990; D'Altroy and Earle 1992). In the Upper Mantaro, the state appears to have appropriated main valley lands, which were underused in the pre-Inka period (Wanka II) because of local conflict. This strategy may have been intended in part to ameliorate resistance to the state occupation. The state farms in the Mantaro are recognizable largely on the basis of three features of the regional archaeological record. Most important is the strong inverse relationship between the distribution of subject settlements and proximity to the regional center, Hatun Xauxa. In essence, virtually the entire subject population resided at least five kilometers away from the center. Within this radius are found 85% of the region's immense state storage facilities (in terms of volume), but only 15% of the region's population. On the east side of the valley, an especially productive zone, a string of storage facilities extends for about 5 km along a hillcrest, where no subject population was settled. At least two sites within the low population density zone yielded extremely high densities of hoes, thought to be used for maize cultivation (Russell 1988), but little to no evidence of the other kinds of household production that typified Wanka II and III sites elsewhere in the region (e.g., spindle whorls, lithics, pottery wasters, bone weaving tools).

In the Calchaquí Valley, although the scale of agricultural production was markedly lower than that in the Mantaro, it may be the case that production was comparable with respect to the region's productivity. In the north end of the valley, the state appears to have developed agricultural fields within the strip of Inka settlements running from Cortaderas north to Tastil. The identification of state farms is based on the association of Inka sites with land improvements, notably long irrigation canals on either side of the Río Portrero drainage, and the lack of associated indigenous santamariana settlements. Current studies by C. Hastorf should provide more detailed insight into these field systems in the near future. Similarly, ongoing research by M. Calderari in the mid-valley may provide information on state agricultural production in that area.

The organization of state agricultural production was fundamentally different in the two regions, both in scale and purposes. The agricultural productivity of the Mantaro formed a linchpin in the empire-wide infrastructure. Agriculture there was intended to produce a huge surplus of food to sustain traveling armies and a large local labor force working for the state. The surplus was stored in over 3000 storehouses. These *qollqa* were distributed throughout the valley, but about half were concentrated within one kilometer of the provincial center of Hatun Xauxa. In contrast, the Calchaquí production was likely intended for consumption in activities that were more locally and temporally focused. The number of storehouses at Inka settlements in the region probably numbers in the low hundreds. Even Ambrosetti's (1907-08) work at La Paya found no more than a few dozen storehouses at this main mid-valley site. At the Inka settlements of Cortaderas and Potrero de Payogasta in the northern end of the valley, structures associated with state storage number fewer than 100 between them.

As a consequence of the differing goals in the two regions, the state personnel charged with overseeing food production for the state likely followed different decision-making criteria. In the Mantaro Valley, the central intent seems to have been to maximize food production. In this valley, huge quantities of food were needed to sustain traveling armies and a large local labor force working for the state. The location of state lands in a prime maize-growing area and the concentration of stone hoes in settlements adjacent to the main storage facilities suggests that the Inkas may, indeed, have focused on production of the preferred crop. Some evidence suggests, however, that the mix of crops produced may have more closely approximated a stable agricultural cycle than an inordinate emphasis on the ritually important maize. The six storehouses test excavated by UMARP yielded 14 different taxa, covering the full range of highland staple crops. Quinoa, not maize, was the predominant taxon recovered (D'Altroy and Hastorf 1984: Table 2). If the crops recovered were representative, at least in a qualitative sense, of the crops grown on state lands, then agricultural managers were taking broad advantage of the locally varied environment, perhaps practicing crop mixing as part of their agricultural strategies. Without more data, it is difficult to sustain this argument. However, the botanical remains recovered from Morris's (1967) excavations in the storehouses at Huánuco Pampa also conform well to the kinds of crops that are best grown locally. Most of the remains recovered were tubers (especially potatoes), and maize was present in much lower quantities.

In the Calchaquí, the scale of production was substantially lower, but agriculture was clearly intensified through important land improvements. As noted above, the fields north of Cortaderas were irrigated with water drawn from the Río Potrero drainage in a series of canals that lined both sides of the narrow valley. The Calchaquí production was likely intended for consumption in activities that were more locally and temporally focused. As just noted, the storage facilities in the southern part of the empire are far more limited than those from the Mantaro region or from Cochabamba, Bolivia, to the north. Future excavations of the Calchaquí storehouses, revealing the crops stored by the state, will tell us more of the agricultural strategies of state managers in the southern part of the empire.

In the Upper Mantaro, the northern Calchaquí, and Huánuco Pampa, the Inkas appear to have appropriated much of their land from areas that were less intensively used, if at all, during the immediately preceding period. This approach must have ameliorated the impact on the agricultural productivity of the local populace and taken some of the sting out of being exploited for labor and other resources. Elsewhere (e.g., Cochabamba, the mid-valley Calchaquí, and Vilcas Waman), the Inkas displaced indigenous populations and supplanted them with colonists (see Lorandi and Boixadós 1987-88). The strategies employed within the two study regions discussed here thus include a reasonable, although partial, sample of the range of approaches used by the state to support its personnel and projects.

*Landed estates*

A discussion of land use under Inka rule should not pass without at least a mention of landed estates. These estates and, more generally, elite resources provide an intriguing contrast to the institutionally held state resources and those of the general populace. The best known of the estates were around Cuzco, in Chucuito and the Yucay Valley (Rostworowski 1962, 1988:243-44; Murra 1978). The development of private manors, especially for the ten royal *panacas* of Cuzco, reflected trends both to transform prime lands into private landholdings and to commandeer personnel for private use.

These lands appear to have been managed like both public and private resources. The Toledan inspections in the Cuzco region indicate that farmers were installed to take care of the royalty's lands, from the emperor Pachacutec forward (Levillier 1940). The demand for productivity in these private resources lay in three related areas: maintenance of the deceased emperor, subsistence support of his descendants, and underwriting provincial elites and their political activities. Thus, the uses of this production mingled public and private domains, since much was consumed in public activities and in support of retainer personnel. This practice may have promoted both high labor input and an interest in risk minimization, in part through diversification of lands in multiple zones. As more work is conducted on landed estates, it will be intriguing to try to determine how labor resources were allocated and land was managed.

Land grants to elites in the vicinity of Quito provide a counterpoint to the holdings of the ethnic Inka nobility (Salomon 1986). The Quiteñan farmlands were apparently intended to draw the local elites into the imperial sphere of control, but they seem to have balked at living on their new lands, perhaps because the private gain demanded too heavy a political concession to the state. Under Inka rule in the Upper Mantaro, Xauxa and Wanka elites held private lands on the eastern slopes used to produce coca and peppers (Vega 1965; Espinoza Soriano 1971). Similarly, the Lupaqa elites of the Lake Titicaca region had direct access to coastal and other resources under Inka dominion (Murra 1972). The genesis of these kinds of resources dedicated to elites may have antedated Tawantinsuyu, but the granting or confirmation of such perquisites suggests the formation of a landed class that was increasingly becoming separated from its constituency.

## Craft Production

The organization of craft production within the Inka empire assumed two forms. First, the general populace, by and large, rendered only its labor through the rotating corvée system either at home communities or at state centers. An example of a craft activity that resulted in intensified household production for state use is the spinning of yarn and the subsequent weaving of rough cloth (*awasqa*) by women. Each family was given wool from state herds annually and was required to weave cloth from it; thus the household gave only its labor, the materials having been supplied to it. Analogous directives were given to peasants to collect undomesticated biota, such as honey and feathers, and render them to the Inkas (Rowe 1946; Murra 1975, 1980a). The state economy thus relied heavily on the productive capacities of the household.

The second form of state production lay in the enclaves of specialist producers, or *mitmaqkuna*. These were colonists forcibly removed from their home locales and resettled in new locations, to work on behalf of the state. Frequently, entire communities were moved. Women (*aqllakuna*) similarly were installed in sequestered quarters in state installations to produce both cloth and chicha for state consumption. The products made by the general producers and the attached specialists were then used by state personnel or distributed by the state through ceremonial largess to favored elites or to individuals who had distinguished themselves in service to the state, such as through military valor.

The creation of specialized enclaves of artisans built upon previous forms of economic production for Andean elites. Before the Inka empire, attached specialists were apparently present in the Moche, Wari, and Chimu states, many concentrated within major urban centers (e.g., Topic 1982, Isbell and McEwan 1991, Russell 1991). Under Inka rule, craft enclaves were developed both within imperial settlements, such as the provincial centers, and at communities established for specific purposes of producing goods for the state. Analyses of the inspections from Huánuco (Helmer 1955-56; Ortiz de Zúñiga 1967, 1972) and Chucuito (Diez de San Miguel 1964) show that the Inkas also required specialized production of certain kinds of commodities at peasant communities especially well-situated with respect to the appropriate natural resources. In the Huánuco region, for example, the distribution of artisans among Chupachu and Queros villages shows that settlements in particular locations specialized in the production of such goods as sandals, rope, or ceramics (see Levine 1987). Thus, while labor assignments were ostensibly to be made on the basis of population, the state clearly took into account environmental variations in making its assignments. Given this situation, in which the state took targeted advantage of existing artisans, artisanal communities, and natural resources, but also created a new array of distinctive specialist producers, it will be useful to try to sort out some of the principles underlying Inka strategies.

*Decision-making in craft production*

In assessing Inka and subject craft production, we need to keep in mind the impacts of both producer concerns and consumer demands, as well as technological and environmental factors. Some analysts suggest that methodological priority should be assigned to the environmental and technological elements of craft production, and that sociopolitical concerns be treated secondarily (e.g., Arnold 1985:19, Rice 1987). But in a political economy in which the means of production are subordinate to consumer interests, this approach may mislead us. Where the state requisitioned all necessary resources and forcibly resettled producers, it makes sense to think simultaneously of environmental, technological, and sociopolitical concerns.

It is possible to distinguish several kinds of demand populations that are pertinent to craft production within an empire assimilating socioeconomic groups of varying complexities (see Brumfiel and Earle 1987, Costin 1990). Among these are, first, a production system driven by relations of household or kin-related consumption, such as that of the simple, contemporary Shipibo-Conibo communities of the Peruvian jungles (DeBoer and Lathrap 1979, DeBoer and Moore 1982). A variant of this is a local household or community production system driven by the demands of communities that do not have direct access to important, localized resources. This situation, which entailed a regional trading network without a market-based economy, apparently was involved in the manufacture and distribution of lithic tools in the Upper Mantaro in late prehistory (Russell 1988). A second form may be found in local responses to a supply and demand market-based economy, such as in the Mediterranean region under Roman rule (Garnsey and Saller 1987). A third alternative consists of production for direct tribute, such as occurred with certain goods under Aztec rule, including cotton cloth and cacao (Berdan 1975, Brumfiel 1987). A fourth relationship results when craft goods are produced on consignment, as was sometimes the case for potters supplying the Roman army and other state personnel (Peacock 1987); this may be seen as a large-scale example of attached specialization. A related fifth situation occurs where a state political economy organizes and controls the artisans as its own workers, such as the specialist *mitmaqkuna* under Inka rule (e.g., Espinoza 1973, 1975, 1987), whose production La Lone (1982) has aptly termed *supply on command*, in contrast to supply and demand. Although not remotely exhaustive of the range of craft organizations (excluding, for example, itinerants, guilds, modern industry), this list probably covers most kinds of artisanal activity under Inka rule.

A main reason for distinguishing these producer-consumer relationships is that sound strategies of production will vary, depending on both consumer demands and the degree of producer autonomy. Arnold's (1985) model of ceramic ecology, for example, underscores a view of specialist potters as agriculturally marginal groups that focus their production strategies on risk minimization. This differs from a strategy that optimizes labor input and economic output, employed by the contemporary potters of Quiche in the Upper Mantaro, as described by Hagstrum (1988, n.d.). Both kinds of decision-making criteria contrast markedly with the principles underlying production directly for the Inka state, where maximization of output, control of distribution, or quality of the product likely drove organizational decisions.

Production for a state economy that has an expansive appetite for products creates different pressures on the producing system than does production for barter or market exchange in a domestic economy. Although the artisans supplying local economies may be able to expand production, it may not be in their interests to do so. Under Inka rule, many were forced to increase their output. What happened when household or community producers were required to produce more for the state than they would if producing for a domestic economy? What happened when producers who traditionally tried to minimize risk or labor input were forced to shift toward maximizing output? How did this affect labor scheduling, or the balance between craft and the agricultural pursuits that most state artisans still likely maintained?

In evaluating the kinds of decisions that went into developing specialized groups of ceramic artisans, it is worthwhile drawing attention to a characteristic of intensification of craft production that partially distinguishes it from agricultural production. Since Boserup's (1965) seminal work, it is a truism in anthropology that intensification of agricultural production tends to produce a decreasing return on investment, evaluated in terms of energy. In contrast, intensification of craft production, through specialization, may provide an increasing yield of output to input of labor up to the point where raw materials become increasingly difficult to procure (see, for example, Rice 1987). This gain may be a consequence of more efficient use of labor through economies of scale, a decrease in competition over raw materials, or technological advances. The intensification of craft production through specialization may therefore have had substantially different effects on the productivity of craft and farm workers producing for the state. How noticeable this difference would have been in the short term is unclear, but it may have been one inducement for the Inkas to shift more toward specialized, *mitmaqkuna* enclaves over the course of the empire.

*Craft production for the Inka state*

The formation of craft enclaves paralleled the establishment of state farms (see Murra 1980a); both represented an effort by the state to establish an economy that did not rely on the productivity of subject labor mobilized through corvée. Among the best-documented craft centers were the pottery making settlements at Cajamarca in the north-central Peruvian central highlands (Espinoza 1973); Cupi (also called Hupi or Milliraya), near Lake Titicaca (Murra 1978, Spurling 1987); and El Potrero-Chaquiago, in northwest Argentina (Lorandi 1984, Williams and Lorandi 1986). The first of these contained members of at least 14 ethnic groups, whereas 100 potters were said to be settled at the second. Even if pottery manufacture were a seasonal occupation, the number of objects that these artisans could have produced is impressive. Archaeological evidence of state-supported weaving, in the form of concentrations of spindle whorls in architectural compounds at Inka settlements, has been recovered from Huánuco Pampa (Morris and Thompson 1985:91-2) and El Potrero-Chaquiago (Williams 1983, Williams and Lorandi 1986). Enclaves of state weavers have also been documented at Lamay, near Cuzco, where a Wanka elite reportedly headed 500 households in a colonist community (Toledo 1940 [1572]:71), and at the just-mentioned Cupi, where 1000 weavers were resident (Murra 1978:418). Similarly, artifacts from a lapidary workshop have been recovered from the site of Pucará de Tilcara, in northern Argentina (Krapovickas 1964) and evidence of metal- and mica-working has been found at Potrero de Payogasta (D'Altroy et al. n.d.).

The administrative organization of the artisanal communities suggests an intense state interest in controlling production. The ceramic and textile enclaves at Cupi provide specific insight into state supervision (Espinoza Soriano 1987, Lorandi pers. comm. 1992). According to a court document of 1583, ceramic production was supervised by an estimated 10-12 *hilacatas* or *kurakas*, probably organized according to the decimal system (Espinoza Soriano 1987:256). The documentation also mentions *mayordomos* (foremen) and *contadores* (accountants). The administrator of the *qompikamayoq* (tapestry weavers) of Cupi was an elite from the Qolla *señorío* who divided up the quotas of work assigned to each artisan. It seems likely that a foreman was responsible for 100 potters or weavers and supervised subordinate *kurakas* (Lorandi pers. comm. 1992).

The formation of such enclaves underscores the state's need to produce most goods used by its personnel near the points of consumption. The costs and difficulties of transportation in the rough Andean terrain would have made prohibitively costly the centralized production and distribution of all but the most elite, sumptuary goods. As a corollary, the development of these production enclaves illustrates the regional and even highly localized organization of state economic decision-making.

Given the complexity of craft organization, the patterns recognized in the Upper Mantaro and Calchaquí may clarify our understanding.[6]

**Upper Mantaro Valley.** In the Mantaro, although most craft production seems to have been organized at the household level, specialization for local exchange was already well underway before the Inka conquest. The best evidence to this effect may be found in ceramics, metals, lithic tools, and textiles. Costin's (1986) and Hagstrum's (1989) complementary analyses have shown that the technology of production in the local ceramic tradition has stayed remarkably stable from late pre-Inka to modern times (see also Costin et al. 1989). Costin's study of the range of Late Intermediate Period ceramic types suggests that the andesite wares (Mantaro Base Roja), which were concentrated in the households of Wanka II elites, were probably manufactured in the southern part of the valley for exchange throughout a region covering several hundred square kilometers. For most of the local ceramic types, however, local potters exploited nearby sources of clay. Labor investment in household pottery tended to be relatively low and, with the exception of the andesite wares, there was little evidence of standardized production. This pattern suggests that ceramic production was, by and large, a complement to an agrarian economy in which households of certain communities, favorably situated with respect to key resources, diversified their activities seasonally to reduce economic risk (Hagstrum n.d.).

With the advent of Inka rule, ceramic production changed both from the bottom up and from the top down. Local change correlates well with shifts in the settlement patterns. In Wanka III, the Wanka II center of Tunanmarca and town of Umpamalca were abandoned, and the sources of clay used in much of their pottery were no longer used (Costin et al. 1989:118-19). The clays used in the ceramics produced at the new Wanka

III town of Marca were more similar to those of nearby Wanka II-III Hatunmarca.[7]

Production of pottery for the state in the Mantaro was organized in a radically different manner; here I will summarize only the key points for understanding decision-making (see D'Altroy and Bishop 1990). Trace element analysis suggests that the state sequestered raw materials sources for its exclusive use. The ceramics made in the state style, which included an array of storage jars, cooking, and serving vessels, were more labor-intensive than any of the previous or contemporaneous local styles (Costin 1986, Hagstrum 1986). The state ceramics appear to have been used primarily in two contexts. They appear as virtually the sole style at state installations, such as Hatun Xauxa, where they constituted 98.0% of the diagnostic collection. The Inka pottery, especially flared-rim jars, also largely supplanted the deep basins that elites had used in ceremonial hospitality under autonomous rule; small serving and cooking vessels were also concentrated in the households of the local elites (Costin 1986). The state interest in pottery manufacture thus focused on the political economy, within which control of the product was central to management.

A number of features of the metallurgical industry, which was intensive in copper and silver, provide insight into the organization of production (see Owen n.d.). Metal production seems to have been divided up spatially by task, as evidence for copper smelting was minimal at all sites studied by the Upper Mantaro Project, whereas there are numerous sheet fragments in both Wanka II and III contexts. Under Inka rule, there was a shift from arsenic bronzes to tin bronzes, paralleling the pattern seen throughout the Andes within Tawantinsuyu. This technological change may have resulted from the state's supply of the tin, from sources in the southern Andes. In an associated change, elite access to silver, the principal metallurgical adornment in Wanka II, decreased radically under the Inkas, probably because the state was tapping off the metal for its own use. Finally, the copper objects produced under Inka dominion shifted from decorative (e.g., disks) toward utilitarian (e.g., tweezers, pins, needles) objects.

With respect to lithics, households in both periods made a wide array of casual flake tools. However, most of the prismatic blade tools, employed in harvesting grasses, were produced in the Wanka II town of Umpamalca or in Wanka III Hatunmarca (Russell 1988). In each period these sites were the principal settlements near the major chert quarry at Pomacancha, suggesting opportunistic activity comparable to that found in the local ceramic industry. Finally, with respect to textile production, Costin (1984) has shown that the density of spindle whorls in Wanka III households was twice that of Wanka II. This difference appears to correlate directly with the state directive in which subject women regularly wove rough cloth (*awasqa*) in their households, using state-supplied wool.

The patterns of craft production in the Upper Mantaro before and under Inka rule draw our attention to several features of decision-making within the subject and state economies. Craft production before Inka rule, where specialized, seems to have been organized along community lines. Those settlements that had close access to sources of raw materials, whether lithic or ceramic, tended to produce goods that were distributed through local exchange networks. With Inka rule, the state intervened only selectively in artisanal activities, notably in crafts that were part of the political economy: metals, prestige ceramics, and textiles. The production of lithic tools, which were essential to agrarian activities, seems to have been utterly ignored by the state. It is intriguing to note in this context that the state center, Hatun Xauxa, was virtually devoid of lithics, whether raw materials, tools, or by-products of manufacture. Similarly, none of the lists of labor assignments described above includes lithic tool production, although the category of lapidary worker may have encompassed this activity. This overall pattern suggests that craft specialization of autochthonous origin among subject communities was treated as part of an overall domestic economy, in which diversification, opportunistic craft production, and perhaps risk reduction were important criteria in organization. In contrast, state craft production was much more focused on materials useful in the political economy, and seems to have emphasized intensification, and control over the quality and distribution of the products.

**The Calchaquí Valley.** Archaeological evidence from northwest Argentina shows that state and subject craft production were integrated in complex ways. Although our work is still in its incipient stages, three features stand out. First, the evidence for craft activities is far more abundant than are the finished products, at least in the residential, plaza, and midden contexts excavated to date. Second, craft production was divided into sets of tasks that were executed at different locations. Third, the state relied far more heavily on products made in local styles than it did in the Mantaro, even in its most impressive administrative facilities. Let me summarize the data on each point briefly.

Apart from ceramics, the craft objects most frequently recovered were beads and other items of personal decoration. Earle's ongoing analysis of these materials shows that they are made of a variety of materials, usually marine shell, but also land snail, stone (especially malachite), bone, and human teeth. In addition, mica sheets were cut into larger disks and simple geometric forms that were perforated, presumably to be sewn onto clothing.

Metal objects were infrequently recovered, all from Potrero de Payogasta and none from the local settlement of Valdéz, which nonetheless yielded abundant evidence for copper production. The metal objects included a small silver clip, gold sheet, and copper scraps.

In contrast to the comparative rarity of finished metal, shell, and mica items in our excavations, P.A.C. (the Proyecto Arqueológico Calchaquí) recovered abundant evidence for their manufacture (Earle n.d.; D'Altroy et al. n.d.). Evidence for metallurgy includes raw materials (copper oxide ores), by-products (e.g., slag, scrap), features (e.g., hearths), and tools (e.g., ceramic crucibles and molds) (E. Howe, M. Hagstrum, pers. comm. 1992). Evidence for shell manufacturing consists largely of manufacturing by-products (e.g., fragments, occasionally with cutting marks, and unfinished beads). Mica manufacture is shown by the concentrations of raw materials, debris, and partially finished disks and pendants broken during manufacture. The distribution of these materials shows that craftwork differed markedly between the state (Potrero de Payogasta) and subject (Valdéz) settlements that we studied. As can be seen in Figure 4, the ceramic crucibles and ore that were used in copper smelting were heavily concentrated in Valdéz (Hagstrum 1992). Lithic production was also high at this site, but evidence for shell- and mica-working was limited. At Potrero de Payogasta, the inverse appears to have been the case. Relatively little evidence for copper ore reduction was encountered, but fine craft working of finished sheet metal, shell, mica, stone was concentrated in a few residential compounds near the most elite households and some distance away from the civic-ceremonial areas (Earle n.d.).[8]

The relative lack of finished metal and lapidary objects, coupled with abundant evidence for their production, is consonant with the chroniclers' explanation of the state's occupation of the south Andes. The ubiquity of mining and processing settlements in northern Chile and Argentina, coupled with a relative lack of large state installations, has suggested to numerous authors that gaining access to mineral resources was the principal rationale for the Inka conquest (e.g., González 1983, Raffino 1983). However, not all of the craft objects produced in the Calchaquí settlements were intended for export. For example, Ambrosetti's excavation of 202 late prehistoric burials at Puerta de La Paya yielded hundreds of imperial Inka-style ceramics, along with bead strings, and 35 metal objects, mostly tin bronze axes, awls, tweezers, and tumis; only one silver and two gold objects were recovered (González 1979).

With respect to ceramics, the production and use of different styles in the Calchaquí Valley under Inka rule is a daunting problem, given the extraordinary array of archaeological types (Calderari and Williams 1991).

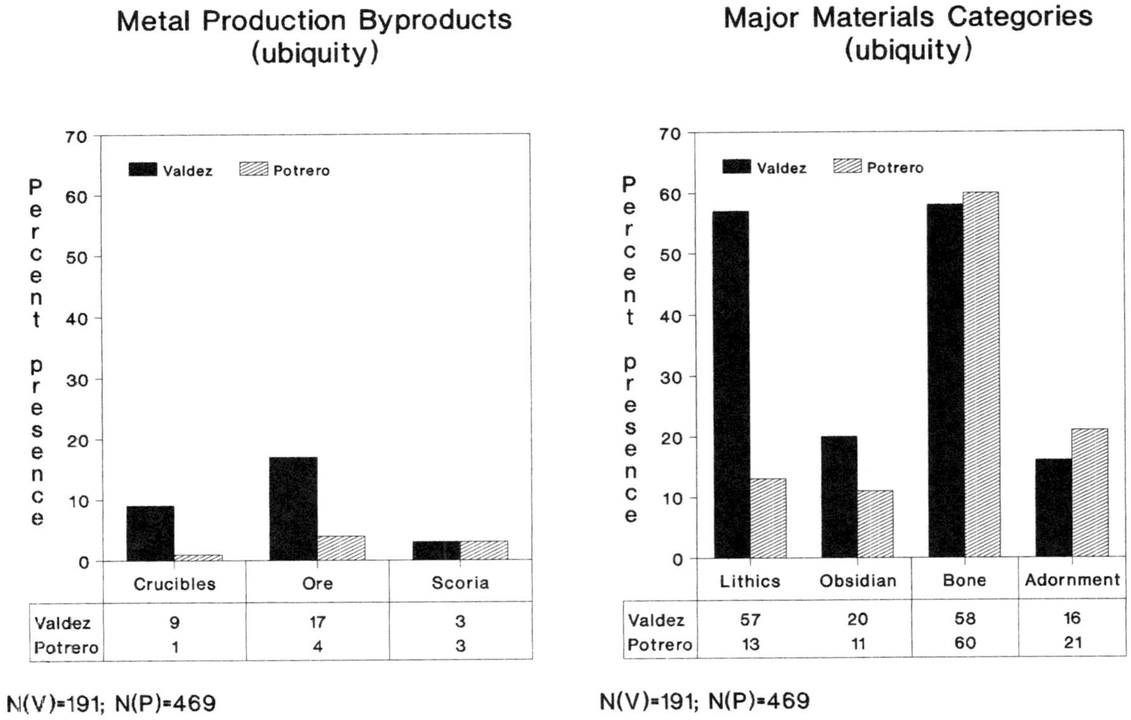

## Metal Production Byproducts
(ubiquity)

|  | Crucibles | Ore | Scoria |
|---|---|---|---|
| Valdez | 9 | 17 | 3 |
| Potrero | 1 | 4 | 3 |

N(V)=191; N(P)=469

## Major Materials Categories
(ubiquity)

|  | Lithics | Obsidian | Bone | Adornment |
|---|---|---|---|---|
| Valdez | 57 | 20 | 58 | 16 |
| Potrero | 13 | 11 | 60 | 21 |

N(V)=191; N(P)=469

Figure 4. Left: the presence of by-products of metal manufacture, as a percentage of excavated proveniences. Right: the presence of the principal kinds of non-ceramic artifacts, as a percentage of excavated proveniences.

Perhaps the most important point for the present analysis is that the proportion of pottery in the Inka state style at Potrero de Payogasta was low, only about 5% of our entire excavated collection (Hagstrum and Calderari, 1990 pers. comm.), although I should note that both Difrieri (1948) and Hyslop (1984) collected about 40% Inka state style pottery in their more limited work at this site. The low proportion of pottery in the state style at Inka installations was widespread in the southern Andes (e.g., Raffino 1982; Calderari and Williams 1991). Where state pottery has been recovered in high densities, it tends to be in particular situations, notably mortuary, elite residence, and public contexts. As is the case elsewhere in the Andes, Inka style pottery is also found in low proportions at numerous other settlements in the Calchaquí, indicating either limited distribution, probably through political affiliations, or some degree of imitation. A final intriguing piece of ceramic production in the Argentine Andes is the pottery apparently made by *mitmaqkuna* -- in their home styles -- at the state center of El Potrero-Chaquiago (Lorandi 1984).

Together, these limited data suggest that craft production in the Argentine part of the empire was organized somewhat differently than was the case in the central Peruvian sierra. State intervention in artisan production focused upon mineral, metal, and ornamental crafts, but assigned certain basic tasks, such as smelting, to local communities. The dominant use of non-Inka pottery at state installations implies that centers drew heavily from production systems that were not directly organized by the state (D'Altroy, Lorandi, and Williams n.d.). Instead, the possibility is very real that the state actually requisitioned certain products directly -- an approach that contravenes the current understanding of the state economy. This explanation seems to make more sense, however, than one in which the state requisitioned raw materials, required the local potters to make pots in the local styles, and then somehow construed this organization as rendering of labor only.

## Conclusion

The formation of the imperial economy was rife with apparent paradoxes. As Murra (1975, 1980a) has described, the Inkas used subject societies both as models for developing state institutions and as structures for implementing state policy. Similarly, as much as incorporation into the Inka state transformed many aspects of subject societies, the stability of traditional economic formations provided the foundations of the state economy. The neat lines between state and subject, or public and private, were additionally blurred in many areas, as the perquisites granted subject elites were often consumed in public activities. Middle-level regional elites often wore several hats: leaders of the local society, self-interested landed gentry, and state managers. At this level especially, there was ample room for conflicting interests to operate in decision-making processes. I have also suggested that *ayllus* were not quite so self-contained and generalized as some models suggest, but often specialized locally even in the sierra. Elites and commoners shared some interests, but conflicted in others; they also had unequal access to resources, both natural and human. A central point of this paper has therefore been that understanding the Inka economy requires addressing a range of different issues simultaneously.

To close, it will be useful to hazard some thoughts concerning decision-making at the levels of policy, middle-level management, and implementation. Clearly, in most of the empire the highest level concerned only the Inka state itself. Although we have only scattered evidence, some of the key elements of economic policy can be inferred. From the state's perspective, two features were probably most relevant in organizing the economy: the nature and amount of the output itself and ensuring compliance in labor investment. Labor input (costs) per se may have been less important in the equation, since many of the costs of intensified production were largely borne by non-state personnel, at least for much of the empire's duration. One central feature of state policy thus followed the standard expectation -- intensification of production through labor investments by the general populace. At some point, however, private labor apparently was perceived as inadequate for state needs. The development of labor cadres appears to have stemmed from joined concerns: the gains in compliance, security, efficiency through scale, and quality control found in specialized production.

A blanket policy was not applied evenly throughout the empire, however. For example, the predominant use of pottery made in local styles in state settlements throughout the southern Andes implies that there was a graded or perhaps staged process entailed in labor investment in state enterprises. In this immense region, the largest of the four quarters of the empire, infrastructural construction, agricultural production, and extraction of mineral wealth took precedence over provisioning of state personnel with at least some of the material goods emblematic of the state's presence. Given that radiocarbon dates regularly assign a century or so to imperial architectural construction in Argentina, we cannot ascribe this pattern simply to a short Inka reign.

The two lower levels of decision-making exhibit a remarkable degree of accommodation to local circumstances. In the case of the state, it appears that the kinds of labor extracted from the local populace coupled targeting of regional environmental variations with overall state goals. That little of the labor extracted from the Chupachu had to do with infrastructural construction or maintenance suggests that the kinds of needs that the state was meeting had shifted more toward service and production of elite goods than building the basics of the state's architecture, at least in the central Andes.

In the private economy, balancing input and output was essential; the subject populace can be seen, quite reasonably, as have emphasized more of an optimizing, risk minimizing, or satisficing approach. On this point, the generalizing documents, which state that the local communities tended to diversify for their sustenance, are concordant with many of the archaeological and documentary data available for the local groups examined in this paper. Two other, less widely described components of the local economies were also important, however. One key feature was the greater diversification of the elite, as opposed to the commoner, resource base. In this regard, economic self-sufficiency can be seen as a function of sociopolitical power. Second, many communities took advantage of specific resources to produce for local exchange systems, for example in lithic and ceramic production in the Upper Mantaro.

The imposition of the state political economy rippled down through the subject economies, all the way to decision-making within the household. The imposition of state rule, especially the exaction of the labor tax, appears to have caused bottlenecks in household labor that probably had to be accommodated at both ends. Thus, although households remained largely self-sufficient, sociopolitical considerations played a role in organizing production and distribution in the private sphere.

In closing, I would like to emphasize the exploratory nature of this paper. Many of the data described here have been examined elsewhere, often in the context of local processes or as examples of the state economy in action. It is my hope that, by focusing on the themes of general process and Andean specifics in a systematic way, this work will stimulate discussion that will advance our understanding of both state economics in general and the economy of the Inka empire in particular.

## Acknowledgments

I thank Liz Brumfiel for her editorial sagacity and Bruce Mannheim for clarifying some intractable Quechua terms. The Peruvian research reported here was conducted by the Upper Mantaro Archaeological Research Project (UMARP), directed by Timothy Earle, Catherine (LeBlanc) Scott, Christine Hastorf, and myself, from 1982 through 1986. Permission to conduct research was granted by the Instituto Nacional de Cultura, Lima, Peru, and was funded principally by the National Science Foundation (BNS 82-03723), the University of California, Columbia University, the University of Minnesota, and the U.C.L.A. Friends of Archaeology. I thank Dr. Ramiro Matos M., Dr. Jeffrey Parsons, Lic. Jorge Silva S., and Dra. Isabel Flores for their generous assistance in facilitating our work. The Argentine research was conducted under the Proyecto Arqueológico Calchaquí (PAC), directed by (United States) the author, Dr. Christine Hastorf, and Dr. Timothy Earle, and by (Argentina) Dr. Ana María Lorandi and Lic. Verónica Williams of the Universidad de Buenos Aires. Permission to conduct this research was granted by the Ministerio de Educación y Cultura (Pcia. Salta), the Museo Antropológico de Salta, the Museo Arqueológico de Cachi, and the Comisión Nacional de Monumentos y Lugares Históricos. I especially thank Sr. Pío Pablo Díaz for his aid in our studies in the Valle Calchaquí. Funding was provided primarily by the National Science Foundation (BNS 88-05471), Columbia University, the University of California, the University of Minnesota, and the Universidad de Buenos Aires. I thank all of my colleagues for sharing their information and insights; any misuse to which they have been put is my responsibility.

## Notes

1. Standard readings of the documentary sources on Inka chronology suggest that the Upper Mantaro was conquered about AD 1460 and northwest Argentina a decade or two later (e.g., Rowe 1946, Tarragó 1978). However, accumulating radiocarbon data point to occupations in both regions that may have begun by AD 1400 or soon thereafter (Bauer, Williams, and D'Altroy in prep.). In the sweep of prehistory, half a century is a brief interval, but its addition to the Inka era doubles the period in which transformations occurred or traditional forms persisted -- a point to keep in mind when assessing the impact of Inka rule on subject communities.

2. An army of this size was present at the time of the Spanish invasion in 1533 (Sancho de la Hoz 1917 [1532-33]).

3. As elegant an organization as the Huánuco visita's slice of time provides us, it needs to be emphasized that the decimal system was effectively applied only in the central part of the empire, where indigenous sociopolitical systems most closely resembled those of the Inkas themselves. Decimal administration may have been marginally important in Ecuador and perhaps absent altogether in much of Bolivia, northern Chile and Argentina. If this was the case, other administrative means must have been used to mobilize labor, but at present, we do not have much written evidence to this end.

4. In assessing this information, we have to keep in mind that almost 70 years had passed since the Spanish conquest and that the indigenous communities had been resettled into ten Toledan *reducciones*, or forced, nucleated settlements situated where the colonial authorities could govern more effectively.

5. Hastorf's (1991) archaeobotanical data show that Xauxa crop mixes did shift toward maize production under Inka rule, but we can not yet specify if changing labor demands or scheduling requirements were implicated in this shift.

6. In this analysis, as in the foregoing, I want to emphasize that I am drawing on the research of my colleagues -- especially Milena Calderari, Cathy Costin, Timothy Earle, Melissa Hagstrum, and Verónica Williams -- and thank them for sharing their information.

7. This pattern of mixed agrarian and craft production suggests a continuing strategy of localized exploitation of raw material sources for part-time production and local exchange. If we refer back for a moment to the Collaguas inspection, we find a parallel circumstance. In the reducción of Tisco-Hanansaya, every one of the 88 households in the ayllus of Collana Malco and Yuamasca held lands, whereas only 11 of the 23 households in Cupi held lands (Tomka 1987: Table 7.0). In contrast, Cupi had the highest proportion of herd-owning households (95.7%, against 73.3% for Collana Malco and 84.6% for Yuamasca). Given that Cupi means *potter*, it appears that this ayllu may have been specialized in ceramic production and herding, with a lesser emphasis on cultivation. Whether Cupi's posited ceramic production was a consequence of autonomous choice or state emphasis is not clear.

8. It should be kept in mind that the contexts excavated at Valdéz more heavily favored middens than did Potrero de Payogasta, so some differences can be expected on this account alone.

## References

Alberti, Giorgio, and Enrique Mayer, eds.
    1974   *Reciprocidad e Intercambio en los Andes Peruanos*. Lima: Instituto de Estudios Peruanos.

Ambrosetti, Juan B.
    1907   Exploraciones arqueológicas en la ciudad prehistórica de "La Paya" (Valle Calchaquí, Provincia de Salta). *Revista de la Universidad de Buenos Aires*, 8 (Sección Antropología, 3), 2 vols. Facultad de Filosofía y Letras. Buenos Aires: M. Biedma e hijo.

Arnold, Dean
    1985   *Ceramic Theory and Cultural Process*. Cambridge: Cambridge University Press.

Bauer, Brian S., Verónica I. Williams, and Terence N. D'Altroy
    n.d.   Radiocarbon Dates and the Expansion of the Inca Empire. (in prep).

Berdan, Frances
    1975   *Trade, Tribute, and Market in the Aztec Empire*. Ph.D. dissertation, University of Texas at Austin. Ann Arbor: University Microfilms.

Berthelot, Jean
    1986   The Extraction of Precious Metals at the Time of the Inka. In J.V. Murra, N. Wachtel, and J. Revel, eds., *Anthropological History of Andean Polities*, pp. 69-88. Cambridge: Cambridge University Press.

Boserup, Ester
    1965   *The Conditions of Agricultural Growth*. Chicago: Aldine.

Brumfiel, Elizabeth M.
    1987   Elite and Utilitarian Crafts in the Aztec State. In E.M. Brumfiel and T.K. Earle, eds., *Specialization, Exchange, and Complex Societies*, pp.102-18. Cambridge: Cambridge University Press.

Brumfiel, Elizabeth M. and Timothy K. Earle
    1987   Specialization, Exchange, and Complex Societies: An Introduction. In E.M. Brumfiel and T.K. Earle, eds., *Specialization, Exchange, and Complex Societies*, pp.1-9. Cambridge: Cambridge University Press.

Brush, Stephen B.
   1976a  Man's Use of an Andean Ecosystem. *Human Ecology* 4(2):14766.
   1977  *Mountain, Field, and Family: The Economy and Human Ecology of an Andean Valley*. Philadelphia: University of Pennsylvania Press.

Calderari, Milena, and Verónica Williams
   1991  Re-evaluación de los Estilos Cerámicos Incaicos en el Noroeste Argentino. *Comechingonia* Año 9. N° esp., 73-95. Córdoba

Cieza de León, Pedro de
   1967 [1553]  *La Crónica del Perú. Segunda Parte*. Lima: Instituto de Estudios Peruanos.

Cobo, Bernabé
   1979 [1653]  *History of the Inca Empire*, Roland Hamilton, transl. Austin: University of Texas Press.

Costin, Cathy L.
   1984  The Organization and Intensity of Spinning and Cloth Production among the Late Prehispaanic Huanca. Paper presented at the 24th Annual Meeting of the Institute for Andean Studies, Berkeley, California.
   1986  *From Chiefdom to Empire State: Ceramic Economy among the Prehispanic Wanka of Highland Peru*. Ph.D. dissertation, University of California, Los Angeles. Ann Arbor: University Microfilms.
   1991  Craft Specialization: Issues in Defining, Documenting, and Explaining the Organization of Production. In M.B. Schiffer, ed., *Archaeological Method and Theory*, vol. 3, pp. 1-56. Tucson: University of Arizona Press.

Costin, Cathy L., and Timothy K. Earle
   1989  Status Distinction and Legitimation of Power as Reflected in Changing Patterns of Consumption in Late Prehispanic Peru. *American Antiquity* 54:691-714.

Costin, Cathy L., Timothy K. Earle, Bruce Owen, and Glenn S. Russell
   1989  Impact of Inka Conquest on Local Technology in the Upper Mantaro Valley, Peru. In S.E. van der Leeuw and R Torrance, eds., *What's New?: A Closer Look at the Process of Innovation*, pp.107-39. London: Unwin and Allen.

D'Altroy, Terence N.
   1987  Transitions in Power: Centralization of Wanka Political Organization under Inka Rule. *Ethnohistory* 34:1:78-102.

1992 *Provincial Power in the Inka Empire.* Washington, DC: Smithsonian Institution Press.

D'Altroy, Terence N., and Ronald A. Bishop
1990 The Provincial Organization of Inka Ceramic Production. *American Antiquity* 55:120-138.

D'Altroy, Terence N., and Timothy K. Earle
1992 Inka Storage Facilities in the Upper Mantaro Valley, Peru. In T.Y. LeVine, ed., *Inka Storage Systems*, pp.176-205. Norman: University of Oklahoma Press.

D'Altroy, Terence N., and Christine A. Hastorf
1984 The Distribution and Contents of Inca State Storehouses in the Xauxa Region of Peru. *American Antiquity* 49:334-349.

D'Altroy, Terence N., Ana María Lorandi, and Verónica I. Williams
n.d. La Producción y el Uso de la Alfarería en la Economía Política Inka. In I. Shimada, ed., *Avanzes en Estudios Cerámicos en los Andes.* (tentative title). Lima: Pontificia Universidad Católica del Perú.

D'Altroy, Terence N., Ana María Lorandi, Verónica Williams, Timothy K. Earle, Christine A. Hastorf
1990 Informe Preliminar: Proyecto Arqueológico Calchaquí. Submitted to Ministerio de Educación y Cultura, Provincia de Salta, Argentina. (ms.)

D'Altroy, Terence N., Ana María Lorandi, Verónica Williams, Christine A. Hastorf, Timothy K. Earle, Elizabeth DeMarrais, Elsie Sandefur, Robert Daniels, Glenn S. Russell, Milena Calderari, Melissa B. Hagstrum, Ellen Howe, and Catherine Heyne
n.d. Inka Imperial Rule in the Valle Calchaquí, Argentina. (ms.)

DeBoer, Warren R., and Donald W. Lathrap
1979 The Making and Breaking of Shipibo-Conibo Ceramics. In C. Kramer, ed., *Ethnoarchaeology: Implications of Ethnography for Archaeology*, pp.102-38. New York: Columbia University Press.

DeBoer, Warren R., and James A. Moore
1982 The Measurement and Meaning of Stylistic Diversity. *Ñawpa Pacha* 20:147-62.

DeNiro, Michael J., and Christine A. Hastorf
1985 Alteration of 15N/14N and 13C/12C Ratios of Plant Matter during the Initial Stages of Diagenesis: Studies using Archaeological Specimens from Peru. *Geochimica et Cosmochimica Acta* 49:97-115.

Deustua, José
    1978    Acceso a recursos en Yanque-Collaguas 1591: Una experiencia estadística. In M. Koth de Paredes and A. Castelli, comp., *Etnohistoria y Antropología Andina*, Primera Jornada del Museo Nacional de Historia (1974), pp.41-51. Lima.

Diez de San Miguel, Garci
    1964 [1567]  *Visita Hecha a la Provincia de Chucuito por Garci Diez de San Miguel en el Año 1567*. Lima: Casa de Cultura.

Difrieri, Horacio
    1948    Las Ruinas del Potrero de Payogasta. *Actes du XXVIII Congrés International des Américanistes*, pp.599-604. Paris.

Earle, Timothy K.
    n.d.    Wealth Finance on the Inka Empire's Edge: The Calchaquí Valley, Argentina. (ms.)

Earle, Timothy K., and Andrew J. Christensen
    1980    *Modelling Prehistoric Economic Systems*. New York: Academic Press.

Earle, Timothy, Terence D'Altroy, Christine Hastorf, Catherine Scott, Cathy Costin, Glenn S. Russell, and Elsie Sandefur
    1987    *Archaeological Field Research in the Upper Mantaro, Peru, 1982-1983: Investigations of Inka Expansion and Exchange*. Los Angeles: University of California, Institute of Archaeology, Monograph 28.

Espinoza Soriano, Waldemar
    1971    Los Huancas, Aliados de la Conquista: Tres Informaciones Inéditas Sobre la Participación Indígena en la Conquista del Perú, 1558-1560-1561. *Anales Científicos de la Universidad de Centro del Perú* 1:3-407. Huancayo.
    1973    Las Colonias de Mitmas Múltiples en Abancay, Siglos XV y XVI. *Revista del Museo Nacional* 39:225-299. Lima.
    1975    Los Mitmas Huayacuntu en Quito o Guarniciones para la Represión Armada, Siglos XV y XVI. *Revista del Museo Nacional* 41: 351-394. Lima.
    1983    Los Mitmas Plateros de Ishma en el País de los Ayamarca, Siglos XV-XIX. *Boletín de Lima* 30 (5): 38-52. Lima.
    1987    Migraciones Internas en el Reino Colla: Tejedores, Plumereros, Alfareros del Estado Imperial Inca. *Chungará* 19:245-89. Arica.

Falcón, Francisco
    1946 [1567] Representación Hecha por el Licenciado Falcón en Concilio Provincial Sobre los Daños y Molestias que se Hacen a

los Indios. In F.A. Loayza, ed., *Los Pequeños Grandes Libros de Historia Americana*, Series 1, T. 10, pp.121-64. Lima: D. Miranda.

Feinman, Gary, Stephen Kowalewski, and Richard Blanton
    1984    Modelling Ceramic Production and Organizational Change in the Pre-Hispanic Valley of Oaxaca, Mexico. In S.E. van der Leeuw and A Prichard, eds., *The Many Dimensions of Pottery: Ceramics in Archaeology and Anthropology*, pp.295-338. Albert Egges van Giffen Instituut voor Prae- en Protohistorie. Amsterdam: University of Amsterdam.

Fonseca Martel, C.
    1974    Modalidades de la Minka. In *Reciprocidad e Intercambio en los Andes Peruanos*, pp. 89-109. Instituto de Estudios Peruanos, Lima.

Garcilaso de la Vega
    1966 [1604] *Royal Commentaries of the Incas and General History of Peru*, 2 parts, H.V. Livermore, transl. Austin: University of Texas Press.

Garnsey, Peter, and Richard Saller
    1987    *The Roman Empire: Economy, Society, and Culture.* Berkeley: University of California Press.

González, Alberto Rex
    1983    Inca Settlement Patterns in a Marginal Province of the Empire: Sociocultural Implications. In E.Z. Vogt and R.M. Leventhal, eds., *Prehistoric Settlement Patterns: Essays in Honor of Gordon R. Willey*, pp.337-60. Cambridge: Harvard University Press.

Guaman Poma de Ayala, Felipe
    1980 [1614] *El Primer Nueva Corónica y Buen Gobierno.* J.V. Murra and R.Adorno, eds., J.I. Urioste, transl. 3 vols. Mexico: Siglo Veintiuno.

Hagstrum, Melissa
    1986    The Technology of Ceramic Production of Wanka and Inka Wares from the Yanamarca Valley, Peru. *Ceramic Notes* 3:1-29.
    1989    *Technological Continuity and Change: Ceramic Ethnoarchaeology in the Peruvian Andes.* Ph.D. dissertation, University of California, Los Angeles. Ann Arbor: University Microfilms.

1992    *Progress Report. Intersecting Technologies: Ceramics, Metallurgy and the Organization of Specialized Craft Production in the Inka State.* (ms.)

n.d.    Household Autonomy in Peasant Craft Specialization. In T. D'Altroy and C. Hastorf, eds., *Empire and Domestic Economy.* Washington, D.C.: Smithsonian Institution Press.

Harris, Olivia
1978    El Parentesco y la Economía Vertical en el Ayllu Laymi (Norte de Potosí) *Avances,* No. 1. La Paz.

Hastorf, Christine A.
1983    *Prehistoric Agricultural Intensification and Political Development in the Jauja Region of Peru.* Ph.D. dissertation, University of California, Los Angeles. Ann Arbor: University Microfilms.
1991    The Effect of the Inka State on Sausa Agricultural Production and Crop Consumption. *American Antiquity* 55:262-90.
1993    *Resources in Power: Agriculture and the Onset of Political Inequality Before the Inca.* Cambridge: Cambridge University Press.

Hastorf, Christine A., and Timothy K. Earle
1985    Intensive Agriculture and the Geography of Political Change in the Upper Mantaro Region of Central Peru. In I. Farrington, ed., *Prehistoric Intensive Agriculture in the Tropics,* pp.569-95. Oxford: British Archaeological Reports, International Series, no. 232.

Helmer, Marie
1955-56 [1549]    "La visitación de los Yndios Chupachos" Inka et encomendero 1549. *Travaux de L'Institut Français d'Etudes Andines* 5:3-50. Lima and Paris.

Hyslop, John
1984    *The Inka Road System.* New York: Academic Press.

Isbell, William H., and Gordon F. McEwan, eds.
1991    *Huari Administrative Structure.* Washington, DC: Dumbarton Oaks.

Julien, Catherine J.
1982    Inca Decimal Administration in the Lake Titicaca Region. In G.A. Collier, R.I. Rosaldo, and J.D. Wirth, eds., *The Inca and Aztec States 1400-1800: Anthropology and History,* pp.119-51. New York: Academic Press.
1988    How Inca Decimal Administration Worked. *Ethnohistory* 35:257-79.

Krapovickas, Pedro
   1964    Un Taller de Lapidario en el Pucará de Tilcara. *Runa*, V. IX, partes 1-2, 1958-59. Buenos Aires.
La Lone, Darrell E.
   1982    The Inca as a Nonmarket Economy: Supply on Command versus Supply and Demand. In J.E. Ericson and T.K. Earle, eds., *Contexts for Prehistoric Exchange*, pp.291-316. New York: Academic Press.
La Lone, Mary B. and Darrell E. La Lone
   1987    The Inka State in the Southern Highlands: State Administrative and Production Enclaves. *Ethnohistory* 34:47-62.
LeBlanc, Catherine
   1981    *Late Prehispanic Huanca Settlement Patterns in the Yanamarca Valley, Peru*. Ph.D. dissertation, University of California, Los Angeles. Ann Arbor: University Microfilms.
Lehman, David
   1982    *Ecology and Exchange in the Andes*. Cambridge: Cambridge University Press.
LeVine, Terry Y.
   1979    Prehispanic Political and Economic Change in Highland Peru: An Ethnohistorical Study of the Mantaro Valley. Unpublished MA Thesis, Archaeology Program, University of California, Los Angeles.
   1987    Inka Labor Service at the Regional Level: The Functional Reality. *Ethnohistory* 34:14-46.
Lorandi, Ana María
   1984    Soñocamayoc: los olleros del Inka en los centros manufactureros del Tucumán. *Revista del Museo de la Plata*, Tomo VII, pp.303-27. Antropología 62. La Plata, Argentina: Universidad Nacional de la Plata, Facultad de Ciencias Naturales y Museo.
Masuda, Shozo, Izumi Shimada, and Craig Morris, eds.
   1985    *Andean Ecology and Civilization: An Interdisciplinary Perspective on Andean Ecological Complementarity*. Tokyo: University of Tokyo Press.
Mitchell, William
   1980    Local Ecology and the State: Implications of Contemporary Quechua Land Use for the Inca Sequence of Agricultural Work. In E.B. Ross, ed., *Beyond the Myths of Culture: Essays in Cultural Materialism*, pp.139-54. New York: Academic Press.

Moore, Sally F.
 1958 *Power and Property in Inca Peru.* New York: Columbia University Press.
Morris, Craig
 1967 *Storage in Tawantinsuyu.* Ph.D. dissertation, Department of Anthropology, University of Chicago.
 1974 Reconstructing Patterns of Nonagricultural Production in the Inca Economy: Archaeology and Documents in Instituted Analysis. In C. Moore, ed., *Reconstructing Complex Societies*, pp.49-68. Supplement to the Bulleting of the American Schools of Orental Research 20.
Morris, Craig, and Donald Thompson
 1985 *Huánuco Pampa: An Inca City and Its Hinterland.* London: Thames and Hudson.
Moseley, Michael E., and Alana Cordy-Collins, eds.
 1990 *The Northern Dynasties: Kingship and Statecraft in Chimor.* Washington, DC: Dumbarton Oaks.
Murra, John V.
 1972 El 'Control Vertical' de un Máximo de Pisos Ecológicos en la Economía de las Sociedades Andinas. In J.V. Murra, ed., *Visita de la Provincia de León de Huánuco en 1562, Iñigo Ortiz de Zúñiga, Visitador*, vol. 2, pp.427-76. Huánuco, Perú: Universidad Nacional Hermilio Valdizán.
 1975 *Formaciones Económicas y Políticas del Mundo Andino.* Lima: Instituto de Estudios Peruanos.
 1978 Los Olleros del Inka: Hacia una Historia y Arqueología del Qollasuyu. In F. Miro Quesada, F. Pease G. Y., and D. Sobrevilla, eds., *Historia, problema, y promesa: Homenaje a Jorge Basadre*, pp.415-23. Lima: Pontificia Universidad Católica del Perú.
 1980a [1956] *The Economic Organization of the Inka State.* Greenwich, Connecticut: JAI Press.
 1980b Derechos a las Tierras en el Tawantinsuyu. *Revista de la Universidad Complutense*, 28(117):273-87. Madrid.
Murúa, Martín de
 1986 [ca. 1605] *Historia General del Perú.* Manuel Ballesteros, ed. Crónicas de América 35. Madrid: Historia 16.
Netherly, Patricia
 1978 *Local Level Lords on the North Coast of Peru.* Ph.D. dissertation, Department of Anthropology, Cornell University, Ithaca, N.Y.

Ortiz de Zúñiga, Iñigo
    1967  [1562]  *Visita de la Provincia de León de Huánuco en 1562, Iñigo Ortiz de Zúñiga, visitador*, J.V. Murra, ed., vol. 1. Huánuco, Perú: Universidad Nacional Hermilio Valdizán.
    1972  [1562]  *Visita de la Provincia de León de Huánuco en 1562, Iñigo Ortiz de Zúñiga, visitador*, J.V. Murra, ed., vol. 2. Huánuco, Perú: Universidad Nacional Hermilio Valdizán.

Patterson, Thomas C.
    1985  Exploitation and Class Formation in the Inca State. *Culture* 1(1):35-42. Montreal.
    1986  Ideology, Class Formation, and Resistance in the Inca State. *Critique of Anthropology* 6(1):75-85. Amsterdam.

Peacock, D.P.S., ed.
    1987  *Pottery and Early Commerce: Characterization and Trade in Roman and Later Ceramics*. New York: Academic Press.

Pease G. Y., Franklin
    1977  Inkarri en Collaguas. In M. Koth de Paredes and A. Castelli, comp., *Etnohistoria y Antropología Andina*, Primera Jornada del Museo Nacional de Historia (1974), pp.37-39. Lima.
    1981  Ayllu y parcialidad. In M. Koth de Paredes and A. Castelli, comp., *Etnohistoria y Antropología Andina*, Segunda Jornada del Museo Nacional de Historia (1979), pp.19-33. Lima.

Polanyi, Karl
    1957  The Economy as Instituted Process. In K. Polanyi, C. Arensberg, and H. Pearson, eds., *Trade and Market in the Early Empires*, pp.243-70. New York: Free Press.

Polo de Ondegardo, Juan
    1916  [1571]  Relación de los Fundamentos Acerca del Notable Daño que Resulta de no Guardar a los Indios sus Fueros. In H.H. Urteaga, ed., *Colección de Libros y Documentos Referentes a la Historia del Perú*, tomo 3, pp.45-188. Lima: Sanmartí.
    1940  [1561]  Informe del Licenciado Juan Polo de Ondegardo al Licenciado Briviesca de Muñatones Sobre la Perpetuidad de las Encomiendas en el Perú. *Revista Histórica* 13:125-96. Lima.

Raffino, Rodolfo
    1983  *Los Inkas del Kollasuyu*, 2d ed. La Plata, Argentina: Ramos Americana Editora.

Rice, Prudence M.
    1987  *Pottery Analysis: A Sourcebook*. Chicago: University of Chicago Press.

Rostworowski de Diez Canseco, María
    1962    Nuevos Datos Sobre Tenecia de Tierras Reales en el Incario. *Revista del Museo Nacional*, T. XXXI, pp. 130-64. Lima.
    1977    *Etnía y Sociedad Costa Peruana Prehispánica*. Lima: Instituto de Estudios Peruanos.
    1978    *Señorios Indígenas de Lima y Canta*. Lima: Instituto de Estudios Peruanos.
    1983    *Estructuras Andinas del Poder*. Lima: Instituto de Estudios Peruanos.
    1988    *Historia del Tahuantinsuyu*. 2d ed. Lima: Instituto de Estudios Peruanos.

Rowe, John H.
    1946    Inca Culture at the Time of the Spanish Conquest. In J. Steward, ed., *Handbook of South American Indians*, vol. 2, pp.183-330. Washington, D.C.: Bureau of American Ethnology, Bulletin 143.

Russell, Glenn S.
    1988    *The Impact of Inka Policy on the Domestic Economy of the Wanka, Peru: Stone Tool Production and Use*. Ph.D.dissertation, Department of Anthropology, University of California. Ann Arbor: University Microfilms.
    1990    Preceramic Through Moche Settlement Pattern Change in the Chicama Valley, Peru. Paper Presented at the 55th Annual Meeting of the Society for American Archaeology, Las Vegas.

Rutz, Henry J., and Benjamin S. Orlove, eds.
    1989    *The Social Economy of Consumption*. Monograph in Economic Anthropology, No. 6. Lanham, MD: University Press of America.

Sahlins, Marshall
    1972    *Stone-Age Economics*. Chicago: Aldine.

Salomon, Frank
    1986    *Native Lords of Quito in the Age of the Incas*. Cambridge: Cambridge University Press.

Sancho de la Hoz, Pedro
    1917 [1532-33] Relación. In H.H. Urteaga, ed., *Colección de Libros y Documentos Referentes a la Historia del Perú*, vol.5, pp.122-202. Lima: Sanmartí.

Sandefur, Elsie C.
    1988    *Andean Zooarchaeology: Animal Use and the Inka Conquest of the Upper Mantaro Valley*. Ph.D. Dissertation, Archae-

ology Program, University of California, Los Angeles. Ann Arbor: University Microfilms.

Spurling, Geoffrey
    1987    Qolla Potters Making Inka Pottery: Ceramic Production at Milliraya. Paper Presented at the 52nd Annual Meeting of the Society for American Archaeology, Toronto.

Stanish, Charles
    1992    *Ancient Andean Political Economy.* Austin: University of Texas Press.

Tarragó, Myriam N.
    1978    Paleoecology of the Calchaquí Valley, Salta Province, Argentine. In D.L. Browman, ed., *Advances in Andean Archaeology*, pp.485-512. The Hague: Mouton.

Toledo, Francisco de
    1940 [1570]    Información Hecha por Orden de Don Francisco de Toledo en su Visita de las Provincias del Peru, en la que Declaran Indios Ancianos Sobre el Derecho de los Caciques y Sobre el Gobierno que Tenían Aquellos Pueblos Antes que los Incas los Conquistasen. In R. Levillier, ed., *Don Francisco de Toledo, supremo organizador del Perú, Su Vida, Su Obra 1515-1582*, vol. II, pp.14-37. Buenos Aires: Espasa Calpe.

Tomka, Steve A.
    1987    Resource Ownership and Utilization Patterns Among the Yanqu-Collaguas as Manifested in the Visita de Yanque-Collaguas, 1591. *Andean Perspective Newsletter* 5:15-23. Institute of Latin American Studies, University of Texas, Austin.

Topic, John
    1982    Lower-Class Social and Economic Organization at Chan Chan. In M.E. Moseley and K.C. Day, eds., *Chan Chan: Andean Desert City*, pp.145-76. Albuquerque: University of New Mexico Press.

Vega, Andrés de
    1965 [1582]    La Descripción que se Hizo en la Provincia de Xauxa por la Instrucción de Su Majestad que a la Dicha Provincia se Invio de Molde. In *Relaciones Geográficas de Indias*, I, pp.166-75. Biblioteca de Autores Españoles, vol. 183. Madrid: Ediciones Atlas.

Wachtel, Nathan
    1977    *The Vision of the Vanquished*, B. and S, Reynolds, transl. New York: Barnes and Noble.
    1982    The *Mitima* of the Cochabamba Valley: The Colonization Policy of Huayna Capac. In G.A. Collier, R.I. Rosaldo, and J.D. Wirth, eds., *The Inca and Aztec States, 1400-1800: Anthropology and History*, pp.199-235. New York: Academic Press.

Williams, Verónica I.
    1983    Evidencia de Actividad Textil en el Establecimiento Incaico Potrero Chaquiago (Provincia de Catamarca). *Relaciones de la Sociedad Argentina de Antropología* 15:49-59.

Williams, Verónica I. and Ana María Lorandi
    1986    Evidencias Funcionales de un Establecimiento Inkaico en el Noroeste Argentino. *Comechingonia* Año 4. Nº esp., 133-48. Córdoba.

Wolf, Eric
    1968    *Sons of the Shaking Earth*. Chicago: University of Chicago Press.

# POLITICAL CHOICES AND ECONOMIC STRATEGIES IN THE VIJAYANAGARA EMPIRE

Carla M. Sinopoli
The University of Michigan

## Introduction

The Vijayanagara empire was a Hindu polity that dominated much of south India from ca. 1340 - 1565 A.D. Throughout that period, Vijayanagara authority expanded from its initial seat of power along the banks of the Tungabhadra River in modern Karnataka to encompass a territory of some 360,000 square kilometers, virtually all of peninsular India south of the Tungabhadra (Stein 1989:2, Figure 1). Approximately 20 rulers from three dynasties led the empire during the 220 years preceding the abandonment of the capital (Smith 1958:318-319). Warfare was chronic throughout the period and the borders of the empire fluctuated in response to local political and military conditions and the success of individual rulers in welding their fragile realm together. The nature of Vijayanagara imperial and economic control also varied considerably over time and space. As a result, it is difficult, in fact impossible, to come up with a single picture of either Vijayanagara polity or economy.

Nonetheless, it is apparent that the Vijayanagara empire heralded a significant change in the organization of south Indian political systems. The empire was characterized by increased militarization, urbanization, and an increasingly monetized economy (Abraham 1979, Stein 1989:xi). In other respects though, Vijayanagara continued the relatively uncentralized patterns of earlier south Indian states and empires. Such continuities can be seen in the largely ritual nature of Vijayanagara kingship (Appadurai 1978, 1981) and the lack of a well-developed bureaucratic or administrative infrastructure (Stein 1989).

Over the past century numerous historians have sought to document and account for Vijayanagara organization. This paper draws heavily on their work and particularly the work of Burton Stein.[1] Since 1979, historical work has been supplemented by extensive archaeological research at the Vijayanagara capital and in its immediate periphery, carried out by the Government of India, the state Government of Karnataka, and international teams of foreign and Indian scholars.[2]

## Research Perspective

In this paper, I will examine some issues of Vijayanagara political economy, drawing on both historical studies and recent archaeological research. My interest is in considering the extent and nature of imperial control over the production and distribution of goods throughout the empire and, in particular, at the capital and its immediate hinterland. I suggest that imperial regulation of the economy was determined by a variety of factors, including: distance from the capital or its outposts, local and centralized political conditions and political actors, the political and economic significance of the good produced, and the existence of other systems of productive regulation, such as endogamous caste organization.

The complex nature of the Vijayanagara political economy is such that it cannot be encompassed by a single term, e.g., "feudal", "market economy", "wealth or staple finance" (Earle 1987) and so on, though each of these has some relevance to different aspects of Vijayanagara's economy. In order to understand imperial economies in general, and Vijayanagara economy in particular, we must move away from such summary descriptions, and instead focus on developing historical understandings of the multiple dimensions of economic and political organization, each of which may show very different organization.

The present study is thus part of an on-going reassessment concerning the nature and political and economic organization of complex societies occurring in anthropology, history, and political and social theory (e.g., Giddens 1984; Mann 1986; Brumfiel and Earle 1987; Miller, Rowlands and Tilley 1989). From this perspective, complex societies are seen as far less centralized, unified, or efficiently organized than many anthropologists and historians have previously assumed them to be. Thus, sociologist M. Mann, has suggested that "societies are constituted of multiple overlapping and intersecting sociospatial networks of power" (1986:1), and are "much *messier* than our theories of them" (1986:3). Mann (1986:24-32) goes on to suggest that in examining ancient states and empires we should consider four sources or dimensions of power: ideology, economy, political and military. I would suggest that we take this division somewhat further, to examine internal variations in each of these dimensions and to recognize that economy, like politics or ideology, is never a unitary phenomenon, but rather is also far messier than our theories of it (also Thomas 1991:28). In the remainder of this paper, I will illustrate this approach through an examination of four diverse economic domains in the context of the historic empire of Vijayanagara.

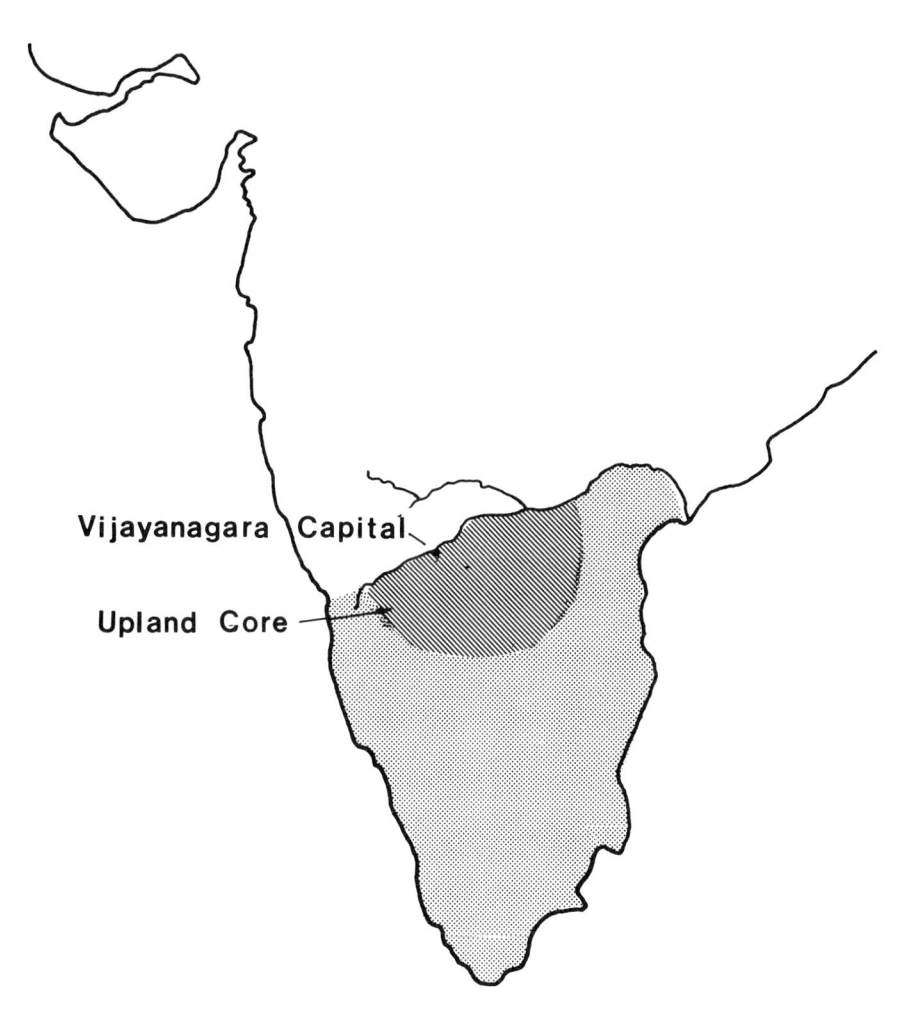

Figure 1. The Vijayanagara empire: Approximate borders.

## Vijayanagara Spatial Organization

Two broad geographic and political areas of the Vijayanagara empire have been distinguished by Stein (1989:58). The heart of the empire was a core area of some 30,000 square kilometers in the semi-arid upland plateaus surrounding the capital[3] (Stein 1989:58). This area was inhabited by Telugu and Kannada speakers, primarily herders and farmers. All land in this zone was owned by the king, and its villages and towns were under the authority of some eighty local chieftains who provided revenue and soldiers to the center (Stein 1989:58). In order to expand the agricultural potential of the core area, imperial and local rulers invested in large scale construction of rain-fed irrigation facilities. Road systems were built to facilitate long distance exchange and the movement of goods into the capital. The Vijayanagara elite also constructed and endowed temples (with tax free lands and cash). Temple leaders, in turn, contributed to the further expansion of agricultural potentials through clearing forested areas and constructing additional irrigation facilities.

This heartland area provided the only secure source of revenue for the empire (Stein 1989:58). The irrigated areas yielded rice and other foodstuffs, and dry farming in the unirrigated uplands produced cotton and dyes for the critically important Vijayanagara textile industry. The region was also a major producer of livestock, important both as food and as beasts of burden for the movement of troops and goods. The security and productivity of the core was, no doubt, in part due to the continuous and highly visible presence of Vijayanagara authority; an Italian visitor to the capital in the early 1400s observed that it housed a permanent force of 90,000 soldiers (Nicolo Conti in Major 1857:6).

Beyond the imperial core lay the highly fertile and productive lowland regions of the empire and its coastal ports. These regions, particularly the Tamil speaking southeast coast of India, were the traditional centers of South India's wealth, with vast and productive rice fields maintained by complex canal irrigation systems. Sea ports on both east and west coasts were crucial to Vijayanagara international trade with China, the Middle East, and Europe (Subrahmanyam 1990:48-62). The lowland regions contained powerful local kingdoms, whose leaders were often unwilling to relinquish their wealth or their status to foreign Vijayanagara conquerors. As will be discussed below, Vijayanagara kings seldom sought to administer these areas directly and received relatively little direct economic benefit from them.

## Vijayanagara Political Economy

As the Vijayanagara elite sought to expand and maintain their empire they faced the dual challenges of how to most effectively absorb and administer distant territories from their capital, and the need to assure continued production and movement of foodstuffs and other goods throughout the empire. Three strategies were employed to administer conquered territories: (1) the support of local political elite and religious institutions, (2) the installation of foreign war lords, and rarely, (3) the creation of state run fortresses or garrisons. These different strategies created a patchwork pattern of imperial government, highly dependent on individual relations between kings and local leaders. Such relations were thus inherently unstable and vulnerable to changing political circumstances.

With the first of these regulatory approaches, local elite continued to control their territories so long as they fulfilled their obligations, of paying honor and goods, to the empire. This allowed Vijayanagara to claim control over territories and receive some of their benefits, at relatively little cost. By supporting local nobility and/or temples and religious leaders, the Vijayanagara conquerors maintained good will, heightened their status as ritual kings and protectors of Hinduism, and did not disrupt local productive relations. The tribute actually transported to the capital was small, but the costs of acquiring it were similarly low.

A second strategy employed by the Vijayanagara elite in administering their empire was the appointment of war lords responsible for maintaining conquered territories. These war lords, or *nayakas*, often Telugu speakers, were most important in the highly fertile and productive coastal regions far from the capital. *Nayakas* were sometimes the sons or close relations of the kings, but were often successful military leaders who were ceded territories in return for their service. The presence of foreign rulers and of the considerable military forces that they controlled served to undercut local systems of leadership and power. *Nayakas* were responsible for collecting the high taxes owed to the empire and transferring them to their rulers. Additional revenues were also collected to support *nayaka* courts and armies. *Nayakas* also engaged in international trade and minted their own currency. The *nayakas*, and there were as many as 200 of them, were extremely important to the rapid expansion and comparatively long-term success of the empire.

Yet, the *nayakas* were also a potent threat to imperial solidarity. Many were able to amass considerable wealth and power into their own hands, and were unwilling to cede either to the distant and often ineffectual imperial capital. The vast majority of wars fought by the empire were fought to retake already conquered territories from rebellious subjects, and the major dynastic transitions within the empire resulted from the overthrow of ruling dynasties by a powerful *nayaka*.

Even in the best of circumstances (from the perspective of the Vijayanagara rulers), it appears that only a very small portion of the wealth of *nayaka* controlled areas ever entered imperial coffers. It may be particularly telling that, although we have records for local revenue officers, no references have been found for any centralized office responsible for collecting and accounting for tribute revenues from the entire empire (Stein 1989:39). Thus, although we know that tax rates were high during the Vijayanagara period, we know far less about what portion of these revenues were actually available to imperial rulers as opposed to the local rulers responsible for their collection. The amounts transferred to the imperial center were likely contingent upon the strength of the king and his ability to coerce payment and loyalty from local elite.

A third political strategy taken by Vijayanagara rulers was the establishment of military outposts or garrisons (Stein 1989:83). Such garrisons were most associated with Krishnadevaraya (1509-1529), king during the third and most effective dynasty of the empire. Krishnadevaraya sought to create an effective and loyal imperial bureaucracy. He constructed garrisons in strategic locations along major trade routes or borders, and staffed them with Islamic and Portuguese mercenaries with loyalties only to their employer (Stein 1989:43). Loyal Brahman officers were recruited to administer the outposts and to collect and account for tax revenues. These Brahmans provided the potential core for an imperial bureaucracy that had not previously existed. The innovative efforts of Krishnadevaraya to centralize the empire were, however, short-lived, and did not extend much beyond his reign and that of his brother and successor, Achyutadevaraya (1529-1542). Assassination attempts and battles for succession occurred during and after Achyutadevaraya's rule. During this period of disorder nayakas and ruling elite throughout the empire asserted their autonomy from centralized control (Stein 1989:68-69).

Concomitant with these strategies of imperial regulation, large temple centers were constructed or expanded throughout the empire. They were the recipients of lands and wealth from Vijayanagara rulers and local leaders, and were a fertile field for negotiations of legitimacy and authority among competing local and imperial elites (Appadurai 1978, 1981). Donative inscriptions at these temples provide a useful record of the changing extent and nature of imperial control in the peripheries. Temple centers were also major foci of craft production and agricultural intensification.

## Approaches to Vijayanagara Economy

These gross divisions of core and periphery or "state"-run and *nayaka*-run territories belie the great complexity and diversity of Vijayanagara political and economic strategies.[4] Along with political and military leaders, were powerful merchant castes and artisan groups, sectarian religious leaders, and village and caste systems of production and authority. Rather than attempt to discuss each of these groups abstractly, I wish to turn to a consideration of some of the goods that they controlled and the role of imperial officials in assuring access to and income from these products.

I will consider four categories of goods: (1) goods important to military activities, i.e., guns, horses, and elephants; (2) goods important to international and internal trade, i.e., textiles; (3) foodstuffs or other agricultural products; and (4) various utilitarian craft goods, including ceramics and stone artifacts, essential to daily activities. The evidence on some of these goods comes from historical references and inscriptions. On others, it comes from archaeological remains found in and around the Vijayanagara capital. I am therefore not dealing with strictly comparable data or strictly comparable scales of analysis, but will, I hope, show some of the potential for considering the nature of diverse economic realms during Vijayanagara times.

## The Archaeological Evidence

I will preface this discussion by considering the nature of the archaeological evidence available from the Vijayanagara capital. The city of Vijayanagara was a large walled city, with a densely populated core that extended over approximately 25 sq. km. Beyond the core lay a defended zone of at least 300 sq. km. which contained aggregated settlements, temples, workshops, and agricultural lands.

The Vijayanagara capital came into existence as an imperial capital in an area where no comparable city had previously existed.[5] Although our demographic estimates are speculative, it is evident that the region was relatively sparsely populated before 1340. By the early 1400s, the capital had a population of at least 200,000 (and perhaps twice that number) and the semi-arid uplands of northern Karnataka had become one of India's most densely settled regions.[6] The capital was abandoned in 1565, following a major military defeat. Caesaro Federici, an Italian traveler to the region only two years after the capital's abandonment, noted that, at Vijayanagara, "the houses stand still, but emptie [sic] and there is dwelling in them nothing ... but Tygres [sic] and other wild beasts" (cited in Sewell 1900:

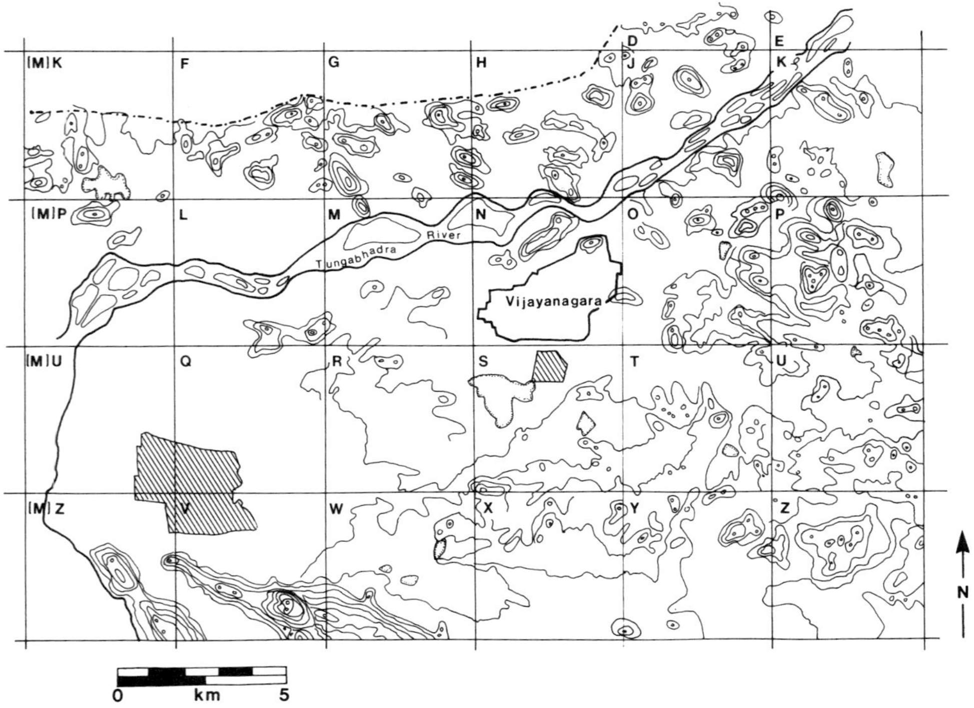

Figure 2. The greater metropolitan region of the Vijayanagara capital.

208). Although the tigers and many of the smaller structures are now gone, the city of Vijayanagara is still largely unoccupied and remarkably well preserved, providing the best example in South Asia of a pre-colonial Hindu imperial city.

Most of the archaeological work carried out at Vijayanagara over the past decade has focused on documenting the city's densely settled core (see Fritz, Michell and Nagaraja Rao 1985; Michell 1990). K. Morrison and I have recently turned our attention to the outer zone of the capital, a 300 sq. km. region that we refer to as Vijayanagara's 'greater metropolitan region' (Figure 2, Morrison and Sinopoli 1992, in press; Sinopoli and Morrison (1991, 1992). We are documenting the archaeological remains in this area through a program of systematic regional survey, in order to examine patterns of urban settlement and economic activities. As of 1992, approximately 60 sq. km. have been sampled and approximately 370 archaeological sites have been located. Included among these are a range of site types: agricultural features, settlements, temples, road segments, and craft production locales.

## Products and Producers

*Military Products*

As heads of a militaristic and highly contentious empire, Vijayanagara rulers were especially concerned with controlling access to the means of warfare: weaponry, cavalry horses, war elephants, and soldiers, including mercenaries. War horses were crucial to Vijayanagara military strategies. The best horses were not bred in India, but were obtained through marine trade from the Middle East. Vijayanagara built no navy to acquire these animals directly. Rather, they sought to monopolize trade in horses with foreign merchants. Fernão Nuniz, a Portuguese horse trader who visited the capital in the 1520s, noted that Krishnadevaraya purchased 13,000 horses per year and:

> He caused horses to be brought from Oromuz [Hormuz] and Adeem [Aden] into his kingdom and thereby gave great profit to the merchants, paying them for the horses just as they asked. He took them dead or alive ... and of those that died at sea they brought him the tail only, and he paid for it just as if it had been alive (Sewell 1900:307).

The king kept the best horses for his own army, reported by Nuniz to contain 6000 horsemen (Sewell 1900:381). The remainder were given or sold to chiefs and war lords throughout the realm. By seeking to control access to horses, Vijayanagara rulers attempted to regulate internal military structure and to limit threats from competing armies. Gifts of horses were used to reward and honor loyal followers, and thus were also important prestige goods that helped to cement relations between imperial rulers and local elite.

Firearms, including cannons and muskets, were similarly obtained through international trade (Rudner 1987:362, Stein 1982:119). In addition, they were produced by local crafts people. Metal workers were responsible for producing swords, javelins, shields, and armor (Ramaswamy 1985b:424-426), and, as will be discussed below, the status of certain metal working communities rose considerably during Vijayanagara times, in recognition of the importance of their labor. The highly valued war elephants came from the forested lowland regions; Vijayanagara rulers sought good relations with local chieftains in these areas in order to insure exclusive access to them (Stein 1989:22-23).

The acquisition and maintenance of the weapons of war was extremely costly. Along with the considerable expenses involved in acquiring and maintaining war animals, secure and substantial road systems were necessary for them to travel to and from the inland capital (Kuppuswamy 1978). We are finding considerable evidence for such roads in our survey. These include raised causeways, substantial pavements, gateways or watchtowers, and the remains of a large bridge that spanned the Tungabhadra. Numerous wells and temples also demarcate major transportation routes. The construction of large scale transportation routes served to facilitate and regulate the movement of people, goods, and information into and out of the capital. The collection of import duties and other taxes was no doubt also made easier by the placement of officers along major routes.

*Trade Goods*

Much of the resources expended by rulers on instruments of war was acquired through the collection of revenues from the international and internal exchange of a variety of goods. Among the most important of these goods were silk and cotton threads and textiles. Textiles were produced throughout the empire in a variety of productive contexts, ranging from household looms to large-scale workshops run by master craftsmen (Ramaswamy 1979, 1985a, 1985b, 1985c). Elaborate textiles were important as garments for high status individuals within the empire, who adopted fashionable Muslim styles for royal presentation (Ramaswamy 1985b:307). Textiles were also critically important goods in international trade (Ramaswamy 1985b:301).

Vijayanagara's rulers did not manage textile production directly, but derived considerable revenue from taxes and tariffs levied on looms, thread, and the sale of cloth (Ramaswamy 1985c:86, Satyanarayana 1980). They sought to assure this revenue through a variety of means. These include royal patronage of the products of particular weaver castes or communities. Noble men and women and the military provided an enormous market for elaborate textiles that contributed to the general expansion of production during this time (Ramaswamy 1985c:69). Nuniz reported that Achyutadevaraya dressed only in fine silk worked with gold, and never wore the same garment twice (in Sewell 1900:383). Royal patronage of weavers also included the granting of benefits such as tax abatements and the bestowal of ritual status and other social privileges. Kings appointed members of weaver castes as officers in major temple centers, which were often centers of textile production (Ramaswamy 1985b:423). Weavers were organized into a range of broad territorial groups, based on caste divisions and techniques of textile production.

The status and wealth of weaving castes, individual artisans, and merchants involved in the textile trade increased substantially during Vijayanagara times. Weaving communities were effective in manipulating their relations with imperial and local officials through collective action including strikes, tax revolts, and mass migrations (Mines 1984). Artisan groups and individuals used their newly acquired wealth to make large scale cash donations to major temple centers throughout the south. Other producers of valued goods, particularly brass, gold, and, to a lesser extent, iron workers, underwent parallel increases in status and wealth during the Vijayanagara period (Ramaswamy 1985b:420). Similar changes seem to have occurred among builders and masons, skilled laborers necessary for constructing the rapidly expanding urban centers and temple complexes of the empire.

Although we have not yet found archaeological evidence for weaving activities in our survey, we have found a small temple complex (VMS-111) that gives important evidence on the status of at least one weaver at the capital. This is a small Shaivite shrine located along a major road into the city. An inscription at this site says that it was built by Nagayya, son of a weaver, in honor of his *guru*. The inscription goes on to state that anyone who comes to the site and says the name of its builder and the god, will have his wish granted. It is interesting to note that the name of the builder,

Adawanidevirappa, refers to a place name some 150 km. away from the capital. Thus, in this small shrine we see evidence for the status and wealth of an individual weaver and his ability to transport that status to the empire's capital.

*Foodstuffs*

Like all kings, Vijayanagara's rulers were greatly concerned with providing a secure subsistence base for their capital. Significant amounts of foodstuffs were likely procured by royal armies for their own consumption as they moved throughout the empire, perhaps for considerable portions of the year. Yet, for the most part it does not appear that substantial quantities of foodstuffs from distant regions ever reached the capital. The most fertile and productive lowland regions of the empire did not feed its core.

Intensification of agricultural production in the semi-arid core area was a major focus of the Vijayanagara rulers. Rulers directly sponsored the construction of major irrigation facilities in the core and encouraged communities and temples to construct others. River-fed canals were built at the capital and massive rain-fed tanks and tank systems were built throughout the core area. These tanks are large stone embankments designed to trap run-off from surrounding slopes and feed it into agricultural fields (Morrison 1989, 1991). Tank systems consist of up to dozen inter-connected embankments that channelled water over vast areas. They required considerable skill and planning in their construction.

Agricultural sites include a variety of erosion control features and terraces and stone embankments. It is abundantly evident in the survey area that virtually every square meter of land that could be farmed was exploited during Vijayanagara times. The size and investment in tank construction varied in proportion to available arable land. These embankments range from about 30 meters long, serving field areas of less than half a hectare, to embankments that were several kilometers long. One of these massive embankments, about 5 km long, was constructed by Krishnadevaraya with the aid of Portuguese engineers. Domingo Pes, a Portuguese visitor to the capital, noted that:

> In the tank I saw so many people at work that there must have been fifteen or twenty thousand men, looking like ants, so that you could not see the ground on which they walked, so many there were (Sewell 1900:245).

When the tank failed to hold water, 60 men and many horses and buffalo were sacrificed to assure its success. Embankments such as this and comparable ones in the metropolitan region provide evidence for considerable imperial investment in agricultural intensification. Many of the smaller embankments and erosion control features likely were sponsored or managed at a much lower level, by temples, villages, or individuals.

*Utilitarian Craft Goods*

The material goods of everyday life, such as earthenware ceramics, leather goods, agricultural tools, or the garments of commoners, receive relatively little mention in Vijayanagara texts. Local tax records indicate that producers of these goods were subject to significant levels of taxation. Taxes were collected by caste or village headmen and then eventually channeled to political rulers.[7] The distance craftspeople lived from political centers likely determined where their taxes went -- whether directly to the imperial capital or channelled through local political elite.

Craftspeople, like all members of Hindu society, were members of endogamous hereditary castes. These castes were, among other things, occupational groups. They also served as regulatory groups, with caste councils responsible for enforcing rules on both the quality of the products and the appropriate behavior of caste members. Reliance on castes to regulate production and behavior is a low cost strategy for political rulers, and seems to have been the dominant practice of the Vijayanagara empire. There are occasional references in texts to the adjudication of inter-caste disputes (Kuppuswamy 1978), but otherwise the producers of low-status goods were largely invisible. As discussed above, such a pattern is in stark contradistinction to what we see for producers of high status and trade goods, including brass and gold workers, weavers, and to a lesser extent, iron workers.

Archaeological data is the main source of evidence for understanding the productive organization of goods that had limited political or symbolic significance for the Vijayanagara state. In our survey we have thus far found evidence for the production of basalt pegs, stone tools, lime plaster, and iron. For each of these crafts, production occurs either in specialized locales outside of settlements or is spatially segregated within settlements. In either case, the scale of production is small and localized, with no evidence for large scale centralized or administered production (Sinopoli 1988).

Basalt pegs are roughly flaked oblong or trapezoidal artifacts, ca. 15-20 cm in length, that were used in construction of structures on sloping sheet rock or outcrops. Two settlements found within the survey contain refuse from peg production and a number of completed pegs. The density of these objects is not great, and it is not clear that they were producing these materials beyond the needs of the community, but production does seem to occur in bounded areas within the sites. The other stone tools found on survey are remains of an expedient flake tool industry. These are found at settlements and in rock shelters or outcrop areas where raw materials were abundant. Lithic tools are not extensively modified and were most likely produced and consumed as needed by individuals who did not have ready access to iron tools.

The three iron working sites identified to date are not associated with settlements.[8] The sites are small, with two consisting only of surface scatters of iron waste, slag, and overfired red brick, and the third of a small furnace structure (ca. 3 x 5 meters in dimension) containing ceramic crucibles and a surrounding slag scatter. Our admittedly limited evidence on craft production thus far indicates a pattern of local production of these essential goods, either in formal workshops, in the case of iron working, plaster, and basalt peg production, or informally on an ad hoc basis, for chipped stone implements.

No ceramic workshops have yet been located in the survey. I have argued elsewhere on the basis of ceramic morphology that it is probable that ceramic production also took place at small scale workshops distributed throughout the metropolitan region (Sinopoli 1988, 1993). A Vijayanagara inscription near the capital does refer to a community known as "Kumbharapura" or "village of the potters", in the metropolitan region; we have not been able to identify its location.

## Discussion

The Vijayanagara political economy was complex and varied considerably over both time and space. Direct imperial control of production or distribution of goods appears limited, restricted to some aspects of international trade at coastal ports, and to agricultural intensification in the imperial core. The geographic core and periphery and different areas of the periphery were regulated in distinct ways. A limited bureaucracy and lack of effective control over local elite and/or *nayakas* led, overall, to very weak control beyond the imperial heartland.

Even within the Karnatak uplands surrounding the capital, there is no evidence that the empire sought to directly control the production of even such politically, symbolically, and economically significant products as textiles. Production and distribution of valued goods was regulated by temples, castes, merchants, and entrepreneurial master weavers. The state attempted to facilitate and encourage production of such goods, but through the bestowal of favors and prestige, rather than through the use of coercive means. Less valued goods received even less imperial interest and were largely regulated by local castes and communities.

Vijayanagara's rulers did benefit considerably from the expanded production and commerce that occurred in the emerging temple and urban centers of south India, and the burgeoning international trade of the period. Even if they only received a small percentage of the taxes, tariffs, and other revenues collected, this still amounted to substantial wealth that could be reinvested in imperial activities. The economic and political strategies taken by Vijayanagara rulers had considerable benefits. Like other empire builders, the builders of Vijayanagara had to balance the costs of continuing to expand the authority of South Asia's last great Hindu empire, with the costs of effectively controlling that empire. They chose the former option, leaving the rulers free to focus their energy and resources on the task of empire building through militaristic conquest, without becoming overwhelmed by the costs of administering and regulating activities of everyday life throughout their realm. While such a decision certainly contributed to the eventual collapse of the empire, Vijayanagara was able to bind together their polity for more than 200 years. In so doing, Vijayanagara's kings ruled over the most effective, durable, and extensive empire in South Indian history.

## Acknowledgments

I would like to acknowledge the Indian Government and the Government of Karnataka for permission to carry out research at Vijayanagara. Thanks also to the American Institute of Indian Studies and particularly Dr. P.R. Mehendiratta for sponsoring this work. The Vijayanagara Metropolitan Survey, co-directed by myself and Kathleen Morrison, has been supported by the Smithsonian Foreign Currency Program (Grant FR00627500), the Wenner Gren Foundation for Anthropological Research (Grant 5044) and the National Geographic Society (Grant 4186-89). I especially thank Kathy Morrison for being a wonderful collaborator and critic. Thanks also to the members of the survey team, especially Mark T. Lycett and the participants from Deccan College, Pune. Ken Hirth, Don Kurtz, Estellie Smith have provided comments on an earlier draft of this paper; I am grateful to them for their advice and suggestions.

## Notes

1. Such studies include the work of Sewell (1900), Nilakanta Sastri and Venkataramanayya (1946), Nilikanta Sastri (1955), Mahalingam (1975), Appadurai (1978, 1981), Stein (1979, 1980, 1982, 1989) among others. It should also be noted that Stein's interpretation is not without its critics; see for example Palat (1987).

2. Reports on recent archaeological work at the Vijayanagara capital can be found in Nagaraja Rao, ed. (1983, 1985), Dallapicolla, ed. (1985), Fritz, Michell and Nagaraja Rao (1986), Sinopoli (1993).

3. In this context, I am following Stein in using the terms "core" and "periphery" to refer to solely geographic zones within the empire, with no necessary implications on political relations or relations of economic dependency.

4. Stein has also pointed out that it is incorrect to think of *nayaka* organization as a "system" of administration. Rather it is more accurate to view these nayakas as each having an individual relation with the Vijayanagara ruler, which is subject to continual renegotiation and manipulation.

5. There were earlier political centers in the region, such as Kampili, Kumata Durga, and probably, Anegundi, located to the north of the Tungabhadra River, but these were on a significantly smaller scale than the Vijayanagara capital.

6. Stein (1989:58) estimates the core area of the empire may have had a population of two million during the early 16th century.

7. The collection of taxes was sometimes entrusted to "tax farmers" who collected taxes owed the state along with an additional amount for their services.

8. One of the iron working sites is located nearby a small but quite elaborate Vijayanagara temple and/or administrative structure to the south of the capital.

## References

Abraham, Meera
    1978    The Currency System and Monetisation in Karnataka in Vijayanagara Times. *Quarterly Journal of the Mythic Society* 69:12-39.

Appadurai, Arjun
    1978    Kings, Sects and Temples in South India, 1350-1700 A.D. In B. Stein, ed., *South Indian Temples: An Analytical Consideration*, pp.47-73. New Delhi: Vikas.
    1981    *Worship and Conflict Under Colonial Rule: A South Indian Case.* Cambridge: Cambridge University Press.

Brumfiel, Elizabeth M. and Timothy K. Earle, eds.
    1987    *Specialization, Exchange and Complex Societies.* Cambridge: Cambridge University Press.

Dallapiccola, Anna L., ed.
    1985    *Vijayanagara: City and Empire.* Wiesbaden: Franz Steiner Verlag.

Earle, Timothy K.
    1987    Specialization and the production of wealth: Hawaiian chiefdoms and the Inka empire. In E.M. Brumfiel and T.K. Earle eds., *Specialization, Exchange and Complex Societies*, pp.64-75. Cambridge: Cambridge University Press.

Fritz, John M., George A. Michell, and M.S. Nagaraja Rao
    1985    *The Royal Center of Vijayanagara: Preliminary Report.* Tucson: University of Arizona Press.

Giddens, Anthony
    1984    *The Constitution of Society.* Berkeley: University of California Press.

Kuppuswamy, G.R.
    1978    Some Aspects of Commercial Policy Under the Vijayanagara Empire. *Quarterly Journal of the Mythic Society* 70:29-40.

Mahalingham, T.V.
    1975    *Administration and Social Life Under Vijayanagara.* 2 vols. Madras: University of Madras Press.

Major, R.H.
    1857    *South India in the Fifteenth Century.* Hakluyt Society. New York: Burt Franklin Publisher.

Mann, Michael
    1986    *The Sources of Social Power, Vol. 1*. Cambridge: Cambridge University Press.
Michell, G.A.
    1990    *Vijayanagara: Architectural Inventory of the Urban Core*. 2 vols. Mysore: Directorate of Archaeology and Museums.
Miller, D., M. Rowlands, and C. Tilley, eds.
    1989    *Domination and Resistance*. London: Unwin Hyman.
Mines, Mattison
    1984    *The Warrior Merchants: Textiles, Trade, and Territory in South India*. Cambridge: Cambridge University Press.
Morrison, Kathleen D.
    1989    Urban Agricultural Production in South India: Agricultural Intensification at Vijayanagara. Paper presented at the 54th annual meeting, Society for American Archaeology, Atlanta.
    1991    Small Scale Agricultural Features: Three Vijayanagara Embankments. In D.V. Devaraj and C.S. Paitl, eds., *Vijayanagara: Progress of Research 1987-88*, pp.81-84. Mysore: Directorate of Archaeology and Museums.
Morrison, Kathleen D. and Carla M. Sinopoli
    in press    Archaeological Survey in the Vijayanagara Metropolitan Region, 1990. In D.V. Devaraj and C.S. Paitl, eds., *Vijayanagara: Progress of Research 1988-91*. Mysore: Directorate of Archaeology and Museums.
    1992    Economic diversity and integration in a pre-colonial Indian empire. *World Archaeology* 23:335-52.
Nagaraja Rao, M.S., ed.
    1983    *Vijayanagara: Progress of Research 1979-83*. Mysore: Directorate of Archaeology and Museums.
    1985    *Vijayanagara: Progress of Research 1983-84*. Mysore: Directorate of Archaeology and Museums.
Nilakanta Sastri, K.A.
    1955    *A History of South India From Prehistoric Times to the Fall of Vijayanagar*. Madras: Oxford University Press.
Nilakanta Sastri, K.A. and N. Venkataramanayya
    1946    Further Sources of Vijayanagara History. Madras: University of Madras.
Palat, Ravi
    1987    The Vijayanagara Empire: Re-integration of the Agrarian Order of Medieval South India, 1336 - 1569. In H. J. M.

Claessen and P. Van de Velde, eds., *Early State Dynamics*, pp.170-86. Leiden: E.J. Brill.

Ramaswamy, Vijaya
- 1979 Some Enquiries into the Condition of Weavers in Medieval South India. *The Indian Historical Review* 6:119-140.
- 1985a Artisans in Vijayanagar society. *The Indian Economic and Social History Review* 22:417-44.
- 1985b The Genesis and Historical Role of the Masterweavers in South Indian Textile Production. *Journal of the Economic and Social History of the Orient* 28:294-325.
- 1985c *Textiles and Weavers in Medieval South India*. New Delhi: Oxford University Press.

Rudner, David W.
- 1987 Religious Gifting and Inland Commerce in Seventeenth Century South India. *The Journal of Asian Studies* 46:361-79.

Satyanarayana, K.
- 1980 Taxation Under the Rayas of Vijayanagara. *Indian History Congress: Proceedings of the 41st Session*, pp.265-70. Bombay: Bombay University.

Sewell, R.
- 1900 *A Forgotten Empire (Vijayanagar)*. London: Swann Sonneschein.

Sinopoli, Carla M.
- 1988 The Organization of Craft Production at Vijayanagara, South India. *American Anthropologist* 90:580-97.
- 1993 *Pots and Palaces: The Archaeological Ceramics of the Noblemen's Quarter of Vijayanagara*. New Delhi: Manohar Press.

Sinopoli, Carla M. and Kathleen D. Morrison
- 1991 The Vijayanagara Metropolitan Survey: The 1988 Season. In D.V. Devaraj and C.S. Patil, eds., *Vijayanagara Progress of Research, 1987-88*, pp.55-69. Mysore: Directorate of Archaeology and Museums.
- 1992 Archaeological Survey at Vijayanagara. *Research and Exploration* 8:237-39.

Smith, Vincent A.
- 1958 *The Oxford History of India*. (Fourth Ed., Percival Spear, ed.). New Delhi: Oxford University Press.

Stein, Burton
- 1979 Integration of the Agrarian System of South India. In R. Frykenberg, ed., *Land Control and Social Structure in Indian History*, pp.178-216. New Delhi: Manohar Press.
- 1980 *Peasant State and Society in Medieval South India*. New Delhi: Oxford University Press.
- 1982 Vijayanagara, ca. 1350-1564. In Tapan Raychaudhuri and Irfan Habib, eds., *The Cambridge Economic History of India Volume I: c.1200-c.1750*, pp.102-24. Cambridge: Cambridge University Press.
- 1989 *The New Cambridge History of India I.2: Vijayanagara*. Cambridge: Cambridge University Press.

Subrahmanyam, Sanjay
- 1990 *The Political Economy of Commerce: Southern India, 1500-1650*. Cambridge: Cambridge University Press.

Thomas, N.
- 1991 *Entangled Objects: Exchange, Material Culture, and Colonialism in the Pacific*. Cambridge: Cambridge University Press.

# STATE ECONOMIC POLICY AND RURAL DEVELOPMENT IN PARAGUAY

### Christina Bolke Turner
### New College of the University of South Florida

In rural Paraguay there are two primary types of land settlement patterns, those occurring spontaneously over time and those directed by government land settlement policies. They are distinct in nature -- physically, socially, and economically. This paper discusses those differences and analyzes how state economic policy influences the direction of their development focusing specifically on cooperatives. This paper also illustrates some of the links between Paraguay's economic policies and the international economic system and development agencies. Two communities are used as case studies, one on the edge of the traditional mini-fundia zone and one in the newly-opened Brazilian frontier zone.

The two case study communities should be considered as examples from opposite ends of a continuum. Minga Guazú ("large cooperative work effort"), formerly Colonia Presidente Stroessner, is a showcase land colony on the Brazilian border and, for this reason, has received more material and developmental support than most colonies. Ñu Pyajhu Guazú ("great new pasture") is an isolated community settled through slow expansion into a sleepy, backwater area in the interior of Caazapá ("beyond the forest"). While both land colonies share typically Paraguayan features, their development has differed radically.

### Ñu Pyajhu Guazú

Ñu Pyajhu Guazú was originally settled by four families who traveled for three days by ox cart to reach the virgin forest although the actual distance involved was only about 45 kilometers. The area was separated from previously settled land by two extensive ranches, the Pirapó River ("Fish Jump" River), then bridge-less, and several swamps. Reportedly, there were two indigenous populations living in the area. The Guayakí immediately fled while the Mby'á remained at the periphery of the tiny settlement for several decades.

The population grew slowly due to its isolation and lack of any infrastructure. Despite Emilio F. Moran's contention (1988:199-212) that

244 ECONOMIC ANTHROPOLOGY OF THE STATE

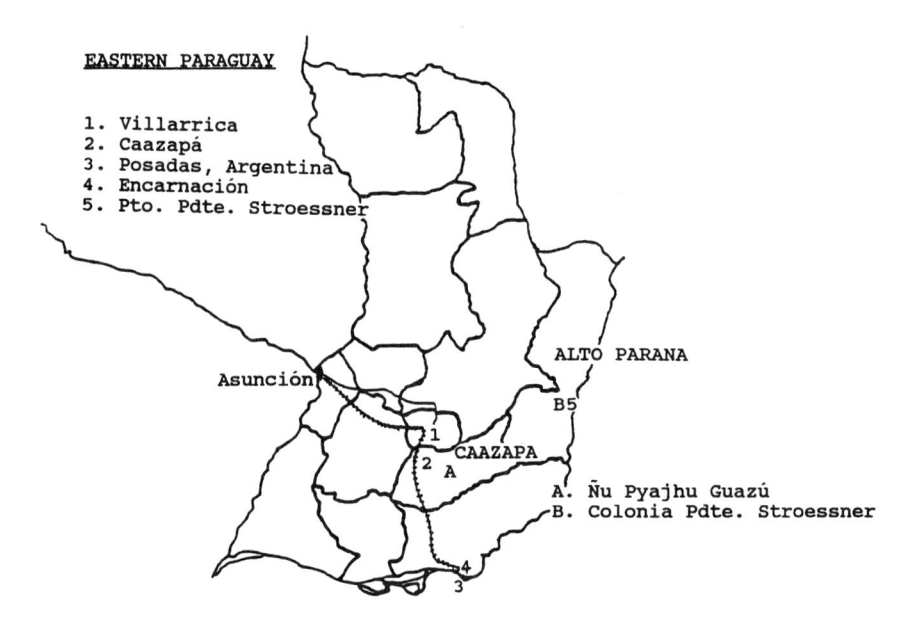

Figure 1. 1959 asphalt road system.

all frontier societies reproduce social stratification and class differences, the community was undifferentiated. This has continued to the present day, and although there are now social status differences, they are minor. (The situation in Minga Guazú does correspond with Moran's hypothesis, and arises from a similar set of circumstances.) This lack of differentiation can be attributed to the wealth of land available for those who were willing to live "beyond the Ricardian margin" (Gudeman 1988:213-216) of non-profitability and subsistence farming, the slow in-migration rate, and the lack of

RURAL DEVELOPMENT IN PARAGUAY 245

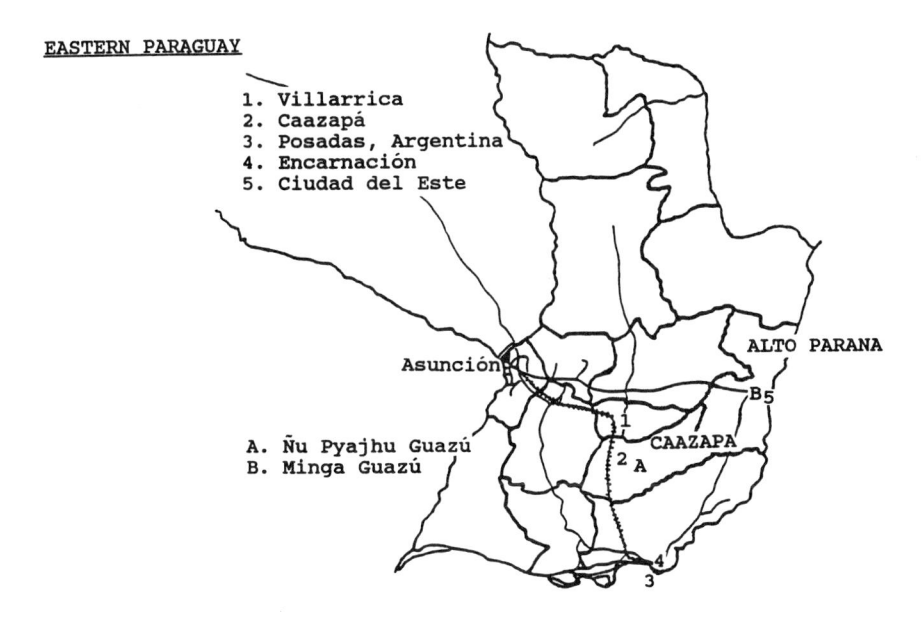

EASTERN PARAGUAY
1. Villarrica
2. Caazapá
3. Posadas, Argentina
4. Encarnación
5. Ciudad del Este

A. Ñu Pyajhu Guazú
B. Minga Guazú

Figure 2. 1990 asphalt road system.

capitalist ventures or wage labor in the area. In fact, young men traditionally walked three or more days to Argentina or Brazil to work a season of wood extraction or *yerba mate* (a type of tea leaf) processing in order to buy their first suit of clothes or to finance their weddings.

During this early period most of the growing population consisted of family members of the early colonists or first generation offspring ready to start their own homesteads. The squatter colony was virtually ignored by the national and departmental governments and *gauchos* (in this usage meaning a lawless horseman outside the reach of the state) roamed freely and unchecked through the countryside. Immigration, by those seeking to escape war service, accelerated slightly during the Chaco War with Bolivia (1932-35). It increased again in 1940 after the Liberal Party in power created a land colony called Colonia Nicolás Argüello. This colony included Ñu Pyajhu Guazú and much of the surrounding area to the north and west. The land was surveyed using existing land claims with space designated for a road, a school, and a communal pasture. The first official school was recognized and a state-salaried teacher was hired for the first and second grades. (The inhabitants had been educating their own children until this time.)

After the Revolution of 1947, there was another influx of colonists due to political persecution by the victorious Colorado Party over their Liberal Party counterparts. These new migrants were almost exclusively relatives of the people already settled in Ñu Pyajhu Guazú for there they could be assured of a safe haven.

By the 1950s there was little unclaimed land available. However, real population density was still low and the majority of the land remained uncleared. But Ñu Pyajhu Guazú was now being linked politically and economically to the state; transportation was improving, and the *gauchos* were brought under control. The Mby'á retreated onto a private landholding beyond the colony. A third and fourth grade were added to the school and permission was required for all public functions. An oratory for Catholic religious services was built in 1956 in a "central" location. In the 1960s the colonists constructed a bridge over the Pirapó River and cut a direct road from the colony to the capital of Caazapá. The road transversed a swamp and a large ranch owned by the major political family in Caazapá, the Sarubbis.[1]

Migration from Ñu Pyajhu Guazú began in the 1970s to neighboring land and to other frontier zones in the 1980s. The community has recently become a peripheral part of a World Bank development project that, by 1990, had completed an improved dirt road. The World Bank project had also made it possible for a large percentage of landowners to receive title to their land (previously, landowners had found it almost impossible to obtain a title due to local graft and the notorious incompetence of the government land reform agency known as the IBR or Institute of Rural Welfare).

Currently, Ñu Pyajhu Guazú has no town center, no stores, bars, restaurants, police, health services, running water, electricity, or public buildings other than the oratory, the school, and a half-finished health post. Other than the teachers' salaries, the government has no monetary investments in the community. The people themselves have built all the public buildings and a feeder road leading to the new World Bank road and continue to maintain them.

There are local political functionaries, but they are subsistence farmers like their neighbors and have no special respect, income, or power. There is some economic activity unrelated to cash cropping but on a very minor scale. No one individual has sufficient income or land to differentiate himself or herself substantially from his or her neighbors. There are no cars, trucks, or tractors. Cotton is the only cash crop for which there is a reasonable market, and it is grown by almost everyone. However, no one monocrops nor would anyone dare to do so even if such an individual had the means because cotton profits do not supply sufficient income and yearly profits are unpredictable. Subsistence farming remains the norm, and subsistence crops are highly diversified.

In the official land registry, Ñu Pyajhu Guazú appears to be a community of "middle" farmers (landholdings being predominantly in the 20 to 50 hectare range). This type of land holding is considered adaptable to mechanized farming with appropriate credit inputs by development agencies. However, without exception, a number of different families work the same land. The holdings that have been split by inheritance have never been officially divided due to the expense involved. Many landholders with large lots freely allow less fortunate relatives and neighbors to use several hectares for farming or for their house lots. There is no one in Ñu Pyajhu Guazú who does not have access to land for subsistence farming although there are many who own no land.

There are differences in how much land each nuclear family has available and there are concomitant social differences, but there has been no class differentiation based on land or economic wealth. Until recently the land has been almost valueless except for marginal subsistence farming, and there has been no history of land speculation by the inhabitants themselves.[2] Every individual in Ñu Pyajhu Guazú can be considered a member of the lower class in Paraguay and is viewed that way by himself and by outsiders.

Despite their isolation, the people of Ñu Pyajhu Guazú have always participated in the national market economy and have continually attempted to improve their cash crop production, diversify their cash crops, develop access to markets and goods, and improve their position in the capitalist system. From the earliest settlement of the zone, cash cropping has intermixed with subsistence. Cash cropping was accelerated with the advent of President Alfredo Stoessner's economic policies encouraging export crops to the detriment of nationally consumable crops.[3]

The people in Ñu Pyajhu Guazú, however, have been always thwarted by lack of infrastructure, markets, reasonable credit, and political will on the part of the regional and national authorities for any real development. When the peasants from this zone managed to surmount these difficulties, they were crushed by state economic policy, political patronage, and *ley mbareté*, i.e., the rule of the strongest.[4]

There are three primary cash crops in Paraguay, wheat, cotton, and soy. Bank credit is regularly available for only soy and cotton. Since soy and wheat both require large land holdings and mechanization to be profitable, cotton is the default crop for most Paraguayan peasants. There are other cash cropping possibilities such as tobacco and bitter orange extract, but the market value varies greatly, they require much more work, and some years there are no buyers in Caazapá. Any perishable crop is out of the question because of poor road conditions and frequent rains. Until 1990, the nearest paved road was 85 kilometers away. It is now about 65 kilometers away. There are no grain silos or cotton gins in the entire department of Caazapá. The nearest market area is the capital of Caazapá and the producers in Ñu Pyajhu Guazú are almost completely dependent upon the *acopiadores*, or middlemen, in Caazapá who set the local price for cotton and other produce. This price is set as low as possible and never reflects national prices. Many years, the peasants of Ñu Pyajhu Guazú have lost money on their crops, if labor costs are included in the equation. They are also, at times, forced to wait several months to receive payment. It is not unknown for an *acopiador* to fail to pay the peasants at all. Of course, this only happens once, but there is effectively no recourse for the vendor, due to the workings of the economic system and *ley mbareté*.

In the past, if there were a poor season, the male head of the household would go to Brazil or Argentina to work in a factory or as a day worker engaged in some type of heavy physical labor and then return during the next farm season. This activity increased during the 1970s as infrastructure and work opportunities improved in South America. This strategy is no longer viable in most cases due to high inflation rates and low wages in Brazil and Argentina. In fact, Argentines are flooding into Paraguay, their former hinterland, in search of economic opportunities. In Ñu Pyajhu Guazú itself, there are few opportunities for obtaining wages. The primary method is to work the *changa*, i.e., to work someone else's field. This is limited to the cotton harvest season and pays very little, the wage sometimes being paid as a percentage of the cotton picked. No one wants to work the *changa*: it is considered to be degrading, only for the poorest of the poor, incompetent farmers, or children looking for pocket money.

The population of Ñu Pyajhu Guazú faces strong political, social, and economic control outside of the community and in any dealings with outsiders within the community. They have no power, no political connections, minimal education, and no economic means. Because of this, they have no leverage in the system of *ley mbareté*, and due to their isolation, they can seek no alternative options. However, within Ñu Pyajhu Guazú itself, the evidence of state control is practically non-existent in every day life. It exists, but only covertly.

Local people tend to work together and take care of their own. This is not precisely in an egalitarian manner, as individuals do try and improve their situation vis-à-vis their neighbors, and there are definite social differences. But if there is a real need, help is given without question. The community organizes itself to provide perceived necessities such as the oratory, road, school, and health post, and everyone contributes labor, materials, or money. Most important, if there is a threat from outside, the entire community provides a common front to meet that threat.

Ñu Pyajhu Guazú is also united spatially. The first inhabitants picked an area of pasture surrounded by forests, and built the first homes around the perimeter of the pasture area. As the population grew, the homesteads formed a ring, which then began filling in towards the center. The pasture and housing space is separated from the crop land by natural fences made of *karaguatá*, a species of pineapple with very sharp, spiny leaves. The effect is a community formed like a bowl with the fencing interlocked behind the houses, a strip of forested area (for construction and firewood) and then the surrounding fields lying outside the rim of the bowl. Until very recently, there were no fences delineating different fields and pastures, and even now fencing is minimal. All the livestock grazes together regardless of the actual land ownership, and the animals are herded toward individual houses every evening.

## Minga Guazú

In 1950, the entire department of Alto Paraná (20,257 km$^2$) had a population of only 9531, or less than 1% of the national population. It had a population density of less than two inhabitants per square kilometer compared to 40 individuals per square kilometer in the *minifundia* zone around Asunción.

At the time of colonization, the land in Alto Paraná had been exploited for a century by foreign capitalists. They extracted *yerba mate* leaves from natural tree stands and various species of valuable woods, but the land had never been farmed except by indigenous populations. The foreign exploitation was conducted from the eastern border using the Paraná River for transport to Brazil or Argentina.

When the first 35 colonists arrived in Minga Guazú in 1959, entry was frequently made from Brazil. Some arrived by means of a new air strip built in 1957 to facilitate development of the colony and its sister river port, Puerto Presidente Stroessner (now called Ciudad del Este). Many arrived by ox cart, but the overland journey was long and arduous. A road to the Brazilian border wasn't completed until 1966.

Minga Guazú was a special colony from the beginning. Between 1957 and 1960, the Paraguayan government passed a series of laws relieving the Institute of Agrarian Reform of responsibility for the new colony and port and placing them under the direction of the Ministry of Interior.[5] The Commission of Administration of Port President Stroessner (CAPPS) was formed to develop and administer the colony. Salesian priest Guido Coronel arrived in 1959 as de facto director of the colony. He was a personal friend and crony of former president Alfredo Stroessner as well as the uncle of Pastor Coronel, Stroessner's Chief of Investigations and most notorious abuser of human rights in Paraguay. For the next 30 years, Father Coronel (known as Pa'i Coronel from the Guaraní word for "priest") used his political and familial connections "to make himself strong" and control the social, economic and religious life of the colonists.

Minga Guazú covered 54,000 hectares laid out in a grid, with the new highway running through the center. Perpendicular feeder roads were designated every two kilometers. The early lots were 25 hectares with a road frontage of 250 meters and a depth of 1000 meters. Later lots were cut to 20 or 10 hectares. Not all of the land was cut into private lots. Large tracts of land were reserved for the Salesian fathers (750 hectares), for the future agricultural school (169 hectares), and the future cooperative (1000 hectares). Some land was sold for speculation although under the law this is illegal in a land colony. The colony included an urban center, apart from the port, and Stroessner had his own 40 hectare lot on the highway.

A special group of agricultural engineers was dispatched to aid the colony and to visit various *minifundia* settlements to encourage settlement in Minga Guazú. Apparently only loyal Colorado Party members were invited, and they frequently received free transportation. The earliest colonists quickly filled the lots closest to the proposed highway and the port city, leaving later arrivals less accessible lots. Later colonists arrived individually, many migrating from other colonies. The colony grew rapidly and by 1963, there were 700 families in Minga Guazú.

During the 1960s, the international highway was completed and the Puente de Amistad ("Friendship Bridge") linking Paraguay with Brazil was inaugurated. A hydro-electric dam, Acaray I, was constructed. This new infrastructure gave the population access to expanded markets and goods, off-farm labor opportunities, electricity, and turned the area into the major growth zone in the country.

In Minga Guazú itself, the colony as a whole was benefitting from every government development plan implemented in Alto Paraná. Alto Paraná itself was targeted to receive more development aid than other areas in Paraguay. In addition, Minga Guazú received aid in the form of food from Caritas Paraguayas ("Paraguayan Charities", an independent international aid group) and aid from the Interamerican Development Bank for farm machinery and tractors. CAPPS built a sawmill that accepted lumber for land payments, and Pa'i Coronel organized and directed the largest cooperative in Paraguay, Cooperative Minga Guazú, from which the colony's current name was derived.

By the early 1970s, there were approximately 11,200 people in the rural area of Minga Guazú and 1800 in the urban center. The port city of Stroessner became the official capital of Alto Paraná and was separated from Minga Guazú at Kilometer 10 (counting from the Brazilian border). Throughout the 1970s and 1980s Minga Guazú was rapidly developing an impressive infrastructure for agricultural production that included 19 grain silos, 18 lumber yards, ceramic, brick, and cement factories, and cotton gins, to list only a few. Concomitantly, the urban infrastructure expanded at a phenomenal rate. By the end of the decade, Minga Guazú could boast of two hospitals, a police station, civil registry and justice of the peace, a post office, a telephone office, an agricultural extension agency, 40 schools, two private Catholic high schools, four technical colleges, and a soccer stadium. In 1989 Minga Guazú applied to become a district and by 1990 the urban center was officially named a municipality and the colony a district, both to be called Minga Guazú.

Minga Guazú was socially and economically stratified from its inception ranging from poor peasants to Pa'i Coronel and his administrators. Some colonists, usually Brazilians, had the resources to mechanize on their own or with a bank loan. Others were able to work through the political system to reap the benefits of international aid programs and national development plans that were dispersed by Pa'i Coronel. The majority were forced to duplicate their traditional subsistence farming practices. Many who had a lot along the highway sold their land to business interests and others sold their land to urban developers who broke the agricultural land into small lots for resale. Population turnover was high and it is estimated that only 20% of the original population remain. Over time, as Minga Guazú became developed and settled, class differences became more defined and noticeable. Those who did well bought more land and improved their holdings, and those who did less well often sold part of their land to pay for the remainder. Frequently, needy relatives from the colonists' original settlement arrived to share one lot, effectively splitting the lot into smaller pieces. As elsewhere in Paraguay, grown children were given land for houses and agricultural plots. This has resulted in a land holding pattern ranging from lots of five hectares or less to those of 100 hectares or more. Today on any *calle* (or feeder road) large mechanized estates with fancy houses intermingle with wood plank home made houses and only partially cleared fields.

The houses are dispersed (except for clumps of relatives), and neighbors have little contact with each other. Since the colonists were drawn from all over Paraguay and include a fair number of Brazilians, Germans, Swiss, and Japanese, the inhabitants were often strangers to each other. At times, they were frequently wary and suspicious of their neighbors' intentions and unsure of each other's political connections. Potential colonizers were frequently forced to affiliate officially with the Colorado Party in order to buy land or own a business. Many people therefore lied about their true political "colors" and, if discovered, were in danger of being forced to leave the colony. The land was then transferred to a more "reliable" owner.[6] The colonists were more directly discouraged from organizing by Pa'i Coronel, who allowed no peasant organizations, no unions, nor even outside Catholic Church organizations.

There are no communal pastures, and every pasture must be fenced to prevent animals straying onto the adjoining property. Although included in the original colony plans, interconnecting roads are nonexistent except for the highway. This effectively cuts every *calle* off from the others, and strings the population along a line that can extend up to 16 kilometers. It also makes public transportation unfeasible, and there is only one *calle* that has an intermittent bus line. Without a truck or tractor, the farmer is dependent upon an *acopiador* to move his produce, and even going to town can sometimes be a difficult proposition. However, a number of colonists have bicycles or motorcycles or are able to flag a ride on the road. On the highway, there are a number of bus lines, always overcrowded.

Due to its location and the growth boom in Alto Paraná, farmers have been able to work either in Ciudad del Este or in one of the factories and silos that now dot the highway. Many work the *changa* for their large land-holding neighbors. Cotton is still an incompletely mechanized crop, and the harvesting is done by hand. This work can be for cash or for use of a tractor for a determined amount of time. Unlike in Ñu Pyajhu Guazú, working the *changa* is common, and it is a source of needed income for many people, even though wages for this work are only marginally higher in this region than elsewhere. Besides cotton, the other major cash crops in Minga Guazú are soy, wheat, and corn. Soy has the largest production, being the most profitable for export, and most bank credit is given for this crop. It is also the only export crop accepted by the Minga Guazú cooperative. International prices and local weather conditions vary too much for wheat to be considered a good risk, and credit resources tend to reflect this. Small farmers are restricted to cotton as a cash crop, but they can reap a better profit than in other parts of the country, since the land is so rich that the yields are quite high. In addition, although small farmers must use an *acopiador*, there are more to choose from and they have less distance to travel, both to load the cotton at the farm and to unload at the cotton gin.

Education is quite variable in Minga Guazú. In Ñu Pyajhu Guazú almost everyone is educated to the grade level that was available at the time they were in school. Only a small minority has had any education beyond the sixth grade, due to the difficulties and expense involved in leaving the community to attend.

In Minga Guazú a number of the *calles* did not have a school until well into the 1970s or 1980s and those that did frequently had less than six grades. The delay can probably be attributed to the fact that the government promised to provide schools but didn't, and the difficulty of organizing a *calle* for community work. This means that there are many young people with little or no education. A few *calles* had schools in the 1960s, although these did not always have six grades at the onset. The colonists that had personal transportation or lived reasonably close to the highway could sometimes afford to send their children to the urban center. Those higher on the socio-economic scale usually have a high school degree, and the colony's administrators and their families tend to have some college or technical training. For the average colonist, however, high school is impossible because, until 1990, there was no public high school, and tuition fees for the Catholic schools were quite high. These differences added to, and continue to add to, the stratification of the population as a whole in Minga Guazú.

State control is much more noticeable in Minga Guazú than Ñu Pyajhu Guazú and is more likely to touch the individual. The political and economic patronage system is fully developed. There is a main Colorado

Party section in the urban center, and 29 different sub-sections are spread throughout the rural areas. While it is true that the rural politicians do not receive a salary, they have more power than those in Ñu Pyajhu Guazú and have economic opportunities unavailable to others, such as obtaining a tractor on good credit terms. Until the 1989 coup that toppled Stroessner, Pa'i Coronel was the leader of the church, of the cooperative, of the education system, and of the colony's administration. He controlled the political system and had his own private garrison of 20 soldiers on Kilometer 20. He made decisions that affected all spheres of an individual's life and forged his own web of political cronies. He decided who could enter the cooperative and who had access to development aid -- even which crops could be grown. Without the approval of the *pa'i*, the individual could even be in danger of losing his lot, as Pa'i Coronel personally approved all land titles and collected all land payments. This entrenched system of *ley mbareté* had ramifications outside of the strictly political or economic, at times dictating who would marry whom or who would be chosen to become godfather to one's children. It even dictated which people were safe friends, as known associates of undesirables were considered suspect.

Land settlement and development have been quite distinct in Ñu Pyajhu Guazú and Minga Guazú (Table 1). Both populations were drawn primarily from a common Paraguayan capitalist-based market economy. It is my contention that state economic policy, itself affected by the world economic system, had a large measure of responsibility in creating and fostering the differences between them.

## State Economic Policy

Former Paraguayan president Stroessner is frequently credited with developing Paraguay and bringing it into the 20th century, but, in fact, his efforts were specifically directed to favored areas and projects in order to take advantage of international development monies while consolidating his position politically and economically. After 1954, the Paraguayan state became synonymous with Stroessner and the Colorado Party machine. Over the years, there were several episodes of mass physical repression, but Stroessner preferred to consolidate and strengthen his regime through a balance of civilian and military patronage. He assigned secondary control of large geographic areas or lucrative business enterprises to his primary supporters (Kleinpenning 1987:156-157). These supporters were expected to form their own tiers of cronies who were coopted by economic considerations or prestige positions of power. Each level of these tiers repeated the

TABLE 1. PHYSICAL, SOCIAL AND ECONOMIC DIFFERENCES

|  | Minga Guazú | Ñu Pyajhu Guazú |
|---|---|---|
| **Physical** | | |
| proximity to asphalt | 1-16 kilometers | 65 kilometers |
| transport | varied and plentiful some private vehicles | very limited no vehicles |
| colony layout | dispersed grid | concentric |
| migration pattern | government directed | spontaneous |
| pasture | fenced | not fenced |
| land holdings | mixed types, sizes | all similar |
| growth | rapid | slow |
| age of settlement | 30 years | 75 years |
| **Social** | | |
| stratification | well developed | minimal |
| local organization | minimal | developed |
| education | uneven | equal |
| neighbors | frequently unknown | known |
| language use | largely bilingual | mainly Guaraní |
| turnover rate | high | low |
| daily state control | noticeable | minimal |
| **Economic** | | |
| access to markets | high | low |
| access to goods | high | low |
| land prices | high | low |
| economic options | varied | very limited |
| wage earning options | varied | migratory |
| cash crops | soy, cotton, wheat, corn | cotton |
| farming system | subsistence, some mechanization and monocropping | subsistence no mechanization or monocropping |
| income differences | marked | minimal |
| land speculation | common | none |
| cooperatives | one long term | several failed |

pattern of control that Stroessner devised -- patronage to those who were most powerful or necessary and repression for dissenters. Every individual became dependent upon Stroessner and the Colorado Party for his or her economic well-being, down to the lowliest rural school teacher. No state jobs were given to non-Colorado Party members. Even employees in the private sector were hired on the basis of whom they knew and who their connections were, even bank tellers and hotel clerks (Masi 1989, Arditi and Rodríquez 1987).

At the time that Stroessner came to power, Paraguay had traditionally been heavily dependent upon Argentina politically and economically. This was due to Paraguay's land-locked position and lack of alternate land-based transportation infrastructure. All exports and imports had to be transported via the Paraguay River through the La Plata River system to the sea (Lewis 1980).

Stroessner wanted to terminate this dependence and embarked upon a state policy of overland expansion eastward to Brazil. Brazil had started a "March to the West" some years earlier and had its own economic rationale for opening the border with Paraguay. Brazil would gain access to land and investment opportunities and could take over Argentina's position of chief importer and exporter in Paraguay. Stroessner's "March to the East" was intended to improve Paraguay's international position vis-à-vis both of his powerful neighbors (Birch 1988). There were domestic benefits as well. This period corresponded with an expanding population, new needs for public lands and higher food production for use in the urban centers (Baer and Birch 1984).

In implementing his new economic policy, Stroessner was aided by the U.S. government and international development agencies. President Dwight D. Eisenhower was concomitantly launching new policies based on the concept of "trade rather than aid," and money became available specifically for internal development in Latin American countries. The benefits to the U.S. were expected to be more foreign investment opportunities and more vigorous international trade (International Cooperation Administration 1956).

A series of development packages were designed and funded by the U.S. with cooperation of the Paraguayan government. Stroessner's official external economic policy and unofficial internal policy differed however. Implementation and maintenance were dependent upon the state's need for control of its general population and maintenance of its supporters' vested interests. This becomes vividly clear when we explore the question of cooperatives in Minga Guazú and Ñu Pyajhu Guazú.

In general, the "March to the East" gave justification for regaining control of foreign owned land, relieved internal land crowding, raised the production level of exportable crops, opened new economic markets with Brazil and provided new jobs. It was approved and encouraged by the international capitalist bankers and development agencies who were relied upon for loans, grants, and support. Perhaps most importantly, it offered new ground for political control (from the ground up, so to speak) and generated substantial new patronage.

Spatially, this new state policy had the effect of creating a new type of frontier zone in Paraguay. Previously, the rural frontier had slowly been expanding within and beyond a triangular area formed by the Paraguay River, the Paraná River and a railroad that ran south from Villarrica. The new economic plan effectively cut off further development of the area running south of Villarrica. This leg had never been well developed nor particularly vibrant. It took until 1990 for the bridge to be inaugurated connecting Encarnación with Posadas, Argentina, and to this day, there are no paved roads within the entire department of Caazapá.

The new frontier in Alto Paraná made a larger triangle delineating Paraguay's borders and left Ñu Pyajhu Guazú in the underdeveloped center (see maps). For the first time in history, Paraguay experienced a boom town, rush-to-the-frontier phenomenon with high expectations of personal gain for the frontiersmen. The majority of the government's development interests were directed towards the newly-opened ground while Caazapá received only peripheral benefits of newly established national institutions such as the agricultural extension agency, development bank, and cooperative development agency.

After 1965, the international economic system and U.S. government economic policies were affecting and directing the changes in Paraguay's cooperative history. The first surge of cooperatives corresponded with a U.S. Agency for International Development (USAID) program for credit and marketing cooperatives. Under the 1967 Agricultural Commodities Sales agreement between the U.S. and Paraguay, a certain percentage of Paraguay's wheat sales profits had to be used for cooperatives. The government was advised to promulgate a revision of existing agricultural cooperative laws, which had been originally designed for foreign colonists such as the Mennonites in the Paraguayan Chaco. This urging was repeated more strongly in following years. The revision in the cooperative laws in 1972 coincided with USAID's Development of Agriculture Cooperatives project designed to reach farmers with less than 21 hectares of land (U.S.A.I.D. 1989). It also resulted in the creation of new agency, the

General Direction of Cooperativism (GDC), to oversee the new cooperatives (Verdecchia 1989:23-29).

While many new cooperatives were constituted, the USAID target group received little or no benefit. The cooperative guidelines and stipulations required a large amount of bureaucratic paperwork, an understanding of bureaucratic processes and the urban milieu, and a governing body that had both time and money to fulfill their roles. This effectively excluded Paraguayan peasants from controlling their own organizations. The majority of peasants in Paraguay cannot read or write well, if at all. They may never have been in the capital much less know the intricacies of Paraguay's abysmal bureaucracy, and frequently they do not speak Spanish.[7] The new law controlled who was organizing cooperatives and how they were organized. In effect, it allowed for the familiar system of power brokerage and patronage to exploit the peasant population and dominate potential trouble- makers through their own organizations. Unofficially, the new cooperative laws controlled and discouraged peasant cooperatives while officially they encouraged and promoted peasant economic organizations. At the same time, the laws allowed Stroessner to take advantage of USAID grant monies to extend his and the state's own power and economic advantage through differential disbursement.

The history of cooperative development in Minga Guazú and Ñu Pyajhu Guazú provides a specific example of how state economic policies affected the direction of development in Stroessner's Paraguay. Cooperatives were a central feature of various international aid projects, were important in both case study sites, and their administration clearly shows the differential application of stated economic policy. It is clear that official policy for consumption abroad differed from unofficial state-dictated domestic implementation. Again, it should be remembered that these two case studies are opposite ends of a spectrum and there are gradations between the extremes.

## Cooperatives in Minga Guazú and Ñu Pyajhu Guazú[8]

The Cooperative Minga Guazú Agro-Industrial, Ltd. was founded in 1967 by Pa'i Coronel. It is the only Paraguayan cooperative with agro-industrial capabilities such as grain silos and processing plants. It also claims to be the largest in Paraguay. The cooperative Pio XII Agricultural Ltd., which was active in the district of Caazapá, was founded in 1953. There were some members from Ñu Pyajhu Guazú, but it did not become popular in Ñu Pyajhu Guazú until 1973.

RURAL DEVELOPMENT IN PARAGUAY 259

In 1976, the departments of Alto Paraná and Caazapá led the country in membership percentages, but despite the high membership, there were only modest levels of recorded capital per member, and Caazapá was by far the lowest. In 1981, Caazapá dramatically outstripped Alto Paraná in membership capital even though its total membership number had dropped significantly. At the same time Minga Guazú had 77% of total assets of all cooperatives in Alto Paraná and, by 1986, had 82.6% of all cooperative membership. During this ten-year span, cooperative membership continued to grow in Alto Paraná while it continued to decline in Caazapá. By 1986 the peasant cooperative had disappeared in Caazapá, and it was the only department to show a deficit in peasant income.

Generally, in this 1976-1986 period, there were more new cooperatives initiated in the Brazilian frontier zone, and the most productive and developed of those cooperatives were in Alto Paraná. Benefitting from its favorable location and outside income that totaled 62.9% of its operating capital (the membership contributed only 37.1%), Minga Guazú had a high income but low efficiency record (González et al. 1987:132-174). This information is available in most cooperative studies. An examination of specific events in the two communities explains these statistics.

While the management of the co-op Minga Guazú denies having received any outside aid or financing, the General Direction of Cooperativism's records indicate just how much special aid the cooperative managers received over the years. In 1973, Minga Guazú received swine production financing from the Swiss Technical Cooperation Mission that was channelled to the co-op through the Paraguayan state. The project included G10,000,000[9] to construct a pig feed plant. The National Bank of Development offered G100,000 in credit to co-op members participating in the project. They also received help from the World Food Program. In 1973, the cooperative also "acquired" 1000 hectares of land running from the International Highway between Kms. 32 and 34 to the Acaray River for use as a ranch and a forest reserve.[10] In 1976, Minga Guazú received credit worth G25,000,000 from the National Development Bank, and the Swiss government offered 100% financing to Minga Guazú for the construction of a milk processing plant. In 1977, the Ranching Fund gave Minga Guazú a loan to build a corn silo and to buy equipment and tractors. In 1980, Minga Guazú bought a soybean processing plant, Massiero S.A., with financing by the Bank of Brazil and the National Development Bank. In 1982, Pa'i Coronel publicly thanked Stroessner for his "constant help" and for his "special intervention" with the Council of Economic Coordination to make available G1,500,000,000 through the National Development

Bank and the Central Bank of Paraguay (for the soybean plant). In 1984, Minga Guazú received bank credit from the National Development Bank and the Paraguayan Commerce Bank of South America. The total amount of credit was not specified in the records. In 1986, Minga Guazú received special permission from the Ministry of Finance to import Brazilian soy, process it, and re-export it through Brazil to European markets. The cooperative also received a free market exchange rate (as opposed to the less favorable official rate) for the importation and exportation of this soy and was taxed at less than one Guaraní per kilo. In 1988, Minga Guazú was caught by the Central Bank of Paraguay using its special free exchange rate to sell soy products to Peru. Pa'i Coronel's response to questioning was that the cooperative was only being a good capitalist venture and selling for the best possible profit. No criminal offense action was initiated. In 1989, the National Development Bank, the Paraguayan Commerce Bank of South America, and Investments of Paraguay all gave bank credit to Minga Guazú which amounted to a total of G1,200,000,000 (Dirección General de Cooperativismo 1990).

This record is probably incomplete since pertinent financial information is missing from every report, but it does serve as a good indicator of the differential disbursement of aid and loan packages, especially when compared with the Pio XII cooperative records.

That the cooperative was inefficiently run, was being used to support a patronage system and the Colorado Party, and cooperative profits were being diverted, is suggested by other entries in the General Direction of Cooperativism's records. For every cooperative management election report, only one list of candidates was presented by Pa'i Coronel and unanimously accepted. Pa'i Coronel was always elected head of the cooperative and a select group of men were always elected to the other governing positions. They were all Colorado Party members (as were most of the cooperative's members) and usually held other positions of power in the land colony infrastructure.

Despite a large membership base and significant levels of development aid and agricultural loans, the common membership can produce only soy to sell through the cooperative and must have land title to do so. The cooperative has no money of its own to buy ordinary farm equipment, tractors, etc. for resale to the general membership. Because of this, only members with private means can take advantage of the status a cooperative has to import without high duty costs.

Over the years, Pa'i Coronel consistently contributed higher and higher sums of money to the cooperative in order to keep its books balanced. This means not only that the cooperative was steadily losing money but also that Pa' i Coronel was making money in some way at an incredible rate. In 1979 he subscribed for G1,508,119 or 10% of the total. In 1985 he subscribed G6,958,119 or over 35% of the total. In 1986 he subscribed G8,058,119 or almost 40% of the total subscriptions to the cooperative.

The history of the cooperative experience in Ñu Pyajhu Guazú offers many contrasts with the Minga Guazú cooperative we have just examined. Early records of cooperatives in Caazapá indicate that there were eight members from Ñu Pyajhu Guazú in the cooperative in 1966. At that time the cooperative was run by a priest called Pa'i Wilfrido Rivas who centralized its operation in the town of Caazapá. Cooperative money bought a truck, warehouse and equipment. According to former members, Pa'i Rivas sold their products, kept the money, and then announced that the cooperative was in debt. "We weren't in debt, but he lied, taking advantage of the ignorant peasants." To pay the "debt", the Pa'i Rivas sold the warehouse. An appeal was made to the new General Direction of Cooperativism (GDC), and Humberto Fernandez intervened to help the co-op members retain some of their assets. Although the co-op was able to continue financially, confidence in it was lost, and it folded.[11]

Pa'i Adolfo Zaracho reanimated the former cooperative members in 1976 by decentralizing the daily operations to the peasant communities and promising to export cotton directly to Switzerland for the best possible profit. The people in Ñu Pyajhu Guazú were excited given the new circumstances, and a majority of the farmers joined. After the first cotton harvest, they were paid for half the crop at the local rate and promised their improved rate and remainder after the export sale was complete. They waited for six months before Pa'i Zaracho held a meeting and announced that there was no money because he hadn't realized how much all the documents and paperwork were going to cost. Many of the farmers from Ñu Pyajhu Guazú dropped out of the cooperative. But Pa'i Zaracho convinced the remainder that, since all of their documents were now in order, they would make huge profits in the future.

The process was repeated the next cotton season. When the priest called an assembly seven months later, he explained that not only had the bank told him that the cooperative had lost all its money, they needed $600 to make up a deficit. No one could believe that they had lost money again. A group of 30 co-op members decided to go to the GDC in person and appeal to Fernandez, who had helped them out before. Fernandez was sympathetic and named Rafael Espinola, Juan Benitez, and Domingo Ayala to replace the financial officers of the cooperative. He also gave them authorization to secure financial records from Pa'i Zaracho.

Espinola, a Ñu Pyajhu Guazú resident, related:

> This was on a Sunday at a meeting in Caazapá. On Monday the three of us went to the cooperative. We were met by the Pa'i, a certain Ibarra (official president of the cooperative), and their people, all with revolvers in their belts. They "made themselves strong". So what could we do? We were ready to give up, but some of the members wanted to pursue it. So we went to Asunción again! Fernandez was really hot! He called Zaracho and told him to come to Asunción immediately...and to bring his books (Turner 1993:210).

This occurred in January 1979 and for almost a full year the two factions in the cooperative battled for control with frequent appeals to the GDC, blistering sermons against the "pseudo- Marxists" trying to take over the cooperative, and a public argument in the streets of Caazapá that ended with Pa'i Zaracho punching Benitez in the face.

By September, the new financial officers were ready to reveal their findings about the irregularities of the preceding two years. A special meeting was held in Caazapá with three GDC representatives, two Colorado Party presidents, and both factions of the Pio XII cooperative. At the meeting it was revealed that: 1) In 1977 the cooperative had a profit of G4,576,995 that was distributed among only five people -- three board members, Pa'i Zaracho, and the cooperative's accountant; 2) A donation of G1,307,691 from the Canadian Catholic Organization for Peace and Development Project had disappeared and a false report prepared and given to the Canadian agency saying that it had been disbursed; 3) In 1978, the second quota from the Canadian project also disappeared; 4) A G5,279,854 loan from the Interamerican Foundation was charged as a debit to the cooperative but had never been disbursed; and 5) A National Development Bank loan for G10,527,000 had been illegally requested and only G3,356,000 had been distributed to the farmers. The financial officers asked to be relieved of those debts not incurred by the actual membership, permission to purge the cooperative of those responsible, and for access to purged board members' documents to clarify where the money went and try to recover it.

By the end of the year, Pa'i Zaracho had lost all control of the cooperative and the governing board became dominated by farmers from Ñu Pyajhu Guazú. From 1980 to 1982, cooperative membership dropped, but the cooperative made excellent profits for the first time. They also continued trying to recover their previous losses that amounted to G12,000,000 and which was discovered to be largely in the coffers of Pa'i Zaracho. They attempted to work through the legal system in Villarrica but there had been no results, and the lawyer appointed by the GDC to help was dragging his feet.

The cooperative was also trying to improve its market position during this period. Early in 1982, some members went to the Agriculture Ministry to ask Minister Hernando Bertoni about defending the cotton price which was set at an official rate of G600 for 10 kilos. Because the cooperative had no trucks of its own, it was still being forced to go through intermediaries and were receiving only G350. The cooperative members never saw Bertoni, but his secretary arranged for a cotton ginner to give them the official rate and to pick up the cotton in Caazapá. On the appointed day, the cooperative's cotton was there, but the trucks weren't. The cooperative was forced to sell to the local *acopiadores* at a much lower rate.

In February of 1982, the military began making arrests for unspecified crimes and vague accusations of communism. Two of the first arrests were men who had been to see Bertoni. They were accused of bothering the minister and of being communists. The people of Ñu Pyajhu Guazú were terrified after two police sweeps through the community had netted most of the governing board and a number of the rank and file membership. A desperate letter was sent to the GDC informing them that Pa'i Zaracho was using his influence as a priest and friend of the local Colorado Party leaders to block legal proceedings. Additionally, the cooperative was being pressured to cease its investigation by arrests of its members. The GDC sent a man to investigate the situation, but apparently the GDC was now worried itself. It was decided that the evidence against Zaracho could not be used as the documents lacked official stamps. Furthermore, it advised members to dissolve and liquidate the Pio XII cooperative, which was done (Dirección General de Cooperativismo 1990, Turner 1993).

In a situation like this it is difficult to point a direct finger of responsibility. Other events occurring in Ñu Pyajhu Guazú during the late 1970s and early 1980s suggest that the community was pushing too hard to improve its position and was perceived as trying to circumvent local authority. This corresponded with various accusations that the Liberal Party in Ñu Pyajhu Guazú was trying "to make itself strong" and a denouncement of the local Colorado sub-section president, who was replaced, for being "soft on Liberals."

After the fall of President Stroessner, several local government functionaries admitted what the peasants already knew, that the government was against cooperatives and had almost completely eliminated them in Caazapá and Guairá by the mid-1980s. Ñu Pyajhu Guazú and other communities were "repressed politically and religiously; they were called 'communists' and the organizers were broken up....[T]he local politicians don't want to give up their control over the peasants" (Turner 1990).

Another consequence of the change of government is the formation of a union at the Minga Guazú cooperative that is agitating for greater control of the organization.[11] A number of new cooperatives and peasant organizations have formed across the country and the national agricultural extension agencies are now encouraging them and helping to create more.

As can be seen, the actual history of these two cooperatives makes quite clear that selective patronage and repression lies behind the official statistics on growth, membership, and profitability of cooperatives. The histories also give lie to the official state explanations of why cooperatives tend to fail in Paraguay. These are that peasants don't know how to work together, aren't interested in investing time and money, lack technical and capitalistic knowledge, and don't pay off their debts. But this rationalization is important to support the status quo and maintain international development agencies' support and continuing aid.

## Conclusion

It is clear that, for the last 35 years, Stroessner's state economic policy has had a two-fold agenda. The government has attempted to improve its economic and political position internally and in the world economic system through development of new frontier areas and higher agricultural export production. This allowed Stroessner to lessen his economic dependence upon his two powerful neighbors, Brazil and Argentina. At the same time, he was able to expand his internal power base and consolidate his political control.

To do so, it was necessary to accept certain dictates from outside economic powers that had their own economic agendas of expansion and control. Stroessner presented an official economic policy for external consumption but implemented it only to the extent that it did not interfere with his own political needs. In order to extend and maintain internal control and protect the entrenched patronage system, the state found it expedient to subvert economic growth and development for some sectors of the population while strengthening others. In some cases, such as in Ñu Pyajhu Guazú, there was a deliberate policy of underdevelopment.

The overall growth of Paraguay's economy has suffered but the wealth of the entrenched elite has not. Where possible, the general population has been controlled spatially, structurally, religiously, and economically. The social life of the Paraguayan populace has been dominated and directed by state economic policies. In Minga Guazú these policies have dramatically stratified the community. In Ñu Pyajhu Guazú they have hindered the development of local class differences while strengthening the dichotomy between the local population and those who control their economic output. In neither case did state economic policy benefit the stated target group, the small, often landless, peasant farmer.

Since the 1989 government coup, there has been an opening for change and a lessening of government repression, but political necessity and international influences remain largely unchanged. Whether the recent "transition to democracy" will substantially change the state's economic policy and allow a more even development remains to be seen. However, historically as capitalism evolves within an internal system, there is an economic imperative to allow more participants into that system to increase production, provide markets, and prevent serious political problems.

## Acknowledgments

Research was funded by a Fulbright, Institute for International Education Dissertation Research grant. I would also like to acknowledge the Peace Corps as my two years of service in Paraguay prepared me with background knowledge of the countryside, crucial linguistic abilities, and many, many Paraguayan friends. Most of all I would like to thank Brian Turner who shares everything with me, including his field notes.

## Notes

1. This was not accomplished, however, with ease. The workers had only shovels and crude tools and the Sarubbi family sent soldiers to prevent the work until they became convinced that the road was in their own best interests.

2. Before Ñu Pyajhu Guazú became an official land colony, there were speculators who claimed to represent the land's absent owner. They attempted, and sometimes succeeded, in selling phony land titles to the squatters.

3. Before 1950 banks would give credit for corn production, and the government would buy both corn and manioc in order to feed the standing army. After 1950, Stroessner turned army recruits out on higher officer's land-holdings to produce their own food and to benefit his military officers.

4. *Ley mbareté* is an integral part of Paraguay's economic, social, legal, and political functioning. It literally means "strong law" but refers to an individual's ability to control events regardless of the law or social mores through personal position, cleverness, or social/political connections. *Ley mbareté* operates throughout all strata of Paraguayan society and a common expression is "*oñemombareté*" or "he or she made himself or herself strong."

5. The Institute of Agrarian Reform was replace by the IBR in 1963. Both agencies were responsible for creating and administering colonies for landless Paraguayan peasants.

6. There are a number of unusual and unexplained land transfers in the land registry files.

7. Approximately 40% of rural Paraguayans are monolingual in Guaraní and about twice that in Caazapá.

8. All data from the General Direction of Cooperativism in the following section was collected by Brian Turner in 1991. See Turner (1993) for additional information.

9. G indicates the Paraguayan unit of money, the Guaraní. In 1973, G126 was equal to $1 at the official exchange rate.

10. There are no records of this transaction in the Minga Guazú land registry for 1973 or any other year. Nor are there records of those lots ever having been sold.

11. This was confirmed orally by Fernandez who said Pio XII failed twice due to bad management and by Carlos Luna who worked with cooperatives in Caazapá and Guairá. "I told Pa'i Rivas that the cooperative belongs to the peasants, not to the Church. Pa'i Rivas said, 'No, the cooperative belongs to the Church.'"

12. Pa'i Coronel "fell" with Stroessner and has recently died.

## References

Arditi, Benjamín and José Carlos Rodríguez
    1987    *La Sociedad a Pesar del Estado: Movimientos Sociales y Recuperación Deomocrática en el Paraguay.* Asunción: El Lector.

Baer, Werner and Melissa Birch
    1984    Expansion of the Economic Frontier: Paraguayan Growth in the 1970s. *World Development* (August):786-91.

Birch, Melissa
    1988    La política pendular: Política de desarrollo del Paraguay en la post-guerra. *Revista Paraguaya de Sociología* 73:73-105.

Dirección General de Cooperativismo
    1990    *Memorias del Consejo de Administración.* Asunción.

Gonzalez, Carlos Alberto, Gladys Casaccia, Mirna Vázquez, and Celso Valázquez
    1987    *Organizaciones Campesinas en el Paraguay.* Asunción: Universidad Católica, Centro Interdisciplinario de Derecho Social y Economia Politica.

Gudeman, Steven
    1988    Frontiers as Marginal Economies. In J.W. Bennett and J.R. Bowen, eds., *Production and Autonomy, Anthropological Studies and Critiques of Development*, pp.213-16. Monographs in Economic Anthropology, No. 5. Lanham, MD: University Press of America.

International Cooperation Administration
  1956  *Some Aspects of Foreign Investments. Investment Opportunities in Paraguay.* Prepared by Frederic R. Fisher, Foreign Trade Specialist. The U.S. Operation Mission to Paraguay. Mimeo.

Kleinpenning, J.M.G.
  1987  *Man and Land in Paraguay.* Amsterdam: Centrum voor Studie en Documetatie van Latijns Amerika.

Lewis, Paul H.
  1980  *Paraguay Under Stroessner.* Chapel Hill: The University of North Carolina Press.

Masi, Fernando
  1989  *Stroessner: La Extinción de un Modelo Político en Paraguay.* Asunción: Ñanduti Vive/Intercontinental Editora.

Moran, Emilio R.
  1988  Social reproduction in agricultural frontiers. In J.W. Bennett and J.R. Bowen, eds., *Production and Autonomy, Anthropological Studies and Critiques of Development*, pp.199-213. Monographs in Economic Anthropology, No. 5. Lanham, MD: University Press of America.

Turner, Brian
  1990  Unpublished field notes.
  1993  *Community Politics and Peasant-State Relations in Paraguay.* Lanham, MD: University Press of America.

U.S.A.I.D.
  1989  *A.I.D. History in Paraguay, 1942-1988.* Asunción: U.S.A.I.D.

Verdecchia, José Miguel A.
  1989  *Algunas Consideraciones Sobre las Condiciones de Exito y Fracaso en Asociaciones Cooperativas Campesinas in el Paraguay.* Asunción: Centro Paraguayo de Estudios Sociológicos.

# INCORPORATION OF WAGE LABOR INTO A FORAGING ECONOMY ON THE PERIPHERY OF THE VENEZUELAN STATE

Ted L. Gragson
University of Georgia

## Introduction

Theories of the state seldom address the process of change associated with capitalist penetration into native cultures, yet unravelling this process is extremely important for understanding how individuals choose a particular course of action under a situation of incomplete knowledge. While the historical and contemporary devastation of native cultures resulting from capitalist penetration should not be minimized, in analyzing these situations, the process of change is frequently overlooked in favor of the consequences of change thus subverting any attempt to understand causation or offer plausible explanations. This failure most likely results from viewing the state as an autonomous vehicle of change exerting its power and authority equally over the areas it incorporates. Present evidence, however, suggests states are less a unitary concept than a vehicle of expression for component subgroups (Bunker 1985, Ostrom 1990, Love 1989).

That states are neither autonomous nor equally powerful within the scope of their authority is evident from the situation of many native groups in South America. Native groups presently living at the periphery of state societies throughout South America have been subject to capitalist penetration in some cases for hundreds of years. Nevertheless, many of these societies have managed to retain customary patterns of production, consumption, and exchange along with their associated social and political institutions (Love 1989). In the course of this article, I will attempt to indicate how state institutions are used as a vehicle of expression for particular subgroups by tracing the development of cattle ranching in the *Llanos de Apure* of southwestern Venezuela. To illustrate how non-participants in this form of capitalist penetration are affected by incomplete knowledge, I will present a formal analysis of the response to subsistence uncertainty among the *ciri khonome* Pumé, a native American group also living in the Llanos de Apure.

## Nature of States and Capitalist Penetration

States operate according to a logic of "capital imperialism" in which core regions accumulate resources by exploiting peripheral regions (Chase-Dunn and Hall 1991, Bunker 1985). States attempt to systematize control and bureaucratic procedures over the heterogeneous peripheral areas they hold subject, but the state is ultimately constrained by the fact it cannot dominate or transform autonomously. The exploitation itself is directed by capitalists who, in the ideal, represent a class extracting surplus value from a mass of free laborers lacking personal means of production. However, the idealized articulation between regions of a state, and the relations between capitalists and laborers, fails to indicate how real individuals act in a situation of capitalist penetration. States simply facilitate and regulate what society allows; thus, the state and the vehicle of capitalism should be viewed as constraint fields within which individuals act (Bunker 1985, Love 1989, Smith 1983).

The idealization of the state as an entity imposing and maintaining order for achieving maximum efficiency out of self-interest comes out of Hobbes' Leviathan. Case studies of modern, centralized states, however, provide evidence of how "irrational" states can be in their control of peripheral areas (Bunker 1985, Ostrom 1990, Chase-Dunn and Hall 1991). This is particularly evident in extractive enterprises such as cattle ranching. Extractive enterprises are geographically peripheral to states because they must be near the natural resources used or exploited, but distance also means the regions with which these enterprises are associated are poorly linked economically, socially, or politically to the state they are members of (Bunker 1985). At the core of a state, efficiency and rationality can be achieved through factors of scale and the benefits deriving from the perpetuation of institutions; neither of these advantages is present in peripheral areas. Distance leads to increased administrative costs for the state, which in turn limit the state's capacity to monitor peripheral areas and sanction defiant individuals or communities (Ostrom 1990). In the real world, efficiency is readily achieved in peripheral areas through informal markets such as those associated with rights to pasture and water in cattle ranching in the absence of state control (or despite it).

## Creating an Informal Market in the Llanos

The first cattle arrived in Venezuela during the 1550s. By 1560, *cimarron* cattle had made their way as far south as the Meta river -- the present political boundary with Colombia -- and by 1630 they were reported as "numerous" in the Llanos de Apure (Carvajal 1956, Otto 1986). Cattle ranching in Venezuela became a significant economic pursuit during the mid- to late 18th century following the collapse of the world cacao market and the increase in local and regional demand for meat, hides, and milk by-products. Meat production relying on the criollo breed of cattle remains to this day the primary objective of cattle ranching throughout the Llanos. The criollo breed produces very small amounts of milk (about 1-2 liters/day), but some cheese (and pigs fed on whey obtained from making cheese) is nevertheless produced seasonally. The State of Apure is presently the second largest supplier of cattle by-products in Venezuela producing 14.9% of all beef (nearly half the entire production for the Llanos region) and 1.2% of all milk products in 1974 (Otto 1986, Mendez Echenique 1985, Carvallo 1985).

The original Venezuelan oligarchy of cattle ranchers consisting of no more than 80 individuals began moving south through the Llanos region from Caracas in the early 1700s. The Llanos of Apure proper came into the reach of this expansion after the founding just north of the Apure river of the Villa de Españoles de San Jaime in 1753. The early *entradas* by ranchers to the Llanos region were made in order to privatize the large herds of cimarron cattle living there (Mirabal 1987, Carvallo 1985, Mirabal and Olivares 1990). Newcomers would found an *hato* by building a corral and a house and take de facto possession of rivers, cattle, and land. An *hato* was legally described as follows in a 1791 census of cattle in the Llanos of Apure:

> Hato: una parcela de 80 varas de cuadro, escogidas ó identificadas para la construcción de casas y corrales y desde la cuál se extiende la pretendida dotación de tierras que mide regularmente media legua a cada viento (Pinto, quoted in Mirabal 1987).

De facto possession could be made a legal possession through the venue of a *composición*. Since the Crown did not involve itself with the granting of *composiciones* by local *cabildos*, title-solicitors could easily use their political and economic standing to influence the final outcome of requests (Mirabal 1987, 1991; Mirabal and Olivares 1990). It is important to note, however, that an *hato* is more than a specified amount of land since it combines private land with a collective use of pasture and water premised on the roundup of cimarron cattle. The state did not legally recognize these communal rights until 1811, 60 years after ranching began in the Llanos. An extra-legal codification (*Derechos de Llanos*) was nevertheless made by a group of ranchers within a matter of 10-15 years of founding the first *hato* in the region (Mirabal 1987).

Both the extra-legal and the legal set of laws codified by the State in 1811 (also called *Derechos de Llanos*) restricted communal rights over pasture and water to a *criador*. Being a *criador* depended upon having a sizable herd of cattle as well as an *hato*, but the exact definition changed over time through manipulation of the *Derechos de Llanos* by influential subgroups and individuals. For example, General Juan Vicente Gomez (dictator of Venezuela from 1908 to 1936) created a cattle monopoly in this way during the early part of the 20th century that persisted until 1970. The *Derechos de Llanos* are still employed to various degrees in peripheral areas and continue to allow control over pasture, water, and land to concentrate into the hands of *criadors* not those of the state (a *criador* is presently defined as a person having a minimum of 100 cows [vacas paridas]) and 2500 ha of land, Carvallo 1985). In 1937, 58% of the land in Venezuela dedicated to cattle ranching was in estates greater than 10,000 ha and was held by only 4% of landholders; 10% of this same land was in estates larger than 100,000 ha held by only 0.1% of landholders (Müller 1990). In 1978, 96% of the land being exploited in the State of Apure was held by 6% of proprietors in ranches larger than 500 ha (Mendez Echenique 1985).

Cattle have always been more valuable than land throughout the Llanos. The creation of an informal market by selected individuals in order to institutionalize the control of cattle resembles the process reported from other areas peripheral to state authority. Webb (1931), for example, describes it for the American Great Plains during the second half of the 19th century. This quote effectively summarizes the process:

> The Easterner, with his background of forest and farm could not always understand the man of the cattle kingdom....Yet the man of the timber and the town made the law for the man of the plain; the plainsman, finding this law unsuited to his needs, broke it, and was called lawless (Webb 1931:206).

Recently, in areas peripheral to the Brazilian State, low population density combined with low production levels have helped maintain an *aviamento* ("squatter") system (Bunker 1985). Title to land and legally sanctioned rules of use and transfer have little value in these areas because informal means such as occupation or use of force supersede judicial means. In the Llanos of Apure, the American Great Plains, and the Brazilian hinterland, use-rights have always been more valuable than entitlements; state administrative centers were distant, and the influence of a solicitor was more important than legal venues in deciding the outcome of encounters. Externalities of resource use such as these are important in determining how rights of use and property are structured since private costs and benefits differ from social costs and benefits (Anderson and Hill 1977).

## Present Situation in the Llanos de Apure

Cimarron cattle in the Llanos de Apure no longer provide the investment incentive to capitalists they did up until the early 1970s, but land does. Most land south of the Capanaparo river today is still open range and, in principal, belongs to the Venezuelan State. Nevertheless, individuals seeking control over a piece of land can first take de facto and later legal possession of it through reliance on the contemporary *Derechos de Llanos* in a process reminiscent of that used during the Colonial period. Individuals seek out a desirable location, build a house, clear a landing strip, and make other improvements to the property. De facto possession is later legalized in a local *ayuntamiento* (municipal government) and the owner can then lease, transfer, or sell the physical basis of wealth. Since most owners are absentee owners, few take an interest in capital improvement of their property beyond the minimum to secure possession.

Large estates are needed for successful cattle ranching throughout the Llanos due to the protracted return on investment and the environmental constraints to this extractive enterprise. Poor quality soils throughout the Llanos lead to native-grass pastures that are marginal in protein and deficient in calcium. Between 96% and 99% of pastures in the State of Apure rely on native grasses (Pérez 1983). The result of nutritionally marginal pastures in the Llanos are herd capacities on the order of 0.2 head/ha, and poorly nourished cattle with reproductive efficiencies on the order of 50 calves per 100 cows and maturity rates between 4 and 6 years. Cattle must consequently be carried for 7-8 years before they can be marketed (White 1956, Rouse 1977).

The major environmental constraint on ranching in the area south of the Capanaparo river is the marked seasonal pattern of rainfall despite an average annual rainfall of 2000 mm. Water is a limiting resource during the dry season since it is only available in highly localized land features, but it is overabundant in the wet season due to extensive flooding. To provide water for their cattle during the dry season drought, ranchers seek control, legal and extra-legal, of *aguadas*, *esteros*, or deep river ponds. Ranchers must also have within their control land above the level of wet-season flooding in order to herd their cattle onto it and thus minimize their losses from predation and drowning (White 1956, Eastwick 1959, Pérez 1983,

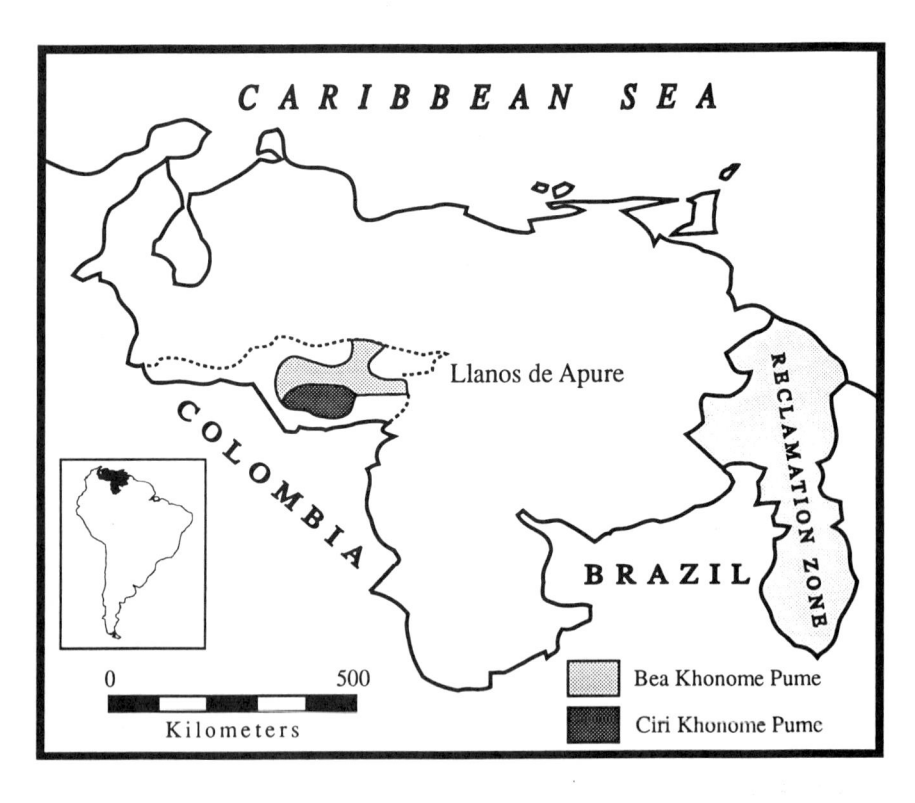

Figure 1. Location of the Pumé in Venezuela.

Tamayo 1987). Most *hatos* in the Llanos de Apure control between 44,000 ha and 350,000 ha, and some as much as 700,000 ha (Mendez Echenique 1985).

## Pumé Response to Subsistence Uncertainty

Most Pumé live in permanent villages along the major rivers of the Llanos of Apure, but a significant fraction of the total population occupy the interfluvial savanna between the Capanaparo and Cinaruco rivers (Figure 1). The Pumé living along the rivers are referred to as *bea khonome* ("river living") Pumé, while those living in the interfluve are referred to as *ciri khonome* ("savanna living") Pumé. *Ciri khonome* Pumé communities contain around 40 people, with each community using approximately 200 km$^2$ of landscape, yielding a population density between 1 person per 3.9 - 5.4 km$^2$. The annual residential pattern of *ciri khonome* Pumé communities comprises a series of moves among at least two semi-permanent settlements and as many as 10 short-duration camps (Gragson 1989). Settlements, camps, and areas of exploitation around them are located with reference to the availability of palm thatching, elevation of the site above the seasonal flood level, location of other Pumé communities, and pressures from local Criollo ranchers.

Since early Colonial times, the Pumé have been characterized as "fishers" as opposed to "hunters" (Gumilla 1970, Rivero 1956, Gragson 1992), but this characterization does not do justice to the scope of their foraging subsistence economy based as it is on fishing, hunting, gathering of wild foods, and some agriculture. The *ciri khonome* Pumé, like other native groups relying on foraging, are not simply concerned with momentary contingencies of how to maximize energetic returns, but are also interested in the variability of returns as it relates to the probability of resource shortfall. Decisions and choices about subsistence are made by weighing the costs and benefits of individual food procurement strategies along with the costs and benefits resulting from linkage with other systems of production such as cattle ranching.

The Pumé have been in contact with state-level representatives since the mid-1700s but without any apparent lasting effects. By the late 1930s, however, Pumé living north of the Capanaparo river began to experience the forces of change associated with cattle ranching (Petrullo 1939). For the Pumé living south of the Capanaparo river where my research has been carried out, the forces of change only became manifest during the late 1970s to early 1980s. To some degree, the cultural differences that distinguish *bea khonome* from *ciri khonome* Pumé probably have their basis in the 40 to 50

TABLE 1. EFFORT AND NET KILOCALORIES FOR PUME
MEN FOR DIFFERENT SUBSISTENCE STRATEGIES

| Strategy | Kcal/hour | Std. Dev. | Min/Day | Kcal Exp.[a] | % Diet |
|---|---|---|---|---|---|
| Fishing | 692 | 658 | 51.7 | 596 | 28.5 |
| Hunting | 1737 | 3023 | 10.4 | 302 | 14.4 |
| Collecting Tubers | 0 | --- | 3.91 | --- | 0 |
| Gardening | 4930 | 5942 | 10.6 | 878 | 41.7 |
| Foraging | 482 | 1264 | 6.2 | 50 | 2.4 |
| Wage Labor | 1098 | 137 | 14.9 | 273 | 13.1 |
| Total | | | 93.9 | 2365 | |

[a] Kcal expected = (Kcal/hour) x (Min/Day)

year difference in onset time of capitalist penetration. The *ciri khonome* Pumé now occasionally engage in wage labor for cattle ranchers, but in contrast to *bea khonome* Pumé who as a rule seasonally migrate north to seek wage labor, most *ciri khonome* Pumé work locally. Wage labor among the *ciri khonome* Pumé can easily be rationalized as a resource strategy because individuals are paid in kind, not in cash. The labor rate for a 10-hour work day in 1987 in the area south of the Capanaparo river was 2 kg of rice and/or pasta, plus one meal consisting of 1 kg of rice and/or pasta, and 0.5 kg of meat.

Of the total amount of time dedicated by the *ciri khonome* Pumé to the various food procurement strategies constituting their subsistence economy, approximately 50% is dedicated to fishing. Fishing events are undertaken 3 to 12 times more frequently than any other type of procurement event (Table 1, Figure 2) and fish provide some 17% of the kilocalories and 64% of the protein consumed on an annual basis (Gragson 1989, 1992). While fishing lakes and ponds during the dry season Pumé often come into contact with *criollo* cattle ranchers who, during this season, locate at these sites to provide drinking water for their cows and to manufacture cheese. The Pumé perceive such cheese stations as a threat to their subsistence and frequently remark on the quantity of fish *criollos* take for their personal consumption. The *criollos* in turn perceive the Pumé as a

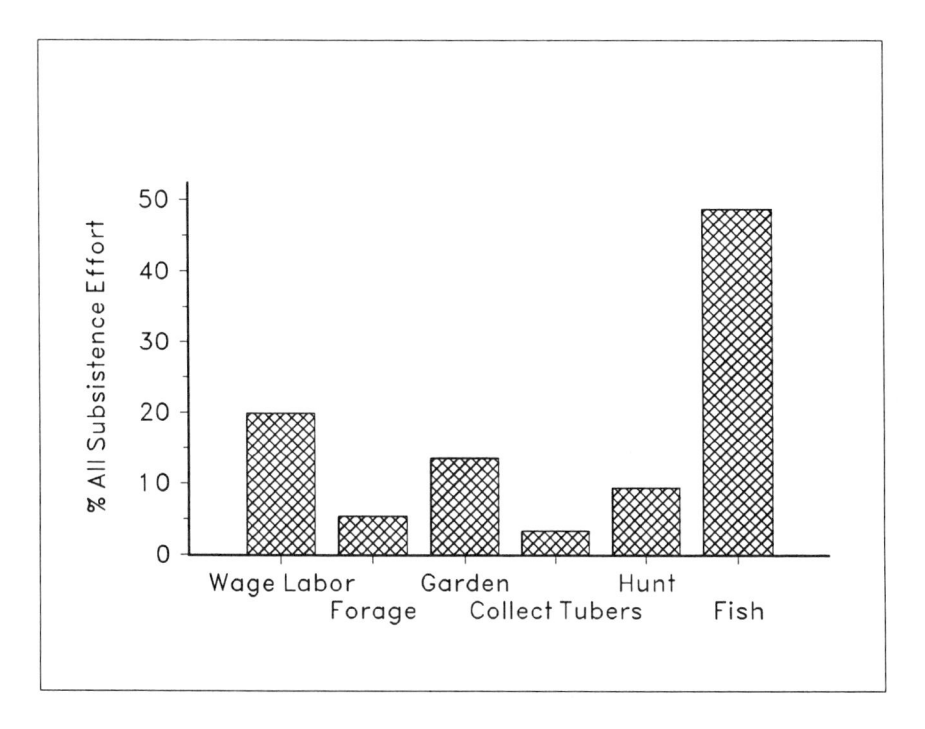

Figure 2. Allocation of effort to subsistence strategies by Pumé men.

threat to their way of life also, because they believe their cattle are killed by the fish poison (*Tephrosia sinapou*) used during the dry season by the Pumé.

Despite the antagonism over dry-season water sources that exists between *criollos* and Pumé, Pumé men dedicate 20% of all time spent on subsistence working for local *criollo* ranchers. An historically documented source of subsistence stress on native communities that is apparent among the Pumé at the present is the significant difference in the duration of traditional food procurement events such as fishing and hunting, and the duration of volunteered or coerced wage labor events (Rivero 1956, Gumilla 1970). Among the *ciri khonome* Pumé, all traditional food procurement events have mean durations on the order of 4 hours, but wage labor events can last up to 12 hours and frequently entail staying away from the native village at a cattle ranch for up to a week at a time. When men are away from the village for 12 hours at a time, they can only provide as food to their family whatever they obtain from wage labor. Men are also unable to

278 ECONOMIC ANTHROPOLOGY OF THE STATE

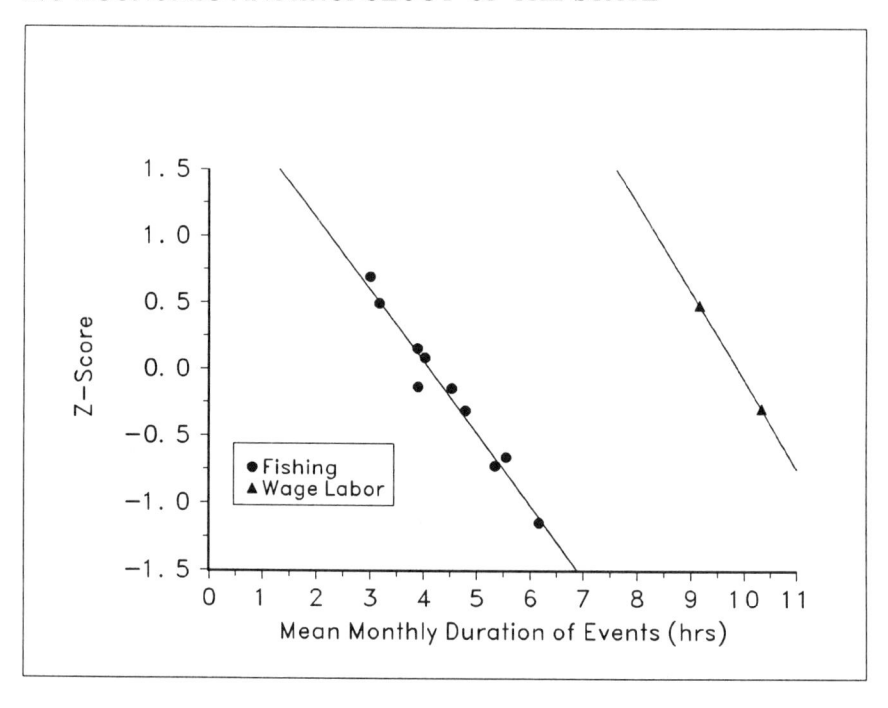

Figure 3. Normalized variance of event duration for fishing and wage labor.

undertake other daytime activities such manufacturing and repairing needed items of material culture such as they could in a traditional schedule. An additional stress factor among the Pumé is that some activities like gardening, more commonly carried out by women in South American native societies, are almost entirely performed by men in Pumé society. A women avoids going to her family's garden to harvest produce unless accompanied by her husband. When Pumé men work for several days continuously, hunger often occurs in a village.

Although fishing and wage labor events are significantly different in duration, the Pumé do not appear to factor this difference into their choice of strategy. When the mean monthly duration of fishing and wage labor events are plotted against their standardized variances (Z), it suggests the Pumé are relatively insensitive to duration overall (Figure 3). (The horizontal displacement of the two scatters reveals the difference in duration between fishing and wage labor events; the linearity of scatter in fishing-event variances along with the similarity between the slopes of both distributions suggests insensitivity to duration -- risk indifferent). The Pumé

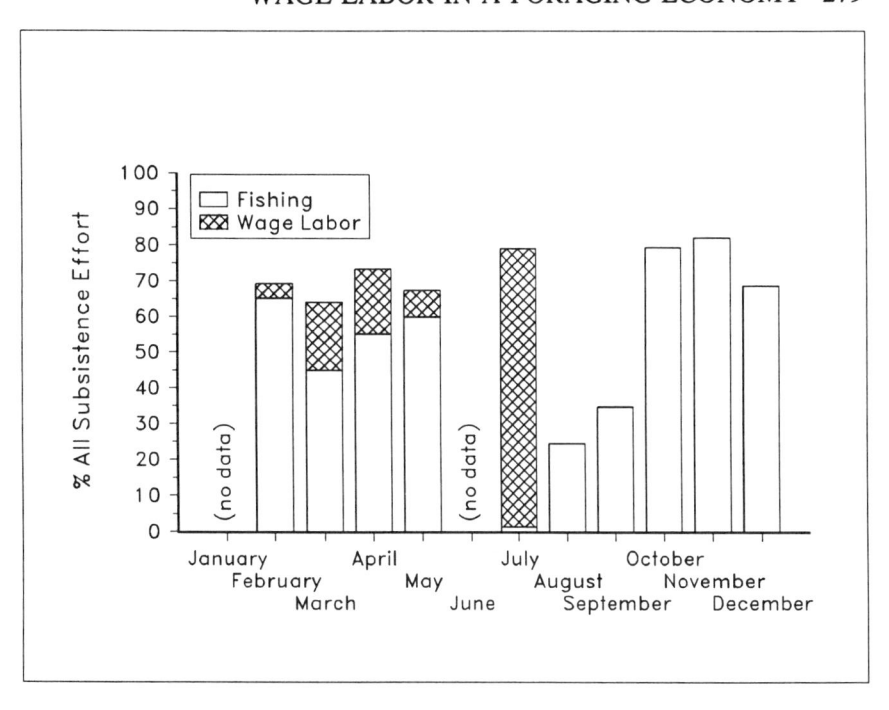

[Figure: bar chart showing % All Subsistence Effort by month, with Fishing and Wage Labor categories]

Figure 4. Monthly effort dedicated by Pumé men to fishing and wage labor.

are currently not concerned over spending 2.4 times longer on wage labor events than on some other subsistence event such as fishing, because the opportunity to work for local cattle ranchers arrives infrequently. Each Pumé man undertakes, on average, about 0.63 wage labor events per month, but will undertake 5.5 fishing events, 1.6 gardening events, and 0.9 hunting events. Local rancher demand for labor is seasonal and for Pumé men it largely consists of cutting posts during the late dry season to build corrals and fences during the early wet season (Figure 4).

Differences in the expected efficiencies of fishing and wage labor events reveal a response on the part of Pumé men that differs from that seen over duration. Mean annual efficiency for fishing is 692 kcal/hr (:net consumable kcals/hr) while that of wage labor events is 1098 kcal/hr. The difference in mean expected efficiency does not appear to be as significant as the difference in the variance around the mean, however. Fishing efficiencies are widely distributed around their means while wage labor event are narrowly distributed (evidenced by the difference in slope of

280 ECONOMIC ANTHROPOLOGY OF THE STATE

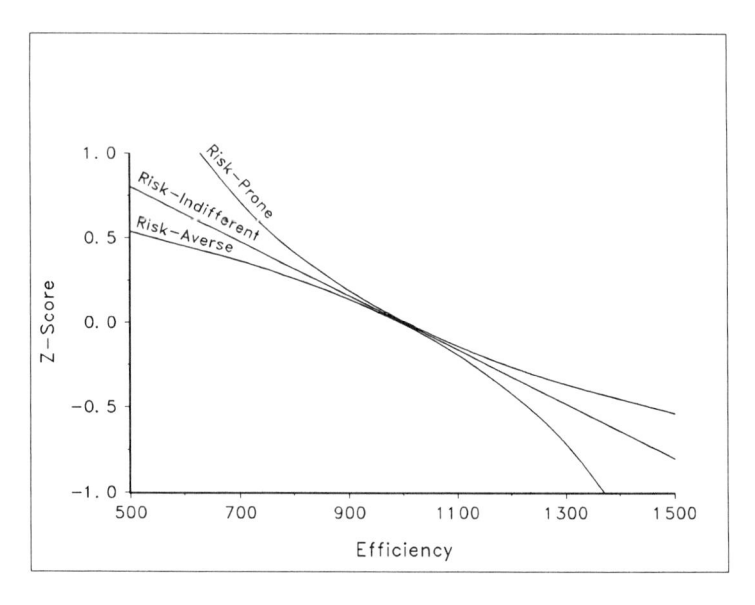

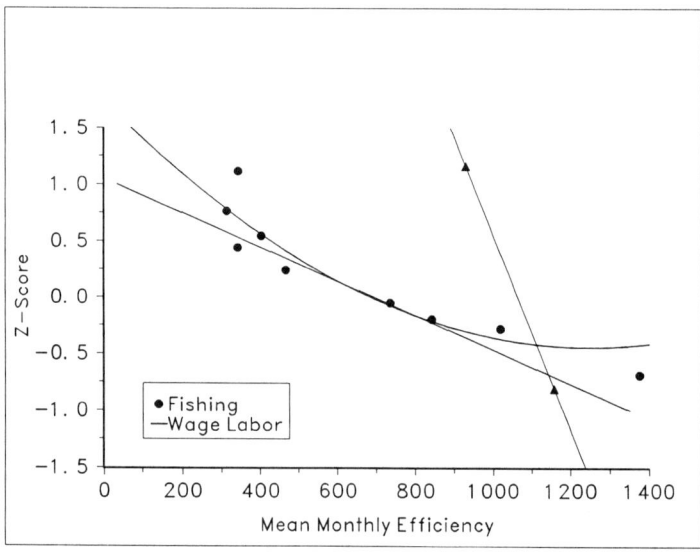

Figure 5. Actual and theoretical normalized variances of monthly fishing and wage labor event efficiencies.

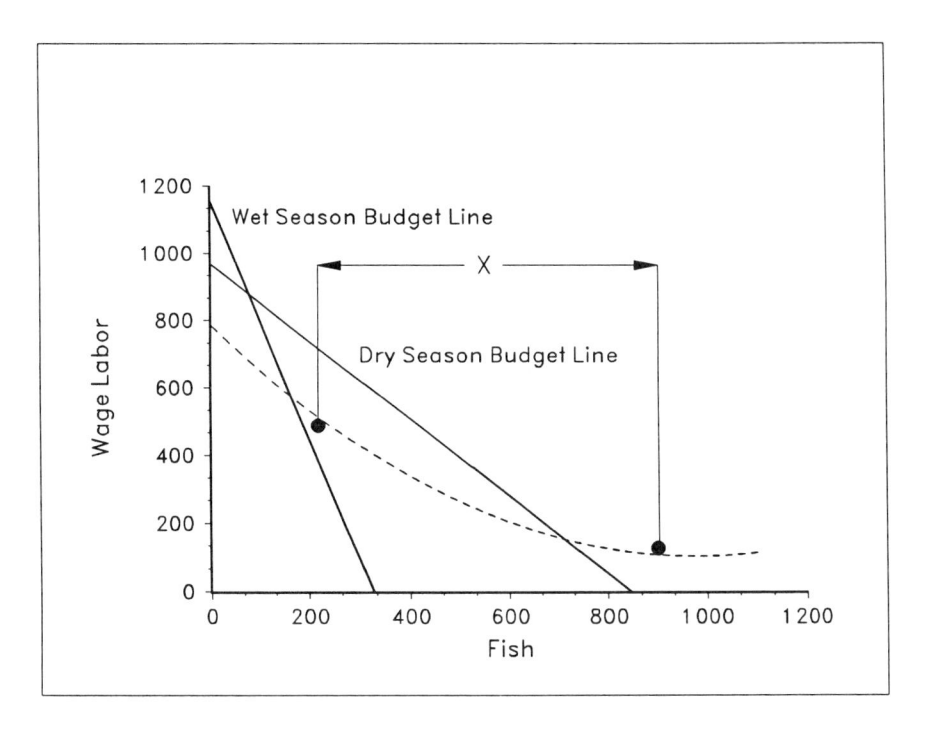

Figure 6. Unit costs of fishing and wage labor versus kilocalories actually obtained.

these two scatters, Figure 5). Certainty about the outcome of any given wage labor event will be high by comparison to that of any fishing event. With respect to fishing events, the Pumé display a risk preference attitude over efficiencies denoted by the concave-upward curve above the straight line of constant variance. (The lower diagram compares the shape of the three possible positions for risk-prone, indifferent and adverse.) On any given fishing event, the Pumé gamble with the possibility of not obtaining the mean expectation on the chance their returns will exceed the mean.

The seasonal cost trade-offs between fishing and wage labor events versus the consumption potential each strategy offers bears directly on why the Pumé choose to undertake wage labor events despite their low efficiencies. The unit cost in time of a kcal obtained by fishing or wage labor increases during the wet season relative to its cost during the dry season

(Figure 6). The shift in price is most dramatic for fish, which increase about 188%. With the change in price of these two resources, there is a corresponding shift in the relative consumption of kcals obtained from either strategy based on time allocation and efficiency. The flat, drawn-out shape of the implied indifference curve suggests kcals obtained from fish or from wage labor are substitutable, although the first impression would probably be that they are complementary. Pumé attitudes about the products of wage labor, regardless of their feelings about *criollos*, bear out the complementarity of kcals derived from fish and commercial products. Rice, pasta, and other goods derived from wage labor events are highly valued by the Pumé for several reasons. Rice and pasta are easily stored for extended periods of time (although they seldom are); unlike garden produce and other natural resources, once rice and pasta procurement costs are "paid" these resources are cheap because they do not require additional processing time; finally, the consumption of rice and pasta provide a difficult-to-quantify, but nevertheless real, sense of physical satisfaction that is very noticeable after days or weeks on a diet consisting only of meat.

## Conclusion

One might expect the Pumé to choose fishing events over wage labor events on the principle of time discounting: fish in hand now are better than rice and pasta later. Fishing rewards accumulate as effort is expended, but the returns on wage labor events become available only after the work is completed and this can take several days if the task is protracted. The Pumé, however, show risk preference over expected efficiency, which is a function of time and quantity. This is a more complex strategy calculation than a single-factor calculation while holding the other constant. The complexity of the decision calculus Pumé undertake in order to be successful foragers is further revealed by the fact that monthly fishing efficiency correlates with depth of landscape inundation (adj. $r^2 = 79\%$, F-score = 34.9), but the actual amount of fish obtained on a daily basis correlates with a complex variable made up of precipitation, landscape flooding, and evaporation (adj. $r^2 = 60\%$, F-score = 14.3). Foragers in the real world choose between alternatives varying in both time commitment and amount since they "do not eat means, they eat sums" (Stephens 1990:30).

In studying native food production systems, it is generally taken for granted that people fully understand the structure of their resources. Given the complexity of information needed to efficiently use resources, the process of resource incorporation probably takes many years (Stearman 1990, Ostrom 1990). Situations such as capitalist penetration may offer a

Love, Thomas F.
    1989    Limits to the Articulation of Modes of Production Approach: The Southwestern Peru. In B.S. Orlove, M.W. Foley, and T.F. Love, eds., *State, Capital, and Rural Society: Anthropological Perspectives on Political Economy in Mexico and the Andes*, pp.147-79. Boulder: Westview Press.

Mendez Echenique
    1985    *Historia del Estado Apure*. Caracas: Miguel Angel García e Hijo, S.R.L.

Mirabal, Adelina C.R.
    1987    *La Formación del Latifundio Ganadero en los Llanos de Apure: 1750-1800*. Biblioteca de la Academia Nacional de la Historia, no. 193. Caracas: Italgráfica, S.R.L
    1991    El Régimen de Tenencia de la Tierra en los Llanos Venezolanos: Figuras Jurídicas, Económicas y Sociales. Paper presented at the 47th International Congress of Americanists, New Orleans.

Mirabal, Adelina R. and Pedro P. Olivares
    1990    *Fray Gregorio de Benaocaz y la Fundación de la Villa de Españoles de San Jaime: Inicio de la Conquista del Llano*. Caracas: Universidad Santa Maria.

Müller, Luis G.
    1990    Evolución Histórica de la Tenencia de la Tierra y del Ganado. In *Evolución Histórica de Barinas*, pp.65-79. Barinas: UNELLEZ.

Ostrom, Elinor
    1990    *Governing the Commons: The Evolution of Institutions for Collective Action*. Cambridge: Cambridge University Press.

Otto, John S.
    1986    Open-range Cattle-ranching in Venezuela and Florida: A Problem in Comparative History. *Comparative Social Research* 9:347-360.

Perez, José E. G.
    1983    *La Planificación Pecuaria en Venezuela*. Caracas: Dirección de Información y Relaciones Públicas de la Gobernación del Dtto. Federal.

Petrullo, Vicenzo M.
    1939    The Yaruros of the Capanaparo River, Venezuela. *Bureau of American Ethnology Bulletin* 123:161-290.

Rivero, P. Juan
    1956    *Historia de las Misiones de los Llanos de Casanare y los Ríos Orinoco y Meta.* Bogota: Editorial Argra.

Rouse, John E.
    1977    *The Criollo: Spanish Cattle in the Americas.* Norman: University of Oklahoma Press.

Smith, Carol A.
    1983    Regional Analysis in World-system Perspective: A Critique of Three Structural Theories of Uneven Development. In S. Ortiz, ed., *Economic Anthropology: Topics and Theories*, pp.307-59. Monographs in Economic Anthropology, No. 1. Lanham, MD: University Press of America.

Stearman, Allyn M.
    1990    The Effects of Settler Incursion on Fish and Game Resources of the Yuquí, a Native Amazonian Society of Eastern Bolivia. *Human Organization* 49:373-385.

Stephens, D. W.
    1990    Risk and Incomplete Information in Behavioral Ecology. In E. Cashdan, ed., *Risk and Uncertainty in Tribal and Peasant Economies*, pp.19-46. Boulder: Westview Press.

Tamayo, Francisco
    1987    *Los Llanos de Venezuela.* Caracas: Monte Avila Editores.

Webb, Walter P.
    1931    *The Great Plains.* Boston: Ginn and Company.

White, C. Langdon
    1956    Cattle Raising: A Way of Life in the Venezuelan Llanos. *The Scientific Monthly* 83:122-129.

# A DIFFERENT DISTINCTION: THE CASE OF ANCIENT GREECE

David B. Small
Lehigh University

## Introduction

The most common type of public/private economic separation in early states is one that pits state and elite interests against non-state provincial elite or, more generally, commoner interests. In other words, the state usually identifies with the central elites in the formation of economic policies. Two well-known examples of this type of public/private distinction are the Aztec and Inka states, where the meshing of elite and state economic interests is clear. In the case of the Aztec (for models see Berdan 1982; Carrasco 1982; Brumfiel 1983, 1987), the central elites were given lands expropriated in conquered territories as well as reclaimed land from Lake Chalco-Xochimilco. The Aztec state established a tribute in luxury goods and sponsored long-distance trade with other states to provide display items that could be used by the elite in status definition within the capital. Among the Inka (Murra 1980, D'Altroy and Earle 1985, Earle et al. 1987, D'Altroy 1992), the elite were likewise the beneficiaries of state policies. As the empire grew, it gave allotments of land and workers to state elite for the production of staples, and it earmarked special enclaves for the production of luxury goods, obviously intended for elite use as well. Within some of their conquered territories the Inka also altered the access to, production and use of luxury goods. In short, there was no distinction between the elites and the governors; economic policies of the state were naturally structured to benefit the elite themselves.

While this model is certainly valid for cultures such as the Inka or Aztec, it is inapplicable to ancient Greece, a culture rarely considered by mainstream archaeologists in the analysis of public/private economic distinctions. Unlike the Inka or Aztec, the separation between public and private in Athens, and most likely in other Greek polis-states as well, was one that opposed state and commoner interests to those of the elite. Even when the Greek states acquired control over other states, as did the Aztec and Inka, they did not direct benefits to the elite, but aided the commoners instead.

Why was this so? The answer lies in the distinctive context of state development in Greece. Unlike the Inka or Aztec, state development in Greece resulted in numerous states, of which there were two types. The state identified either with individual cities, such as Athens or Corinth, or larger confederations of communities. Both types of states developed within a larger preexisting web of elite interaction, the nodes of which were the many interpolital sanctuaries and not the urban centers themselves. These sanctuaries provided strong alternative non-state contexts for the conduct of elite commercial transactions and thereby marginalized elite enterprises in the development of state economic policies.

To support this argument, I will first examine the separate economic roles of the economic elite and the state. Then, I will explain why Greece demonstrated such an unusual public/private distinction by locating the role of both elites and the states within the special context of Greek state formation.

## The Development of Greek Political Structure

Much of the argument in this paper rests upon the reader's acquaintance with some of the more salient features of the political and social history of Greece. For readers who might not be familiar with this narrative, I provide a brief outline of the major developments.[1] My concern here is with social change and development, not with individuals or military operations. In no way is this intended as anything but a representation of the chronological developments. Those familiar with Greek archaeology and history will immediately recognize that I have abandoned the usual ceramic chronological definitions. This has been done to simplify the narrative.

*1125 - 800 B.C.*

This period begins with the fall of the Mycenaean palaces such as Mycenae or Pylos, and it continues with important demographic, economic, and social changes. While the Mycenaean world had numerous contacts with the larger kingdoms to the east and the peoples in the west, post-Mycenaean Greece became more isolated. This period has produced few, if any, artifacts that would have come from the Near East or Egypt. The population declined. Survey in different regions of Greece has defined an abrupt fall-off in population, sometimes as great as 75% (McDonald and Rapp 1972). The population shifted; by 1000 B.C. Greeks from all different parts of the mainland appear to have migrated to the shores of western Anatolia.

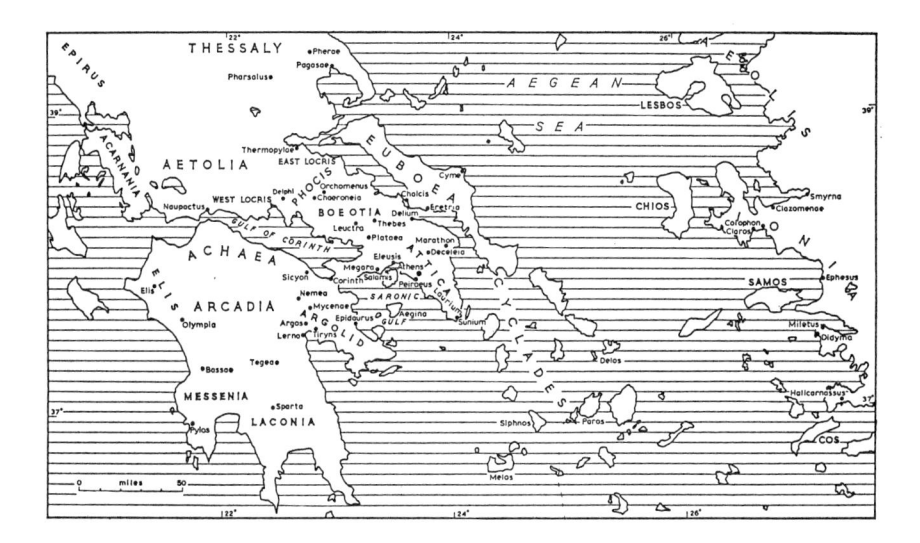

Figure 1. Map of Ancient Greece with principal sites. By permission of W.W. Norton Publishers.

Although our information is still spotty, it would appear that much of the remaining population lived in small villages, such as Karphi on Crete (Pendlebury et al. 1939). Hierarchical distribution in these villages is not easily distinguished. House size is relatively uniform and contemporary burials shed little light on any possible hierarchies.[2]

Emerging social differentiation is noticeable shortly after 1000 B.C. Ironworking was introduced to Greece around 1000 B.C. from Cyprus and a recent study of its depositional pattern (Morris 1989) has demonstrated how emerging elites used iron objects in burial contexts to differentiate themselves from the rest of the community. By 925 B.C. overseas trade was reestablished, and social differentiation was intensifying with greater competition now between elites. The graves from this period contain bronze, gold and ivory, from regions outside Greece.

While our image of the social and political structure from this early period is dim, some overall observations seem to apply. Analysis of the values displayed in the Homeric poems (Austin and Vidal-Naquet 1977:36-48, Finley 1978a), i.e., oral epics, put into writing probably in the late 8th century B.C., argues strongly that the elites considered themselves aristocrats. The chiefs were probably the *basileis*, or "gift devouring princes" mentioned by the 7th century poet, Hesiod (1978:97, lines 38-39). Study of cemeteries from this period appears to demonstrate that these elite comprised 1/4 to 1/3 of the population (Morris 1989). Power was most likely generated through land tenure, gift secured alliances with peer elites, or lesser elite households, and control over dependents. The primary relation of production appears to have been close to our concept of landlord and serf (Finley 1981, Garnsey and Morris 1989).

*800 - 600 B.C.*

Several dramatic developments in Greek civilization took place in these two centuries. There was a further increase in foreign contact and trade, with the establishment of trading emporia in the Near East, and with the spread of Greek settlements into the western Mediterranean and the Black Sea. This period is also marked by the introduction of the alphabet and the rise of sanctuaries, especially interstate ones, such as Olympia and Delphi. The most noticeable event which occurred was state formation. The formation of the state can be detected as early as the 8th century B.C., and its development followed two different paths (for review see Garnsey and Morris 1989, Morris 1989).

The first was the polis-state. Throughout large parts of the Greek world there was a growing proliferation of small autonomous cities that at different times laid claim to a distinct territory, fortified their urban areas, built temples to patron deities, enacted distinctive law codes, organized citizen armies, and based citizenship and participation in the political process on ownership of land. Sections of western and northern Greece on the other hand, appear to have experienced a different type of state development, the *ethnos*. In an *ethnos*, the state was not coterminous with a single community but rose out of a confederation of several. The powers of the *ethnos* were the same as those of the polis-state. State affairs were usually conducted at a sanctuary, which became the traditional congregational center for members from the participant communities. An excellent example would be the *ethnos* of Aetolia. This consisted of a loose federation of different scattered villages, with a political and religious center at Thermon.

Figure 2. The extent of the polis-state (shaded and of the ethnos-state (unshaded) in Greece, 750-500 B.C. By permission of University of California Press.

*600 - 338 B.C.*

This period saw the continuing development of the polis-state. In some cities, such as Athens, the commoners broke the serf relationship they held with the old elites, and forced labor was now beginning to be performed by chattel slaves from other states (Finley 1980: Ch. 2). On the other hand, well into the later part of the fourth century B.C., the ethnos-state continued to exhibit examples of landlord-serf relationships of production.[3] The hold on political power in this period was weak, with shifting forms of government in the polis-state. The sixth century, often called the age of tyranny, witnessed the height of political coups by non-established elites. And, throughout the period, the political forms in the polis-states were shifting back and forth from oligarchies to tyrannies, to democracies. The situation did not begin to stabilize until 338 B.C., when Greece effectively became a province of Macedonia.

## Elite and State Interests

Those not acquainted with the academic context of the debate over the role of the elite in Greek state economics could easily become casualties in the continuing cross-fire between those who see the ancient Mediterranean economies as best explained on their own terms and those who see them capable of assessment with models pertinent to more current cultures.[4] To explain as clearly as possible some of the salient features of the economy of ancient Greece, I will first examine separately both the economic world of the Greek elite and that of the Greek states. Let us begin with the more difficult of the two: the Greek elite.

*Evidence for Elite Commercial Involvement*

It will come as no surprise that the wealth of ancient Greece was essentially based on agriculture (exceptions are few, but see Engels 1990). As far as we can determine, the Greek elite owned large estates, on which they grew winter wheat and barley, legumes, such as broad beans and chick peas, as well as lentils, olives, and grapes. (Gallant 1989:396) Livestock included sheep, goats, cattle and pigs. We have known for some time that in fourth century Athens (and, most likely, in other states and periods as well), several elites owned workshops (Hasebroek 1933:72-76). These workshops relied primarily upon slave labor. The goods produced included flour, bedsteads, knives, leather goods, flutes, dyes, sailcloths, and shields. We cannot say how large these enterprises were, although references might indicate that they could be as large as 120 slaves (although this has been doubted, Hasebroek 1933:73).

Interstate trade was an additional source of income. There are several lines of evidence that support the argument that the elite were active in this type of commerce from at least the Archaic (ca. 700 B.C.) period and probably earlier (Morris 1986, 1989). We know that long-distance trade existed. There are obvious trade goods in the early (ca. 900 B.C.) archaeological record, such as imported pottery -- both Greek and otherwise. Greek traders were present in cities such as Naucratis in Egypt or El Mina in Syria, from the early years (ca. 750 B.C.) of the Archaic age (for overview see Boardman 1980). We also have epic accounts of elite activity in trade probably as early as the 8th century.

This involvement in trade may really have started as early as the 9th century (Morris 1989), when the elite would have been positioned to trade, because, unlike non-elites, they would have had the benefit of relations that had risen out of inter-elite gift-exchange in Greece and because seaborne transport (which appears the principal kind) would have been very costly and thereby limited to the more wealthy families (Morris 1986, 1989). Greek merchant vessels do not appear in the art historical record until the late Archaic period (ca. 500 B.C.), and therefore early long-distance commerce had to have been carried out through the use of pentekonters, oared warships, traditionally owned by the elite and used in the elite pursuits of piracy, warfare, marriage alliances, diplomacy, and travel to religious and athletic festivals. The historical record also demonstrates that Greek elites were known to be travelers, with such early (ca. 600 B.C.) notables as Solon traveling to Egypt and the kingdom of Lydia. Epic poems, such as those of Homer or the 7th century Boiotian poet, Hesiod, also demonstrate that the ideal early farmer, i.e., owning a house, land, draft animal, and at least one slave, is engaged in commerce during the slow agricultural months (Bravo 1983). The elite must have been just as active, for Hesiod advises, "Praise a small ship, but put your produce in a large one" (1978:126-27, line 643).

*The Commodities*

Just what were the elite were trading? It is quite likely that they were importing luxury items, such as ivory from Egypt or textiles from Phoenicia, marble from parts of Greece, or exporting products, such as flutes, shields, and knives from their own workshops. To this must also be added the possible importation of slaves from Sicily and the Black Sea region. Non-luxury items, besides slaves, would have included grain, and at least before 900 B.C., iron (Morris 1989).

A look at the grain and marble trade provides some insight into the driving forces behind and the conduct of the elite within commercial transactions. To understand the interest of the Greek elite in shipping grain we first have to understand the environmental and climatic context of Greece and the eastern Mediterranean in general (Garnsey 1988; Halstead 1981, 1988; Gallant 1989). There was an annual shifting need to import grain throughout the Greek world. Each year different parts of Greece experienced agricultural shortfalls and surpluses. There were two reasons for this. Greece and the eastern Mediterranean were characterized by both climatic fluctuation (Garnsey 1988, Gallant 1989). These microenvironments react differently to annual climatic variation. Some are adversely affected, while others are not. Consequently, each year different parts of Greece would either meet local needs or even produce a surplus, while others would suffer from crop shortfalls. Another cause for periodic agricultural shortfall was warfare. The history of ancient Greece is one of constant aggression by different city-states campaigning against their neighbors. One of the chief military tactics was the destruction of the enemies' crops to starve them into surrender.

There were several ways in which people could protect themselves against these uncertainties. Several authors (Gallant 1989, Garnsey 1988, Halstead 1981) have elaborated upon the use of grain storage, diversified planting, and so on, but one of the most recognizable and most frequently reported methods of meeting agricultural uncertainty was the importation of grain from other parts of Greece, or even from other parts of the eastern Mediterranean. Because their land holdings were larger than those of the Greek peasant, the elites themselves must have been actively engaged in this agricultural exchange. Herman (1987) has pulled together the sources for this type of commerce, and although our evidence is restricted to a few inscriptions and mentions of the shipment of grain between elites in some Athenian court cases, he is probably correct in arguing that this evidence represents "merely the tip of an iceberg" (Herman 1987:82).

Although not often thought as having been connected with the elite, marble was an important bulk commodity in the Archaic period (650-550 B.C.) (Snodgrass 1983). The use of marble in elaborate tomb monuments and statues that would have adorned a tomb as well, makes marble an excellent example of a prestige commodity. In the Archaic period marble appears in the archaeological record in two contexts. The first is in the form of male (*kouroi*) and female (*korai*) statues. These statues appear as early as 650 B.C. and were used by the elite as tomb monuments or honorific dedications. The second use of marble, in building, began around 550 B.C., and again the elite were agents in its use. For example, Herodotus (1927:128-29, sections 125-30) relates that the Alkmaeonids, an aristocratic Athenian family, refurbished the temple of Apollo at Delphi around 525 B.C. in marble that was obtained from the island of Paros. Even though we do not have close control over the provenance of some of this marble, the fact that large regions of Greece did not have supplies of good white marble, while others (notably the Cycladic islands) did, would almost force us to reconstruct systems of marble shipment.

How extensive was this trade? Even with Snodgrass' conservative reconstructions, we are left with at least 40,000 tons of marble shipped in the Archaic period to cover just the statuary alone. This would translate into at least ca. 350 blocks per year of marble about 3/4 ton each traveling around the Mediterranean for use just in statue sculpting. This, of course, underestimates the marble trade, because it excludes marble used in building construction as the Archaic period develops.

Snodgrass' model of procurement and use demonstrates well the position of the elite in this active trade. There were five steps: client commissions artist, artist goes to marble source, artist pays quarry-owner and contractor for extracting marble, artist pays for land and sea transport of part-worked statue, client pays artist's and assistant's maintenance for period of work. In this reconstruction, the elite are involved in the shipment of marble at both ends. The elite client must have paid the artist in the initial stages of the enterprise so that he could have paid to journey to the quarry and pay for eventual extraction and shipment of the marble itself. At the other end, the elite would also have paid for the upkeep of the artist and assistants while they were working on the stone after they had brought it to the place of erection. Snodgrass estimates that this could easily have been up to a complete year for a life-sized work.

*Modes of Exchange*

The network through which most of this trade flowed was that of ritualized friendship (Herman 1987; also, Humphreys 1978:168). According to Herman (1987:10), ritualized friendship is broadly defined as "...a bond of solidarity manifesting itself in an exchange of goods and services between individuals originating from separate units." In Greece in particular, ritualized friendship's actors were the Greek elite, and its "separate units" were the Greek states. This bond could be passed on to succeeding generations. We have evidence for ritualized friendship as early as 1000 B.C (Morris 1989) and as late as the Hellenistic (after 338 B.C.). Its initiation was accomplished through a ritual that followed a sequence of "a declaration, an exchange of objects, feasting, and again, the taking of oaths" (Herman 1987:56). The validity of the alliance rested more upon the exchange and the declaration that the other parts of the ritual.

Ritualized friendship was one of the major forces behind elite long-distance commercial transactions. Sources attest to the use of this bond in the transfer of surplus grain, as well as other supplies such as timber, and even the transfer of estates (Herman 1987: Ch. 4). Most of the sources come from fourth-century Athenian court speeches, which mention donations of grain and timber between ritualized friends in Athens and Macedonia and the Black Sea. But Herman (1987:63) is undoubtedly right in arguing that the enterprise was far greater than what we see.

While the elite were certainly involved in this long distance commerce, there are some qualifying factors to discuss in regard to the manner of their involvement. There is much evidence to support the argument that the elite were involved in intercommunity commerce, but not actually actively engaged in the every-day haggling of trading. The earliest to argue this effectively was Hasebroek (1933), who supported his claim with reference to values stated by Greek philosophers and poets, such as Homer and Hesiod.

In a somewhat different interpretation, Mele (1979) argues that the very fact that poems such as Homer's propose that Greeks should not engage themselves in trade indicates that the elite did, and were in the process of trying to defend their own particular type of commerce. He argues that these works are the product of a social strategy proposed by the elite to thwart attempts by non-elite merchants to gain power in Greek commerce. Mele sees the eighth and seventh centuries B.C. as a time of crisis where the aristocratic concept of commerce as *prexis*, i.e., private elite activity, is being pitted against non-aristocrats who conduct business in specialized *emporia*, i.e., ports of trade such as Naucratis in Egypt, rather than between peer elites. The object of this trade, according to Mele, was to trade agricultural surplus for decorated pottery, a prestige good sought after by what Mele would consider the developing merchant class. This was all part of a larger social strategy to weaken the elite, as seen by the passage of sumptuary laws in Corinth and Athens.

On the other hand, there is strong evidence that the elite were actively involved in trade. Humphreys (1978:167) notes that in the Archaic period, "Little but an ideological hairline divided the noble who voyages in order to come home loaded with valuable gifts...or to exchange iron for copper...from the 'commander or sailor out for gain..., always thinking about his cargo'".[5] Whether or not a man such as Odysseus saw himself as a trader or aristocrat, he would have been involved in the exchange of goods. If an aristocrat, then the goods were exchanged within an overarching system of peer exchange, rather than within the context of haggling negotiations.

Bravo (1974) extends the observation that the elite were actively involved in trade and argues that the elite were not only involved in loaning money to traders, i.e., involvement at a distance, but were actively using agents to direct their own commerce. The argument stems from an interpretation of a letter written on a lead tablet around 500 B.C., apparently from an elite's agent. In the letter, Archillodoros addresses both his son, Protagores, and Anaxagores, his economic patron, protesting that he and his cargo have been seized by Matasys, apparently as a reprisal for injury

Anaxagores at one time inflicted on Matasys. Bravo argues here that Anaxagores is a landed elite engaged in commerce through commercial agents such as Archillodoros.

Bravo's concern here is with the Archaic period, but it may very well be that in the later Classical period Greek elite were engaged in such commerce on an even more active level. Millett's (1983) observation of the larger context of lending in Athens demonstrates that wealthy Athenian citizens, who loaned money in maritime loan transactions, were probably more than just estate owners. These loans involved the lending of money from a wealthy Athenian to an *emporos* (merchant) or *naukleros* (shipowner). Rates of interest were high (10.5% - 30% recorded), but this was mostly the result of stipulations that the borrower would not have to pay back the loan, if the ship did not reach the port safely. The amount invested ranged from 1000 - 4500 drachmae. Millett (1983:52) argues that, "The indications are that the complexity of maritime credit made it an unsuitable field for casual lenders without practical experience in trading," and supports this with reference to lenders in the speeches of Demosthenes. One of the better known is *Against Apaturius* (Demosthenes 1936:205) in which the speaker claims, "I, men of the jury, have by now been for a long time engaged in foreign trade, and up to a certain time risked the sea in my own person; it is not quite seven years since I gave up voyaging, and, having a moderate capital, I try to put it to work by making loans on adventures overseas." The evidence could not be clearer.

*The Economics of the City-State*

We know very little about the economic polices of the ethnos-state. Relations of production remained at the landlord-serf level well into the Hellenistic period (Finley 1980, Morris 1989). What policies there were must have been controlled by elite interests. The polis-state, on the other hand, demonstrates a separation between elite and state interests. The greatest share of information on the economic policies of the Greek polis-states comes from historical documentation from ancient Athens. But the information from other states is consonant with what we see in Athens and leaves room for us to argue that, in economic policies, the Greek polis-states were broadly similar. The Greek polis-states had very little, if any, integrated economic policy. Our information tells us that this type of state acted economically, but this action was restricted to disparate roles and contexts (Humphreys 1978: Chs.6,8). In order to clarify this, I will examine the economic roles of the Greek polis-state, and consider how this state operated when it engaged in foreign activity.

The economic interests of the polis-state revolved mainly around collecting revenue, providing for its citizens, and supporting its army. As a collector of revenue, the state gathered income, in the case of Athens at least, from state ownership of mines, taxation and the imposition of imperial tribute. Athens is probably typical in her taxation policy in that she directly taxed not citizens, but resident foreigners or *metics*. The rich were taxed indirectly, through a liturgy system, which called upon the wealthy to support state activities, such as athletic, religious, or dramatic festivals. This system was open, in that it required the rich to provide for the state, but it did not set any minimum or maximum amount that the rich could spend on these activities, leaving the support of public functions open to elite competitive display. Athens also placed a tax on the use of its harbor, the Peiraeus. The tax appears to have been a flat rate of 2% for entering and leaving.

All in all, the purpose of taxation was rather limited. It was used solely as a measure to gain revenue, rather than a possible lever to give Athenians a commercial advantage. This is seen in the use of the harbor tax itself, which, instead of being manipulated to favor Athenian shippers, fell equally upon all who used the harbor, whether Athenian or not.

In their roles as providers for their own citizens, the Greek polis-states were actively engaged in securing grain to feed the population in times of shortfall. Athens at least, was also paying citizens to participate in state functions, such as the public assembly, the law courts, and militarily, to row in the navy. While we can not be sure that other Greek states were supporting their own citizens in a fashion equal to that of Athens, we do know that many states were at least actively involved in securing needed grain. There remains a small record of economic treaties between different states, either preserved on stone as inscriptions or mentioned in other historical texts (compiled by Hasebroek 1933:110-117 and more recently by Garnsey 1988:71-74), which must represent something more extensive.

These treaties differ very much from what we are accustomed to calling economic treaties today in that they had a very limited and special purpose. What Hasebroek demonstrated in 1933 is still accepted by scholars today (Finley 1973: Ch.6): the purpose of concluding economic treaties between Greek polis-states was limited to securing a consistent supply of imported grain and other necessities, with any further economic benefit being strictly secondary. This was perfectly consonant with what were seen by the Athenian philosophers as the proper interests of the city. As Hasebroek records (1933:111-12), the proper interests of the statesman are: state revenue and expenditure, war, home defense, the grain supply, and the silver mines. There is no mention of an elaborate foreign economic policy;

rather, attention should be paid to supplying the state with necessary imported grain. This would explain the bias in the epigraphical record towards treaties concluded between Greek states and kings in the Black Sea region. The Black Sea was one of the chief regions that supplied the Greek states with imported grain. Typical of these types of treaties is that which is mentioned by Demosthenes in his speech, *Against Leptines* (Demosthenes 1954:467, lines 36-40) where mid-fourth-century Athens concludes a treaty with Leucon I of Bosphorus (a kingdom on the southern shore of the Black Sea). In this treaty, Leucon removed the duty from those ships carrying goods to Athens (obviously grain) and guaranteed that merchants sailing to Athens be allowed to load their ships first.

Treaties between two different states were one means of controlling imports of grain and securing additional produce as needed. Another method was to regulate what could be exported. Solon was perhaps the first Athenian to enact a law that affected Athenian exports (see Garnsey 1988:107-110). His law prohibited the shipping of grain outside Athens. It further appears that by the fourth century there was a permanent ban on the export of other necessary materials from Athens (Hasebroek 1933:112-113). These included not only grain, but also shipbuilding materials such as wax, rope, pitch, and timber. And Athens was not alone. Hasebroek (1933:148) notes that cities such as Selymbria also prohibited the export of necessities, here domestic grain, in time of agricultural shortage.

*Colonization*

The economic role of the Greek polis-state should also be considered in relation to two aspects of foreign policy in Greek history: colonialism and imperialism. Greek colonization began in the eighth century B.C. and eventually saw colonies in as far flung regions as the Black Sea, Spain, Italy, Sicily and Africa. It is a difficult subject (for overview see Austin and Vidal-Naquet 1977:61-68). Greek colonies do not resemble more modern colonial establishments, where the colony remains controlled by the colonizing country, as a source of economic and political benefit. Greek colonies, once established, were independent polities, whose relationship with the mother city was limited to a few religious ties at most.

As Garnsey and Morris argue (1989:102), if there was an economic policy governing the establishment of colonies, it was probably "...often a response to a short-term crisis," and as they demonstrate, the crisis was famine. For example, the establishment by Thera of the colony, Cyrene, in Libya was preceded by a drought of seven years, at which time Thera then forced one son per household to migrate, under penalty of death.

forced one son per household to migrate, under penalty of death.

There were, however, other Greek establishments in foreign countries that had obvious economic goals. Whether or not they represent a convergence of elite interests from different states or a direct state policy however is open to question. This type of establishment is best classified as an emporium or "port-of-trade". Two notable examples of this type of city stand out: Naucratis in Egypt and Pithekoussai off the western coast of Campania. Naucratis was said to have been established as a port of trade for east Greek traders from different states in Ionia. Pithekoussai was established by Euboians from Eretria and Chalcis. In both cases, the function of these trading ports was to gain access to goods in each region, in Egypt luxury goods and grain, in Italy, most likely iron ore. The problem for us is assessing to what degree the establishment of this type of colony was correlated with state policies. In my assessment there are strong arguments for a distinct lack of correlation. Naucratis and Pithekoussai have multiple founders, coming from more than one state. Goods that these colonies were seeking, with the possible exception of grain from Egypt (which very well might have been a secondary interest), were goods that were sought after chiefly by the economic elite. Finally, as Snodgrass notes (1980:41) Pithekoussai has very few characteristics of a Greek polis-state. Its very poor soil conditions and very early settlement date (ca. 770 B.C.) suggest that it was not established on a polis-state model. Evidently, it was established by non-state means.

*Imperialism*

The best documented and longest example of Greek state imperialism is the first Athenian empire. During the period between the end of the Persian Wars (478 B.C.) and the termination of the Peloponnesian War (404 B.C.), Athens controlled what can be called an empire, which incorporated at least 200 polities. As leader of this group of city-states, Athens both controlled their foreign policies and, at times, their internal affairs. Here we see the Greek polis-state in its economic role of supporting an army. Athens' army was the fleet that both controlled and guarded her empire. Although member states were initially required to supply warships as tribute, as the empire progressed, most of the states paid a monetary tribute. In 413 B.C. this tribute was replaced with a 5% harbor tax on all harbors of all the member states.

The example of Athens and her empire supplies an important additional facet in the model of public/private economic interests. The Athenian elite did not benefit from Athens' control of the empire, as we

Aztec. The primary beneficiaries were the Athenian lower classes (Finley 1978b). The lower classes of Athenian citizens would have benefitted directly from the opportunity to colonize territories that were confiscated from rebelling member states, or from receipt of rent from lands that were likewise confiscated from member states but not occupied by Athenians. Additional benefits would have come from money earned from rowing in the large navy that policed the empire, money earned from participation in public office (indirectly supported by tribute money from the empire), possible work in the dockyards, and release from famine. The empire ensured that additional grain would be available to Athens in years of shortfall.

It is not clear how, if at all, the empire helped the elite. The only possible advantage that they might have had is seen in a rare glimpse of the confiscation of lands held by elite Athenians outside Attica (Athens' hinterland). In 415 B.C. some very prominent Athenians were convicted of profanation of the Eleusinian Mysteries and mutilation of the hermes (semi-sacred standing representations of Hermes). Punitive measures included the confiscation and sale of the condemned's estates. The states that lay outside Athens included those in Euboea, Thasos, Abydos on the Hellespont, and Ophryneion in the Troad (near Troy), all parts of the Athenian empire. The case for the empire providing the means by which Athenian elite could gain extra state property is inconclusive, however. Ownership of these lands could easily have been obtained through normal ritualized friendship alliances, rather than through imperial agency.

The empire of Athens in no way gave economic advantage to Athenian traders and thereby to Athenian elites, who were either indirectly or directly involved in interstate commerce. There were no navigation acts, no preferential treatment for Athenian shippers, no protective tariffs, no attempts to remove some of the commerce of the empire to Athens itself. Athens did attempt to control the import and export of grain from some of its subject cities, but this was more politically inspired than anything else. This was an empire that saw itself only in military and political roles.

**The Elite, The State, and Economic Policy**

To summarize the argument so far, the Greek elite owned large estates, some with craft workshops, and engaged in interpolital commerce through a network of ritualized friendship. The elite were interested in luxury goods, but also grain and marble. It may well be that the values of elite culture kept some elites at a respectable distance from the actual process of trading. But values change from context to context and we do not know those of the harbor or market. Millett's argument is strong: the experience required for maritime lending must have necessitated that several elites who loaned to traders were actively engaged in trade themselves.

On the other hand, the Greek polis-state was a loose grouping of several different economic policies, each embedded in a specific context, but not forming an integrated whole. The polis-state appeared uninterested in the economic benefit of its own elite, ignoring opportunities to tip the scales in their favor through uneven taxation or more aggressive polices, even when it controlled an empire. In fact, the state would often set itself in opposition to elite economic interest by restricting its own elite from selling their surplus grain in other communities.

That the economic policy of Athens actually aided the non-elites rather than its wealthier citizens produces a very unusual model of public and private economic distinctions. There were two very separate spheres. The public economy joined the commoners and the state; the private comprised the state's elite.

*Explanations*

Why was this so? There have been very few attempts to address this question. Humphreys (1978: Chs. 6,7) argues that the split between state and private elite economies, in ancient Athens at least, is the result of a strong ideological separation of different functional contexts, such as politics, religion, and economics. She further adds that the apparent economic interests of the elites did not involve them in state policies. Humphreys' reconstruction of social structure is insightful, but it doesn't aid us here in seeking a beginning for the structure itself. In addition, her interest is primarily with Athens. As I have argued elsewhere (Small 1987), an examination of the context of public assembly in many Greek states demonstrates that there was a strong ideological separation between different contexts of interaction within these different communities as well, at least until the middle years of the Roman empire. Athens was not alone.

Morris' model (1987, 1989; Garnsey and Morris 1989) concerns the development of the Greek states and is directed towards political developments and general concepts of relations of production and should thereby have some explanatory force in regard to our observations. Following Finley's earlier lead (1981:97-166), Morris argues that many ancient Greek polis-states developed through a strong elite/commoner opposition. As he states, "...the most remarkable feature of the *polis* was the solidarity of the citizen body as a whole against elite interests, culminating in the Classical Athenian democracy...." (1989:514). Morris sees the early stages of the opposition of the elite and citizen body in the elite use of iron as a prestige item by elites before 900 B.C. to differentiate themselves from non-elites. Accordingly, regions that demonstrate a use of iron as a prestige item go on later to witness the development of the polis-state. The prime mover, according to Morris, is this very early trend towards elite/non-elite polarization.

There is some strength in this argument, for antagonism between the state and elites is a common feature in many Greek states, but the model fails to assist in our case. Our distinctive public/private opposition appears to have existed in several different Greek polis-states including oligarchies, democracies, and tyrannies. Morris' argument does not address polarity in states which were not democratic, whose political formations do not so neatly match his model of elite-commoner opposition. Instead, he lumps all states together in a large paradigm of social opposition.

*An Alternative Model*

The underlying cause for the particular type of separation between public and private economies in Greece lies at an interpolital systemic level, one that affected most Greek states in a similar fashion, whatever their political constitutions. The particular trajectory of state development in ancient Greece, as opposed to that of states such as the Aztec and Inka, produced a context within which polis-states like Athens developed such a distinctive public/private split. My argument is that the context of ritualized friendship and elite economic interaction had a profound and lasting effect on the economic development of the Greek polis-states. These developing states never expressed the economic interests of the elite, because one of the most important contexts for the conduct of elite economic interchange lay outside the physical definition of the polis-state, in the interstate sanctuaries.

Herman (1987:Ch. 3) argues that the major context for the creation of ties of ritualized friendship was warfare. Historical documentation supplies numerous examples of how various elite Greeks concluded pacts of friendship before or after military activity. As Herman points out, ancient Greek historians take it for granted that allied commanders were ritualized friends. Sometimes the leaders of opposing sides established relationships after battle through guest-friendship alliances. Most notable examples are those that come from Greek contact with the nobility of the Persian empire.

But this analysis rests upon textual documentation, which for ancient Greece is seriously biased towards accounts of military activity. There is good reason to claim that the most common context for the initiation of bonds of ritualized friendship was not the battlefield, but the inter-state sanctuary. First, we have historical documentation that demonstrates that the initiation of ritualized friendship and its reactivation were important affairs in the interstate sanctuaries. As Herman himself points out, Isocrates states that:

> Having proclaimed a truce and resolved our pending quarrels, we come together in one place, where, as we make our prayers and sacrifices in common, we are reminded of the kinship which exists among us and are make to feel more kindly towards each other for the future, reviving old *xeniai* (ritualized friendships) and establishing new ones (Herman 1987:45).

In addition to this textual argument, the archaeological record at the sanctuary of Olympia demonstrates that it was probably an early center for Peloponnesian gift exchange, part of the initiation ritual for ritual friendship, as early as the ninth century B.C (Langdon 1987). There is no reason to argue that this did not continue into later periods as well, as the fame of this sanctuary grew.

There are also extremely cogent arguments to be made that the very nature of the interstate sanctuary made it the best context for the initiation and utilization of bonds of ritualized friendship. These interstate sanctuaries would have been the very foci for a major share of the initialization and the perpetuation of the institution of ritualized friendship. Sanctuaries presented advantages over meetings that might take place on the field of war. Their contexts were more neutral, incorporating less antagonism than combat. They included many more parties, from different parts of the Greek world, than a military context could ever supply. Sanctuaries also presented a more scheduled and more frequent opportunity for elite contacts. For example, the four most prominent interstate sanctuaries were Olympia, Delphi, Isthmia, and Nemea. These four were often referred to as an athletic *periodos*, for they were scheduled in a four-year sequence so that an athlete could participate in at least one per year over a four-year period. When we combine these four with the larger group of sanctuaries that elites would have visited (for example, Dodona, Didyma, Delos, Mt. Mykale, Ephesos, Samos, Paestum, and many others), it is clear that they would have offered an opportunity for elite gathering at least two to three times a year.

The above arguments are forceful points for the preference of sanctuaries over military contexts, but there is an additional observation that is perhaps the most cogent -- that is, the timing of the sanctuary festivals. From what we can gather, the major festivals were held after the summer's harvest. Olympia, for example, was scheduled for either the second or third full moon after the summer solstice. This was the very time that Hesiod recommended for overseas trading of agricultural goods, and it meant that the elites were coming to the sanctuaries and learning which regions in Greece had a good or bad harvest that year. This was invaluable information for an elite who would be looking to trade some agricultural surplus from his own lands.

*Sanctuaries -- The Power of the Context*

To understand just how special sanctuaries were for the elite, we may examine the best known, Olympia. The archaeological record at Olympia incorporates a variety of buildings and monuments (reports in the hundreds, for overview see Finley and Pleket 1976; Morgan 1990:Ch. 2 with notes; Mallwitz 1988). Religious activities centered around the temples of Zeus, Hera, and the Metroum. Athletic activity was housed in the stadium, where the contests were held, and training and practice buildings, such as the gymnasium and *palaestra* (an exercise yard). Housing and shelter were provided by the various *stoas, bouleteria*, and the Leonidium, an actual hotel or hostel. Within the precinct were also numerous honorific monuments erected for the victors in different contests. These must have been quite numerous, for the Greek travel-writer Pauasanias could still count more than 200 in the 2nd century A.D., when he visited the site.

The sanctuary was visited every four years by a range of Greeks, from spectators to contestants. But in the main, the symbolism of the sanctuary objectified the distinct position of the Greek elite. The majority of the athletic contestants were from the wealthier strata of Greek society, who could afford not only to take the time off to come to the sanctuaries, but also the expense of athletic training and of the journey often from such distant cities as Phasis on the eastern edge of the Black Sea or Hemeroscopium on the eastern coast of Spain.

The interstate sanctuaries were outside the territories of almost all the participant individuals and expressed a symbolic "marginality" (Morgan 1990:223-33), providing a weak context for state-correlated activity. State symbolism was kept at a minimum at Olympia. Its presence was seen in the twelve treasuries, or state-erected display buildings, that were erected along the north side of the precinct. In no way, however, could this presence match that of the various attending elites, who must have come from far more numerous polities. It was the individual, especially the elite, who received the major attention at the interstate sanctuary.

The power of this special context can not be overstated. Archaeologists elsewhere have argued that individual contexts, constructed within a definitive boundary, and composed of materials, both portable and architectural, have important, powerful connections with the larger structure of society (Leone 1984, Jameson 1987). Others have demonstrated equally well that the manipulation of individual contexts, such as votive or burial, plays an important part in growth in at least prestate societies (Parker Pearson 1984, Hodder 1984). In addition, Morris' (1987, 1989) and Humphreys' work (1980) with early and Archaic period Greek burials have effectively shown how the force of a single context can effect Greek state development.

This removed sanctuary setting of elite interaction had a strong impact on polis-state development in Greece. We have evidence that the connection between sanctuaries and Greek communities was strong. Snodgrass (1977) demonstrates how, as early as the 9th and 8th centuries B.C., there was a shift in the use of metals for elite burial goods within the individual state to metal for dedications in interstate sanctuaries themselves. Morgan (1990:203-04) has also shown that private dedications at sanctuaries rise just at the time that states were forming in Greece. She sees this as a context of elite competition for power within the emerging states, which intensified over time. In addition, although Morgan does not agree that the sanctuaries served as contexts for political emulation, and thereby state development, the case has been forwarded by both Snodgrass (1986) and Renfrew (1986). Furthermore, intercommunity sanctuaries played an important role in the development of the ethnos-state. An Achaian ethnos of twelve cities was connected by a central sanctuary at Aegira. Sanctuaries also played a role in the formation of leagues of polis-states. In Ionia the Greek polis-states met at the interstate sanctuary, the Panionion on Mt. Mykale, to discuss matters of foreign relations. The development of the Greek state therefore was not divorced from the context of the interstate sanctuary, but incorporated it within the trajectory of state development.

My view of the effect of the sanctuaries on polis-state formation differs from these previous studies. Herman sees the major effect of ritualized friendship on the state as political (1987:163-64), but I would argue that it was economic. Discussion so far has outlined the power of ritualized friendship in elite commerce, its focus within the sanctuaries, and the non-state character of the sanctuaries themselves. These observations lead us to conclude that the particular disjunction and even opposition of state and elite economic interests in numerous Greek polis-states resulted from the physical and ideological separation of elite economics from the polis-states. Thus, this unusual form of public/private economic distinction is fully understandable when one considers the larger context of Greek state formation.

## Conclusion

The purpose of the paper was to introduce an atypical form of public/private economic distinction to the general archaeological study of past states. State development in Greece was clearly different. A myriad of historical sources has demonstrated that the polis-state and elite economic activity found homes with different social systems. Greek elites conducted business through a network of ritualized friends that spanned state boundaries. The tradition of ritualized friendship began as early as 1000 B.C. and continued at least until Hellenistic (post-338 B.C.) times. The reason for its durability must have been the unique Greek feature of interstate sanctuaries. These sanctuaries provided a strong context for ritualized friendship and facilitated an elite commerce that did not identify with any single polis-state's interests. This created a vacuum within the polis-states, which consequently began to ally with the interests of the commoners in their economic decisions.

If ancient Greece had not preserved this system of interstate sanctuaries, the situation would have been remarkably different. The principal contexts for elite commercial transaction would then have been marriages or funerals located within the space of the state. In these contexts it would have been much harder to preserve the private tradition of ritualized friendship between elites of different states. The sanctuaries provided advantages of neutrality and a greater mix of people, which a state never could. In these changed circumstances the state, rather than ritualized friendship would have become the primary organ for elite commercial enterprises, and Greece might have eventually resembled to a greater degree the states of the Aztec or the Inka.

## Acknowledgments

I would like to express my gratitude to Elizabeth Brumfiel, Anthony Snodgrass and Nicola Tannenbaum, who were kind enough to read through earlier drafts of this paper and offer constructive suggestions for its improvement. Any deficiency in this paper is the result of my own stubbornness rather than the suggestions of others.

## Notes

1. Those interested in further reading may initially refer to Austin and Vidal-Naquet 1977, Snodgrass 1980, or Morris 1987.

2. Morris (1987:110-139) argues that the burial record demonstrates a distinction between elites and commoners. But his analysis is extremely problematic (see Humphreys 1990).

3. Garnsey and Morris (Morris 1989, Garnsey and Morris 1989:101) note that this relationship continued in Sparta and parts of Crete, which demonstrates examples of polis-states. Morris would refer to these polis-states as "intermediate states". His choice of terms betrays an assumed common teleology for all forms of Greek state formation. This has not been adequately demonstrated.

4. The best constructs for reading ancient history have been an issue of intense debate since the late nineteenth century German argument over a primitivist interpretation of ancient economics. There are numerous reviews of this debate. See Austin and Vidal-Naquet 1977:3-11 and bibliography on 28-29. More recent reviews are contained in Cartledge 1983 and Engels 1990, Chapter 1.

5. Morris (1986:6) is probably right to reply that, for the Greeks, the ideology was thicker than Humphreys implies, but his argument misinterprets the purpose of Humphreys' full argument. Humphreys (1978:160) goes on to argue that historical argument should not be based too strongly on a consideration of ancient values.

## References

Austin, M. and Vidal-Naquet, P.
    1977    *Economic and Social History of Ancient Greece: An Introduction.* Berkeley: University of California Press.

Berdan, F.
    1982    *The Aztecs of Central Mexico: An Imperial Society.* New York: Holt, Rinehart and Winston.

Boardman, J.
    1980    *The Greeks Overseas: Their Early Colonies and Trade.* (2nd ed.). London: Thames and Hudson.

Bravo, B.
    1974    Une Lettre sur Plomb de Beresan: Colonisation et Modes de Contact dans le Pont. *Dialogues d'Histoire Ancienne* 1:111-187.
    1983    Le Commerce des Céréales chez les Grecques de l'epoque archaique. In P. Garnsey and C. Whittaker, eds., *Trade and Famine in Classical Antiquity*, pp.17-29. Cambridge: Cambridge Philological Society.

Brumfiel, Elizabeth M.
    1983    Aztec State Making: Ecology, Structure, and the Origin of the State. *American Anthropologist* 85:261-84.
    1987    Elite and Utilitarian Crafts in the Aztec State. In E.M. Brumfiel and T.K. Earle, eds., *Specialization, Exchange, and Complex Societies*, pp. 102-18. Cambridge: Cambridge University Press.

Carrasco, Pedro
    1982    The Political Economy of the Aztec and Inca States. In G. Collier, R. Rosaldo, and J. Wirth, eds., *The Inca and Aztec States 1400-1800: Anthropology and History*, pp.23-42. New York: Academic Press.

Cartledge, P.
    1983    "Trade and Politics" revisited: Archaic Greece. In P. Garnsey, K. Hopkins, and C.R. Whittaker, eds., *Trade in the Ancient Economy*, pp.1-15. Cambridge: Cambridge University Press.

D'Altroy, Terence N.
    1992    *Provincial Power in the Inka Empire.* Washington, D.C.: Smithsonian Institution Press.

D'Altroy, Terence N. and Timothy Earle
- 1985 State Finance, Wealth Finance, and Storage in the Inka Political Economy. *Current Anthropology* 26:187-206.

Demosthenes
- 1936 *Private Orations, Vol. III.* A.T. Murray transl. Cambridge: Harvard University Press.
- 1954 *Orationes.* S.H. Butcher, ed. Oxford: Clarendon Press.

Earle, Timothy et al.
- 1987 *Archaeological Field Research in the Upper Mantaro, Peru, 1982-1983: Investigation of Inka Expansion and Exchange.* Los Angeles: Institute of Archaeology, University of California, Los Angeles.

Engels, D.
- 1990 *Roman Corinth: An Alternative Model for the Classical City.* Chicago: University of Chicago Press.

Finley, M.
- 1973 *The Ancient Economy.* London: Chatto and Windus.
- 1978a *The World of Odysseus.* London: Chatto and Windus.
- 1978b The Fifth-Century Athenian Empire: A Balance-Sheet. In P. Garnsey and C. Whittaker, eds., *Imperialism in the Ancient World*, pp.103-26. Cambridge: Cambridge University Press.
- 1980 *Ancient Slavery and Modern Ideology.* London: Chatto and Windus.
- 1981 Was Greek Civilisation Based on Slave Labor? In B.D. Shaw and R. Saller, eds., *Economy and Society in Ancient Greece*, pp.97-115. London: Chatto and Windus.

Finley, M. and Pleket, H.
- 1976 *The Olympic Games: The First Thousand Years.* London: Chatto and Windus.

Gallant, T.
- 1989 Crisis and Response: Risk-Buffering Behavior in Hellenistic Greek Communities. *Journal of Interdisciplinary History* 19:393-413.

Garnsey, P.
- 1988 *Famine and Food Supply in the Graeco-Roman World: Responses to Risk and Crisis.* Cambridge: Cambridge University Press.

Garnsey, P. and Morris, I.
- 1989 Risk and the Polis: the Evolution of Institutionalised Responses to Food Supply Problems in the Ancient Greek

State. In P. Halstead and J. O'Shea, eds., *Bad Year Economics: Cultural Responses to Risk and Uncertainty*, pp.98-105. Cambridge: Cambridge University Press.

Halstead, P.
- 1981 From Determinism to Uncertainty: Social Storage and the Rise of the Minoan Palace. In A. Sheridan and G. Bailey, eds., *Economic Archaeology: Towards an Integration of Ecological and Social Approaches*, pp.187-213. Oxford: British Archaeological Reports International Series, 96.
- 1988 On the Redistribution and the Origin of Minoan- Mycenaean Palatial Economies. In E. French and K. Wardle, eds., *Problems in Greek Prehistory*. Bristol: Bristol University Press.

Hasebroek, J.
- 1933 *Trade and Politics in Ancient Greece*. London: Bell.

Herman, G.
- 1987 *Ritualised Friendship and the Greek City*. Cambridge: Cambridge University Press.

Herodotus
- 1927 *Historiae*. Charles Hude, ed. Oxford: Clarendon Press.

Hesiod
- 1978 *Works and Days*. M.L. West, ed. Oxford: Clarendon Press.

Hodder, Ian
- 1984 Burials, Houses, Women and Men in the European Neolithic. In D. Miller and C. Tilley, eds., *Ideology, Power and Prehistory*, pp.51-68. Cambridge: Cambridge University Press.

Humphreys, S.
- 1978 *Anthropology and the Greeks*. London: Routledge and Kegan Paul.
- 1980 Family Tombs and Tomb Cult in Ancient Athens -- Tradition or Traditionalism? *Journal of Hellenic Studies* 100:96-110.
- 1990 Review of: Burial and Ancient Society: The Rise of the Greek City-State, by Ian Morris. *Helios* 17:263-268.

Jameson, R.
- 1987 Purity and Power at the Victorian Dinner Party. In I. Hodder, ed., *The Archaeology of Contextual Meanings*, pp.55-65. Cambridge: Cambridge University Press.

Langdon, S.
- 1987 Gift Exchange in the Geometric Sanctuaries. In T. Linders and G. Nordquist, eds., *Gifts to the Gods: Proceedings of*

Leone, Mark
    *the Uppsala Symposium 1985*, pp.107-13. Uppsala: Uppsala University Press.
    1984    Interpreting Ideology in Historical Archaeology: The William Paca Garden in Annapolis, Maryland. In D. Miller and C. Tilley, eds., *Ideology, Power and Prehistory*, pp.25-36. Cambridge: Cambridge University Press.

McDonald, W., and Rapp, G.
    1972    *The Minnesota Messenia Expedition. Reconstructing a Bronze Age Regional Environment*. Minneapolis: University of Minnesota Press.

Mallwitz, A.
    1988    Cult and Competition Locations at Olympia. In W. Raschke, ed., T*he Archaeology of the Olympics: The Olympics and Other Festivals in Antiquity*, pp.79-109. Madison: University of Wisconsin Press.

Mele, A.
    1979    *Il Commercio Greco Arcaico. Prexis ed Emporie*. Naples.

Millett, P.
    1983    Maritime Loans and the Structure of Credit in Fourth-Century Athens. In P. Garnsey, K. Hopkins and C. Whittaker, eds., *Trade in the Ancient Economy*, pp.36-52. Berkeley: University of California Press.

Morgan, C.
    1990    *Athletes and Oracles: The Transformation of Olympia and Delphi in the Eighth Century B.C.*. Cambridge: Cambridge University Press.

Morris, I.
    1986    Gift and Commodity in Archaic Greece. *Man* 21:1-17.
    1987    *Burial and Ancient Society: The Rise of the Greek City-State*. Cambridge: Cambridge University Press.
    1989    Circulation, Deposition and the Formation of the Greek Iron Age. *Man* 24:502-519.

Murra, John V.
    1980    *The Economic Organization of the Inka State*. Greenwich, CT: JAI Press.

Parker Pearson, M.
    1984    Economic and Ideological Change: Cyclical Growth in the Pre-state Societies of Jutland. In D. Miller and C. Tilley, eds., *Ideology, Power and Prehistory*, pp.69-92. Cambridge: Cambridge University Press.

Pendlebury, A., et al.
- 1939 Excavation in the Plain of Lasithi III. Karphi. *Annual of the British School at Athens* 38:57-145.

Renfrew, Colin
- 1986 Introduction: Peer Polity Interaction and Socio-Political Change. In C. Renfrew and J. Cherry, eds., *Peer Polity Interaction and Socio-Political Change*, pp.1-18. Cambridge: Cambridge University Press.

Small, David
- 1987 Social Correlations to the Greek Cavea in the Roman Period. In S. Macready and F. Thompson, eds., *Roman Architecture in the Greek World*, pp.85-93. London: Society of Antiquaries.

Snodgrass, A.
- 1977 *Archaeology and the Rise of the Greek State*. Cambridge: Cambridge University Press.
- 1980 *Archaic Greece: The Age of Experiment*. Berkeley: University of California Press.
- 1983 Heavy Freight in Archaic Greece. In P. Garnsey, K. Hopkins, and C. Whittaker, eds., *Trade in the Ancient Economy*, pp.16-26. Berkeley: University of California Press.
- 1986 Interaction by Design: the Greek City State. In C. Renfrew and J. Cherry, eds., *Peer Polity Interaction and Socio-Political Change*, pp.47-58. Cambridge: Cambridge University Press.

# SUBSISTENCE AND THE STATE: THE CASE OF PORFIRIAN MEXICO

Judith E. Marti
California State University, Northridge

One of the main problems facing developing nations, particularly at early stages of industrialization, is that of providing cheap subsistence goods and basic services to its poor, urban populations. Economically, serving this population is crucial because out of its ranks comes the bulk of the labor force, an important component of the nation's industrialization programs. Historically, serving this population has been the purview of municipal government. Thus, questions about subsistence goods maintenance policies can best be answered by studying the decisions at the municipal level. In this paper, I will examine how the municipal governments of Mexico City and Guadalajara -- Mexico's two largest cities -- dealt with the problem of subsistence during the Porfiriato (1877-1910), the period leading up to the Mexican Revolution.

Subsistence maintenance has often been examined from an institutional perspective -- studying the organization of governments and their relations to the governed. The data from Porfirian Mexico suggests that an examination of processes can also be rewarding, that is, approaching the problem as one of change in relations over time. In addition, this approach sheds light on the little understood yet important aspect of governing in developing nations: the dynamics of decision-making.

Mexico, in its early stages of development, has proved to be an ideal choice for studying these dynamics. From the War of Independence (1810-1821), to the beginning of the Porfirio Díaz presidency (1877), political instability, corruption, rebellions, wars, even foreign interventions and a French emperor, drained the national treasury and crippled the economy. With no money to run the government, one administration after another adopted a variety of unsuccessful policies aimed at increasing revenues (Cumberland 1968, Bazant 1979, Vanderwood 1981).

On arriving to power, the Porfirio Díaz administration embarked on a program of industrialization and modernization to solve Mexico's problems of severe economic stagnation and monetary insolvency (Katz 1981, El Colegio de México n.d.). Implementation of this policy required capital and labor. Since the government could not raise revenues by taxing a population either overtaxed or too poor, it sought revenues-producing capital in foreign loans (Turlington 1930). As for labor, the government sought to recruit from its large population which was migrating to the cities in search of work.

Mexico's two largest urban areas, Mexico City and Guadalajara, attracted people seeking work. This migrant population was poor, and it increased very rapidly, placing an enormous strain on the municipal governments' ability to provide basic goods and services. The municipal governments' obligation toward the citizenry was enormous. On the one hand, the *ayuntamientos* (city governments) had to provide services for and make cheap goods available to that population. On the other, they had to look for revenues to support these social policies at a time when resources were scarce. To solve the dilemma, these municipal governments developed a number of policies and strategies to maximize subsistence goods and revenues.

A principal component of the solution were the merchants, public market vendors, and street vendors, whose main function was to provide goods and services to the general public. These strategies, however, were not free from problems. Because these groups -- merchants, public market vendors and street vendors -- were competing with each other for customers, they often came into conflict. As a consequence, the municipal governments had to act as mediators, creating a host of new problems and giving the impression of ineffectiveness and chaos.

An examination of the records might give the impression that the municipal governments of Mexico City and Guadalajara lacked the skill to cope with the monumental problems at hand, and even more generally, that governments in developing nations are unable to cope with some of the problems of their own making. Nonetheless, a careful study of municipal decisions and the policies motivating these decisions give a very different picture.

To discern policy at the municipal level, the researcher needs to examine the day to day decision-making process recorded in the official government documents for the municipalities of Mexico City and Guadalajara. The importance of public markets and street vendors for the municipality, and the nature of the city government's ties to the federal government, can be found in government publications, such as the *Boletín Oficial del Consejo Superior de Gobierno del Distrito Federal*. Non-government documents (contemporary photographs, travelers' reports, newspaper accounts, etc.) give us a glimpse of the large numbers of street vendors, including children, who managed to escape regulation (and taxation). For day-to-day governmental decision-making, internal government records are particularly revealing; the correspondence between large merchants, market vendors, street vendors, and city and state government officials document the conflicts among these groups. Debates and rulings on these conflicts are recorded in interdepartmental memos between the various branches of government and the minutes of city council (*cabildo*) meetings, including secret sessions of the *cabildo* (*Actas de Cabildo Originales de Sesiones Secretas*). In these sessions, the *cabildos* examined, on a case by case basis, petitions, letters, complaints, about taxation, rents, and so on. Newspapers tend to reflect the "official" government position toward vendors, an attitude which was often at variance with government actions (Marti, 1990).

When rulings of the municipal government are looked at individually, it appears that it was working under a highly arbitrary, even conflicting style of policymaking, and management. In some cases, the municipal government chose to ignore complaints, a clearly *laissez faire* policy. In other cases, it bent or reinterpreted market laws in favor of vendors, evidence of aggressive actions in favor of vending. In still others, the municipal government only weakly enforced the laws, and gave the appearance of an ineffectual government. Yet, when the municipality's handling of conflicts is viewed as a whole, a pattern appears, a regularity in decision-making that points to an effort to maximize revenues when possible, and keep public market and street vendors viable, by protecting them against conflicting interest groups, and even subsidizing them if necessary.

A study of the regularities that emerge in decision-making in the municipal governments of Mexico City and Guadalajara, has led me to posit the existence of three policies at the municipal level, a *revenue maximization policy*, a *subsistence goods maximization policy*, and one of *compliance with the federal leadership*. These policies were meant to solve the problems of raising revenues to pay for costs; of providing basic subsistence goods and services for a growing, poor population; and of maintaining the federal government's patronage.

*The revenue maximization policy* was directed to the need to raise funds to pay for municipal services. Under this policy, as might be expected, the *cabildo* often supported large merchants at the expense of street and public market vendors. Large merchants were, after all, a major source of municipal revenues, and as such they were supported by their ayuntamientos. But the municipal governments could not maximize this group's function as a source of revenue, for in so doing they would jeopardize this upper class's function as a power base for the Díaz regime. Thus, municipal governments had to turn to public market and street vendors for revenues. In fact, this group turned out to be a dependable and not inconsiderable source for revenues. The vendor sector of the economy could be counted on to provide the city with between 5% and 10% of total revenues without costing the city more than about 1% of its total expenditures -- monies spent on market repairs, tax collection, etc. (*Memoria* 1880, etc). Market and street vendors thus also needed to be protected under the revenue maximization policy, even from large merchants. But neither could the municipal governments maximize this group's function as a source of revenue, for in so doing they would overtax it and thus jeopardize their use as providers of basic goods for an industrial labor force. The municipal governments were thus caught in a conflicting position between the wealthier merchants on one side, and public market and street vendors on the other. Both sides needed to be protected and neither could be alienated under the revenue maximization policy.

*The subsistence goods maximization policy* aimed to promote any sector that met an industrial work force's needs for cheap goods. Under this policy, the municipal government would be expected to rule favorably toward any sector that guaranteed industry a sufficient supply of labor, by providing a cheap source of basic food stuffs, etc. Working under the subsistence goods maximization policy, the municipal government often supported street and public market vendors, suppliers of cheap goods, even at the expense of large merchants. But just as they did under the revenue maximization policy, municipal governments faced the problem of supporting opposing interest groups while implementing the maximization of subsistence goods policy. Obviously, protection of public market and street vendors was mandated according to the maximization of subsistence goods policy, as the main source of basic goods for a poor labor force. But the wealthier classes also benefited directly from implementation of the maximization of subsistence goods policy. Industry depended on laborers who, in turn, depended on vendors in order to subsist. To jeopardize the existence of the vendor sector of the economy would also endanger the interests of wealthier groups, especially industrial owners, the cities' main source of revenues.

*The policy of compliance with the federal leadership* was adopted so that local officials could maintain a tenable relationship with the federal government, function effectively, and attain some security in their jobs. Under this policy the local government would be expected to publicly support federal goals and to reiterate the official rhetoric of the Díaz regime. Although local officials had some degree of autonomy in making local decisions, the Díaz government sought increasingly to tighten its control on local affairs. Under a March 26, 1903 law, the political governor and municipal administration of the Distrito Federal were placed under the charge of the president of Mexico who, in turn, appointed three functionaries, salaried by the federal government, to oversee the local government. "With this change...the *ayuntamientos* will feel like they are losing an old friend, almost a father. But they will accept it with courage because they know it is compensated for with the arrival of a powerful protector, who has in his hands all the elements to persevere toward progress..." (*Boletín Oficial*, 3 July, 1903, p. 3). That the president of the city council, Juan Bribiesca, and many of its members were able to survive the political reorganization (*Boletín Oficial*, 1900-1910, pp. various), and continue in day-to-day decision making on local matters, including those concerning vendors and local merchants, attests to their political savvy. Working under the compliance policy, official statements made to local newspapers echoed the federal goals of progress and modernization. But municipal governments faced the same problem of supporting opposing interest groups that they did under the subsistence goods and revenue maximization policies. Thus, street vendors, who did not fit the image of a modern, progressive nation, were publicly denigrated to appease federal government goals while, at the same time, were supported under municipal government policies and rulings so as to keep the city running.

As policies, revenue maximization, subsistence goods maximization and compliance are solutions to opposing demands on the municipality -- to raise revenues, to feed the poor, and to maintain a working relationship with the federal government. The seeming contradictions in government actions in individual cases; the apparent inconsistent rulings in conflicts between large merchants, industrialists, street, and market vendors; the fickle support of opposing interest groups; the discrepancy between the municipal governments' official stance and rulings and actions can now be explained in terms of the applications of these policies.

## Case Studies

From the municipal governments' point of view, juggling alternative policies to serve opposing groups was part of the work-day. From the position of merchants, public market, and street vendors, the situation was less than felicitous. Case studies help clarify the application of policies as it benefited one or another group.

One case illustrates well how apparently arbitrary and contradictory actions taken by municipal governments were in reality evidence of rational decision-making. In this particular case, government first appears to be undertaking a *laissez faire* policy, then aggressively governing; but when analyzed it becomes clear that in both instances, the government was working under the revenue maximization policy.

Market vendors from the Mercado Corona, in Guadalajara, appealed to the governor of the state of Jalisco (AHJ, Gobernación, n/c, "Señor Gobernador: los subscritos," 1910). They sought the removal of street vendors who were selling in front of their market. The municipal government of Guadalajara, they stated, was ignoring their complaints about unfair competition from street vendors. The municipal government, in choosing to ignore the complaints, appeared to be working under a clearly *laissez faire* policy. When pressed by the governor's office to make a ruling, the municipal government reversed its style of governing, bending the law and even reinterpreting market law in what then appeared to be aggressive governing in favor of street vending. The *cabildo* ruled against the market vendors -- they would not remove street vendors from the market area. In both its approaches, city government tried to keep market vendors and street vendors functioning under its revenue maximization policy.

The municipal government's handling of the case reveals the process of governing as a juggling of conflicting interest groups. By first ignoring the complaints, the municipal government tried unsuccessfully to avoid siding with either of two opposing groups, both revenue producers. By their inaction, they meant to keep street and market vendors functioning side by side, albeit acrimoniously. When pressed to rule, the municipal government was forced to protect street vendors actively and keep them viable to maximize revenues. At the same time, the city sought not to alienate market vendors by keeping its policy of revenue maximization hidden. In an interdepartmental memo to the governor, the municipal government noted the considerable funds accruing from street vending. But, when officially replying to the complaining market vendors, the importance of revenues collected from street vendors, the overriding reason for the negative ruling, was omitted. Instead, the municipal government chose to argue on legal grounds for its ruling, thus avoiding alienating either party.

The application of different government policies can also explain other inconsistencies and contradictions in government actions that emerge from the historical data. For instance, the policies of subsistence goods maximization and of compliance can explain the discrepancy between the publicly stated, official, adversarial view of the municipal government toward street vendors, with privately held, actual, subsidy of this sector of the economy. The difference between word and deed is clearly seen in a comparison of the newspaper portrayals, which usually presented an adversarial relationship between the municipality and vendors, with the internal government records that document vendor protection.

Newspapers blamed, directly or indirectly, the street vendors for many social problems. Street fairs in Guadalajara, for example, with probably the greatest concentration of street vendors, were said by one newspaper, to be run by "the lowest class of the populace" and said to be "only good for dissipation and laziness. The monies are spent...on cockfights, not commerce." Street fairs were also said to be a blight on the image of a modern, progressive city, catchwords of the Porfirio Díaz regime: "Besides," continued the newspaper editorial, "this stains the image of the second city in Mexico...this is not what a civilized city should have" (BPE, *El Correo de Jalisco*, 16 July 1895, p. 1).

Newspapers also depicted market vendors as victims of municipal government policies and actions. In Guadalajara, some vendors sold goods from the Portal of San Agustín, a structure which consisted of a row of tiny shops protected by a portal held up by large columns. The city of Guadalajara, according to one editorial, planned to remove the structure by first demolishing the columns and portal, then removing the shops at a latter date. Because the shops were so small, vendors tended to rent the portal columns outside their shops, where they displayed and sold the bulk of their goods. "The local gossip is that this is malicious," read the editorial, "because the value of the little shops will decrease, and the city government will have to pay less indemnity to the properties. Is it fair and honest," the newspaper asked, "that those that indemnify, first make the property less valuable in order to pay less indemnification?" (BPE, *El Paladín*, 23 September 1900, p. 2).

This image of a tough approach toward vendors by city government can be partially explained by city governments' ties to the federal government. Although local governments had a degree of autonomy to make rulings on local matters, local officials depended on the patronage of the national leadership. Thus, official statements aired in local newspapers, echoed the federal goals of progress and modernization, under the compliance policy, goals in which street vendors in particular hardly fit. On the local level, public statements of a tough approach toward street vendors served to keep from alienating wealthy merchants and jeopardizing their function in the municipal governments policy of revenue maximization.

Yet, from the municipal records -- such as city council meetings, internal government memos, correspondence between vendors, merchants and the various departments of city government -- another picture emerges. Municipal governments often stood in partisan relationships toward vendors, ruling in favor of street and market vendors, thus protecting them from bigger and more powerful interests, such as large merchants, or favoring street vendors over market vendors, as we have just seen.

In fact, there is evidence that in many cases the municipal government was actually subsidizing market vendors to keep them viable. Public market records show that many vendors in the public markets of Mexico City were not paying the full market fees each month, but were consistently in arrears. In protecting street vendors by, in a sense, subsidizing them, the municipalities were working under the policy of subsistence goods maximization.

In addition, market vendors who complained to the municipal government that payment of market fees put their livelihood in jeopardy had their fees reduced or even waved for periods of time, sometimes up to a year. In one case, a market vendor was successfully able to argue for two fee reductions. Her first request, for a reduction by half, was granted. But even with this reduction, she argued, "I just have money for living." (AHMG, Mercados, exp. 14, 1893). In order to keep her viable, the city ruled to allow her to pay only a portion of the market tax each month. By making fee reduction allowances, the city was in effect subsidized vendors so they could continue providing cheap goods -- an example of a ruling made under the subsistence goods maximization policy.

These contradictory images, the public acknowledgment of the importance of large merchants and the more hidden support of street and public market vendors; the discrepancy between the official, adversarial view of the municipal government toward street and public market vendors with the governments' subsidy of this sector of the economy; the apparent inconsistencies in rulings dealing with conflicts between large merchants, industrialists, street, and market vendors, can be understood as applications of the municipal governments' revenue maximization, subsistence goods maximization and compliance policies. These policies were crucial to solving the governments' problem of subsistence maintenance, of guaranteeing cheap subsistence goods and collecting revenues to provide basic services to a poor urban population.

## Concluding Remarks

Finally, these policies also throw some light onto the municipal governments' views of the nature of government. The process of governing can best be seen when the competing needs of large merchants, public market vendors, and street vendors are brought into conflict with one another. The municipal government was inevitably drawn into these conflicts as mediator and judge. When first examined, government rulings appear to be arbitrary -- full of contradictions and inconsistencies. But, when seen as implementations of government policies, some measure of consistency is brought in. In those rulings that affected merchants, market vendors and street vendors, the municipal government sought not to alienate any of the conflicting parties. And in its public stance, the municipal government also sought not to alienate the federal government and wealthy merchants. The municipal government's main role in subsistence maintenance was not fixed but rather a continual juggling of opposing interest groups with conflicting demands.

## Acknowledgments

This paper is based on archival research conducted in 1985-1988 in Mexico City and Guadalajara with the aid of a UCLA Mexus Research Award. I wish to thank Timothy Earle, Allen Johnson, Susan Scrimshaw, Robert N. Burr, Juan Gómez-Quiñones, Elizabeth Brumfiel, Charles Hickson, Mari Womack, and Barbara Feezor-Stewart, for their valuable insights and thoughtful criticisms. I am also very appreciative to my research assistants in the field, Maestra Celina G. Becerra, Maestro Alejandro Solís, Sra. Ana Elena Magís.

## Archives Cited

Guadalajara, Jalisco:

    AHJ -- Archivo Histórico de Jalisco
    AHMG -- Archivo Histórico Municipal de Guadalajara
    BPE -- Biblioteca Pública del Estado de Jalisco

## References

Bazant, Jan
    1979    *A Concise History of Mexico from Hidalgo to Cárdenas 1805-1940.* Reprinted with corrections. Cambridge: Cambridge University Press.

*"Boletín Oficial" del Consejo Superior de Gobierno del Distrito Federal.*
    1903-1911 (various).

El Colegio de México
    n.d.    *Estadísticas Económicas del Porfiriato: Fuerza de Trabajo y Actividad Económica por Sectores. Seminario de Historia Moderna de México.* Mexico City: El Colegio de México.

Cumberland, Charles C.
    1968    *Mexico: The Struggle for Modernity.* Latin American Histories. Oxford: Oxford University Press.

Katz, Friedrich
    1981    *The Secret War in Mexico: Europe, The United States and the Mexican Revolution.* Chicago: The University of Chicago Press.

Marti, Judith E.
    1990    *Subsistence and the State: Municipal Government Policies and Urban Markets in Developing Nations, The Case of Mexico City and Guadalajara, 1877-1910.* Unpublished Ph.D. dissertation. The University of California, Los Angeles.

*Memoria que el Ayuntamiento constitucional de 1879 presenta a sus comitentes.*
    1880    Mexico City: Imprenta de Francisco Díaz de León.

Turlington, Edgar W.
    1930    *Mexico and Her Foreign Creditors.* New York: Columbia University Press.

Vanderwood, Paul.
    1981    *Disorder and Progress: Bandits, Police, and Mexican Development.* Lincoln: University of Nebraska Press.

# ECOLOGY AND POLITICS IN THE PUEBLA BASIN OF MEXICO

Sheldon Smith
University of Wisconsin-La Crosse

## Introduction

Those with an active commitment to economic development and the preservation of the environment will not be surprised when this paper shows that these two values are in contradiction to each other. Decisions concerning development and environmental protection are made at various levels in the political institutions of each nation state. Compromises are made between partisans of development and partisans of environmental protection. But in the real world, the economic needs of the human community dominate over the needs of the environment. This paper describes how a political movement born of a fear of a loss of jobs due to the implementation of environmental laws blocked the national agency SEDUE from effectively protecting the environment in Puebla, Mexico. A subtext of this paper is that the structure of municipal government makes it difficult for national agencies to achieve environmental goals. The paper extends Etzioni's analytical "I/We" construct to the environment (Etzioni 1987).

## Stewardship of Human and Environmental Resources: Synthesis of Human Systems Ecology and Socioeconomics

This paper adds to the paradigm of human systems ecology by extending Amitai Etzioni's I/We from culture to nature (Etzioni 1987, Bennett 1976, Smith and Reeves 1989). Etzioni argues that human behavior cannot be reduced to rational economic acts based on the profit motive alone, but that in human behavior there is also a moral dimension, an I/We paradigm. Amitai Etzioni's socioeconomics attempts the development of a morally structured theory of economics which better explains human-human interaction in hopes of developing social policy which balances economic (I) and community (We) needs. Etzioni's socioeconomics does not, however, address the relationships of humans to their environments. The human systems ecology paradigm does address the relationship of humans to nature, but it does not explicitly state the moral (or political) component of that many stranded relationship (Smith and Reeves 1989).

In Etzioni's work, human behavior can be reduced to two bundles: the economic and the moral. These two bundles cannot be collapsed into one other (Etzioni 1987). Paradigmatically, socioeconomics combines neoclassical economics, with its emphasis on the first bundle of rational decision making based on competition, with a second moral and sociological bundle (Etzioni 1987).

Extending Etzioni's I/We paradigm to the human/ecology interface produces the Stewardship model. The Stewardship model also has two irreducible bundles. One is the economic component based on the "I" value, and is similar to the neoclassical "maximization" concept translated to mean "development". The second or "moral dimension" is based on our relationships to each other within and between human communities. The Stewardship maxim is, we are free to increase or to maximize the yield of a given environment (I) so long as what we do benefits all communities and, if imitated by them, does not destroy that environment (the "We"). This type of economic process is one of "sustained development". Sustained development is increased yield within the limits set by nature and resources and equitably distributed to all participating communities.

The Stewardship model can be used to highlight the problems of development and adaptation in a variety of world regions with a variety of distinct political economies. In this paper, I will focus the model on the analysis of the region of the Puebla Basin in south-central Mexico. Puebla is the name of a state in Mexico, a geographic region, as well as an old colonial city dating to the 16th century which administers the state and valley of Puebla.

The following analysis follows a series of feedback loops through the Puebla Basin using Bennett's (1976: 38) model of human ecology: 1) The first feedback loop corresponds to the economy of a society and concerns the transformation of aspects of the physical environment into energy and goods and with trade relations; 2) the second feedback loop concerns demographics: population expansion, contraction and immigration; 3) the third feedback loop concerns to the cultural/symbolic side of human/environment inter-relationships; 4) the fourth feedback loop concerns those aspect of the human/environment interface causing biological trauma to the human population in the form of health problems; 5) the fifth feedback loop concerns technology; 6) the final feedback loop concerns the political/bureaucratic institutions of a society.

Other models can be used and the specific ordering of the loops followed is arbitrary. Because of the interconnections between the loops, it is possible to use a completely different ordering and yield roughly the same analysis. This writer's primary interest has been in feedback loops 1, 2, and 6. The other feedback loops are, therefore, only minimally represented.

## Feedback Loop #1 Economy of Puebla: Involution in the Valley of Puebla[1]

The economy of the valley basin of Puebla is geared towards the production of goods for export. In the valley of Puebla there is a heavy emphasis on lumbering, agriculture, mining, and coffee which are the major local resources which are transformed into energy and goods. Volkswagen of Mexico is a major economic institution in the region. There are also several textile firms which were founded in the early 19th century (Thompson 1989). The following details ecological damage to the environment by the economic institutions of the Puebla Basin.

*Agriculture and the Environment*

Puebla is a major agricultural region producing a wide variety of goods. However, in recent years, two dominant and linked problems are becoming very serious. One is the decreasing production of food in favor of exportable products, such as strawberries (for Los Angeles, California), and the second is the increase in groundwater contamination due to the use of herbicides and pesticides and chemical fertilizers. These two problems are colliding with the population explosion.

Coffee production is one of the major income producers for the state of Puebla. In 1989, 5000 small producers exported coffee to the United States, England, France, and Spain, helped by the Coffee Advisory of Puebla, created by Governor Mariano Piña Olaya. In June of 1989, a shipment of 45,000 Quintales brought in seven million dollars to the economy of the northern sierra (*Sol* 1989:4/25).

The vital economic role of coffee is undermined by the impact of coffee production on ecology. In late February, 1989, residents of the Colonia de Hidalgo of the community of Huauchinango in northern Puebla protested "grave contamination" of the water supply by coffee producers. The threat of coffee contamination affects 3000 people. The pollution is produced when the wastes from coffee processing (removing the husk from the bean) are dumped into streams. The women of the community complained that there is no potable water and that the local river where they wash their clothes and bathe, the Arroyo Amarillo (Yellow Arroyo), has gotten so black it has been renamed Arroyo Negro (Black Arroyo). When the women wash their clothing, it comes out smelling so badly the clothes cannot be worn. In addition, all of the fish in the stream have died. The people of the village requested that the coffee producers be forced to move elsewhere. Nearby, coffee growers pollute the San Marcos and Necaxa rivers to the point where the aquatic life in the rivers is dying. In 1990, a severe frost killed the coffee crop in the Sierra Norte, producing vast economic hardship but ironically cleaning the rivers for the first time

## 328 ECONOMIC ANTHROPOLOGY OF THE STATE

in a decade. Non-coffee growers in the region are currently celebrating the cleanliness of the local water supply while Governor Piña Olaya supports the coffee growers with subsidies. New trees are being planted and it is hoped they will be in production by 1995 (*Sol* 1991/8/10).

In addition to chemical contamination of the environment, there is increased hunger. Because of a shift towards the production of export commodities, more and more food is purchased abroad. According to lawyer Carlos Veraza, president of the State Federation of Small Property Owners of Puebla, speaking to a delegation of CONASUPO, the consumption of locally produced grains has diminished 30%, meat by 40%, milk by 28%, and plantains by 28% over the last decade (*Sol* 1989/4/22). In addition, there are more than 40 million poor in the country who cannot afford to buy imported foods. In the last six years, the population of the country increased by ten million. The population of Mexico is more poorly fed now than a decade ago; last year the country had to import 54% of what it consumed (*Sol* 1989/4/22).

One reason for the substitution of imported foods for domestically grown ones is the conscious shift towards export production by farmers or the abandonment of land due to the low price paid for agricultural products by the government. For example, over 2,000 acres of land in Oaxaca were not worked in 1989 due to a lack of rain and low prices paid by the Agricultural Board (*Gabinete Agropecuario*). The prices paid to farmers for agricultural products are only a third of their value on the international market. For example, corn is priced in old Mexican pesos) by the government at $370 a kilo, rice at $238 a kilo, sorghum at $225, wheat at $270, barley $225, beans $525, soybeans $408. Informants from the abandoned region explained that they have to pay $600.00 pesos for a kilo of corn and that rice costs $995. Beans, which has an official price of $525 go for up to $1500 in the markets of the Mixteca Alta and up to $2000 in Ixcaquixtla (*Sol* 1989/4/25). Thus the incentive to grow food for local consumption has been destroyed.

Once locked into export production, farmers also tend to use increasingly greater amounts of chemicals to increase production.[2] Members of the environmental group, *Puebla Verde* have attacked the use of pesticides, fertilizers, and herbicides in the home and field. They argue that pesticides which are outlawed in the United States are used in Mexico. For example, the product BHC, which was absolutely prohibited in the United States, is still used in Mexico for agriculture and in creams and shampoos. The International Pesticide Action Network found that there are twelve pesticides commonly used in Mexico which are outlawed in the United States, Japan, and in the European Economic Community because the chemicals produce cancer, mutations, and other problems. Among the drugs mentioned were BHC, Toxafeno, and Endrin (*Sol* 1988/11/20).

There is a great demand for water for irrigation by farmers of local communities throughout Puebla. However, run-off from these farms into lakes has killed fish and destroyed the fishing economies of the same communities. The reservoir of Valsequillo has been badly contaminated and water use for irrigation has vastly reduced its usefulness for domestic purposes. There is also considerable water pollution from industry. Atlixco, a major city to the south of Puebla, was found to have high levels of contamination in the well water, particularly detergents (*Sol* 1989/3/10). A study of 35 wells in the *municipio* of Puebla showed that the network of water distribution is contaminated with bacteria, human and animal fecal material, and industrial chemicals. The water produces diarrhea, dysentery, hepatitis, and typhoid (*Sol* 1989/3/15).

*Forestry Production and Deforestation*

Deforestation in the valley of Puebla has become extremely serious over the last two decades. Particularly serious is deforestation in the northern half of the state in the Sierra del Norte and further south on the piedmont slopes of the two volcanoes of Popocatepetl and Ixtaccihuatl and in a variety of woodland parks throughout the state of Puebla. Complicating the situation is the distribution of many forest lands to peasants during the 1930s and 1940s in the form of state controlled *ejidos* or collectives. These properties are difficult for the state to manage due to the lack of titles and because they are the only sources of income for many. The *ejido* lands also have important symbolic attributes to the poor which make it difficult for the federal or state governments interfere in any way with their uses. *Ejiditarios*, the cultivators of *ejidos*, often rent plots of land to be used for lumbering, or cut timber on their plots to sell to wood manufacturers in the state or outside of it. More insidious are the "*contrabundistas*" or smugglers of wood products who steal into the forests of the *ejido* owners, public park lands, and private estates to steal lumber. The smugglers are often well armed with machine guns and outgun the local police and army units. The forests are also being destroyed by firewood cutters and small self-employed lumbermen who cut trees for export.

There have been increased complaints by local farmers, mostly *ejiditarios*, about the destruction of local forests. In December of 1988, farmers in the regions of Popocatepetl and Ixtaccihuatl denounced to *Puebla Verde* deforestation on the two volcanoes. In January, 1989, *ejido* owners complained regarding the extensive destruction of forests which was reported to the Secretariat for Agricultural Development (SARH). The "rational" exploitation of forests by peasants was being destroyed by wood cutters. Later in January, *ejido* owners complained of armed smugglers cutting down trees. In February 1989, local populations reported the destruction of national parks located on Ixtac-Popocatepetl; the governor of the state recommended more police and the military, but the army is not armed well enough to protect against the smugglers of wood with their machine guns (*Sol* 1989/2/19).

One of the problems is that the local governments of the *municipios* of the forested zones are virtually independent of the state and federal government. SEDUE, SARH, and the governor of the state are hamstrung in trying to protect the forest, or otherwise protecting the environment, due to the powerful tradition of respect for the autonomy of the local governments. Clandestine wood cutters use the corruption of the local officials in certain *municipios* to cut the forests. In one instance, *ejidatarios* stopped three lumbering trucks and took the lumber to SARH representatives, but little happened due to a lack of cooperation by the officials. The Civic Forestry Committee of Amozoc, A. C, denounced the use of trees to make charcoal and even showed SEDUE representatives where the charcoal ovens were. Despite the "denouncements" (*denuncias*) to SARH, SARH cannot exert enough local authority to stop the destruction (*Sol* 1989/3/14).

There is interaction between farming and deforestation since the cutting of the forests is affecting the aquifer under the entire valley (*Sol* 1989/3/18). The reduced flow of water is producing a political response. On Friday, April 21, 1989, a group of 150 peasants from the Regional Union of Irrigation Wells of Tehuacan (*Union Regional de Sociedades de Pozos de Irrigacion del Valle de Tehuacan*), blocked four access roads to SARH near Cholula and would not allow anyone enter or leave for two hours, and partially blocked the offices for another six hours after. They demanded the right to dig several new wells and irrigation tubes and for the government to continue work on new filtration galleries. They argued that the Tehuacan Valley has had four years of scarce rainfall and there has been a serious decrease in water available for farming (*Sol* 1989/3/18).

### Feedback Loop #2: Demographics

Fueling the environmental problems of the Puebla region has been a demographic explosion. Birth indices have dropped from 3.5 to 2.3/100, but they must fall to 1.8 before the population begins to achieve balance with resources (*Sol* 1990/9/17). Due to natural internal increase and immigration, the population of the valley of Puebla has doubled over the last two decades. The population of the city of Puebla was 700,000 in 1960; it had expanded to over 2,000,000 by 1989. The region of Puebla grew by one million persons immigrating from Mexico City in less than one year because of the earthquake of 1985. Thousands come from the countryside fleeing hunger and economic underdevelopment. Crowding has led to increased poverty and a variety of diseases and hunger. It has also led to increased environmental destruction. However, these are problems not unique to Puebla but occur throughout Mexico.

Negative economic growth combined with population expansion is producing poverty. Studies by the National Institute of Nutrition shows that 80 out 100 Mexican families are living in poverty, while 30 out of 100 are living in extreme poverty (Sol 1988/7/9). There are 85 million inhabitants in Mexico; of them 50 million live in urban municipal centers of over 150,000 people, such as Puebla. The capital of Mexico City has 22 million people and other concentrations of people are developing in Guadalajara and Monterrey. There are 35 million poor Mexicans in 130 thousand rural communities without any municipal services and with no possibility of achieving improvements (Sol 1988/11/23).

One of the major problems brought on by the population explosion is the demand for potable water. In November, 1988, with the help of federal, state, and municipal agencies, the Committee for Drinking Water of the city of Puebla, formed by the eleven "presidents" of the city's eleven "barrios", made a study of how to improve the aquifers of the city and the capture of water from various wells. What they discovered was that the expense of drilling new wells may be beyond the capacity of the city.

### Feedback Loop #3: Cultural Symbolism

Mexican culture is largely urban with strong metaphysical Aristotelian component due to the influence of the Catholic Church. Possibly it is this urban Catholicism which led historically to the destruction of environments in Latin America. But there is also a highly intellectual aspect to Mexican culture originating in the same urban component which has produced Mexican literature, art, and poetry. Abstraction and abstract ideas are common to Mexican thought. While the history of Mexico's relationship to the environment has been largely exploitative and extractive (the hacienda and the mine), in the last decade there has been a radical shift in this orientation. Borrowing largely from American and European models of human ecology, and depending on their own observations, Mexican environmental and political leaders developed a theoretical vision of the human relationship to the environment. This has been expressed recently in the Law of Ecological Equilibrium.

The Law of Ecological Equilibrium is similar to the United States Environmental Act in the Stewardship command to protect natural resources. However, the American law is more pragmatic reflecting American culture which deals with causal relationships in a mechanistic fashion. The Mexican view is more holistic, mythical, poetical, and powerful. The Mexican environmental act is more all encompassing and philosophical than the American one. It accepts the idea of development and ecology being naturally related to one another, and this axiom is expressed in the creation of the Mexican analogue to the American Environmental Protection Agency, the *Secretaria de Desarrollo Urbano e Ecología* (the Secretariat of Urban Development and Ecology). The philosophical structuring of SEDUE reflects both the urban and ecological ideology of modern Mexico. In the American governmental bureaucracy, the cabinet post of Housing and Urban Development, with its concern with urban systems, and the Environmental Protection Agency, with its concern with nature, are intellectually and ideologically in opposite corners. Mexican leaders have formally brought the American anti-thesis (ecology vs. development) into a synthesis, a concern with feedback connections between systems, cultural and natural.

The intellectual vision one gets of modern Mexico's new law is akin to the philosophy of "deep ecology". However, the actual implementation of the philosophy is quite another matter. This is, in large part, a consequence of the structuring of the Mexican government and PRI. While in recent years there has been movement in the direction of a multi-party democracy, the fact is that Mexico is still a one-party state. The structure of the one-party system and its implications for local politics will be discussed under Feedback Loop #6.

### Feedback Loop 6: Institutional Responses To Involution

The city of Puebla is hard pressed to meet the demands of the population due to population growth and some of the environmental issues we have examined. On one occasion, Mayor Pacheco Pullido declared that the city was only able to meet half of the demands for service because it was so underfunded. He said that factors of "gigantism" are making further growth questionable. The city is growing in an "exaggerated" fashion every day. Social problems are becoming political. The exigencies of delivering municipal services multiply from one month to the next.

According to the mayor, what makes the situation difficult is that the municipal government of Puebla must operate on a continuous deficit, not only because expenditures are greater than collections, but because of the small subsidies paid out to the public and the archaic structures of government. In 1989-1990, the income to the city was about 50,000,000 pesos and it will cost 65,000,000 pesos to meet the population's demand for services, producing a deficit of 15,000,000 pesos each year. In the meantime, the capacity of the infrastructure of city services has been cut in half. The system carrying water through the city produces a network of 280 miles of pipes, or the distance from Puebla to Laredo on the Texas border, and these are disintegrating. There are 92 wells and 940 kilometers of drainage tubes. The municipal government has a fiscal mess because the financial equilibrium is broken (*Sol* 1989: 2/13).

This picture can be repeated throughout all of modern Mexico and has led the federal government to move in the direction of stewardship.

*Federal Laws and Bureaucracies*

The concept of stewardship of the environment is well developed in Mexico and dates to the late 1960s. The rapid expansion of Mexico City from three million inhabitants in 1960 to nearly seven million in 1970 drew public attention to the problems of urbanization and pollution (Mumme, Bath, Assetto 1988:12). The United States National Environmental Policy Act of 1969 stimulated the administration of Luis Echeverría Alvarez to pass the *Ley Federal para Prevenir y Controlar la Contaminación Ambiental* (Federal Law to Prevent and Control Air Pollution) in 1971. A constitutional amendment gave authority to the Secretaria de Salubridad y Asistencia (SAA) to regulate air, water, and soil pollution. Another law concerning air polution was passed in 1971, and in 1973, a law controlling water pollution was also passed (Mumme, Bath, Assetto 1988:13). Other laws were passed during the Echeverría administration towards the stewardship of the environment, and steps were taken to encourage the decentralization of industrial development and human settlement. A special agency was developed within the SSA, the *Subsecretaria de Mejoramiento del Ambiente* (the Subsecretariat for Environmental Improvement). However, despite all of the new laws, environmental policy had a low priority in the Echeverría administration. The concepts of stewardship were largely the product of the government's techno-political elite and had mostly symbolic intent (Mumme, Bath, Assetto 1988: 14).

Under the administration of José López Portillo (1977-1982), the SMA was reorganized into three quasi-autonomous subunits dealing with air, water and soil pollution, but little else was achieved. However, public concern and pressure from the United States forced the government of Mexico to take environmental issues more seriously. Especially critical was the rapid development of the oil fields of the Gulf of Mexico after 1977 and its impact on marine, land resources, contamination of rivers and estuaries, and erosion. There were also peasant mass movements against PEMEX (Mumme, Bath, and Assetto 1988: 15).

In response, the López Portillo administration wrote environmental considerations into the *Plan Nacional de Desarrollo Urbano* (National Plan of Urban Development) (1978), *Plan Nacional de Desarrollo Industrial* (National Plan of Industrial Development) (1979), and *Plan Global de Desarrollo* (Global Development Plan) (1980) emphasizing the decentralization of industry and population. A new Dirección General de Ecología Urbana was created within the Secretaria de Asentamientos Humanos y Obras Públicas (SAHOP). But a national congress on the environment, convened in Mexico City in 1980 by the Escuela Nacional de Ciencias Biológicas of the Instituto Politécnico Nacional, declared the new laws "a dead letter" (Mumme, Bath, and Assetto 1988: 17).

In 1982, at the end of the Portillo administration, Mexico passed a new law which brought together many older laws and reinforced them (Mumme, Bath, Assetto 1988: 17). It was called the Law of Ecological Equilibrium and Protection of the Environment. A new bureaucracy was created at the beginning of the de la Madrid administration to enforce the new national law. It was called the Secretaria de Desarrollo Urbano e Ecología (the Secretariat of Urban Development and Ecology). The politicians who created both the new law of ecological equilibrium and SEDUE, as the new secretariat is commonly labeled, were acting on the most advanced theories of ecology and development, viewing Mexican efforts at urban development as directly tied to the deterioration of the environment. The new law was part of the "we" ethic which is strongly rooted in Mexican culture and the Mexican constitution of 1917, a nationalistic document which is highly protective of human communities and environments (Purcell 1990: 399).

In addition to SEDUE, there are several other bureaucracies whose functions parallel or duplicate those of SEDUE, such as SARH, the Secretaria de Agricultura y Recursos Hidráulicos (the Secretariat of Agriculture and Irrigation Resources). Another overlapping agency is SAHOP. For the most part, SEDUE and SARH cooperate but overlap in jurisdictions, along with other bureaucracies, such as the Secretariat for Agricultural Development and PEMEX.

SEDUE, SARH and other Mexican bureaucracies are much like agencies in the United States Executive branch, and their directors are appointed by the president of Mexico. They are located in Mexico City and have branches in the states and cities of Mexico. The integration of the federal bureaucracies with the states and *municipios* has presented policy makers in Mexico City with major problems (Mumme, Bath, and Assetto 1988: 28-29). Particularly difficult has been the implementation of environmental policies, for it is at the local level of the *municipio* or municipality that SEDUE, SARH and other cabinet level agencies must operate. Each agency has local state representatives appointed from Mexico City having offices in the state capitals.

*The* Ayuntamiento *and* Caciquismo

In order to succeed, federal agencies must have the cooperation of the political heads of the *municipio* (municipal) government, called the *ayuntamiento*. Ayuntamientos, which are like county governments, are ruled by a publicly elected *Presidente* or mayor, and a set of *corregidores* or "managers" (direct translation, but the term is early colonial and has an aristocratic meaning in Mexican Spanish). The managers are members of the *cabildo* of the *ayuntamiento*. Because the corregidores are elected, the *ayuntamiento* of Mexico and elsewhere in Latin America was one of the few formally democratic institutions in otherwise authoritarian states. However, the dominance of the Institutional Revolutionary Party of Mexico (PRI) has led to the development of *caciquismo* (bossism) at the local level.

In the election of 1989, PRI won 15 of the 20 positions in the *Cabildo*; three were won by PAN, one by the Frente Cardenista, and one by the Partido Popular Socialista. This apparently democratic election belies the underlying structure of the Mexican political machine. The PRI candidates for the election had been pre-selected by the local *caciques* (bosses). In Puebla (the city and the state), as in other Mexican cities (and states), membership of the *cabildo* of the *ayuntamiento* is largely controlled by a small clique, locally called the *cupola*. The *cupola* is a network of high ranking PRI politicians, mostly lawyers, who hold membership in the *Asociación de Abogados de Puebla*. The *cupola* is connected into the key economic institutions of Puebla including the state and local governments, Volkswagen of Mexico (the largest employer in the region), large commercial banks, state run businesses, large universities, and the major unions. The *cupola* is reminiscent of the "little saucepan" (*panelinha*) described by Anthony Leeds in his study of Brazilian cities and is probably a widespread, though little studied, institution throughout Latin America (Leeds 1965). It is this "preselection" of candidates at national, state, and local levels which Mexicans complain about as being anti-democratic. The elections appear democratic but, in fact, are not because the population has little choice in candidates. The same appears to be true of the other parties, however.

A powerful government dispensing favors to the electorate will inevitably lead to corruption. In Puebla, as in other Mexican cities, the tight mesh between "city hall" and the PRI has led to corruption. The *caciques* reward their followers with patronage in the form of jobs. But, administrative positions in city government pay poorly and office holders inevitably find other means of augmenting income. The relationship between patronage and corruption, low pay and the need to tap sources of revenue, leads to the common acceptance of all involved in bribes and payoffs.

The problems that emerge with new Law of Ecological Equilibrium, are much like problems that plague the Mexican political economy in all of its domains and have plagued it for fifty years, those of what Mexicans call *caciquismo* and Americans would call "machine politics." Given the fact that the "machine" allocates positions of power to individuals, and these must garner votes among constituents, favors must be traded. There are many *caciques* strategically located throughout the *ayuntamiento* political structure who owe their power to some faction of the Puebla electorate. Trying to attack any problem is extremely frustrating because success usually depends on having the support of all of the various factions, each of which usually has a different vested (I) interest. The tendency is, then, for the *corrigidores* of the *ayuntamiento* to turn their backs on those who break the laws; for the national agencies to pound on the doors of the lawbreakers; for these to threaten strike if threats get too serious, and for the national and state governments to pretend nothing is happening and that they are succeeding in their mandates (We), often through symbolic behavior (e.g., the construction of ecology parks).

In addition, there is the structure of the distribution of largesse by the federal government. Typically, funds are donated down from the President of the republic to governor of the state. The governor, in this case Piña Olaya, then donates funds to the presidents of the *ayuntamientos*.

To add to the complexity of the above, there are 217 *municipios* and, thus, 217 *ayuntamientos* throughout the state of Puebla, each with its local construction of *caciques* and connections to local power structures and PRI. The power structure of each *municipio* differs depending on the local economy. In some districts, the agricultural *ejidos* (cooperative farming estates) dominate and in others industrial unions (*sindicatos*) and in yet others businessmen and industrialists dominate through local chambers of commerce. SARH, SEDUE, the governor, the presidente, and other members of the "elite" government structure, must play intricate political games with the various local political *caciques* to achieve minimal public goals.

The state of Puebla, the city of Puebla, the 217 *municipios*, the governor, the president, the *ayuntamientos*, and the hundreds of *caciques* face two very real problems: achieving economic development to obtain jobs (the I) and solving environmental issues (the We). At times these two sets of policy goals: jobs and environmental protection, contradict each other at the local level.

*SEDUE as Don Quixote: The Attempt to Impose the Law of Ecological Equilibrium*

Representatives of SEDUE began to deal with environmental issues in the mid-1980s. On the one hand, SEDUE officials had the symbolic support of all local political leaders from the governor on down to the presidents of the *ayuntamientos*. On the other hand, the problem of *caciquismo* led to SEDUE sparring with windmills.

Pollution of local soils and water is a consequence of mass disregard for the environment by almost all processing plants throughout the Valley of Puebla, ranging from coffee growers to Volkswagen makers. SEDUE has closed a large number of firms over the last three years, but its impact on a business is largely a consequence of the importance of the firm in question to the economy of the valley. Outsiders and small businesses are much more likely to get their hands slapped than local large private corporations or state run companies. And even outsiders rarely pay attention to the laws. In July of 1988, SEDUE shut down the heavy machinery of General Minerals, which belongs to Grupo Lamosa of Monterrey and Materiales Primas of Ahuazotepec, S.A. The machinery was destroying the rivers and river banks near Zacatlan in the north of the state. SEDUE had the cooperation of the *ayuntamiento* of Zacatlan. However, SEDUE was not successful with the same problem in nearby *municipio* of Ahuazotepec where the president of the *ayuntamiento* also owned the major truck line which was transporting minerals from Puebla to Monterrey, Mexico (*Sol* 1988/7/9).

By August of 1989, SEDUE had shut down 65 contaminating businesses ranging from textile firms, ceramics, wood manufacturing, grease and oil service stations, and sections of Volkswagen of Mexico. SEDUE also angered labor unions and business leaders. In September, one of the union leaders complained that SEDUE had put over 40 families out of work by shutting down one textile firm.

As we have seen, the deforestation of the valley is tied to the water supply problem and that both are critical ecological problems. The Governor of the state of Puebla has attempted to protect the forests in a variety of ways but is unable to stop the destruction by small-holders, commercial lumber companies, and well armed smugglers. As the following demonstrates, federal and state agencies do not have the resources stop those who make their livings by preying on the forests of Mexico.

In early 1989, the governor of the state of Puebla, with the help of the military, developed a special arm of the police to protect the forests (*Sol* 1989/ 1/26). The "attack" on the forests by lumbermen in the form of contraband was denounced by political leaders. Twelve *casetas de vigilencia* (small blockhouses) were built to house policemen who would protect the forests. Local small farmers (*ejiditarios*) denounced lumbermen and forest interests for destroying their environments (*Sol* 1989/1/26). The twelve *casetas* were to function in strategic forest regions such as Huauchinango, Acateno, Carretera Huauchinango, Pozo Rica, Zaragoza and Teziuitlan, Tlapacoya, Zacatepec, Empalme, Tepeaca, Santa Rita Tlahuapan, Azumbilla, Las Palomas Acatlan, and Coxcatlan. SARH, SEDUE, SEFA, the army, and the Secretary of National Defense were to participate. One peasant leader, Antonio Móntez García, from the region of Texmelucan, pleaded for state intervention to protect the forests from destruction (*Sol* 1989/1/26). The program was planned and developed by the Advisory Coordinator State Forests with representatives of peasant farmers, cattle ranchers, small proprietors, and communities in the forests, as well as other agricultural authorities and state legislators. The president of the Advisory Council for State Forests, who is also director of the Secretariat of Agricultural Development, announced that he would ask for a voluntary tax of 5000 pesos per meter of lumber in order to accelerate the official programs. The forestry director of the Secretariat of Agricultural Development, Engineer Edgar Tapia Simon, who is also secretary of the Advisor Council, projected a cost of 1,284,522,000 pesos for the project. The project would focus on contraband logs which are stolen from national forests. In addition, the Director of Public Security of the State and the subprocurator proposed the creation of a special State Forestry Police for the task (*Sol* 1989:1/26).

In February of 1989, The Civic Committee of Amozoc, a town in the northern Sierra, announced a program suspending all cutting of timber in the region. It recommended suspension of all lumbering activities for five years in the nearby forests. The only exception would be a local paper factory, a few artisan business, and businesses which make furniture (*Sol* 1989:2/7).

In March, Governor Piña Olaya began an intense struggle against the clandestine lumbermen by setting up three more "houses of vigilance" in the National Park Ixtac-Popocatepetl and through the creation of a State Forestry Police with 96 policemen and 34 technical and supervisory personnel. But these new forces were unable to stop the continued destruction to the forests.

A series of tree planting projects were organized by SEDUE, SARH, *Patronato Puebla Verde*, and the office of the Governor for the Puebla region. The tree planting projects were an extensive attempt to begin to reforest the Valley of Puebla and its cities. One characteristic of the planting project was the inclusion of industrialists and other businessmen as participants. One of the planting projects was the development of the Ecological Park of the Revolution with trees donated by C. Atoyac, a cement factory. In November of 1988, 40 industries in the industrial park and another 35 industries in the industrial corridor "Quetzalcoatl" of San Martin Texmelucan initiated a Program for the Reforestation of the Industrial Zone. One industrialist donated 60,000 trees. These were to be planted in the industrial park which was to receive the name of Puebla 2000. Local leaders saw this as one of many possible ways of achieving ecological equilibrium and avoiding the inevitable damage to the environment and human health (*Sol* 1988:11/17). The governor of the state, Mariano Piña Olaya, the Secretary of the Economy, a delegation from SEDUE, the Mexican Institute of Chemical Engineers of Puebla, also participated in the plan to reforest the industrial zone.

But all of this activity was ineffective in stemming the destruction of the forests. Almost a year after the project to protect the forests was announced, a group of *ejidatarios* denounced the destruction of the forests directly to Governor Mariano Piña Olaya at a meeting of the Forest Producers and Industrialists of the Northern Sierra. They were led by a young *ejidatario*, Eliseo Flores García, president of the Union of *Ejidatarios* of the Northern Sierra. According to García, the governor's "Forestry Plan for Puebla" had never functioned and that the forests continued to be cut down, "forgotten objects of illegal enrichment for a few government functionaries." García angered the functionaries and representatives of the lumber firms, but he was applauded by the *ejiditarios*. He warned the governor that the *caciques* of the northern Sierra were only interested in their own advantage and that it was impossible to re-forest the region with the depredations continuing. He felt that the government treated the *ejidatarios* like children, but that these were the only ones who could protect the forest: "We want freedom and support to help the forest recuperate" (*Sol* 1989:8/25).

The planting of trees and the creation of "revolutionary parks of ecology" are largely symbolic activities. They do not prevent the tremendous destruction to the forest resources of the state of Puebla. That damage is done primarily by lumbermen representing powerful companies or poor farmers and foresters, both of whom manage to infiltrate the forests and destroy them tree by tree.

The above summary shows how SEDUE was unable to achieve implementation of the Laws of Ecological Equilibrium for largely political reasons originating in the economy. The following is a detailed study of one of the political movements in the city of Puebla which grew to block SEDUE and other Federal agencies from carrying out the Law of Ecological Equilibrium.

*Air Pollution, Taxi Cabs, Combis, Street Peddlers and Marxist Students: SEDUE and the October 28th Movement*

The origins of the October 28th Movement lie in UNESCO's 1985 recognition of the City of Puebla as "patrimony of mankind." This recognition led the *Ayuntamiento* of Puebla, under leadership of Mayor Pacheco Pullido, to outlaw *tianguis* (*tianguis* is a term referring to the places where street peddlers set up their stalls, but it is now used to refer to the peddlers, themselves) from downtown Puebla. There was also an all out effort initiated to preserve the several square block region around the Zocalo, the city center. The street vendors were compelled to set up their stalls on the outskirts of the city in a specially constructed plaza near the bus station (CAPU). However, the vendors did not accept their new status. In 1987, during the Volkswagen strike which closed down the city of Puebla, the vendors protested in front of the Palacio del Presidente (City Hall) in the Zocalo. Many of the vendors are of Indian background and considered the attempt to force them out of town to be racist and fascist. Pacheco Pullido spoke to the vendors promising them to help make their new quarters more economically worthwhile. But the mass of the population of Puebla shops in the downtown, and the new markets on the outskirts of the city are not easily reached, and they are dusty and uncomfortable with little shade. The police began a constant battle to force the street vendors out of the downtown. The vendors considered police actions as a form of political harassment and asked protection from their own union, which forms a part of PRI. On one date in 1989 it was estimated that as many as 6,000 peddlers had invaded the heart of the city (*Sol* 1989:10/28).

In the mid-1980s, the ecological movement and the objective of rebuilding and protecting the downtown of Puebla became bound together. The Congress of the state of Puebla went on record that the city of Puebla should obey the Law of Ecological Equilibrium and passed a law, "The Regulation of Construction in the City of Puebla," a legal document written by local public and private agencies to stop "anarchistic" urban construction which dates back to 1935. Urban development was further brought under control with a new State Law of Ecological Equilibrium (passed by the State of Puebla), which was a local version of the federal Law of Ecological Equilibrium. The new law was meant to allow the development of an equilibrium-oriented urban system. The new law was to have as its objective ecological conservation and protection of the environment. The new rules controlled the disposition of telephone, gas, electric, road, and other networks, as well as construction material.

In the same years, 1985-1988, the city leaders of Puebla began to grapple with the variety of environmental issues discussed earlier. The most critical issue came to be the problem of air pollution. This issue had two sides: 1) controlling air pollution from taxis, combis (micro-buses), and trucks, and 2) planting trees to produce oxygen. The first issue became merged with the tianguis issue and the reconstruction of downtown Puebla. The second issue became a symbol of ecological success, masking the real failure of SEDUE, SARH, the governor and the mayor.

In late 1988 and during 1989, SEDUE and government agencies of the state and city of Puebla orchestrated a major attempt to gain control over air pollution. Photographs appeared in the *Sol de Puebla* showing buses and taxis contaminating the air. One special focus was CAPU, the new bus station and open air market where ambulatory merchants were forced in the mid-1980s. The ambulatory merchants, bus drivers, taxi cab drivers, and Marxist university students from the Autonomous University of Puebla, organized to protest the "fascist" activities of the government. The *Agrupación 28 de Octubre* or October 28th Movement, was organized to protest the passenger rates received by drivers, anti-pollution and anti-ambulatory merchant policy measures of the city and state governments. In November and December of 1988, the October 28th Group invaded the town and blocked the Central Bus Terminal, CAPU, and blocked the intersections of downtown Puebla causing traffic to come to a standstill. On several occasions, the drivers of the *Sistema de Transporte Colectivo de Puebla* (System of Collective Transport of Puebla) used V.W. microbuses to "invade" the city and cut off transit demanding the intervention of the state Director of Transportation to solve their problems.

In San Martín Texmelucan, an industrial town, the gasoline and diesel industry was paralyzed when SEDUE closed down the petrochemical plant "Independencia" January 10th. By the 12th, the plant was open again but SEDUE was suddenly very quiet about proceeding against PEMEX to force the processing of better non-polluting fuels. The PEMEX workers' union were not particularly interested in improving the efficiency of automobiles but in preserving their jobs. It is thought that the *caciques* of the PEMEX union had put pressure on the *ayuntamiento* of Puebla to disregard SEDUE.

SEDUE officials lamented that, in one attempt to improve auto-emissions, about 3000 vehicles were analyzed (out of 200,000 which exist in the state of Puebla). Out of these, about a third were polluting, and the owners took corrective measures. But these represented drivers who voluntarily came to have their auto emissions checked and were but a small proportion of the total number of drivers. The director of SEDUE complained that a more drastic non-voluntary verification campaign was necessary. The following day, a strike of bus drivers once again paralyzed the city (*Sol* 1989:2/21). The strike was organized by the October 28th Movement. It was followed by another Oct 28th strike within a few days which included peddlers, taxi drivers, bus and combi drivers, and Marxist university students. Drivers parked their vehicles at the intersections of the city effectively closing the city down. The strike was in part a protest in order to increase passenger rates and in part a protest against the threat to impose fines on polluting vehicles and the "discrimination" against the peddlers.

In late January, 1989, an article appeared in the *Sol de Puebla* which inflated the developing leftist/rightist rhetoric over the environment. *Sol de Puebla* published a talk by Espinoza Iglesias, an important business leader, which argued that there was a worldwide trend away from state organized institutions. Espinoza Iglesias is one of the chief architects of the Organization Mary Street Jenkins, a foundation which helped fund the reconstruction of the colonial Mercado la Victoria, museums, and the *Parque Ecológico de la Revolución Mexicana*. The Ecological Park is tied to *Patronato Puebla Verde*. The speech thus gave the ecology movement of Puebla a distinctively pro-business caste, whether fairly or unfairly.

*Puebla Verde*, the citizens' ecology group, denounced the activities of the October 28th Movement. Arguing that *Puebla Verde* had the support of General Law of Ecological Equilibrium behind it, members of *Puebla Verde* exhorted fellow citizens to exercise their rights under Article 189 of the Constitution to denounce anyone who destroyed the ecological balance of nature to SEDUE or other federal or local government agents. Article 192 of the General Law of Ecological Equilibrium and Protection of the Environment specifies that SEDUE shall act to evaluate the denunciation of the citizens within 30 days. In 1988, the *Sol de Puebla* and *Puebla Verde*, had denounced a wide variety of private and public corporations and businesses, such as HYLSA, PEMEX, Automanufacturas S.A. de C. V., Companía Minera Autlan, Papelera Poblana, Aceitera el Paradiso, various textile plants, and urban truck and bus lines because of noise, smoke, and gas, as well as the October 28th Movement (*Sol* 1988: 11/10-16)

In this context, the October 28th Movement took its next turn. One of the directors of the October 28th Movement, Rubén Sarbia, known as Simitrio, denounced the increasing influence of the right, focusing on SEDUE. Several more strikes occurred closing down the city's downtown and angering the population. In early February, 1989, Gumaro Amaro Ramírez, one of the leaders of the October 28th Movement (and President of the Housewives Union) was assassinated. On February 23, there was a dramatic protest led by October 28th Movement leaders, including Simitrio. They were joined by Rector Malpica of the Autonomous University of Puebla and Marxist university students. The Rector expressed hope that the region would not return back to "*pistolerismo*" of 1972 and 1974. The demonstrators included taxi and combi drivers who once again closed down the city. The demonstration was a protest against the government's lack of action in finding the murderer of Gumaro Amaro. The strike angered the residents of Puebla (*Sol* 1989:2/23).

Just prior to the strike, Rector Malpica of U.A.P had been accused of malfeasance in office due to overspending the university's budget by $5,312,000,000 (pesos) in anticipation of subsidies. After the strike, the government of Piña Olaya lent the money to the University to pay its debt. Rector Malpica was also accused of leading a group of faculty to destabilize the university (*Sol* 1989:2/28).

In May, members of the October 28th Movement kidnapped an industrialist, Rudolfo Kliffich Suter. He was injured but escaped by paying his captors one hundred American dollars. The state asked the courts for the authority to arrest the leaders of the October 28th Movement: Simitrio, Fransisco Molina, Telesforo Zamorano and other persons involved in the kidnapping. Later, Simitrio stated he had nothing to do with the kidnapping and that he was the victim of right wing political manipulation. Later in the week, representatives of business enterprises of Puebla argued that the leaders of the October 28th Movement should be prosecuted for breaking the law (*Sol* 1989:5/15). Simitrio attacked the government accusing it of siding with right wing interests to destroy the October 28th Movement. The October 28th Movement marched into downtown Puebla with hundreds of drivers and street vendors and blocked traffic with 52 buses from the Estrella de Oro line. The demonstration was a protest against Simitrio's being persecuted by the government and against the firing of 26 bus drivers whose buses had been used to block up the city. According to the *Sol de Puebla*, the protest led to total chaos (*Sol* 1989:5/19).

A week later, the October 28th Movement protested in support of Simitrio and demanded an end to hostilities towards the movement by the government. Among the protesters were personnel of the university hospital of the Universidad Autónoma de Puebla, made up of PRI supporters. Hundreds of vehicles were trapped by the protest (*Sol* 1989: 5/25). In late May, a counter-protest and demonstration occurred led by members of an "*Ejidetario Transportista*", a transport collective of the National Confederation of Peasants, who were angry with the October 28th Movement. Members of the collective accused October 28th drivers of taking over their routes. The protest was also against the Traffic Police for selling protection (*Sol* 1989:5/28).

In July, Simitrio was arrested for the killing of Gumaro Amaro Ramírez. Simitrio accused the government of right wing activities for supporting private enterprise and trying to destroy his organization's reputation. He argued that he had been framed, but an investigation revealed that Simitrio had hired an out-of-work plumber, who had become a street vendor, to assassinate Gumaro Amaro. Simitrio is presently languishing in a Mexico City jail.

### Conclusions: Politics, Economic Development, and Ecology

The approach used in this paper is "human systems ecology," a research technique pioneered by John W. Bennett in his study of southern Saskatchewan (Bennett 1968). The strategy is to collect data on the interaction of human systems within a single region.[3] I have attempted a similar approach on the coast of Guatemala in the 1960s, in the region around Medellin, Colombia, in the early 1980s, and currently in the basin of Puebla, Mexico.

Human systems ecology forces the researcher to begin asking questions about the interaction between political, economic, social, ideological, and ecological systems through time. Studies of environmental issues which are solely ecological, it seems to me, fail to grasp the true complexities of protecting the earth's ecosystems. This study of Puebla demonstrates the need to move beyond the study of the damage we humans are doing to the earth's ecosystems to study the basic institutions which lay down the rules controlling human behavior.

As this paper demonstrates, there is tremendous damage to the environment in the state of Puebla, Mexico, but responsibility is not easily laid at the front door of industrialists, farmers, cab drivers, politicians, or any other single category or agency of human endeavor. Mexico has a comprehensive national law protecting its environments: the Law of Ecological Equilibrium. Educated Mexicans are more aware of the quality of the interconnections between economic and ecological systems than most Americans because the relationship between economic growth and visible damage to the environment is evident everywhere.

But no one obeys the law. Passing laws at international levels will not help and passing more local laws, as the people of Puebla have attempted, will also not help. This paper shows that two different institutional complexes are involved: the economic and the political. To solve its ecological problems, Puebla needs a healthy economy, and it needs a healthy political system. It has neither. Millions of jobs have been lost over the last decade due to the downturn in the Mexican economy and the international debt (*Sol* 1988:7/13). The political system is unable to cope because of the in-grown structure of *caciquismo* at the national and local levels.

PRI was brought into being 65 years ago to create a stable political system in Mexico. Compared to other Latin American countries, Mexico has enjoyed a high level of stability. However, the economy paid a price. PRI took a statist strategy to Mexican economic development. Corruption within state political and economic institutions became a way of life and influenced the average Mexican's perception of reality. Mexican citizens developed the attitude that neither industrialists nor the state acted responsibly in the treatment of human beings or environments, and an exploitative world view became widespread. How could one ask a poor wood cutter to stop chopping down trees when he knew that the mayor of his town was in cahoots with a textile manufacturer to dump dyes in the local river?

During the last two decades, evidence began to accumulate that, despite Mexico's rapid economic growth prior to 1980, the coupling of PRI, the state, and the Mexican economy was not healthy. While the rich grew richer, the poor stayed where they were, and the ecosystem deteriorated. In the 1980s, with the economy slipping badly, the evidence grew even further: PRI's statist strategy was not working.

Returning to the I/We paradigm, I argue that Mexico is an example of a society which pushed the "We" or moral button for historic reasons having to do with the exploitation of Mexico's peoples and environments.[4] PRI was created as a one-party corporatist structure which included all political categories (except the Catholic church and private business until the 1950s). While the Mexican government attempted to legislate into existence laws protecting both people and environments, they have fallen far short of the ideal. The failure of PRI is the consequence of everyone having rights within a political entity and few having responsibilities backed by the state. It is questionable that such a system can legislate responsibility. In such a society, the party which runs the state depends on the political support of all of its members: businessmen, taxi drivers, street peddlers, peasants, loggers, lawyer-politicians, university students, and housewives. Laws are easily passed (which is why Mexicans refer to their government as *una papeleria*, a paper factory) which protect women, workers, children, environments. But when someone breaks the law, the state finds itself in the situation of punishing a person or category of persons whose support the party and the state needs.[5]

In 1988, Carlos Salinas de Gortari was elected President of Mexico. Almost simultaneously, the Soviet Union and the East European socialist countries began to come apart. The Mexican electorate drew parallels between what it read about the political economies and environments of Eastern Europe and the Soviet Union and their own political economies and environments. When the Soviet Union collapsed in 1991, Salinas de Gortari was already well on his way to reforming Mexico's political and economic systems. The PRI has initiated reforms to privatize Mexico's economy and to create a true multi-party democracy. Political reforms are in their infancy. PRI leaders fear bringing about a multi-party democracy before a free-market economy has emerged citing the political instability of the Commonwealth of Independent States as their reasons for being cautious. However, the reforms towards privatization are moving swiftly (Mexico had 1155 state run enterprises in 1981; it now has 29, Purcell 1992: 55).

This paper has concentrated on the relationship between *caciquismo* in Puebla and the federal government's inability to protect Puebla's environment from its own people. It will be years before the new policies will influence the feedback relationships to the environment. Is there any reason for hope?

I wrote at the beginning that economic development and protection of the environment are contradictory processes. I do not see any way out of this dilemma. Economic growth is a necessary part of development, and growth is going to change environments, sometimes drastically. People will put their own survival first. However, the ecological damage which has occurred to Mexico and many other developing countries goes far beyond survival and jobs. It is the consequence of corruption in the political system, which in turn is the consequence of tying political and economic systems too closely together. What happened in Mexico is that the regulators of the legal system also benefitted from a growing economy and turned their backs on entrepreneurs who wanted to take risks with environments and lives.

It is apparent that the separation between political and economic systems is a starting point.[6] The leaders of *Puebla Verde* argue that it is imperative that those who are responsible for environmental damage are made responsible, which cannot happen in one party state forms of political organization.

There are new social movements in predominantly developing countries of the world, much like that in Mexico. The movements are generally anti-statist and demand free-markets and pluralistic democratically elected governments. After more than two decades of statist strategies to the solution to development, people in developing countries are abandoning single party, centrally planned governments. One of the forces driving the new movements is the great environmental damage for which no one seems to be responsible since, in these countries, the state has been all. But that is changing.

## Notes

1. By involution I mean two things: 1) the tendency of humans to adapt to deteriorating environments (Bennett 1976); and 2) "a process whereby the upper ranks of an evolving but hierarchically organized system evolves by drawing increased amounts of energy not only from its environment but from its own lower ranks inducing entropy in the lower ranks of the hierarchy" (Smith 1986:118).

2. *Ejidetarios* and other small farmers who produce food tend not to use the same chemicals because of their expense and the low prices paid for food products by the Mexican government.

3. Bennett developed the term "socionatural" to describe a region in terms of its complex human and ecological interaction. The term "socionatural" draws attention to a fact anthropologists understand well: cultures transform and are transformed by regions. The relationships are many-stranded; they are economic, political, psychological, historical, sociological, and more. Human systems ecology is the study of the interaction of these systems and the transformations which take place as these various systems act upon one another.

4. One could also argue that in the 1980s, the United States pushed the "I" button. Currently, Americans appear to be moving away from the right at the same time that Mexicans are moving away from the left. Both movements have the same reasons: damage to human communities and their environments.

5. In 1988, when I first began research on Puebla, meat packers working for the Hormel company in Dubuque, Iowa, threatened to shut down the city during a strike. The governor of the state threatened to use the National Guard. He argued that strikers did not have the right to threaten

others' rights. When I got to Puebla, strikers from Volkswagen of Mexico had shut down the city by blockading all of the roads coming into the city. Governor Piña Olaya commented over the radio that he had no right to stop them from expressing their political opinions.

6. Is it possible for poor people to protect their environments? In an earlier study near Medellín, Colombia, I found that coffee growers in the small town of Jardín were very careful of their ecosystems. Jardín had a history of small coffee farmers who shared resources and had an interest in protecting what they owned. While there was some corruption, the coffee farmers of the valley had some degree of control over the political structure of the town. Unlike most Latin Americans, they were not controlled by more powerful economic interests (Smith and Smith 1989).

## References

Bennett, John
    1976    *The Ecological Transition*. Chicago: Aldine.
Etzioni Amitai
    1988    *The Moral Dimension: Toward a New Economics*. New York: The Free Press.
Leeds, Anthony
    1965    Brazilian Careers and Social Structure: A Case History and Model. In D. Heath and R.N. Adams, eds., *Contemporary Cultures and Societies of Latin America*, pp.379-404. New York: Random House
Mumme, Stephen P., R. Bath & V. J. Assetto
    1988    Political Development and Environmental Policy in Mexico. *Latin American Research Review* 23:7-34.
Purcell, Susan Kaufman
    1990    Mexico. In H.J. Wiarda and H.F. Kline, eds., *Latin American Politics and Development*, pp.395-419. Boulder: Westview Press.
    1992    Mexico's New Economic Vitality. *Current History* 91(563): 54-59.
Smith, Sheldon
    1986    Entrepreneurial Agriculture and the Involution of Agricultural Dynamics in the Americas. In S.M. Greenfield and A. Stricken, eds., *Entrepreneurship and Social Change*, pp.96-123. Monographs in Economic Anthropology, No. 2. Lanham, MD: University Press of America.

Smith, Sheldon and Richard Smith
    1989       Horizontal and Vertical Linkages in Highland Antioquia, Colombia. In S. Smith and E. Reeves, eds., *Human Systems Ecology*, pp.170-201. Boulder: Westview Press.

Smith, Sheldon and Edward Reeves, eds.
    1989       *Human Systems Ecology: Essays on the Integration of Political Economy, Adaptation, and Socionatural Regions*. Boulder: Westview Press.

*Sol de Puebla*
    1987-1991 (references are to year, month, and day of publication).

Thompson, Guy
    1989       *Puebla de Los Angeles*. Boulder: Westview Press.